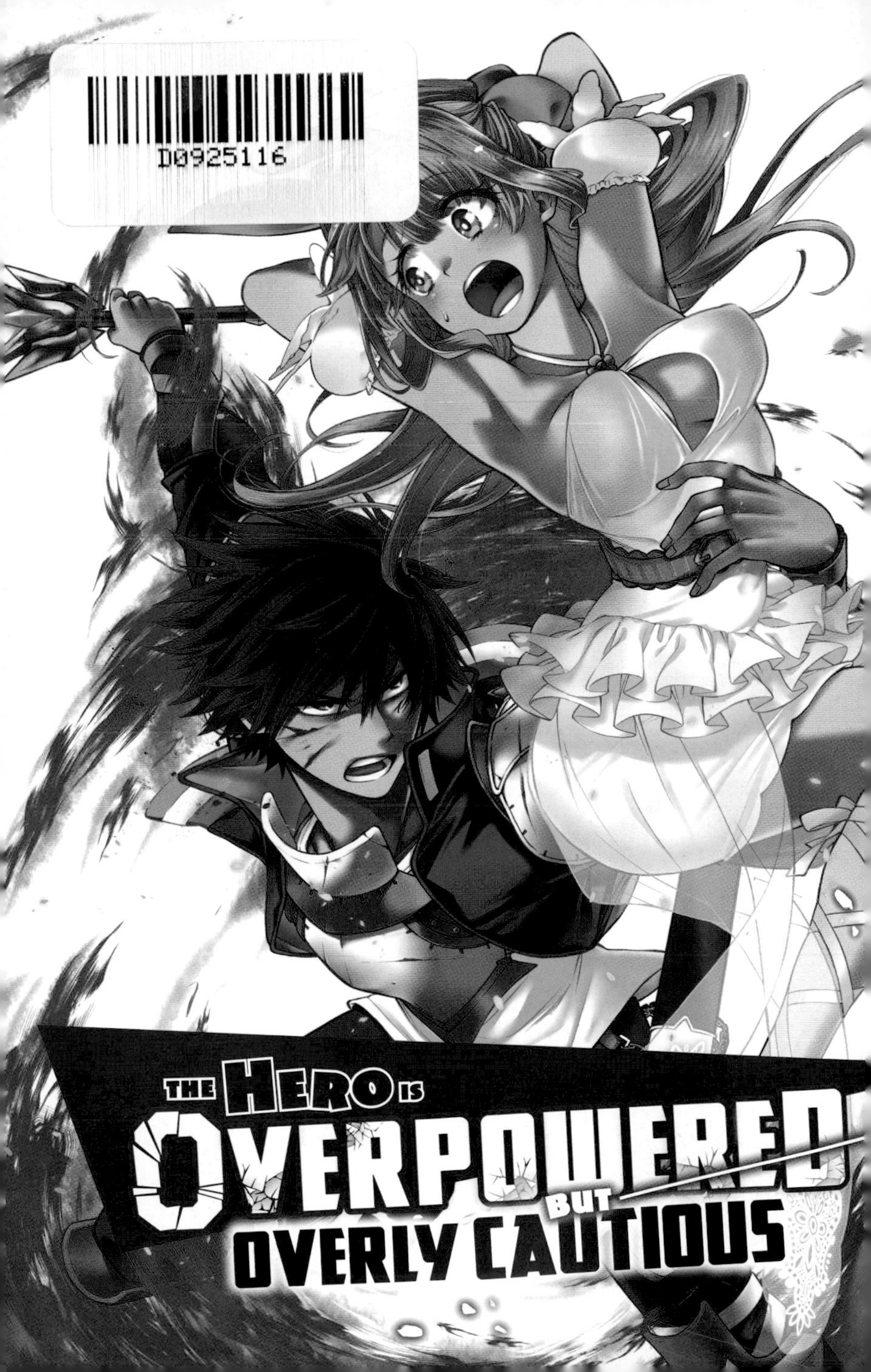
THE HERO IS
OVERPOWERED
BUT
OVERLY CAUTIOUS

CONTENTS

THE HERO IS OVERPOWERED BUT OVERLY CAUTIOUS

5

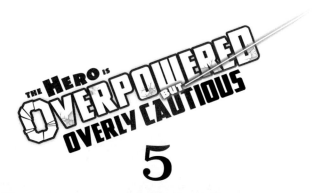

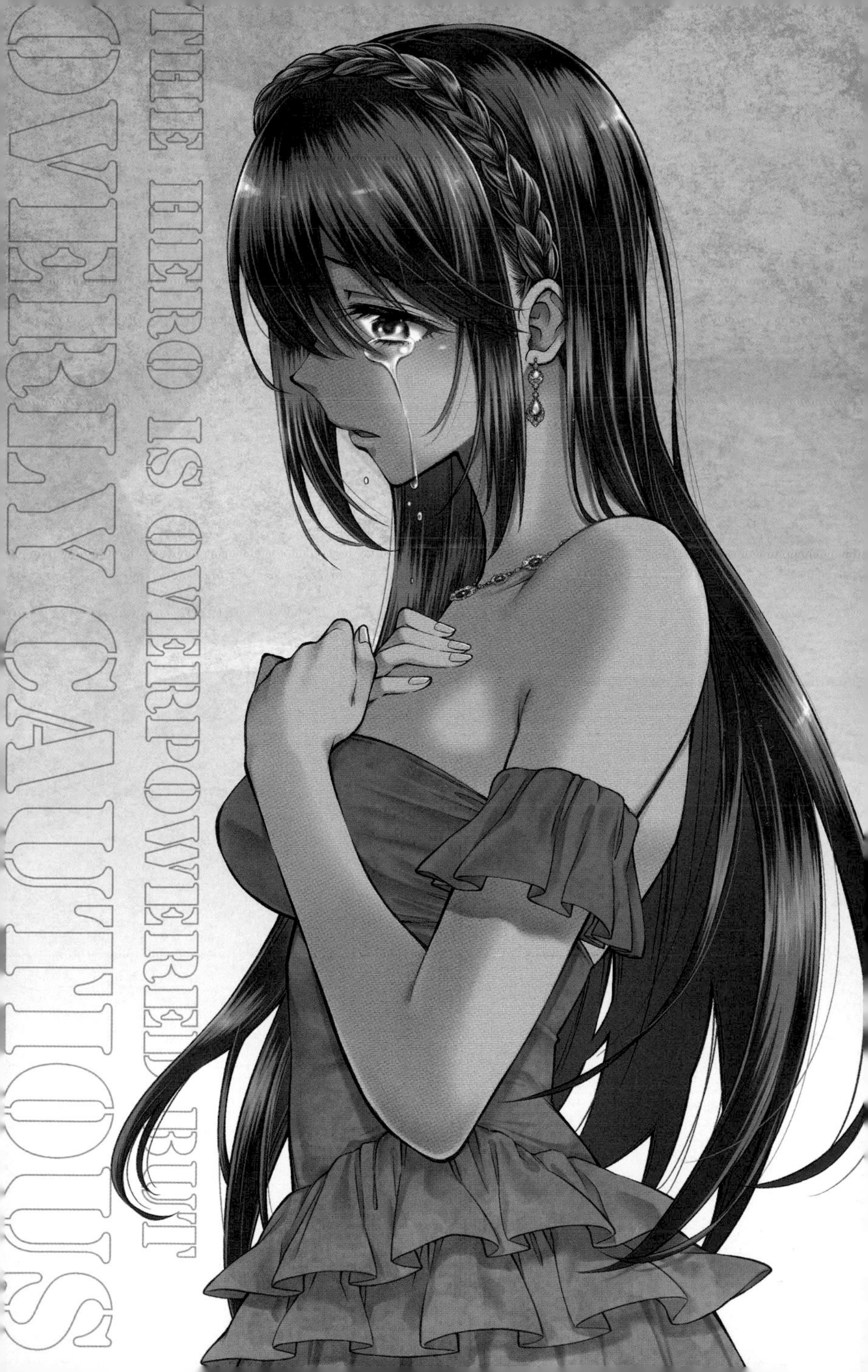
THE HERO IS OVERPOWERED BUT
OVERLY CAUTIOUS

THE HERO IS OVERPOWERED BUT
OVERLY CAUTIOUS

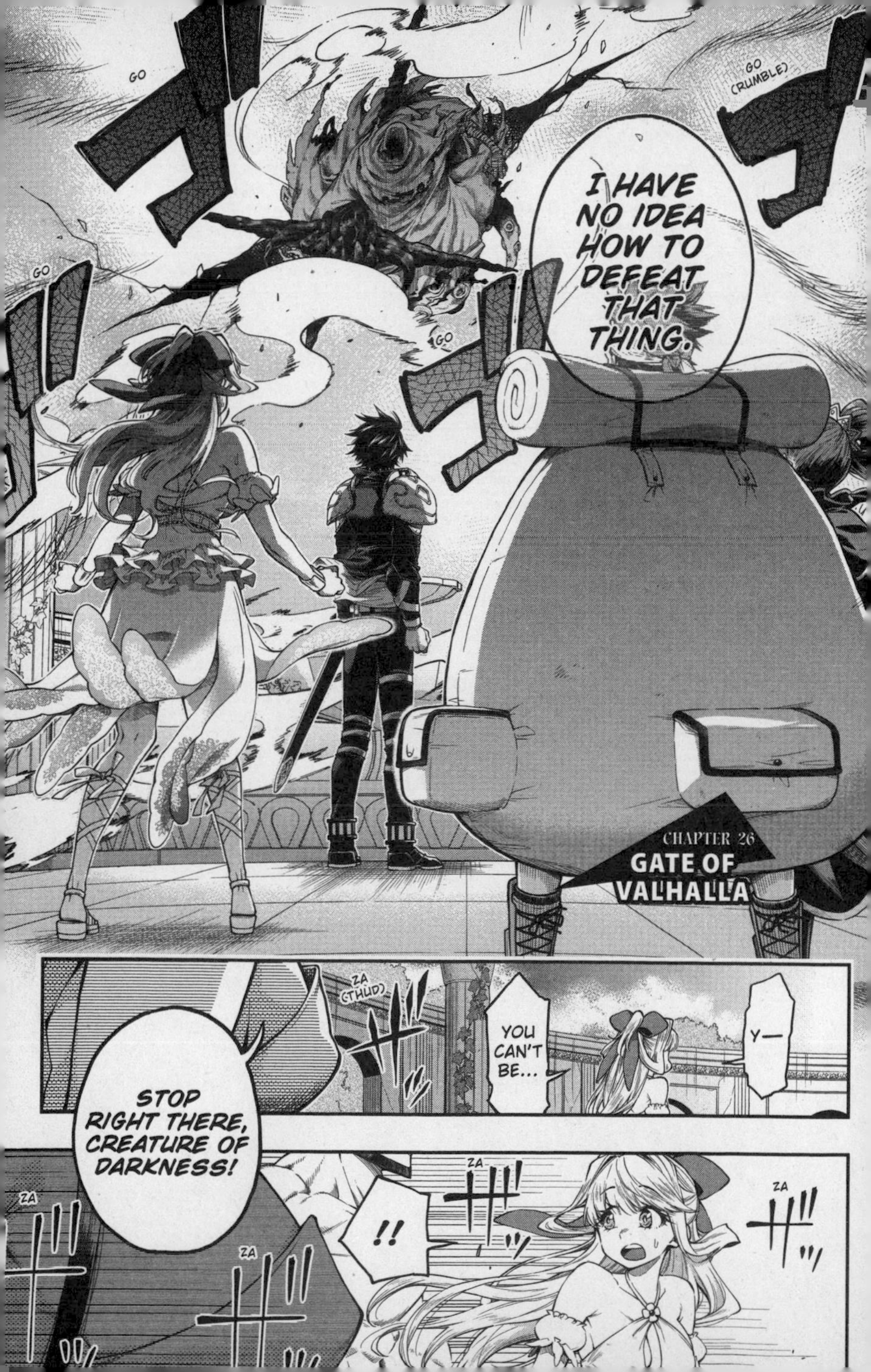
GO
GO (RUMBLE)
I HAVE NO IDEA HOW TO DEFEAT THAT THING.
GO
GO
CHAPTER 26
GATE OF VALHALLA
Y—
YOU CAN'T BE...
ZA (THUD)
ZA
ZA
!!
STOP RIGHT THERE, CREATURE OF DARKNESS!
ZA
ZA

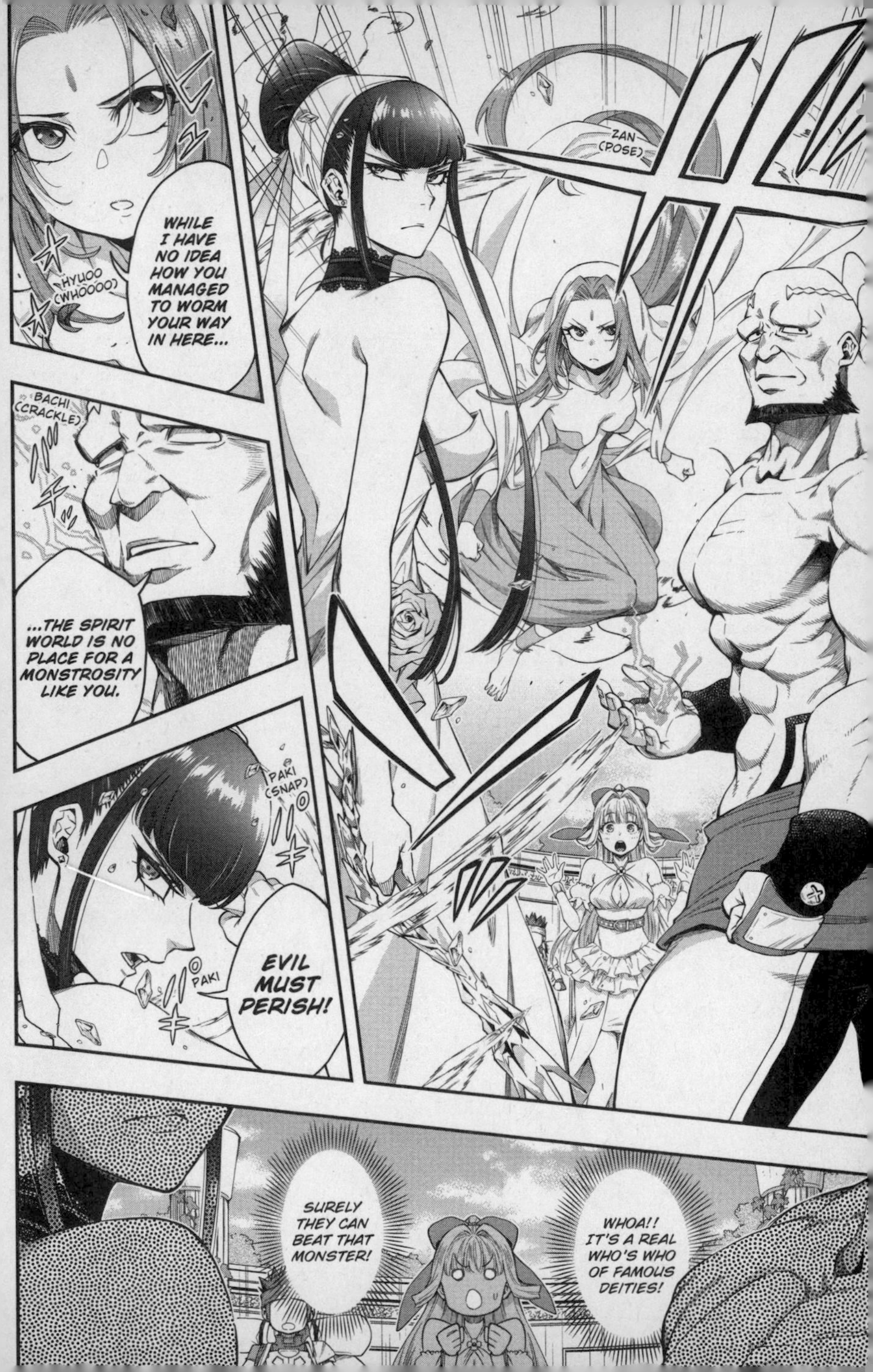
ZAN
(POSE)
HYUOO
(WHOOOO)
WHILE I HAVE NO IDEA HOW YOU MANAGED TO WORM YOUR WAY IN HERE...
BACHI
(CRACKLE)
...THE SPIRIT WORLD IS NO PLACE FOR A MONSTROSITY LIKE YOU.
PAKI
(SNAP)
PAKI
EVIL MUST PERISH!
WHOA!! IT'S A REAL WHO'S WHO OF FAMOUS DEITIES!
SURELY THEY CAN BEAT THAT MONSTER!

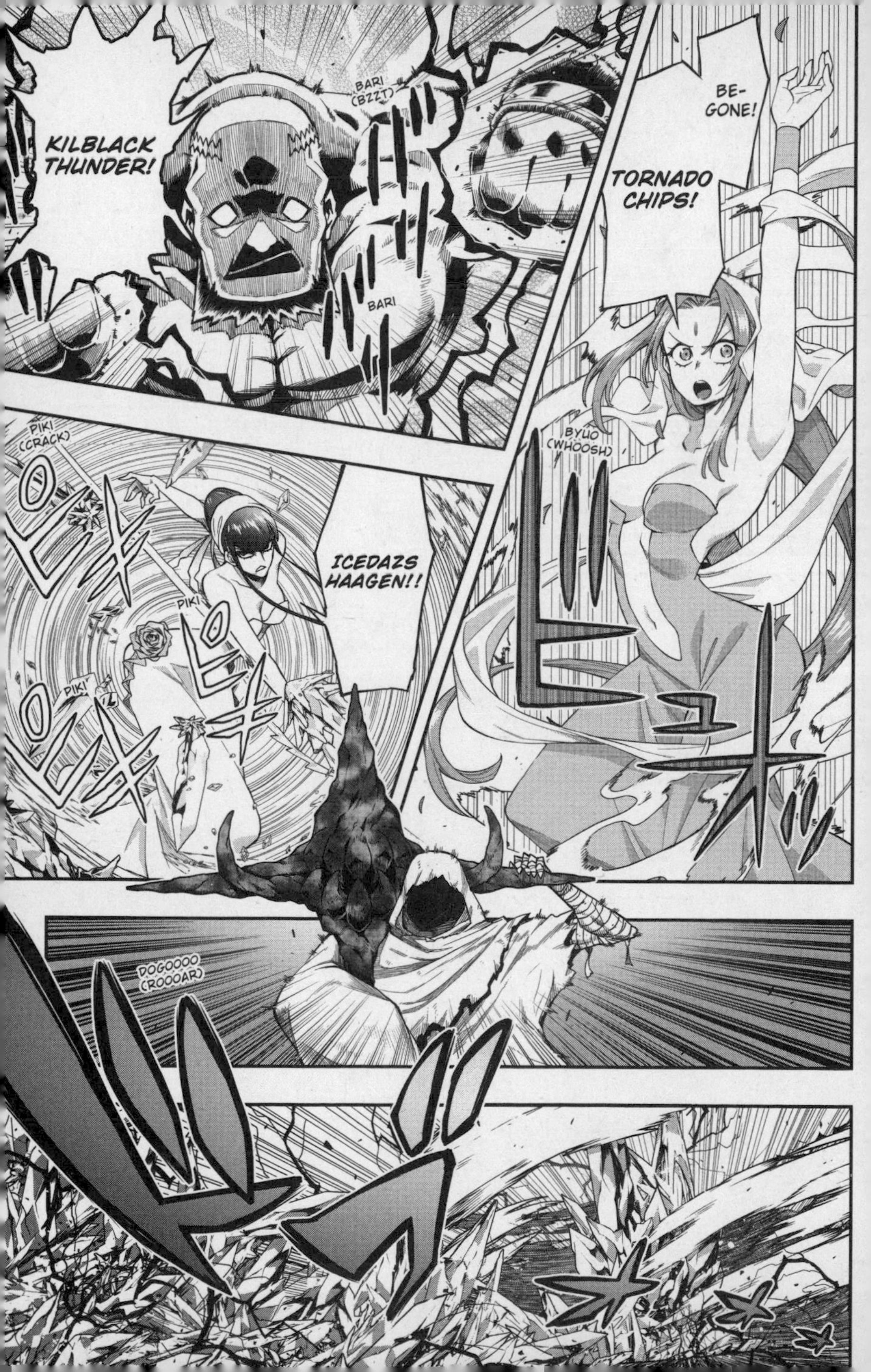
BE-GONE!
TORNADO CHIPS!
BYUO (WHOOSH)
KILBLACK THUNDER!
BARI (BZZT)
BARI
PIKI (CRACK)
ICEDAZS HAAGEN!!
PIKI
PIKI
DOGOOOO (ROOOAR)

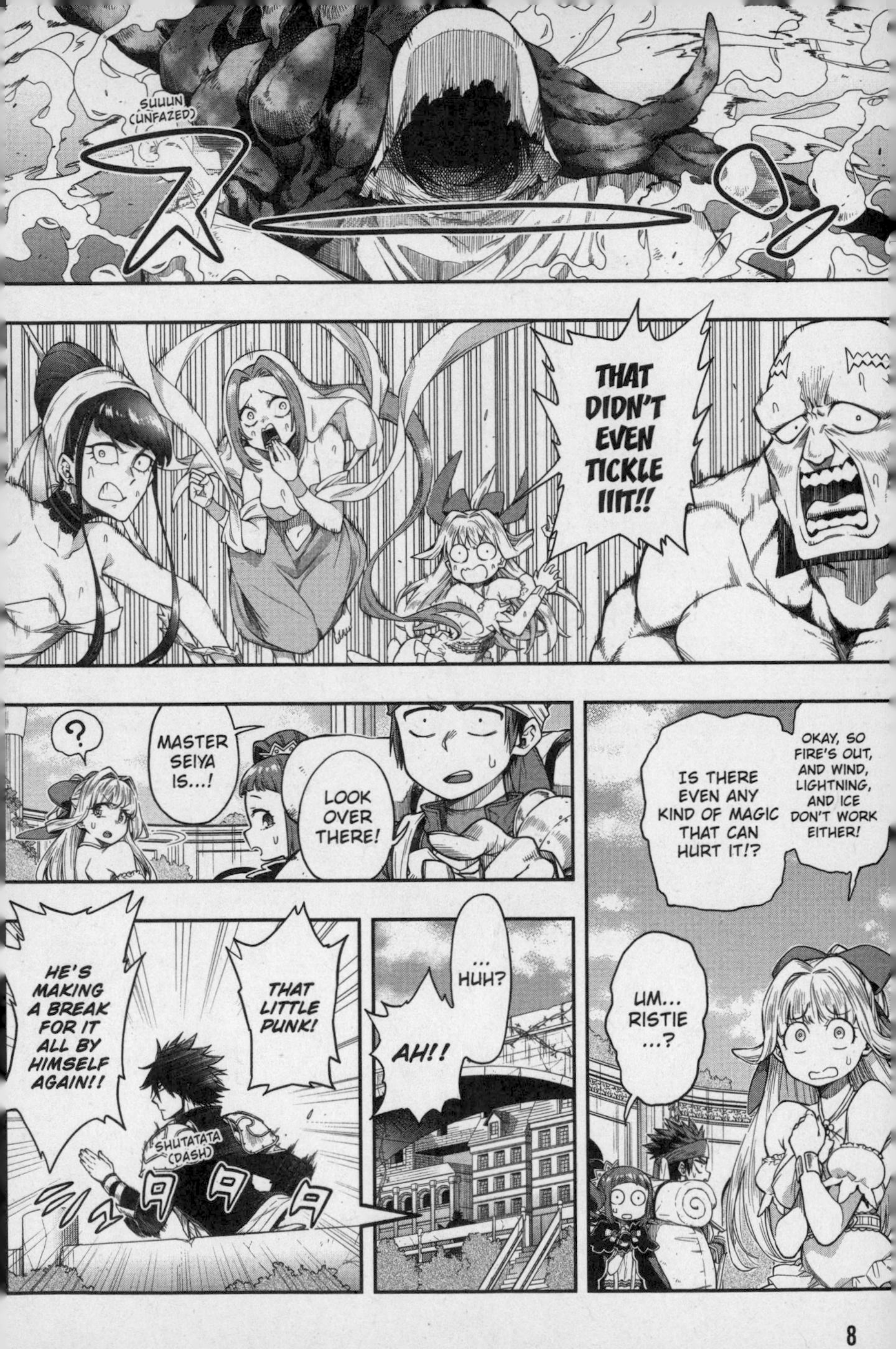
SUUUN (UNFAZED)
THAT DIDN'T EVEN TICKLE IIIT!!
OKAY, SO FIRE'S OUT, AND WIND, LIGHTNING, AND ICE DON'T WORK EITHER!
IS THERE EVEN ANY KIND OF MAGIC THAT CAN HURT IT!?
UM... RISTIE ...?
LOOK OVER THERE!
?
MASTER SEIYA IS...!
... HUH?
AH!!
THAT LITTLE PUNK!
HE'S MAKING A BREAK FOR IT ALL BY HIMSELF AGAIN!!
SHUTATATA (DASH)

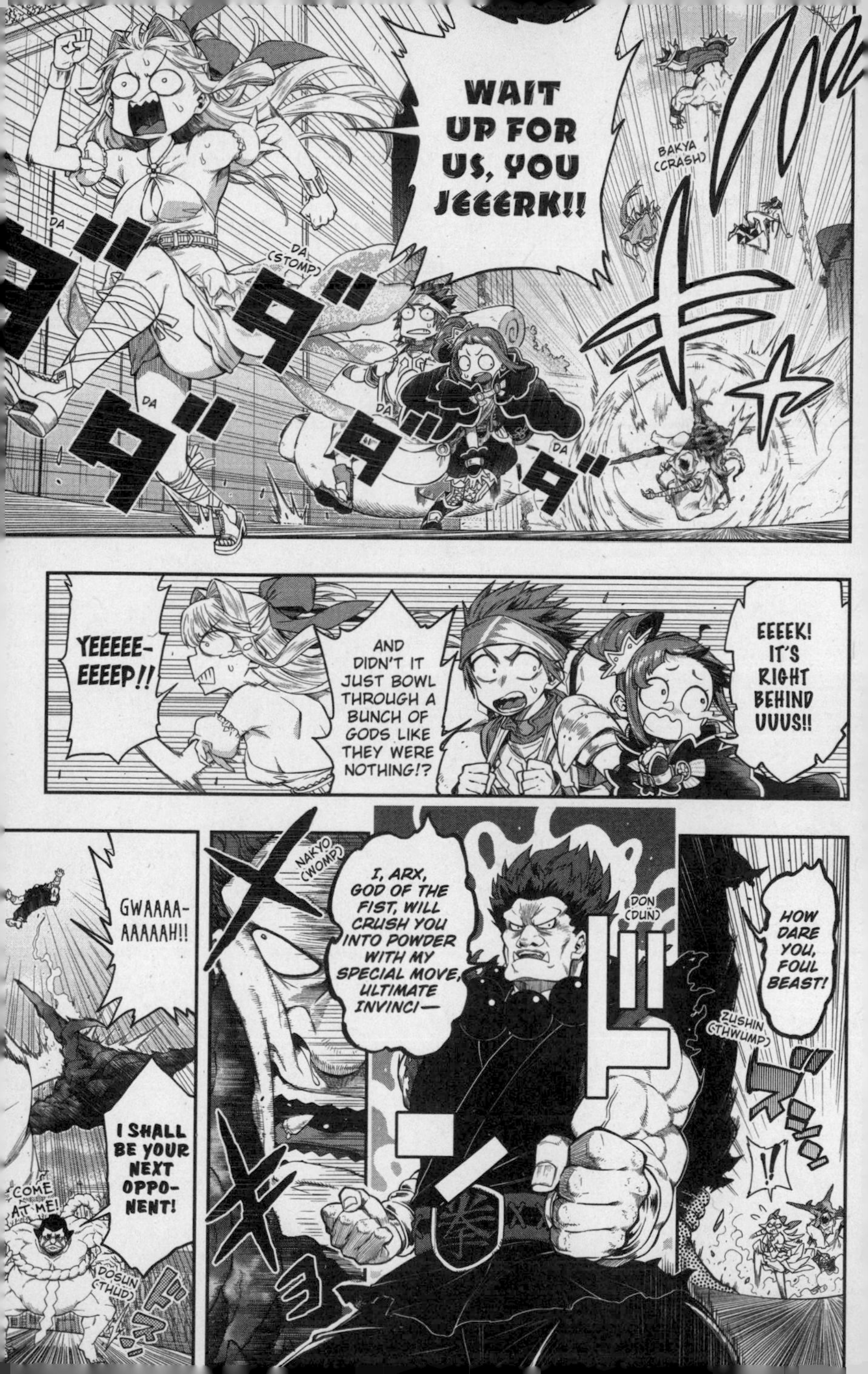
BAKYA (CRASH)
WAIT UP FOR US, YOU JEEERK!!
DA (STOMP)
DA
DA
DA
DA
EEEEK! IT'S RIGHT BEHIND UUUS!!
AND DIDN'T IT JUST BOWL THROUGH A BUNCH OF GODS LIKE THEY WERE NOTHING!?
YEEEEE-EEEEP!!
HOW DARE YOU, FOUL BEAST!
ZUSHIN (THWUMP)
!!
DON (DUN)
I, ARX, GOD OF THE FIST, WILL CRUSH YOU INTO POWDER WITH MY SPECIAL MOVE, ULTIMATE INVINCI—
NAKYO (WOMP)
GWAAAA-AAAAAH!!
I SHALL BE YOUR NEXT OPPO-NENT!
COME AT ME!
DOSUN (THUD)

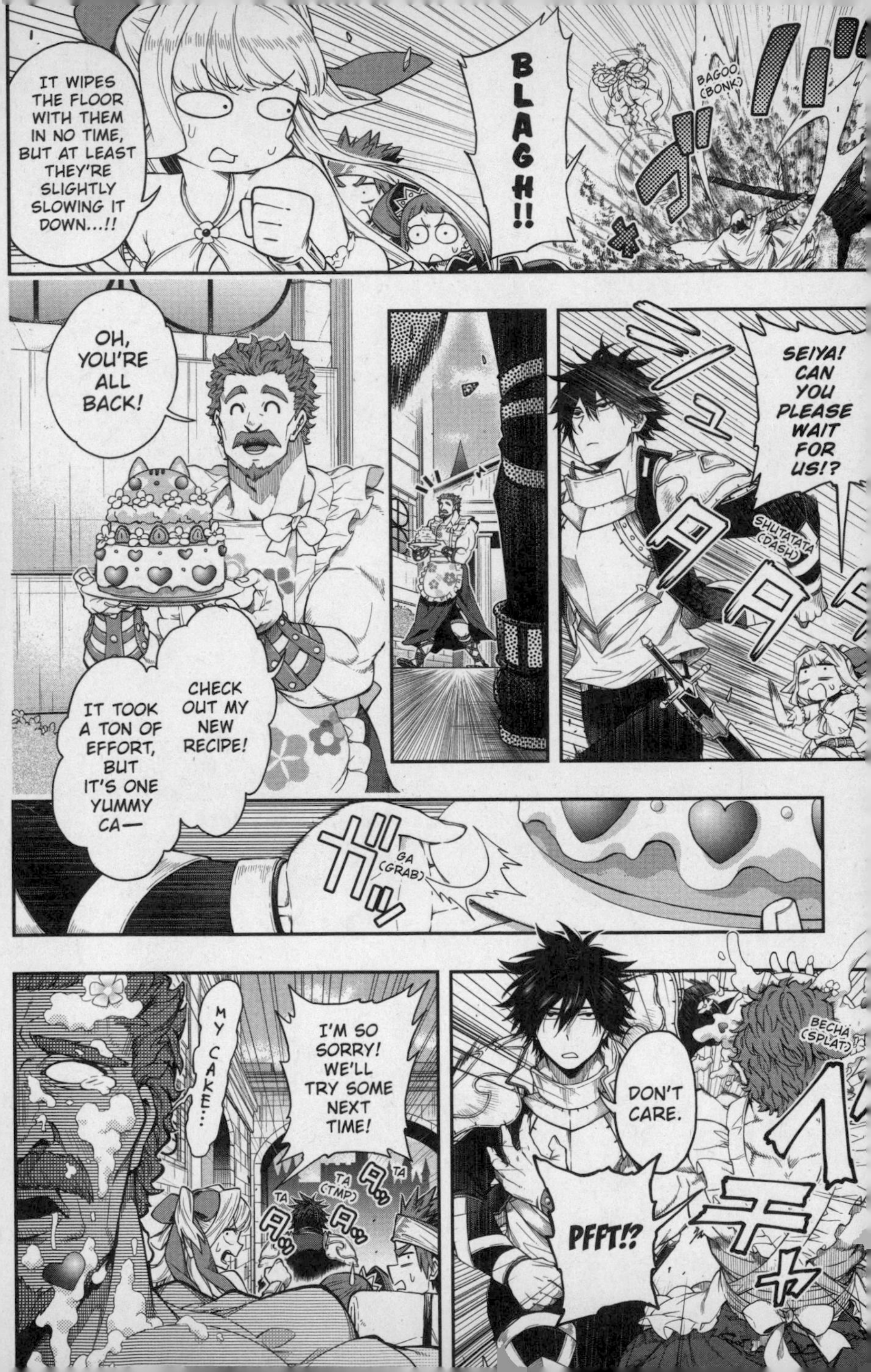
BAGOO (BONK)
BLAGH!!
IT WIPES THE FLOOR WITH THEM IN NO TIME, BUT AT LEAST THEY'RE SLIGHTLY SLOWING IT DOWN...!!
SEIYA! CAN YOU PLEASE WAIT FOR US!?
SHUTATATA (DASH)
OH, YOU'RE ALL BACK!
CHECK OUT MY NEW RECIPE!
IT TOOK A TON OF EFFORT, BUT IT'S ONE YUMMY CA—
GA (GRAB)
BECHA (SPLAT)
DON'T CARE.
PFFT!?
I'M SO SORRY! WE'LL TRY SOME NEXT TIME!
MY CAKE...
TA
TA (TMP)
TA

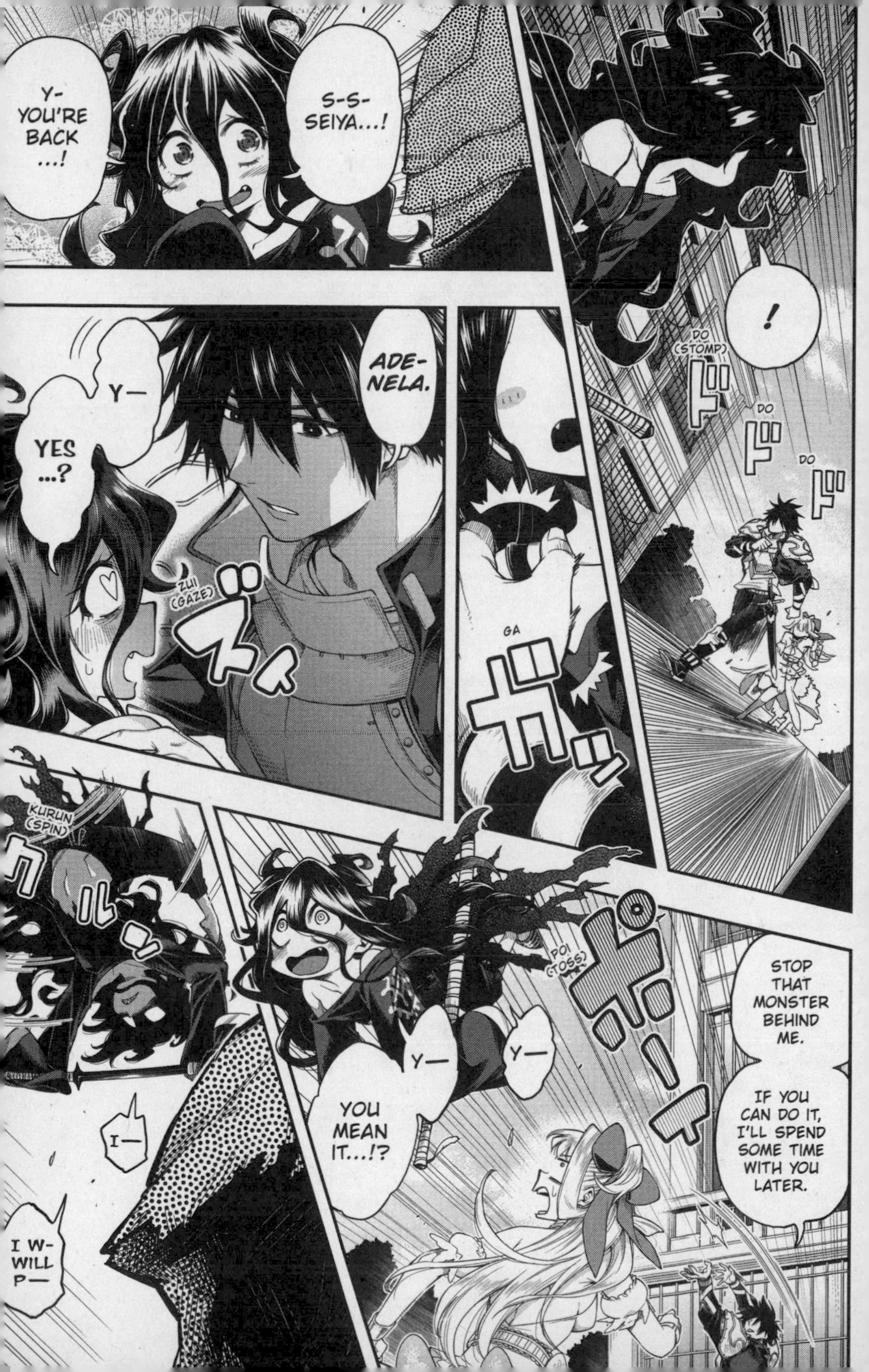
!
DO (STOMP)
DO
DO
S-S-SEIYA...!
Y-YOU'RE BACK...!
GA
ADE-NELA.
Y— YES...?
ZUI (GAZE)
POI (TOSS)
STOP THAT MONSTER BEHIND ME.
IF YOU CAN DO IT, I'LL SPEND SOME TIME WITH YOU LATER.
Y—
Y—
YOU MEAN IT...!?
KURUN (SPIN)
I—
I W-WILL P—

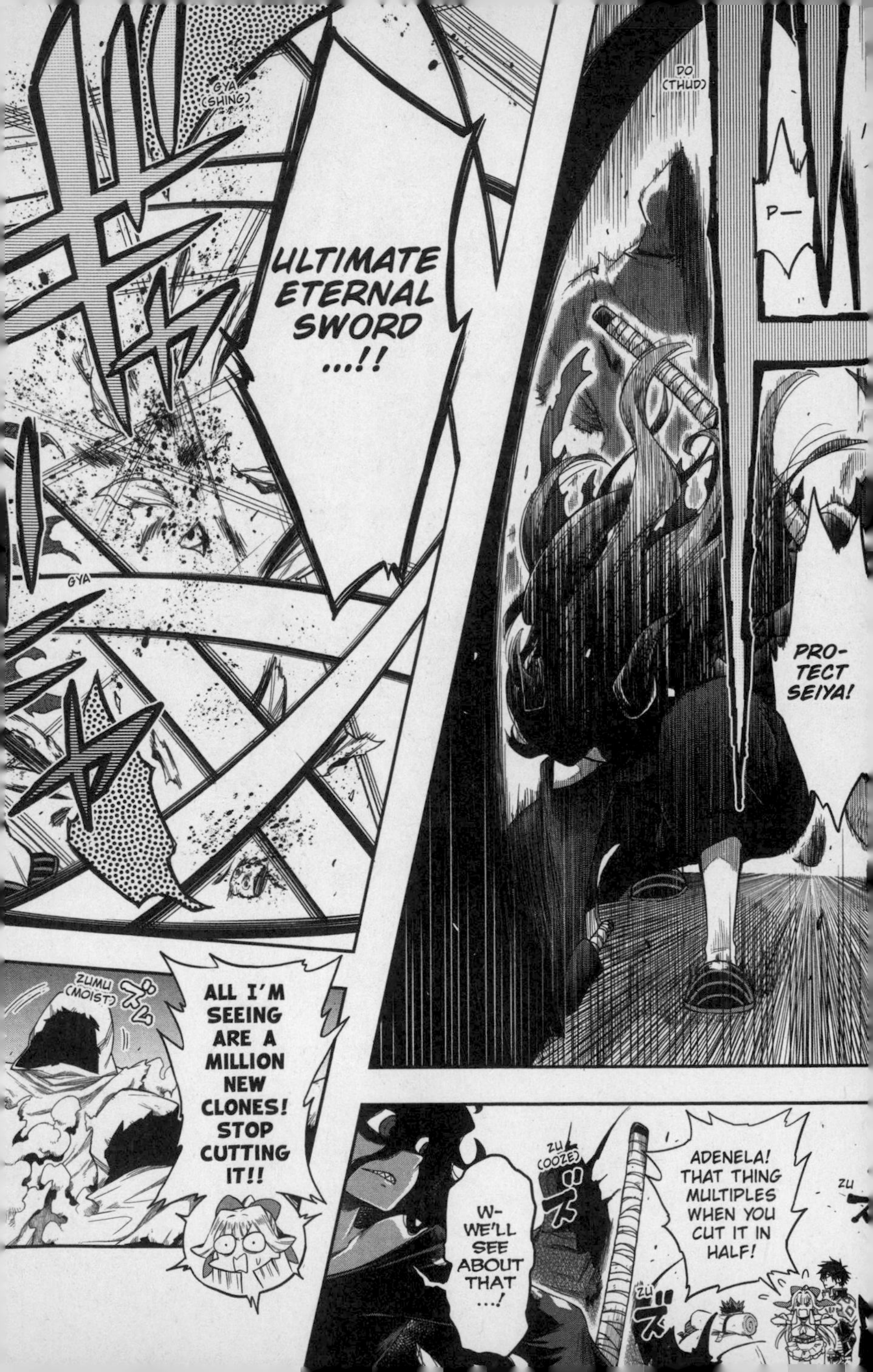
DO
(THUD)
P—
PRO-
TECT
SEIYA!
GYA
(SHING)
ULTIMATE
ETERNAL
SWORD
...!!
GYA
ZU
ADENELA! THAT THING MULTIPLES WHEN YOU CUT IT IN HALF!
ZU
(OOZE)
W-WE'LL SEE ABOUT THAT ...!
ZU
ZUMU
(MOIST)
ALL I'M SEEING ARE A MILLION NEW CLONES! STOP CUTTING IT!!

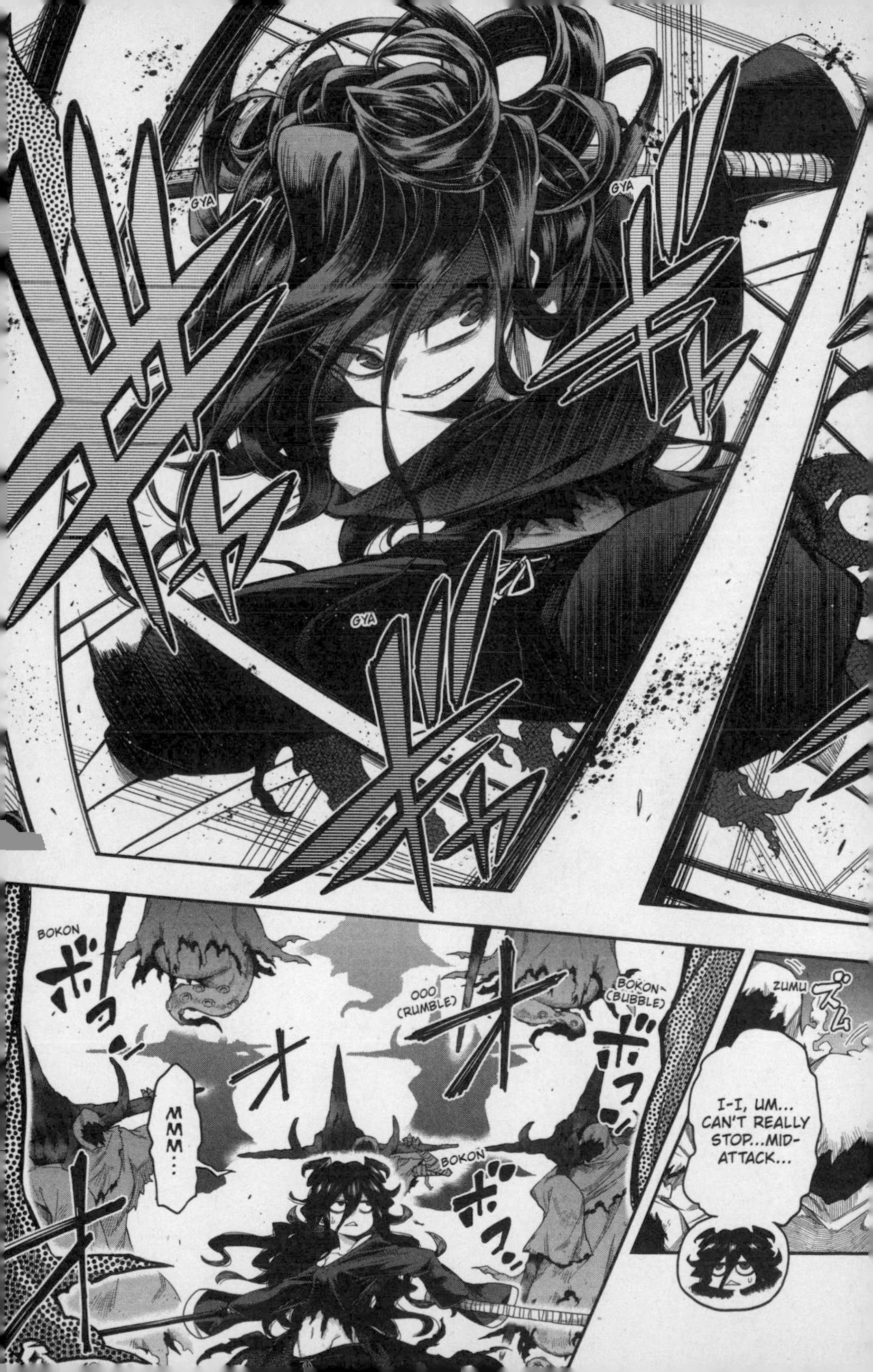
GYA
GYA
GYA
ZUMU
I-I, UM... CAN'T REALLY STOP...MID-ATTACK...
BOKON (BUBBLE)
OOO (RUMBLE)
BOKON
MMM...
BOKON

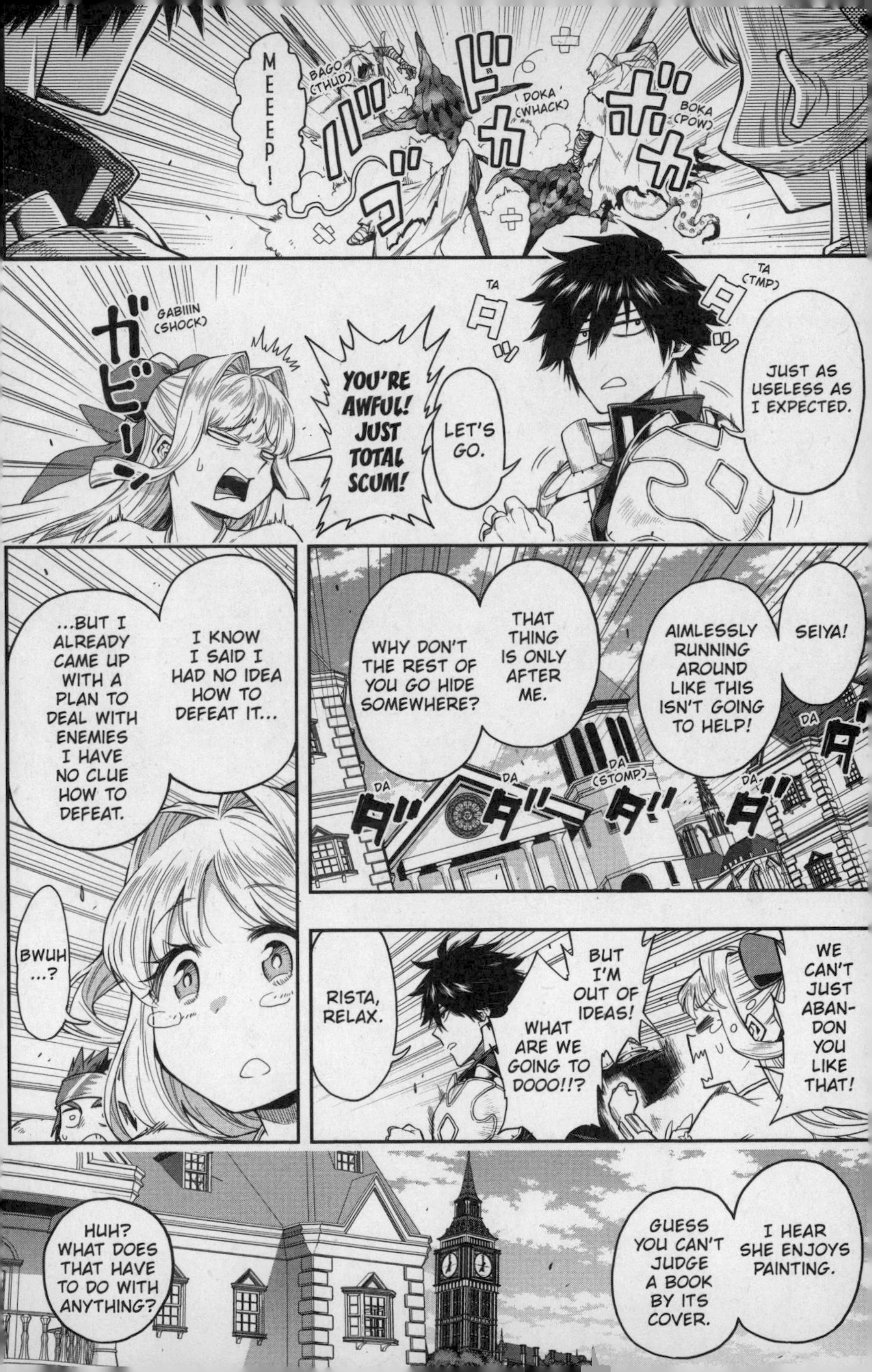
BOKA (POW)
DOKA (WHACK)
BAGO (THUD)
MEEEP!
TA (TMP)
JUST AS USELESS AS I EXPECTED.
TA
LET'S GO.
YOU'RE AWFUL! JUST TOTAL SCUM!
GABIIIN (SHOCK)
SEIYA!
AIMLESSLY RUNNING AROUND LIKE THIS ISN'T GOING TO HELP!
THAT THING IS ONLY AFTER ME.
WHY DON'T THE REST OF YOU GO HIDE SOMEWHERE?
DA
DA (STOMP)
DA
DA
WE CAN'T JUST ABAN-DON YOU LIKE THAT!
BUT I'M OUT OF IDEAS!
WHAT ARE WE GOING TO DOOO!!?
RISTA, RELAX.
I KNOW I SAID I HAD NO IDEA HOW TO DEFEAT IT...
...BUT I ALREADY CAME UP WITH A PLAN TO DEAL WITH ENEMIES I HAVE NO CLUE HOW TO DEFEAT.
BWUH ...?
I HEAR SHE ENJOYS PAINTING.
GUESS YOU CAN'T JUDGE A BOOK BY ITS COVER.
HUH? WHAT DOES THAT HAVE TO DO WITH ANYTHING?

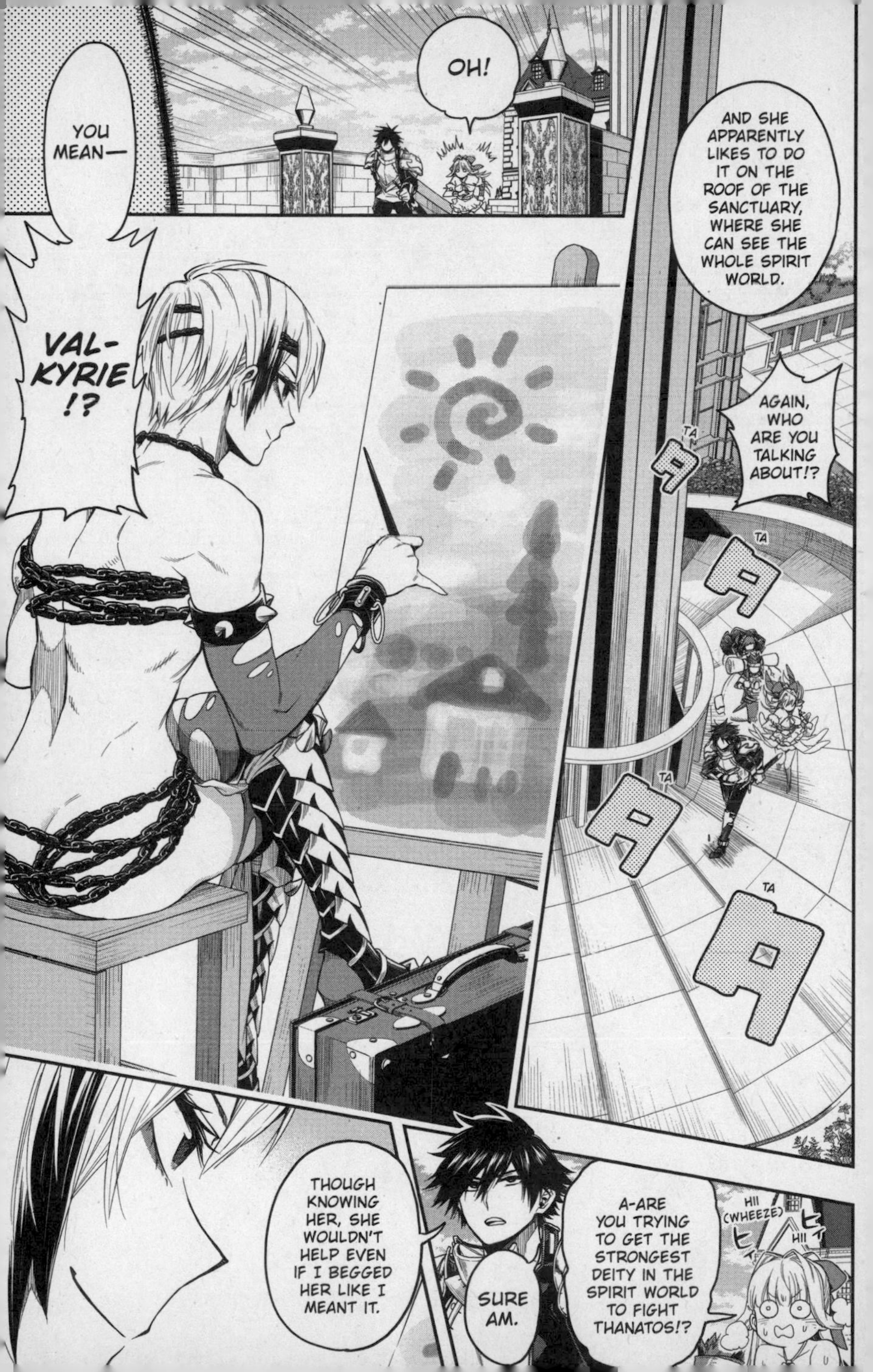
AND SHE APPARENTLY LIKES TO DO IT ON THE ROOF OF THE SANCTUARY, WHERE SHE CAN SEE THE WHOLE SPIRIT WORLD.
AGAIN, WHO ARE YOU TALKING ABOUT!?
TA
TA
TA
TA
OH!
YOU MEAN—
VAL-KYRIE!?
HII (WHEEZE)
HII
A-ARE YOU TRYING TO GET THE STRONGEST DEITY IN THE SPIRIT WORLD TO FIGHT THANATOS!?
SURE AM.
THOUGH KNOWING HER, SHE WOULDN'T HELP EVEN IF I BEGGED HER LIKE I MEANT IT.

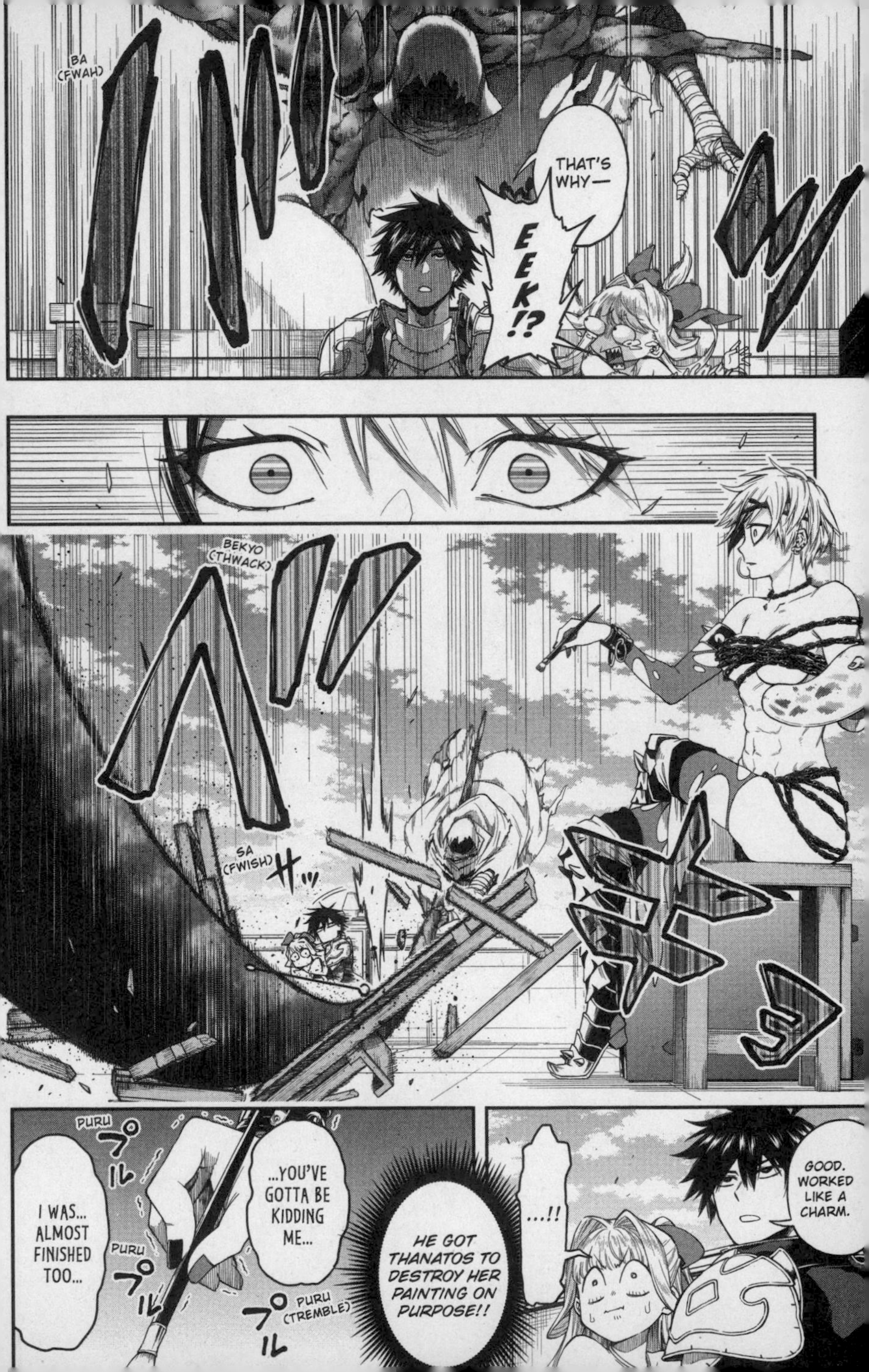
THAT'S WHY—
EEK!?
BA (FWAH)
BEKYO (THWACK)
SA (FWISH)
GOOD. WORKED LIKE A CHARM.
...!!
HE GOT THANATOS TO DESTROY HER PAINTING ON PURPOSE!!
...YOU'VE GOTTA BE KIDDING ME...
PURU
I WAS... ALMOST FINISHED TOO...
PURU
PURU (TREMBLE)

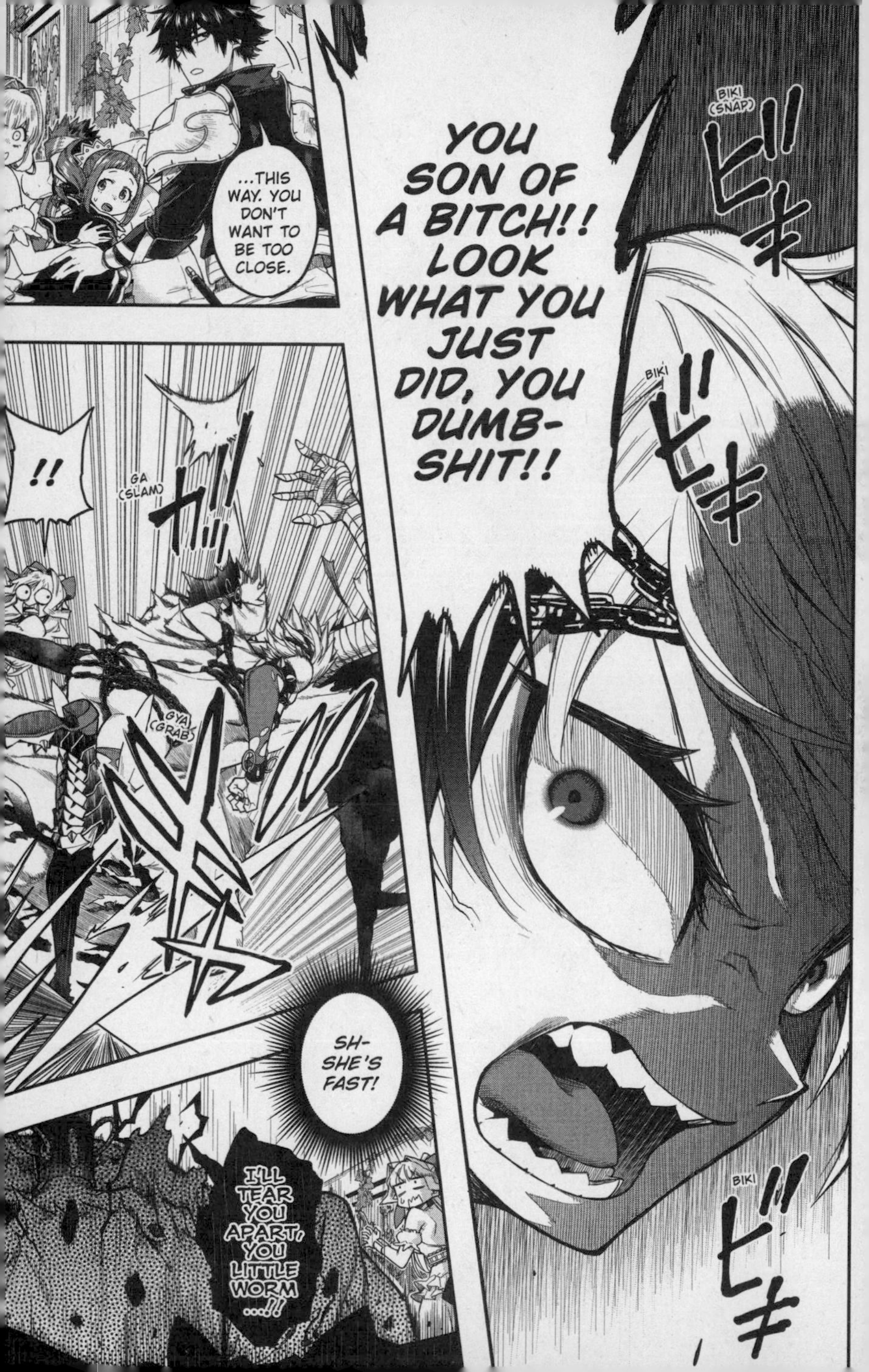
BIKI (SNAP)
YOU SON OF A BITCH!! LOOK WHAT YOU JUST DID, YOU DUMB-SHIT!!
BIKI
BIKI
...THIS WAY. YOU DON'T WANT TO BE TOO CLOSE.
!!
GA (SLAM)
GYA (GRAB)
SH-SHE'S FAST!
I'LL TEAR YOU APART, YOU LITTLE WORM...!!

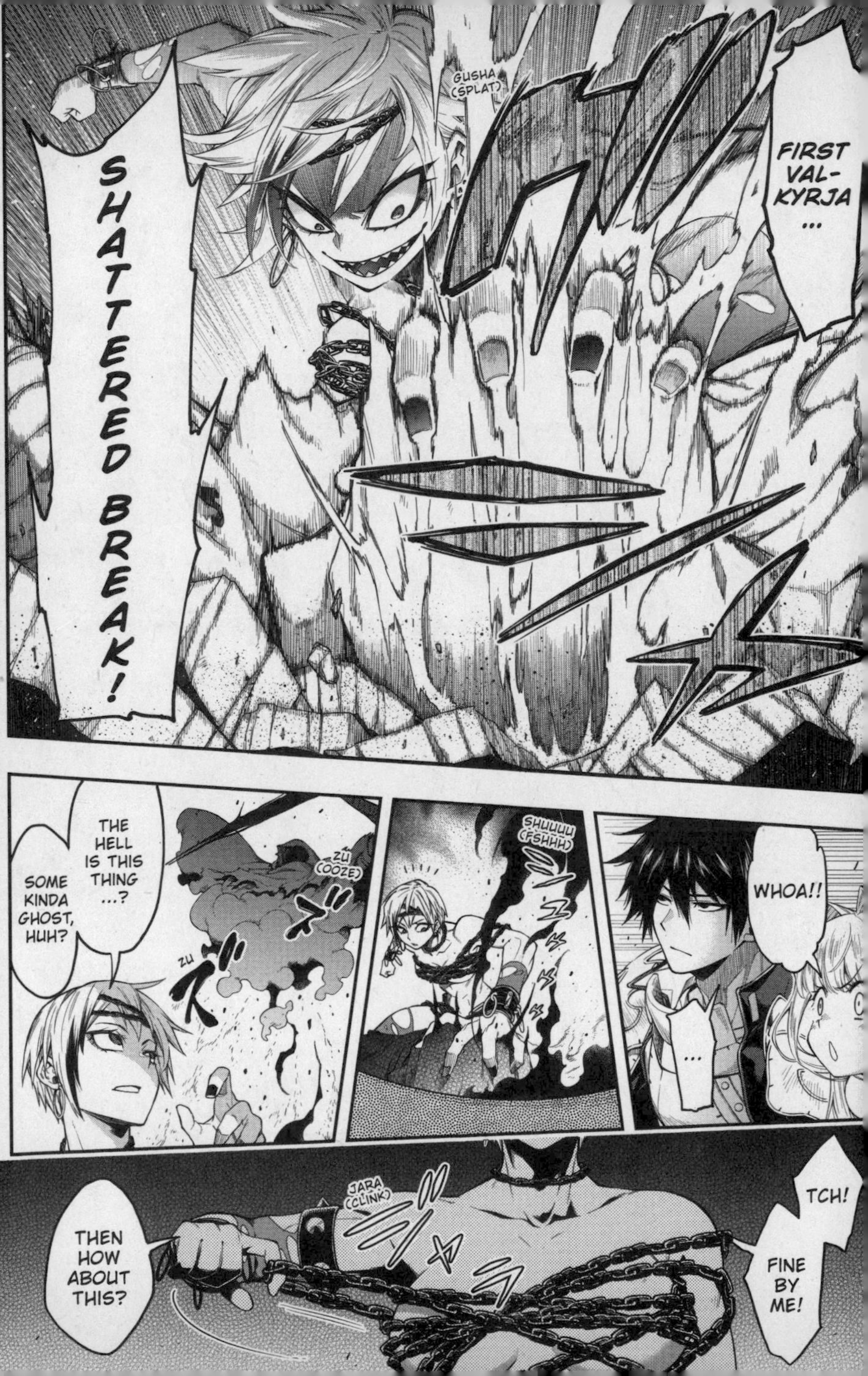
FIRST VAL-KYRJA ...
GUSHA (SPLAT)
SHATTERED BREAK!
WHOA!!
...
SHUUUU (FSHHH)
ZU (OOZE)
ZU
THE HELL IS THIS THING ...?
SOME KINDA GHOST, HUH?
TCH!
FINE BY ME!
JARA (CLINK)
THEN HOW ABOUT THIS?

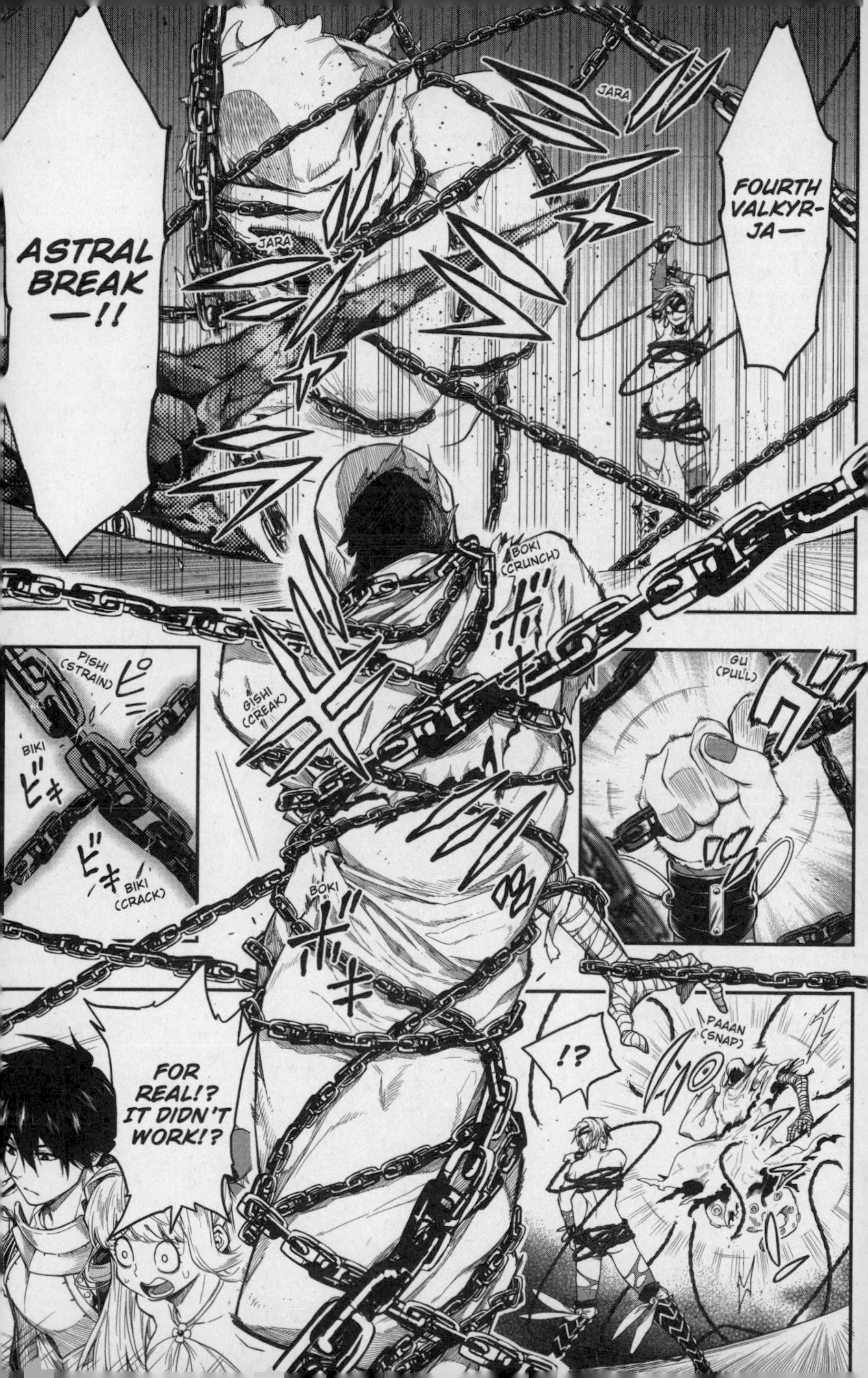

JARA
FOURTH VALKYR-JA—
JARA
ASTRAL BREAK—!!
BOKI (CRUNCH)
GU (PULL)
GISHI (CREAK)
PISHI (STRAIN)
BIKI
BIKI (CRACK)
BOKI
PAAAN (SNAP)
!?
FOR REAL!? IT DIDN'T WORK!?

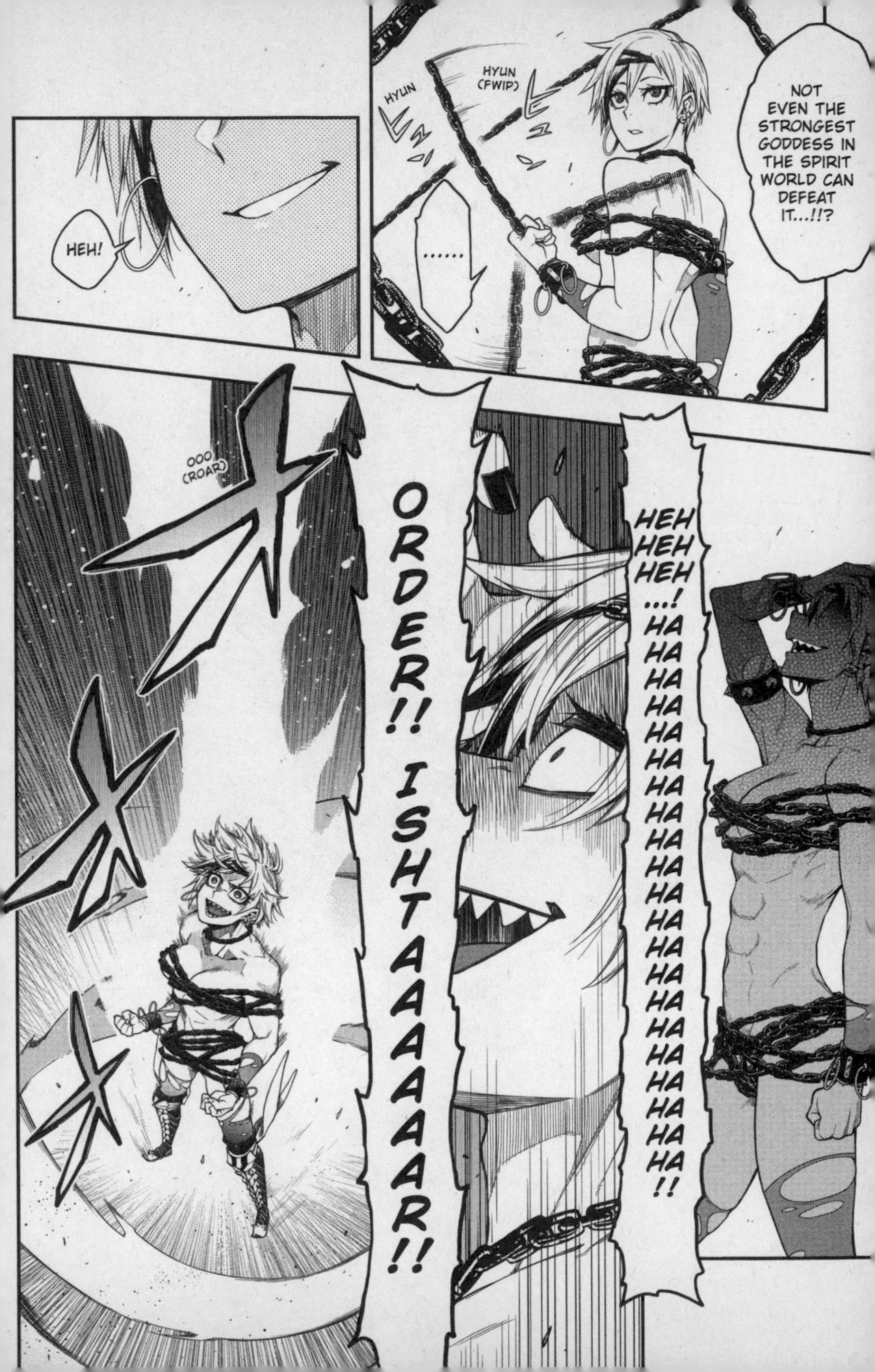
NOT EVEN THE STRONGEST GODDESS IN THE SPIRIT WORLD CAN DEFEAT IT...!!?
HYUN (FWIP)
HYUN
......
HEH!
HEH HEH HEH ...! HA HA HA HA HA HA HA HA HA HA HA HA HA HA HA HA HA HA HA HA HA HA HA HA!!
ORDER!! ISHTAAAAAAAR!!
OOO (ROAR)

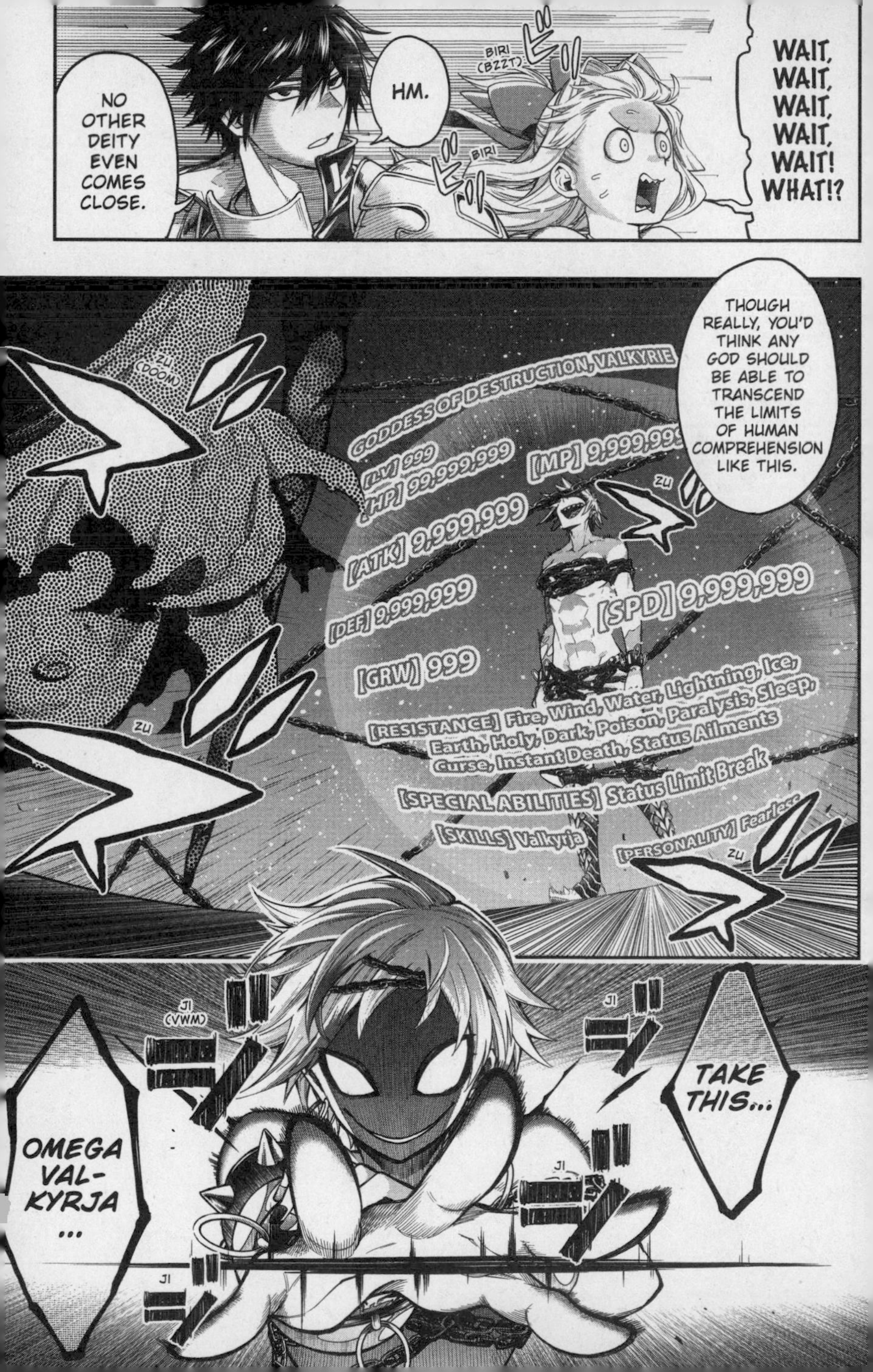

WAIT, WAIT, WAIT, WAIT, WAIT! WHAT!?
BIRI (BZZT)
BIRI
HM.
NO OTHER DEITY EVEN COMES CLOSE.
THOUGH REALLY, YOU'D THINK ANY GOD SHOULD BE ABLE TO TRANSCEND THE LIMITS OF HUMAN COMPREHENSION LIKE THIS.
ZU
GODDESS OF DESTRUCTION, VALKYRIE
[LV] 999
[HP] 99,999,999
[MP] 9,999,999
[ATK] 9,999,999
[DEF] 9,999,999
[SPD] 9,999,999
[GRW] 999
[RESISTANCE] Fire, Wind, Water, Lightning, Ice, Earth, Holy, Dark, Poison, Paralysis, Sleep, Curse, Instant Death, Status Ailments
[SPECIAL ABILITIES] Status Limit Break
[SKILLS] Valkyrja
[PERSONALITY] Fearless
ZU (DOOM)
ZU
ZU
JI
TAKE THIS...
JI (VWM)
JI
JI
OMEGA VAL-KYRJA ...

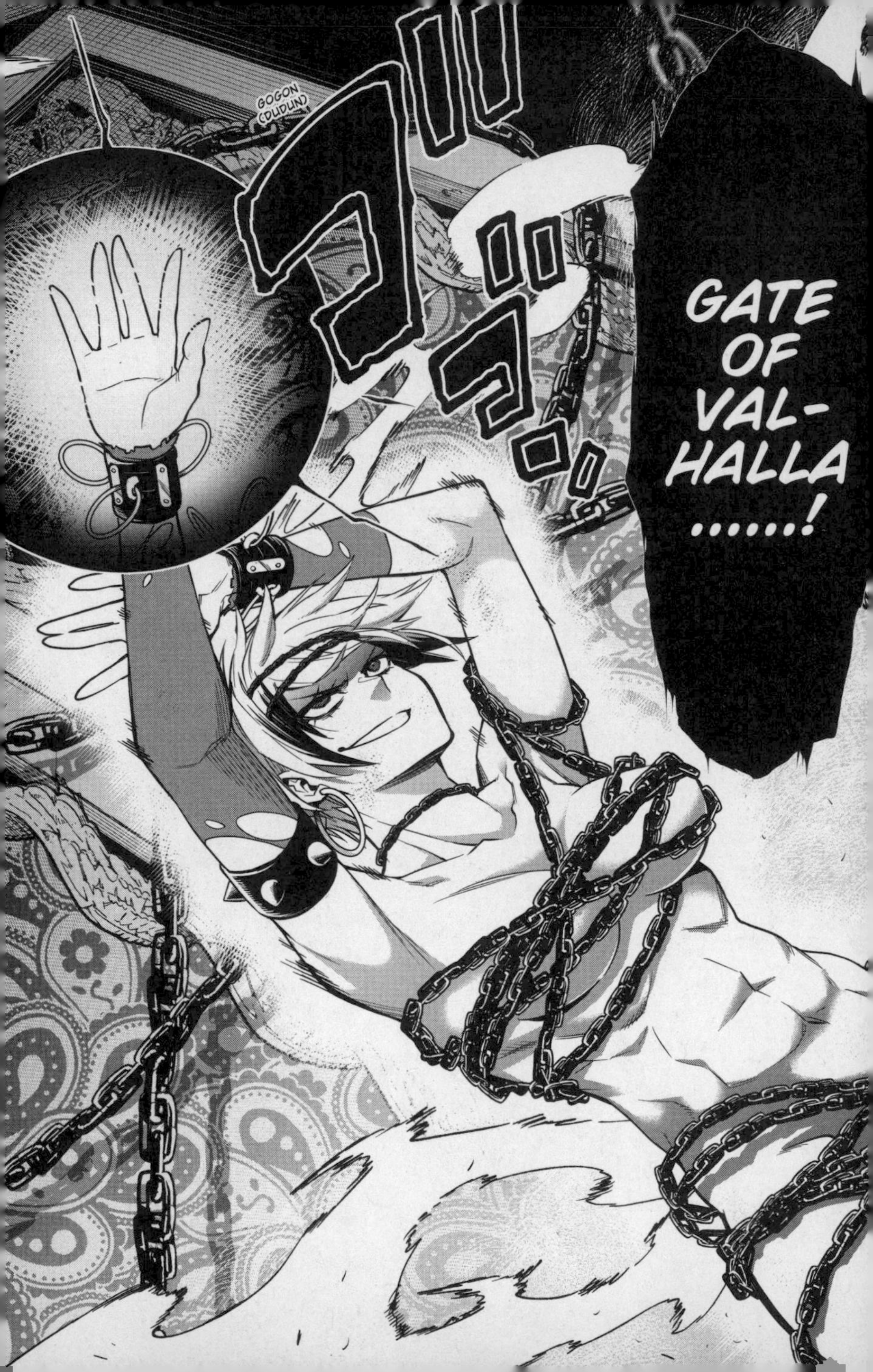
GOGON (DUDUN)
GATE OF VAL-HALLA ......!

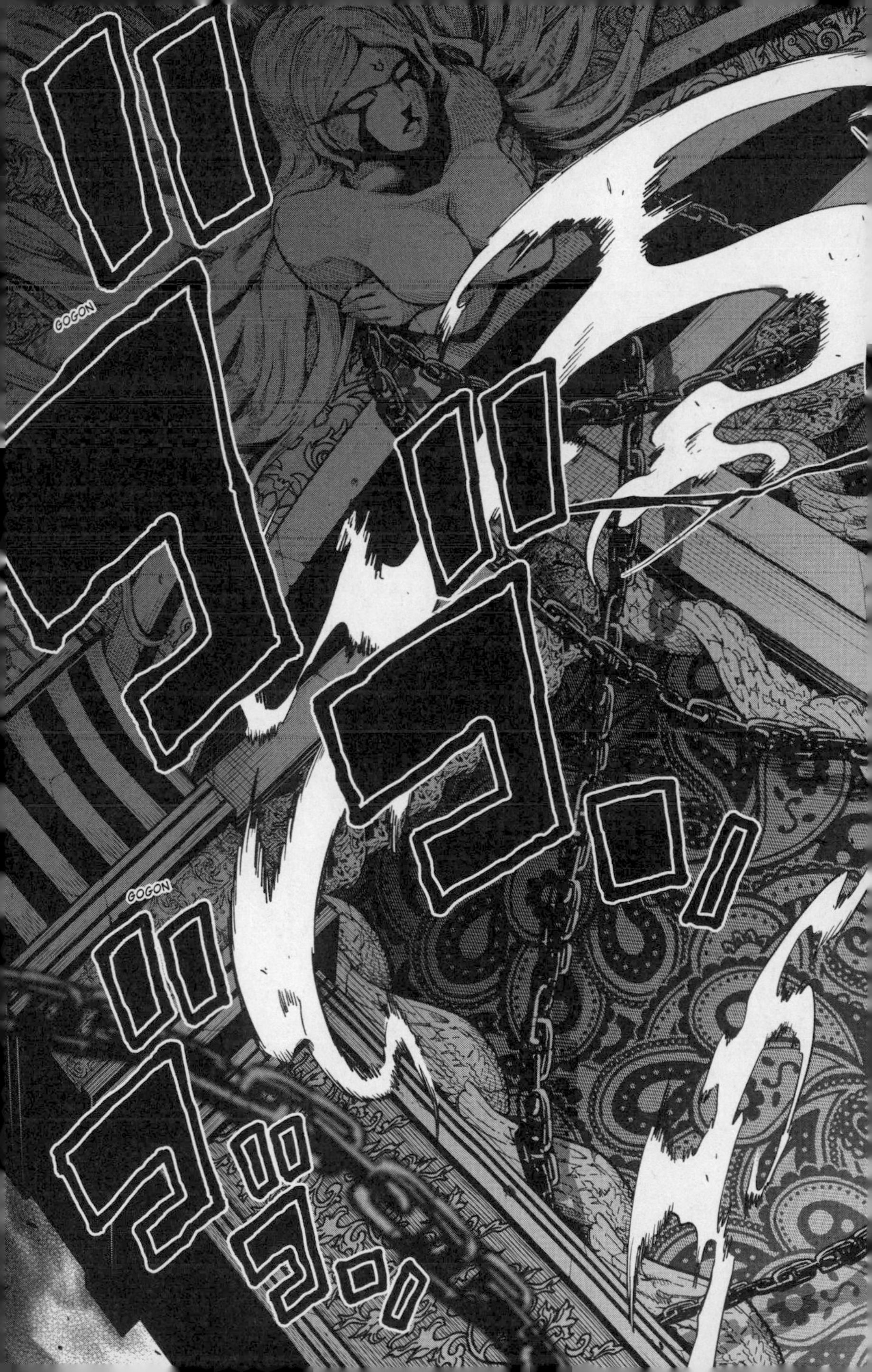
GOGON
GOGON

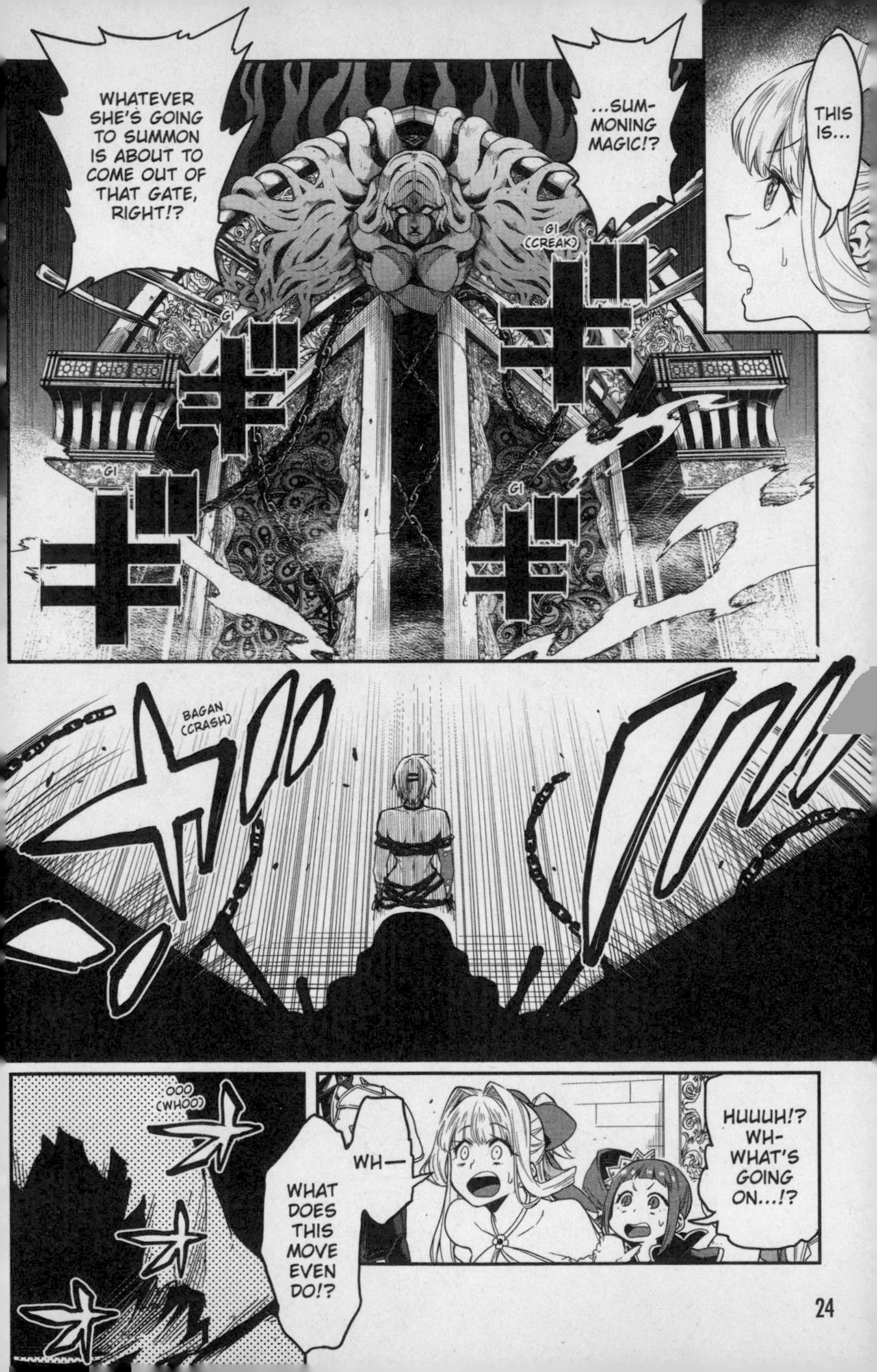
THIS IS...
...SUM-MONING MAGIC!?
WHATEVER SHE'S GOING TO SUMMON IS ABOUT TO COME OUT OF THAT GATE, RIGHT!?
GI (CREAK)
GI
GI
GI
BAGAN (CRASH)
HUUUH!? WH-WHAT'S GOING ON...!?
WH—
WHAT DOES THIS MOVE EVEN DO!?
OOO (WHOO)

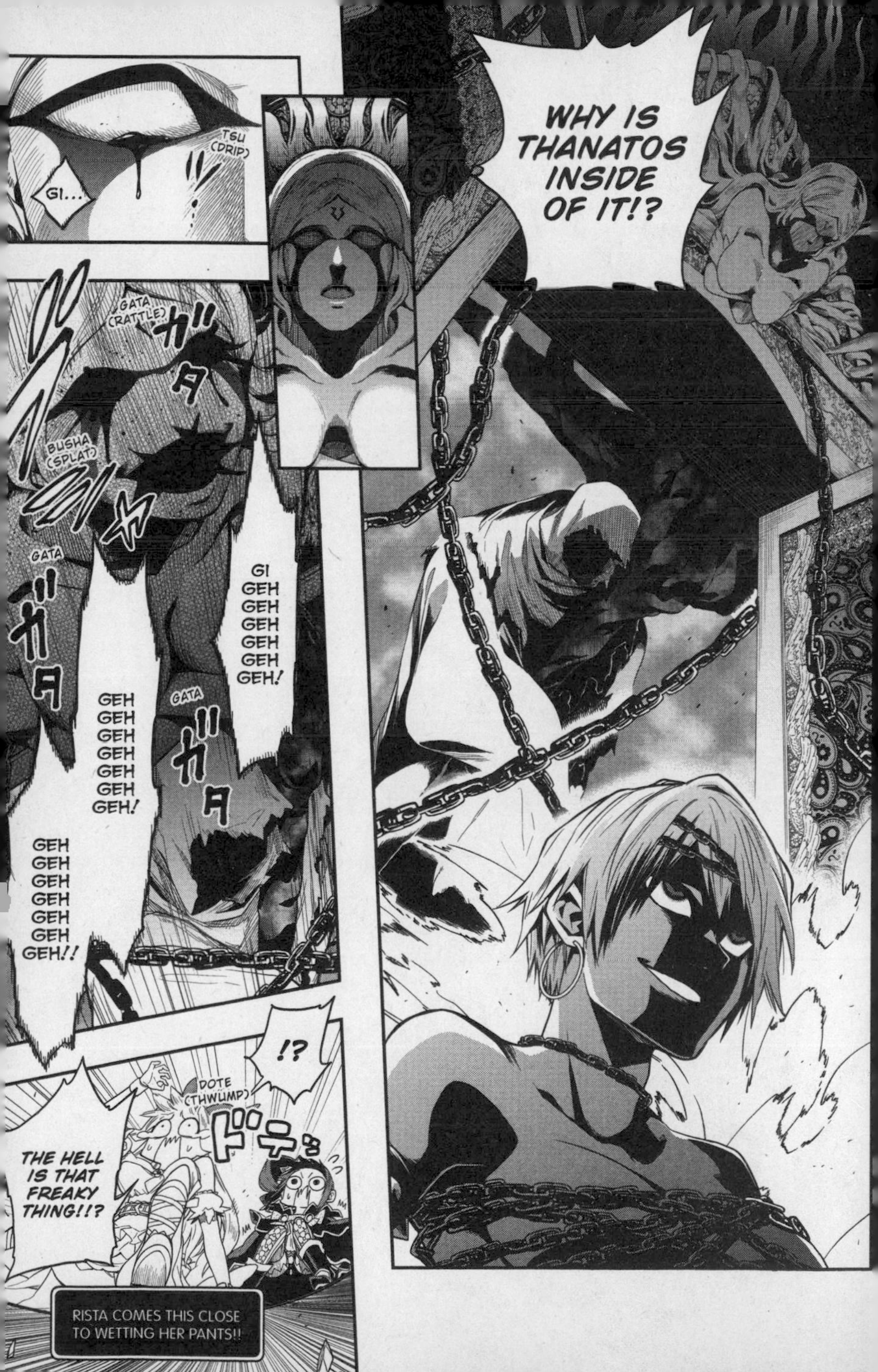
WHY IS THANATOS INSIDE OF IT!?
TSU (DRIP)
GI...
GATA (RATTLE)
BUSHA (SPLAT)
GATA
GI GEH GEH GEH GEH GEH GEH!
GATA
GEH GEH GEH GEH GEH GEH GEH!
GEH GEH GEH GEH GEH GEH GEH!!
!?
DOTE (THWUMP)
THE HELL IS THAT FREAKY THING!!?
RISTA COMES THIS CLOSE TO WETTING HER PANTS!!

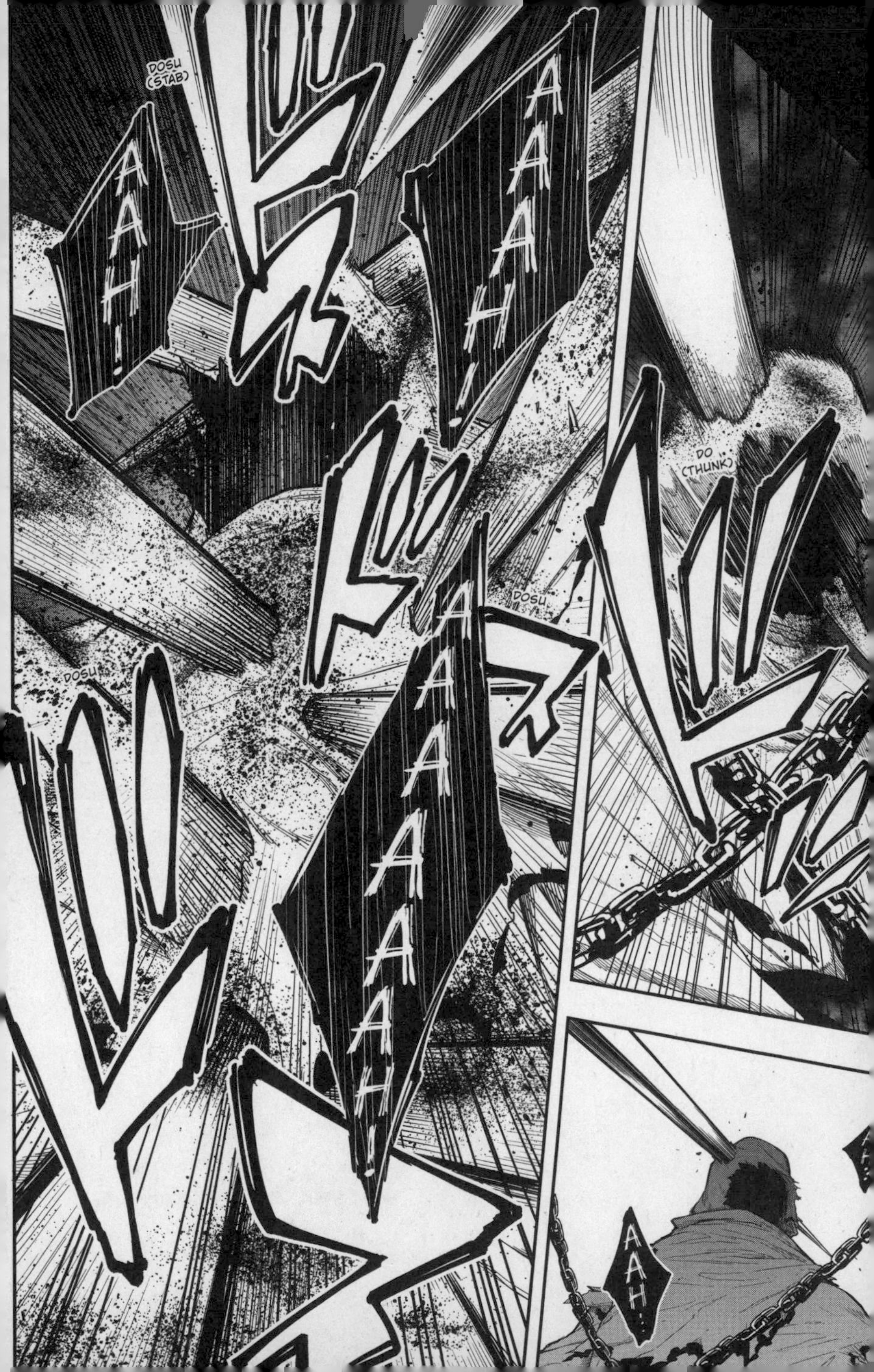
DO
(THUNK)
AAAH!!
DOSU
(STAB)
AAH!
DOSU
AAAAAAAH!!
DOSU
AAH!

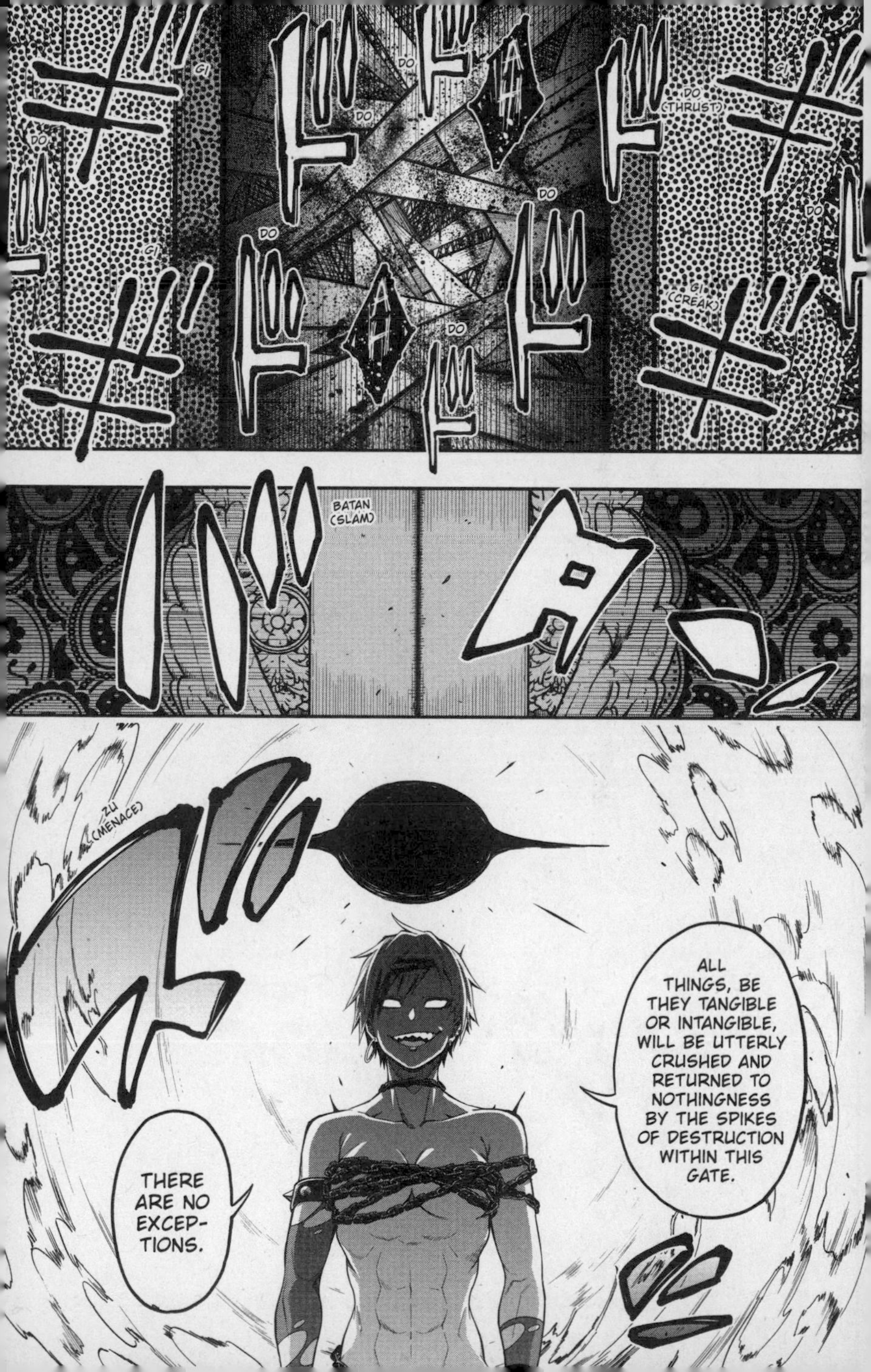
GI
DO (THRUST)
DO
GI (CREAK)
DO
DO
DO
DO
GI
DO
GI
BATAN (SLAM)
ALL THINGS, BE THEY TANGIBLE OR INTANGIBLE, WILL BE UTTERLY CRUSHED AND RETURNED TO NOTHINGNESS BY THE SPIKES OF DESTRUCTION WITHIN THIS GATE.
THERE ARE NO EXCEP-TIONS.
ZU (MENACE)

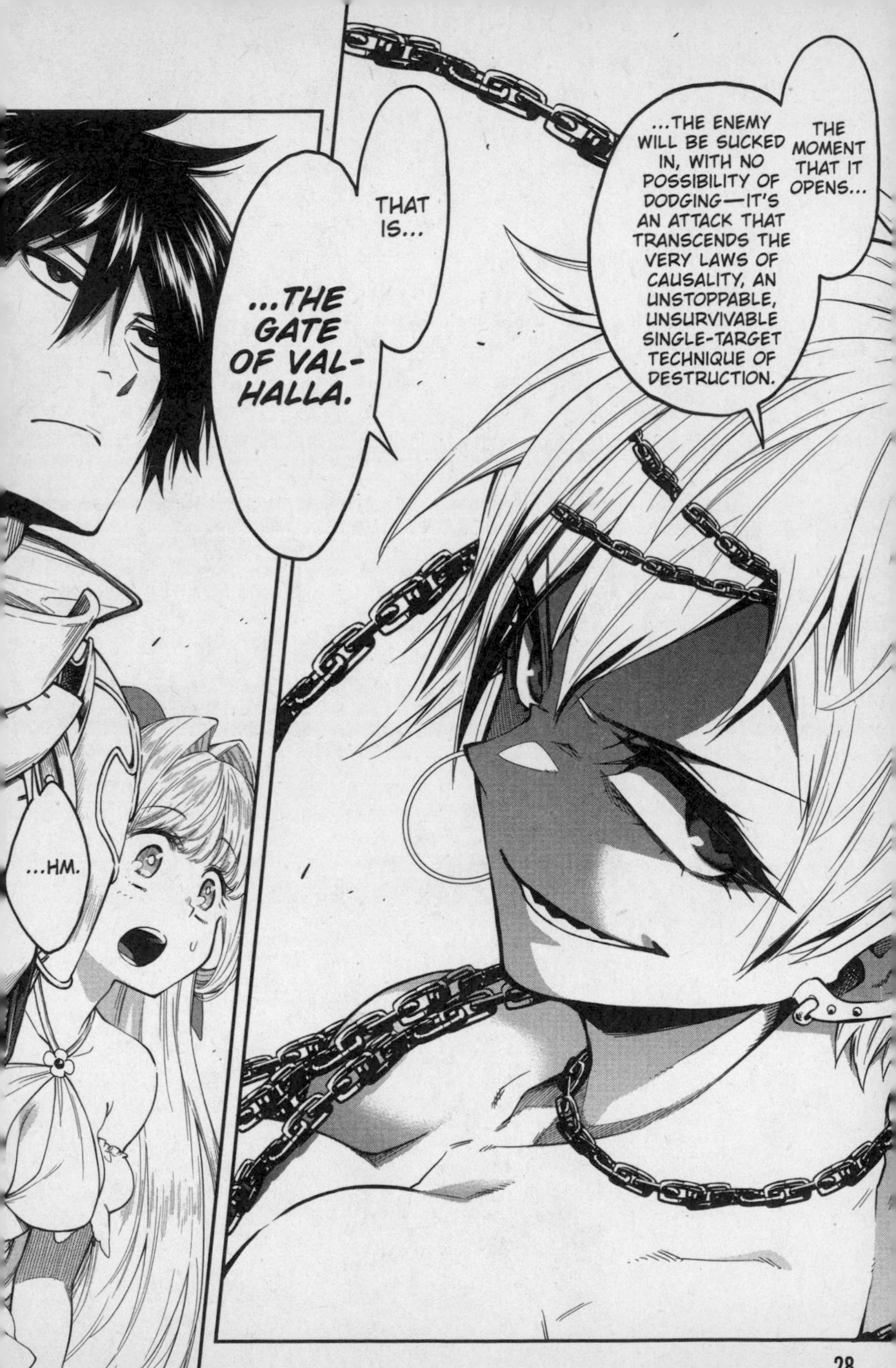
THE MOMENT THAT IT OPENS...
...THE ENEMY WILL BE SUCKED IN, WITH NO POSSIBILITY OF DODGING—IT'S AN ATTACK THAT TRANSCENDS THE VERY LAWS OF CAUSALITY, AN UNSTOPPABLE, UNSURVIVABLE SINGLE-TARGET TECHNIQUE OF DESTRUCTION.
THAT IS...
...THE GATE OF VAL-HALLA.
...HM.

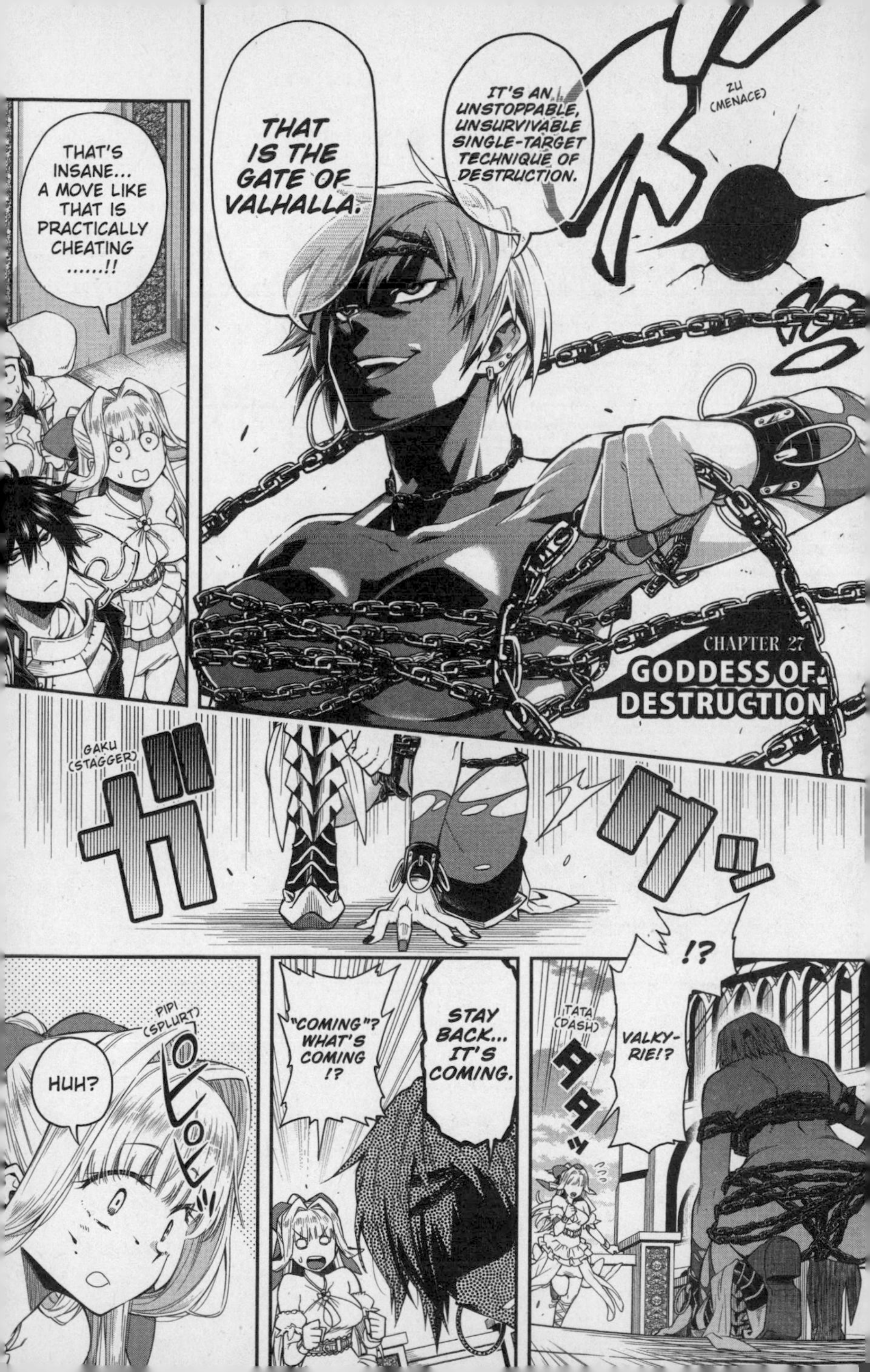
ZU (MENACE)
IT'S AN UNSTOPPABLE, UNSURVIVABLE SINGLE-TARGET TECHNIQUE OF DESTRUCTION.
THAT IS THE GATE OF VALHALLA.
CHAPTER 27
GODDESS OF DESTRUCTION
THAT'S INSANE... A MOVE LIKE THAT IS PRACTICALLY CHEATING ......!!
GAKU (STAGGER)
!?
VALKY-RIE!?
TATA (DASH)
STAY BACK... IT'S COMING.
"COMING"? WHAT'S COMING !?
PIPI (SPLURT)
HUH?

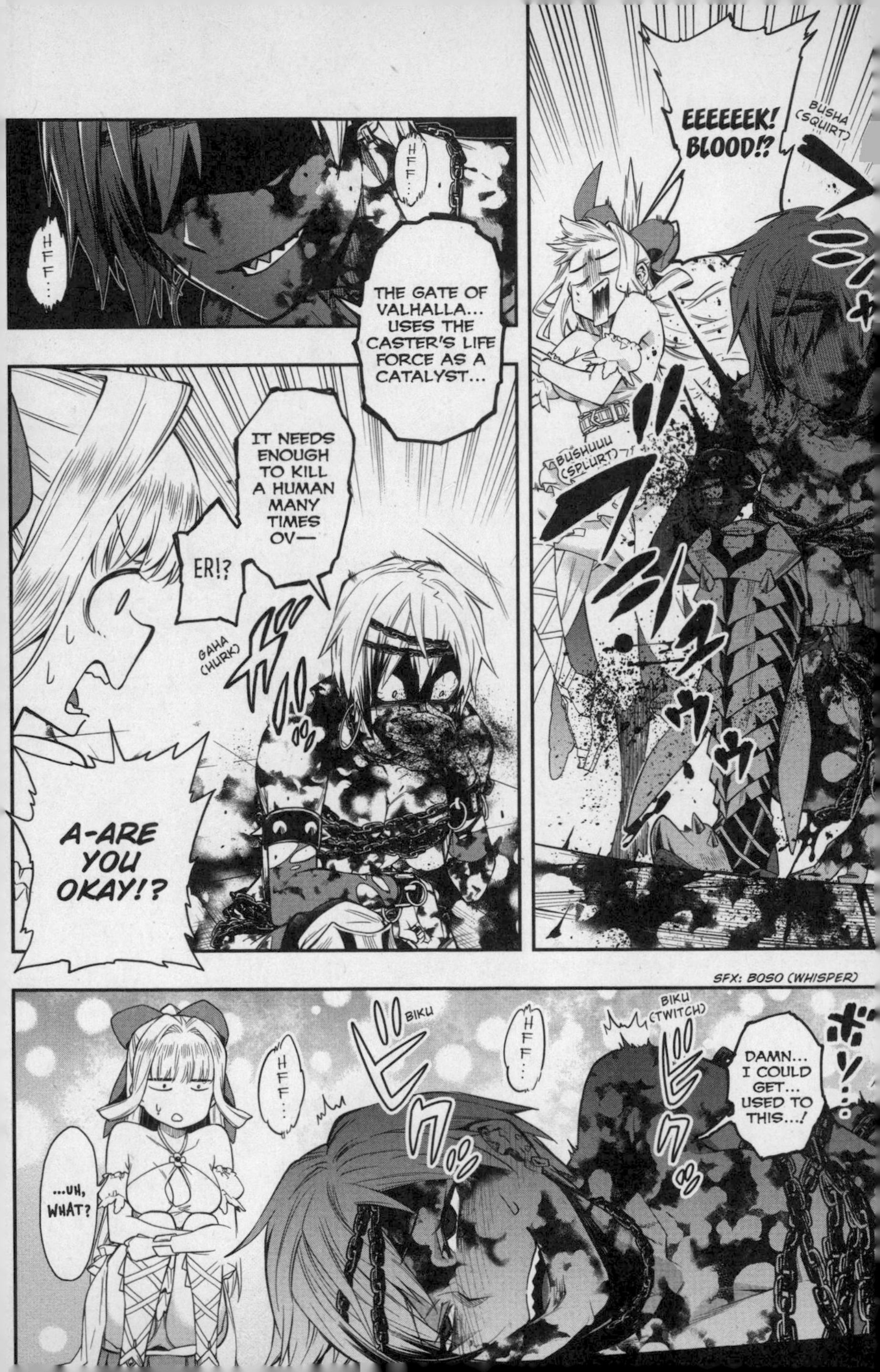
EEEEEEK! BLOOD!?
BUSHA (SQUIRT)
BUSHUUU (SPLURT)
HFF...
HFF...
THE GATE OF VALHALLA... USES THE CASTER'S LIFE FORCE AS A CATALYST...
IT NEEDS ENOUGH TO KILL A HUMAN MANY TIMES OV—
ER!?
GAHA (HURK)
A-ARE YOU OKAY!?
SFX: BOSO (WHISPER)
DAMN... I COULD GET... USED TO THIS...!
BIKU (TWITCH)
HFF...
BIKU
HFF...
...UH, WHAT?

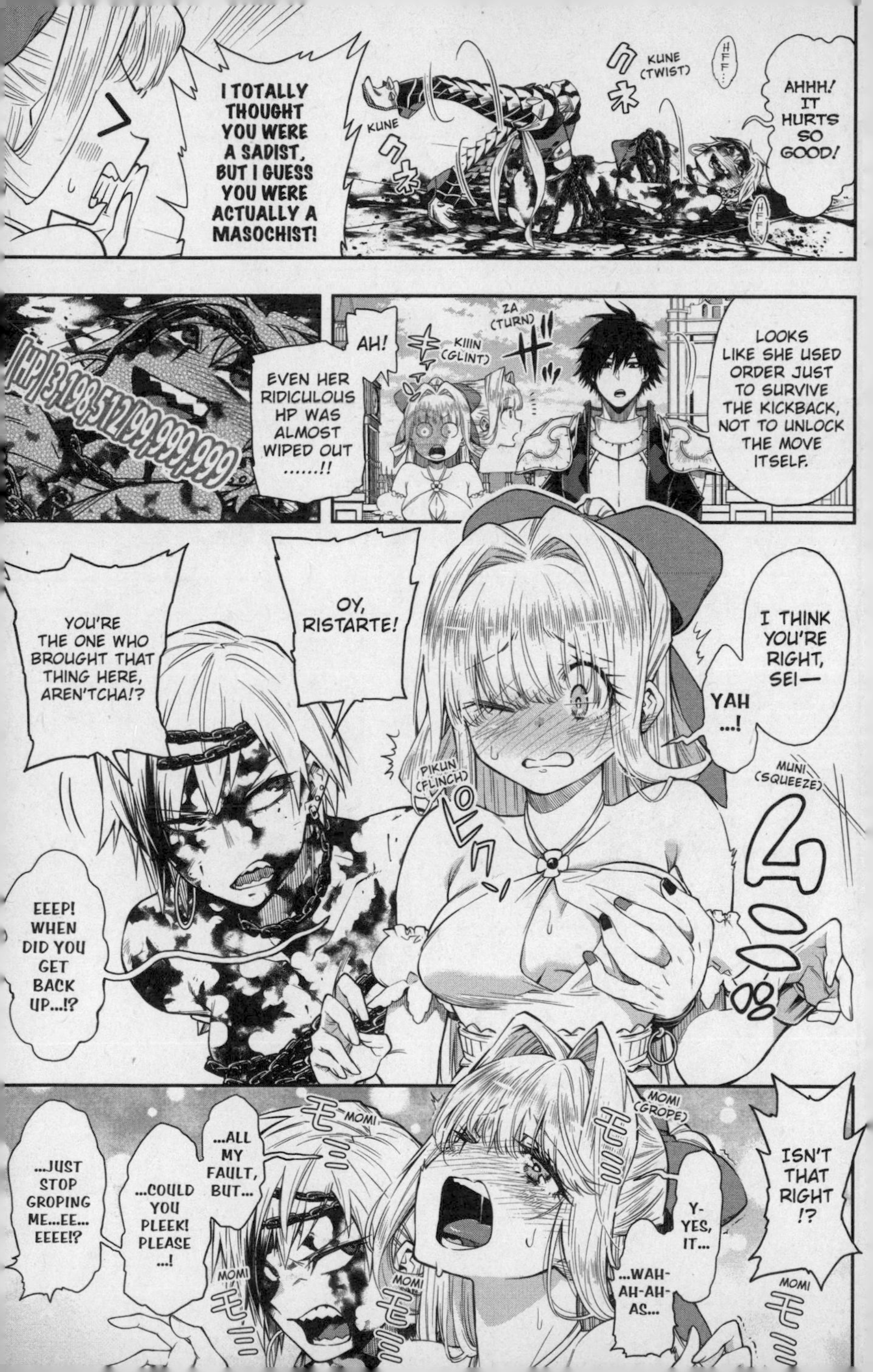
AHHH! IT HURTS SO GOOD!
HFF...
KUNE (TWIST)
KUNE
HFF...
I TOTALLY THOUGHT YOU WERE A SADIST, BUT I GUESS YOU WERE ACTUALLY A MASOCHIST!
LOOKS LIKE SHE USED ORDER JUST TO SURVIVE THE KICKBACK, NOT TO UNLOCK THE MOVE ITSELF.
ZA (TURN)
KIIIN (GLINT)
AH!
EVEN HER RIDICULOUS HP WAS ALMOST WIPED OUT ......!!
[HP] 3,198,512/99,999,999
I THINK YOU'RE RIGHT, SEI—
YAH ...!
MUNI (SQUEEZE)
PIKUN (FLINCH)
OY, RISTARTE!
YOU'RE THE ONE WHO BROUGHT THAT THING HERE, AREN'TCHA!?
EEEP! WHEN DID YOU GET BACK UP...!?
ISN'T THAT RIGHT !?
MOMI (GROPE)
MOMI
Y-YES, IT...
...WAH-AH-AH-AS...
MOMI
...ALL MY FAULT, BUT...
MOMI
...COULD YOU PLEEK! PLEASE ...!
...JUST STOP GROPING ME...EE... EEEE!?

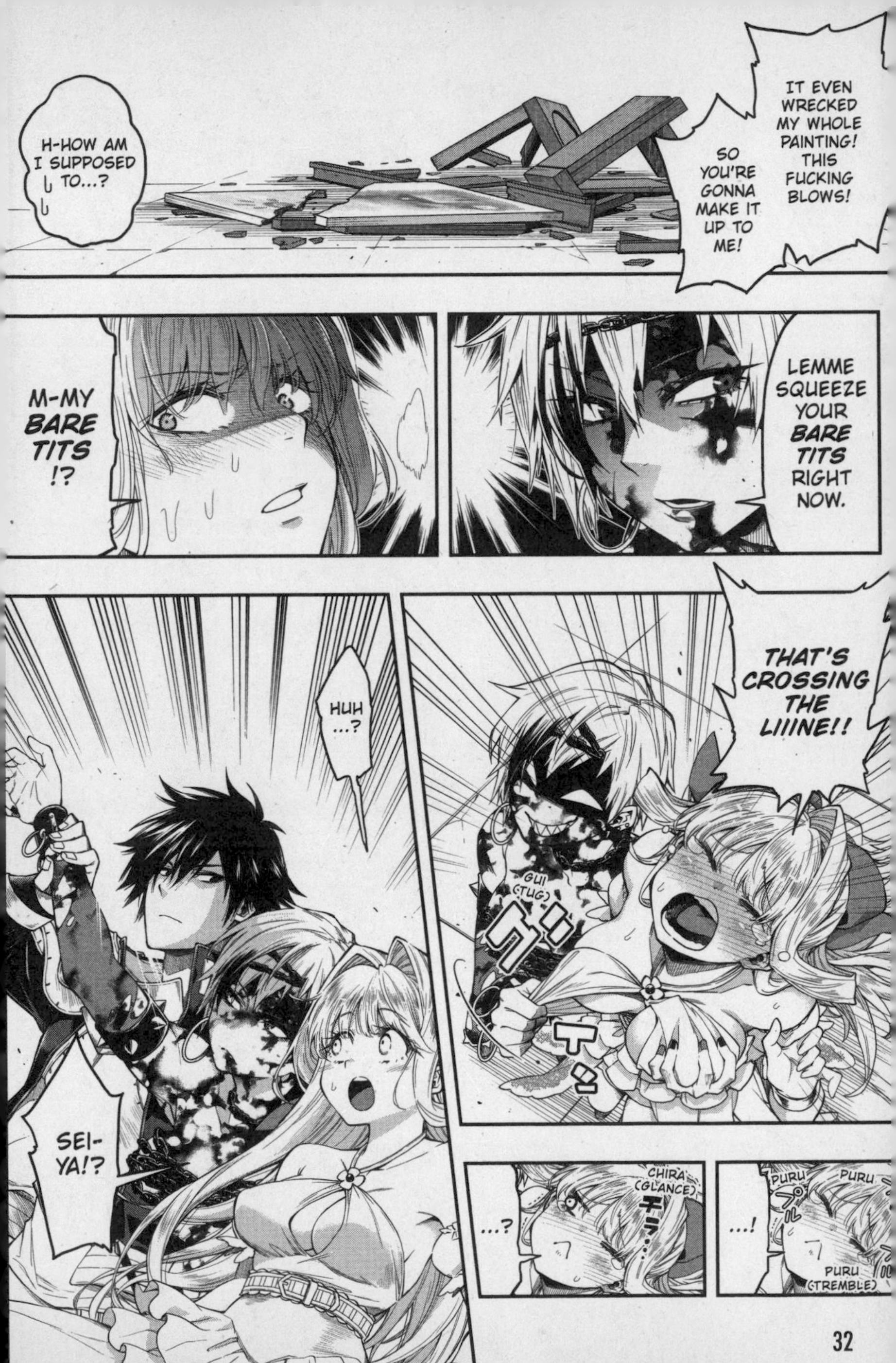
IT EVEN WRECKED MY WHOLE PAINTING! THIS FUCKING BLOWS!
SO YOU'RE GONNA MAKE IT UP TO ME!
H-HOW AM I SUPPOSED TO...?
LEMME SQUEEZE YOUR BARE TITS RIGHT NOW.
M-MY BARE TITS !?
THAT'S CROSSING THE LIIINE!!
GUI (TUG)
PURU PURU
...!
PURU (TREMBLE)
CHIRA (GLANCE)
...?
HUH ...?
SEI-YA!?

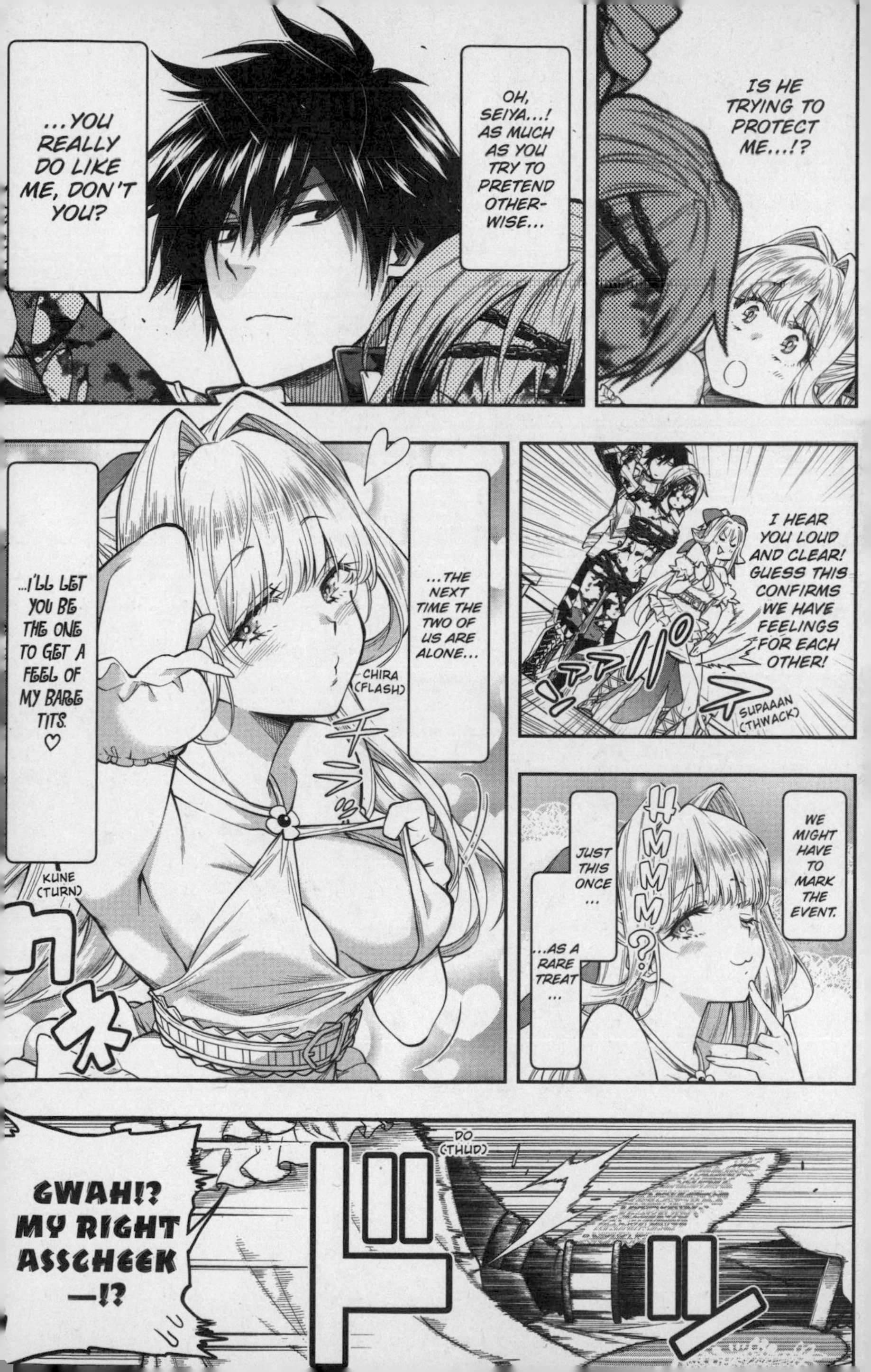
IS HE TRYING TO PROTECT ME...!?
OH, SEIYA...! AS MUCH AS YOU TRY TO PRETEND OTHER-WISE...
...YOU REALLY DO LIKE ME, DON'T YOU?
I HEAR YOU LOUD AND CLEAR! GUESS THIS CONFIRMS WE HAVE FEELINGS FOR EACH OTHER!
SUPAAAN (THWACK)
WE MIGHT HAVE TO MARK THE EVENT.
HMMM?
JUST THIS ONCE...
...AS A RARE TREAT...
...THE NEXT TIME THE TWO OF US ARE ALONE...
CHIRA (FLASH)
...I'LL LET YOU BE THE ONE TO GET A FEEL OF MY BARE TITS. ♡
KUNE (TURN)
DO (THUD)
GWAH!? MY RIGHT ASSCHEEK—!?

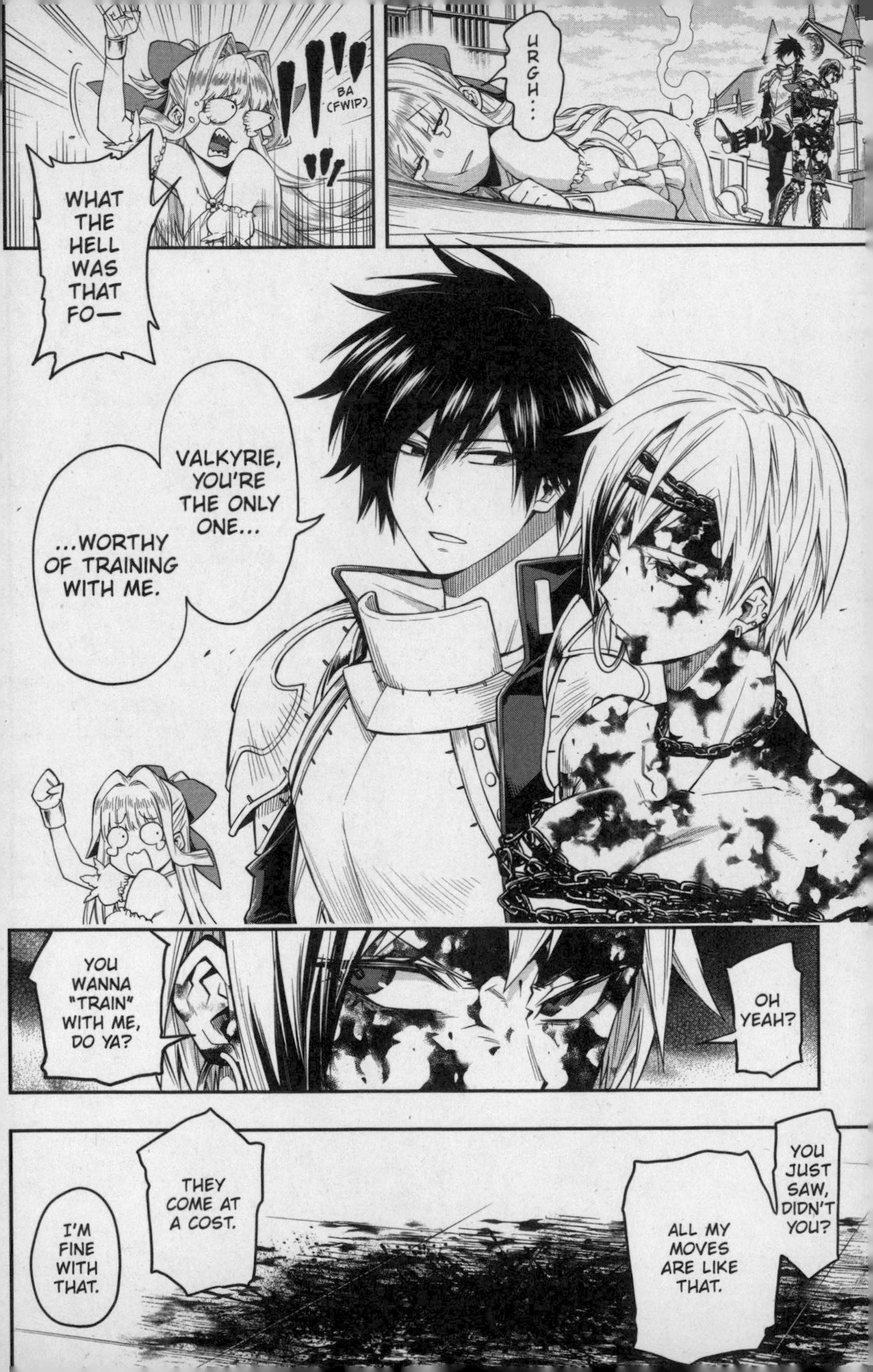
URGH...
BA (FWIP)
WHAT THE HELL WAS THAT FO—
VALKYRIE, YOU'RE THE ONLY ONE...
...WORTHY OF TRAINING WITH ME.
OH YEAH?
YOU WANNA "TRAIN" WITH ME, DO YA?
YOU JUST SAW, DIDN'T YOU?
ALL MY MOVES ARE LIKE THAT.
THEY COME AT A COST.
I'M FINE WITH THAT.

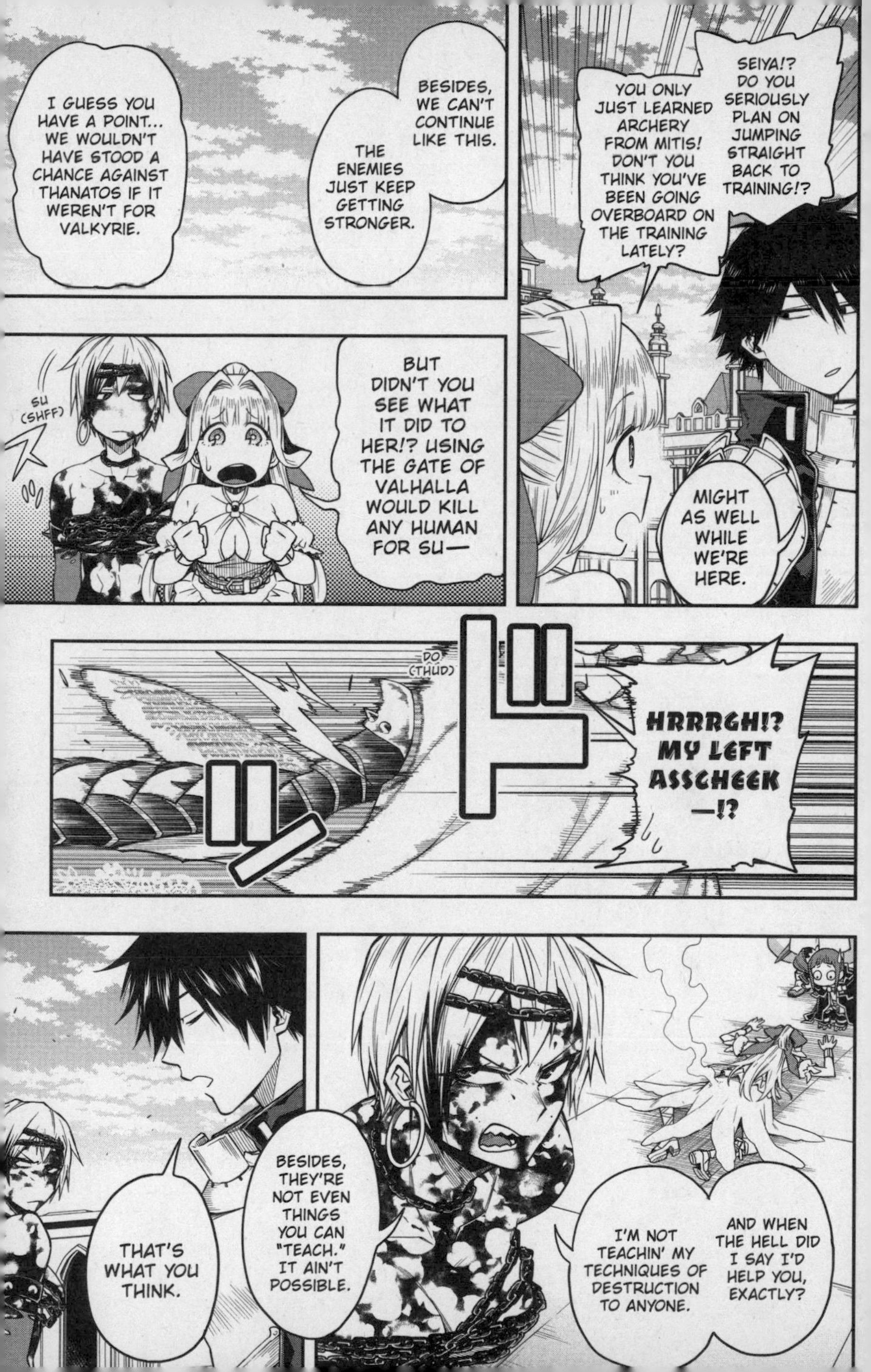
SEIYA!? DO YOU SERIOUSLY PLAN ON JUMPING STRAIGHT BACK TO TRAINING!?
YOU ONLY JUST LEARNED ARCHERY FROM MITIS! DON'T YOU THINK YOU'VE BEEN GOING OVERBOARD ON THE TRAINING LATELY?
MIGHT AS WELL WHILE WE'RE HERE.
BESIDES, WE CAN'T CONTINUE LIKE THIS.
THE ENEMIES JUST KEEP GETTING STRONGER.
I GUESS YOU HAVE A POINT... WE WOULDN'T HAVE STOOD A CHANCE AGAINST THANATOS IF IT WEREN'T FOR VALKYRIE.
BUT DIDN'T YOU SEE WHAT IT DID TO HER!? USING THE GATE OF VALHALLA WOULD KILL ANY HUMAN FOR SU—
SU (SHFF)
DO (THUD)
HRRRGH!? MY LEFT ASSCHEEK—!?
AND WHEN THE HELL DID I SAY I'D HELP YOU, EXACTLY?
I'M NOT TEACHIN' MY TECHNIQUES OF DESTRUCTION TO ANYONE.
BESIDES, THEY'RE NOT EVEN THINGS YOU CAN "TEACH." IT AIN'T POSSIBLE.
THAT'S WHAT YOU THINK.

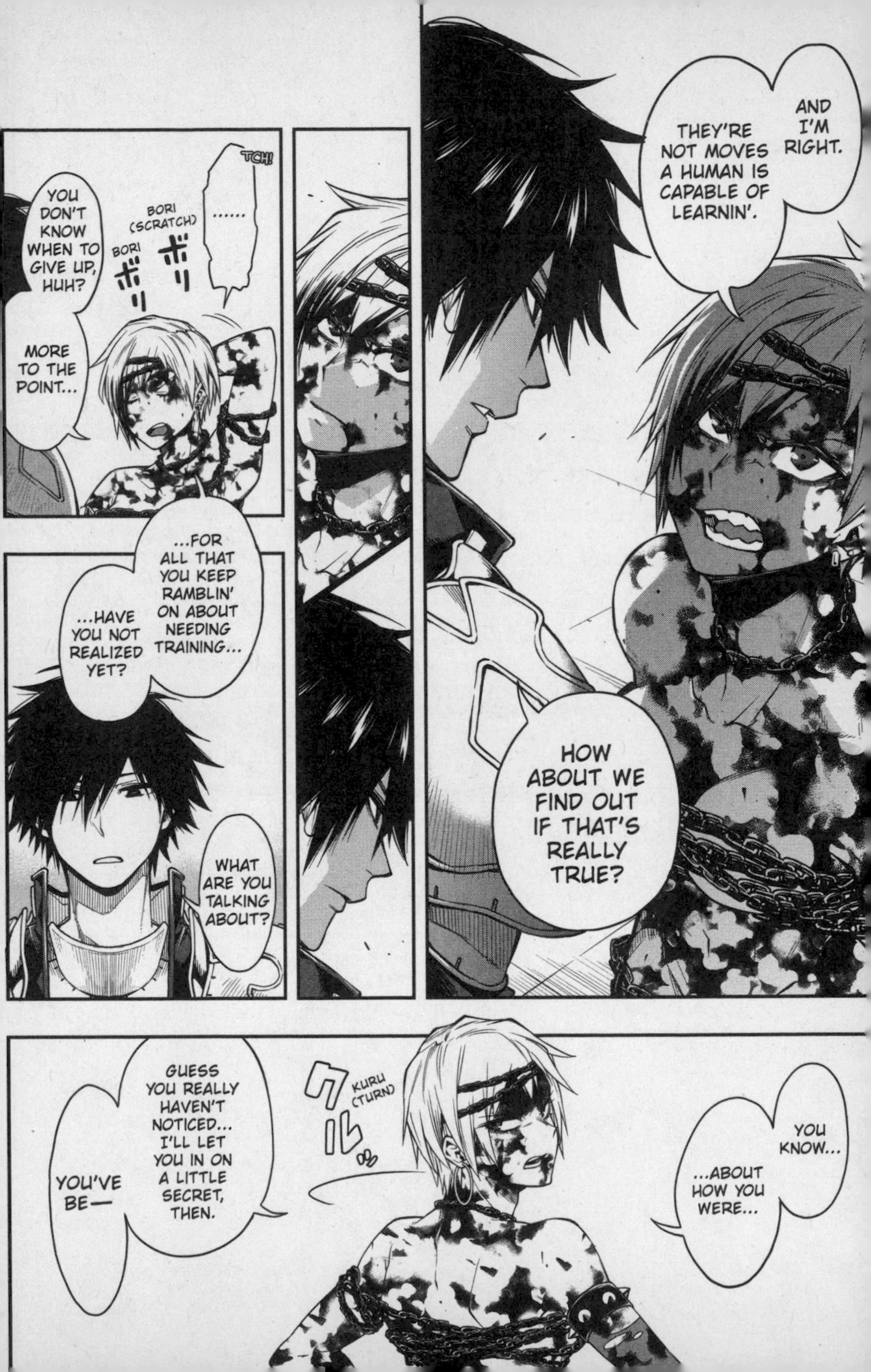
AND I'M RIGHT.
THEY'RE NOT MOVES A HUMAN IS CAPABLE OF LEARNIN'.
HOW ABOUT WE FIND OUT IF THAT'S REALLY TRUE?
TCH!
......
ボリ BORI (SCRATCH)
ボリ BORI
YOU DON'T KNOW WHEN TO GIVE UP, HUH?
MORE TO THE POINT...
...FOR ALL THAT YOU KEEP RAMBLIN' ON ABOUT NEEDING TRAINING...
...HAVE YOU NOT REALIZED YET?
WHAT ARE YOU TALKING ABOUT?
YOU KNOW...
...ABOUT HOW YOU WERE...
クル KURU (TURN)
GUESS YOU REALLY HAVEN'T NOTICED... I'LL LET YOU IN ON A LITTLE SECRET, THEN.
YOU'VE BE—

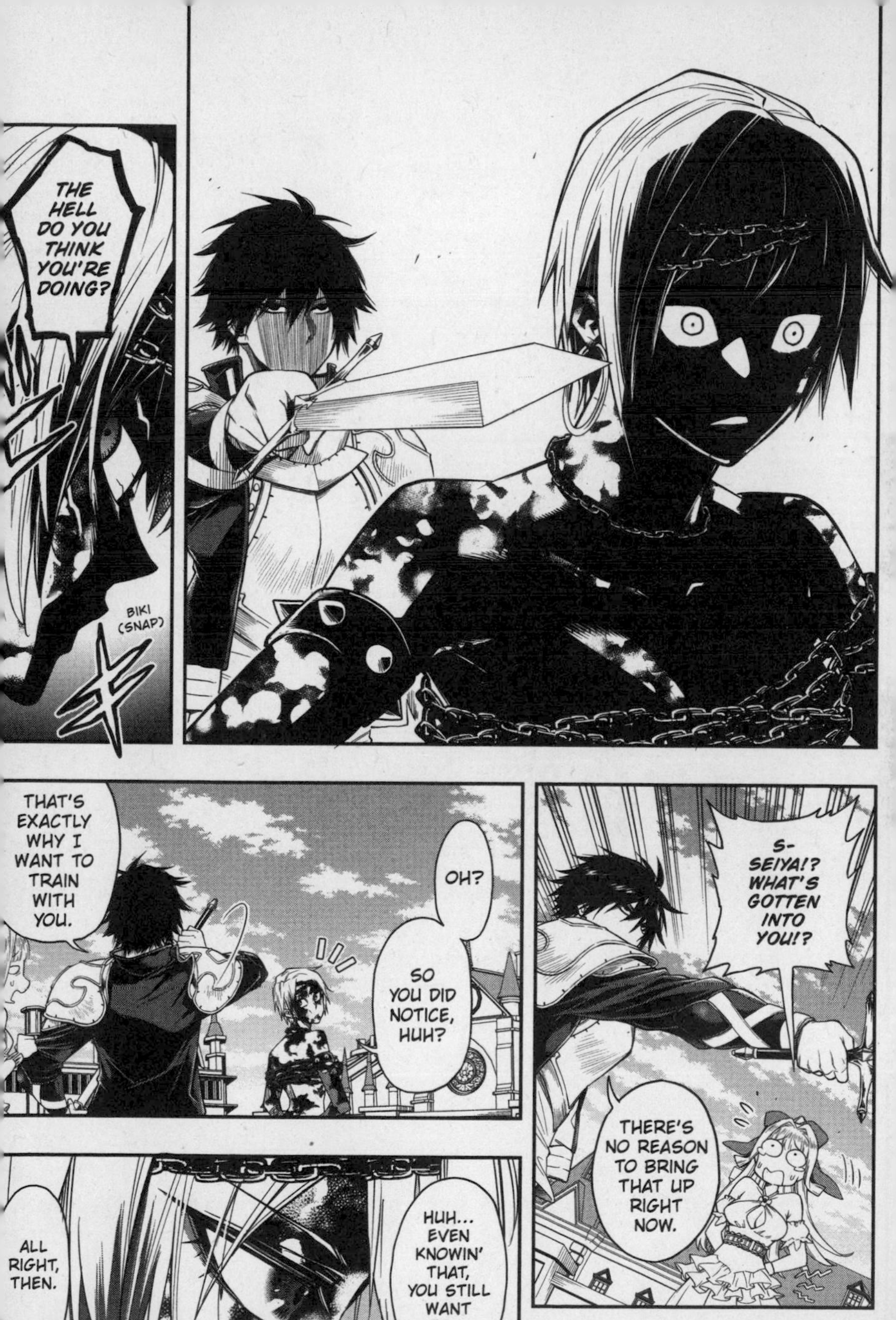
THE HELL DO YOU THINK YOU'RE DOING?
BIKI (SNAP)
S-SEIYA!? WHAT'S GOTTEN INTO YOU!?
THERE'S NO REASON TO BRING THAT UP RIGHT NOW.
OH?
SO YOU DID NOTICE, HUH?
THAT'S EXACTLY WHY I WANT TO TRAIN WITH YOU.
HUH... EVEN KNOWIN' THAT, YOU STILL WANT TO...
ALL RIGHT, THEN.

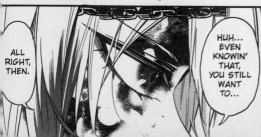

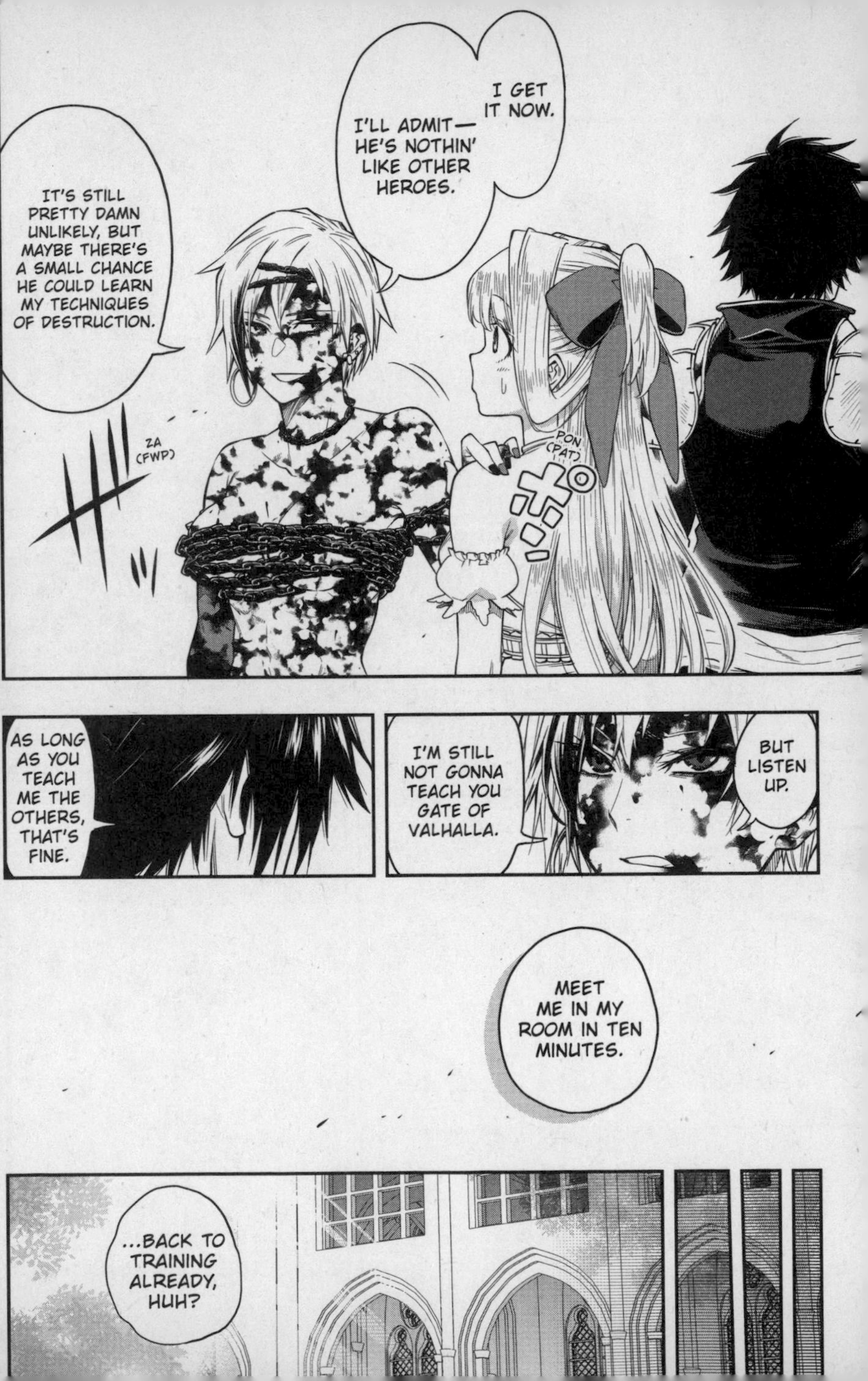
I GET IT NOW.
I'LL ADMIT— HE'S NOTHIN' LIKE OTHER HEROES.
IT'S STILL PRETTY DAMN UNLIKELY, BUT MAYBE THERE'S A SMALL CHANCE HE COULD LEARN MY TECHNIQUES OF DESTRUCTION.
PON (PAT)
ZA (FWP)
BUT LISTEN UP.
I'M STILL NOT GONNA TEACH YOU GATE OF VALHALLA.
AS LONG AS YOU TEACH ME THE OTHERS, THAT'S FINE.
MEET ME IN MY ROOM IN TEN MINUTES.
...BACK TO TRAINING ALREADY, HUH?

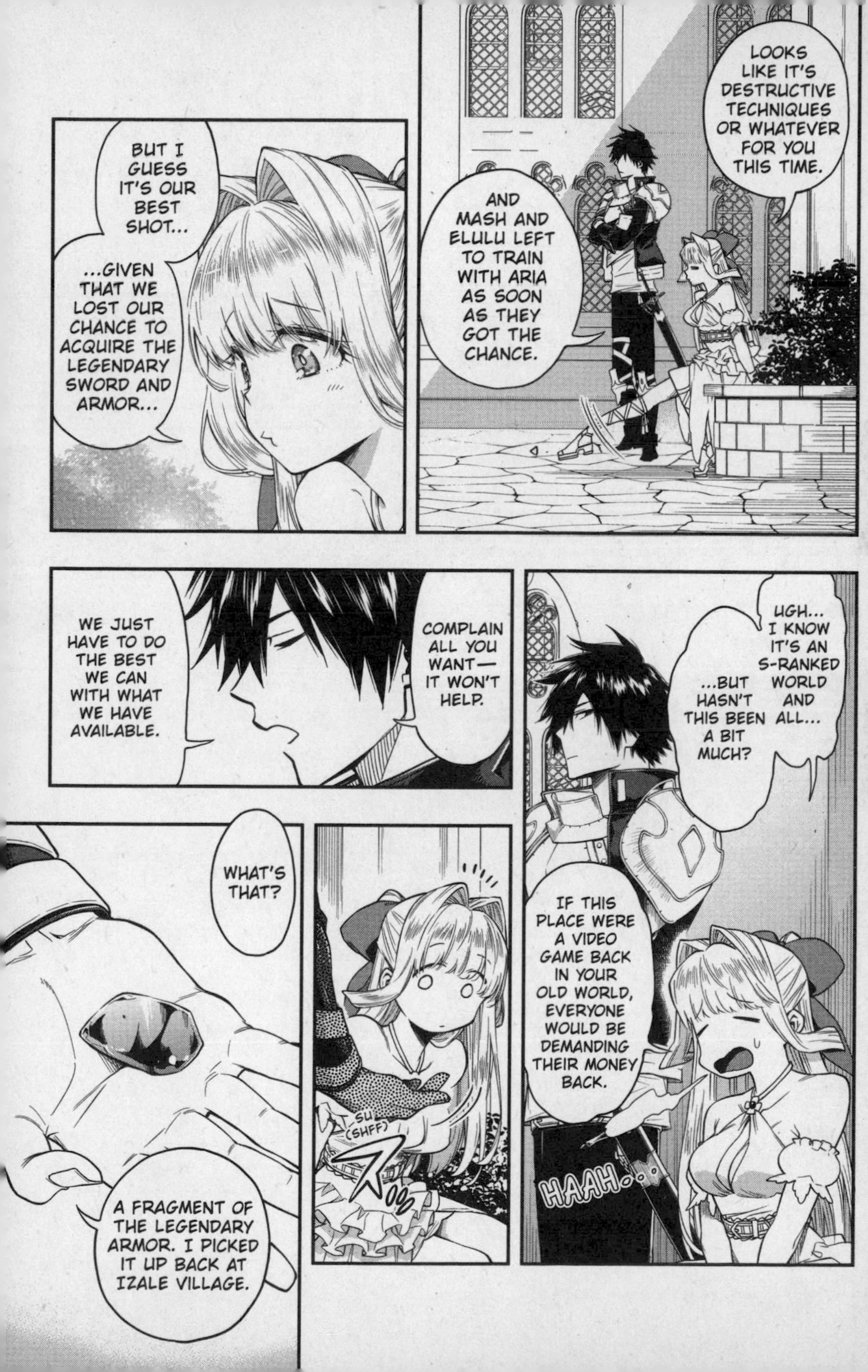
LOOKS LIKE IT'S DESTRUCTIVE TECHNIQUES OR WHATEVER FOR YOU THIS TIME.
AND MASH AND ELULU LEFT TO TRAIN WITH ARIA AS SOON AS THEY GOT THE CHANCE.
BUT I GUESS IT'S OUR BEST SHOT...
...GIVEN THAT WE LOST OUR CHANCE TO ACQUIRE THE LEGENDARY SWORD AND ARMOR...
UGH... I KNOW IT'S AN S-RANKED WORLD AND ALL...
...BUT HASN'T THIS BEEN A BIT MUCH?
IF THIS PLACE WERE A VIDEO GAME BACK IN YOUR OLD WORLD, EVERYONE WOULD BE DEMANDING THEIR MONEY BACK.
HAAH...
COMPLAIN ALL YOU WANT— IT WON'T HELP.
WE JUST HAVE TO DO THE BEST WE CAN WITH WHAT WE HAVE AVAILABLE.
WHAT'S THAT?
SU (SHFF)
A FRAGMENT OF THE LEGENDARY ARMOR. I PICKED IT UP BACK AT IZALE VILLAGE.

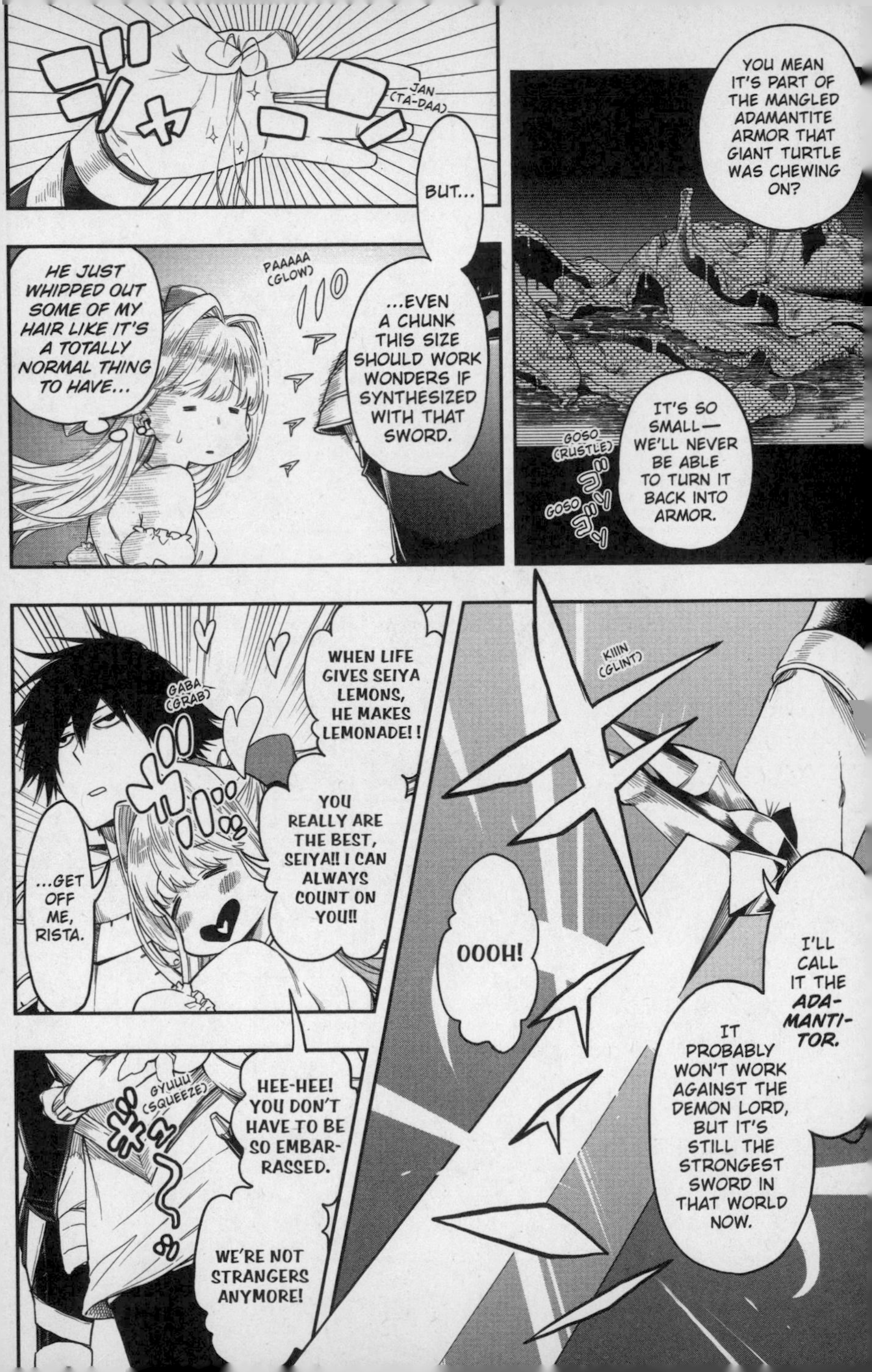
YOU MEAN IT'S PART OF THE MANGLED ADAMANTITE ARMOR THAT GIANT TURTLE WAS CHEWING ON?
IT'S SO SMALL— WE'LL NEVER BE ABLE TO TURN IT BACK INTO ARMOR.
GOSO (RUSTLE)
GOSO
JAN (TA-DAA)
BUT...
...EVEN A CHUNK THIS SIZE SHOULD WORK WONDERS IF SYNTHESIZED WITH THAT SWORD.
PAAAAA (GLOW)
HE JUST WHIPPED OUT SOME OF MY HAIR LIKE IT'S A TOTALLY NORMAL THING TO HAVE...
KIIIN (GLINT)
I'LL CALL IT THE ADAMANTITOR.
IT PROBABLY WON'T WORK AGAINST THE DEMON LORD, BUT IT'S STILL THE STRONGEST SWORD IN THAT WORLD NOW.
OOOH!
WHEN LIFE GIVES SEIYA LEMONS, HE MAKES LEMONADE!!
YOU REALLY ARE THE BEST, SEIYA!! I CAN ALWAYS COUNT ON YOU!!
GABA (GRAB)
...GET OFF ME, RISTA.
HEE-HEE! YOU DON'T HAVE TO BE SO EMBARRASSED.
WE'RE NOT STRANGERS ANYMORE!
GYUUU (SQUEEZE)

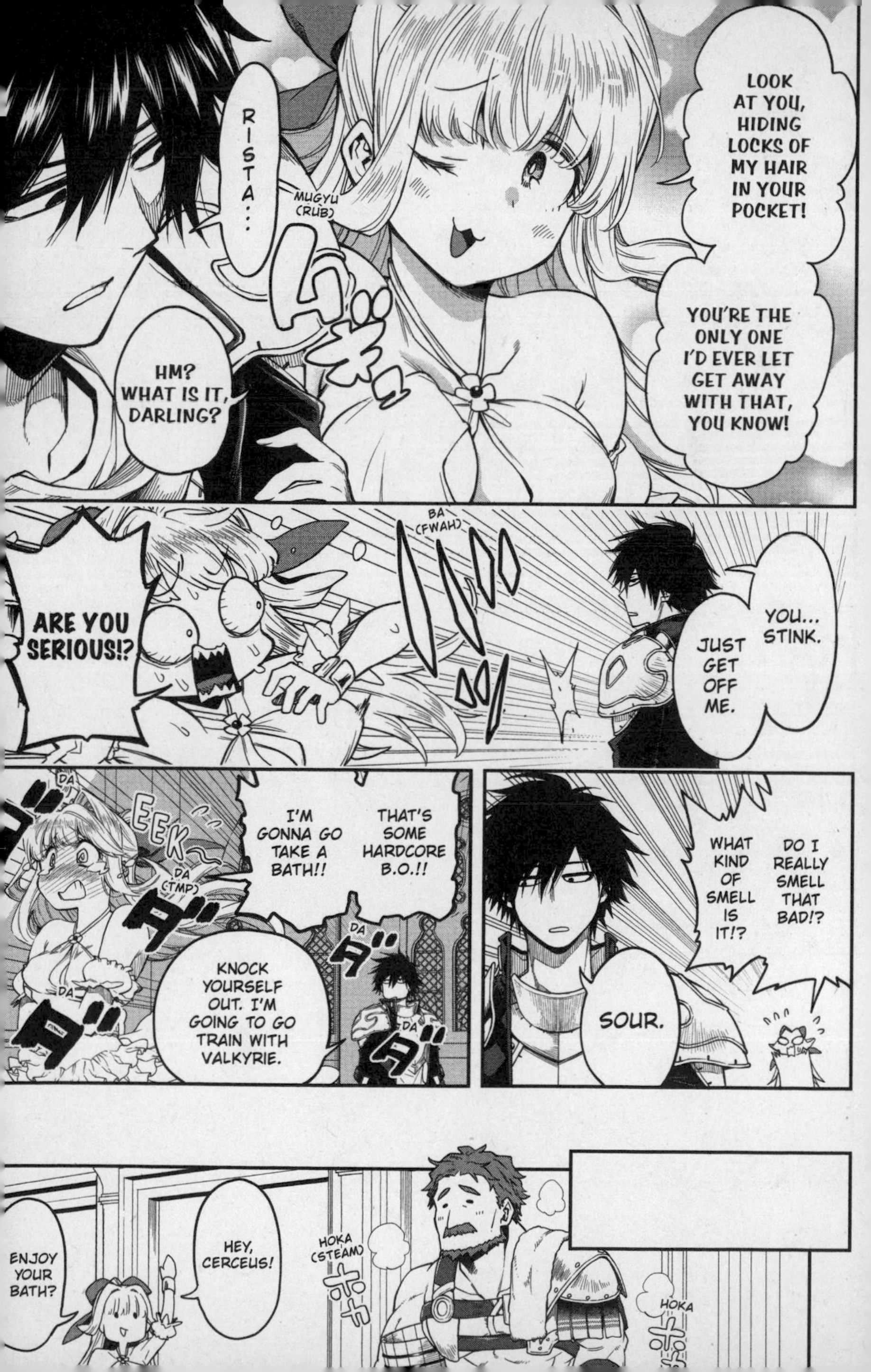
LOOK AT YOU, HIDING LOCKS OF MY HAIR IN YOUR POCKET!
YOU'RE THE ONLY ONE I'D EVER LET GET AWAY WITH THAT, YOU KNOW!
RISTA...
MUGYU (RUB)
HM? WHAT IS IT, DARLING?
BA (FWAH)
YOU... STINK.
JUST GET OFF ME.
ARE YOU SERIOUS!?
DO I REALLY SMELL THAT BAD!?
WHAT KIND OF SMELL IS IT!?
SOUR.
THAT'S SOME HARDCORE B.O.!!
I'M GONNA GO TAKE A BATH!!
EEK
DA
DA (TMP)
DA
KNOCK YOURSELF OUT. I'M GOING TO GO TRAIN WITH VALKYRIE.
DA
DA
HOKA
HOKA (STEAM)
HEY, CERCEUS!
ENJOY YOUR BATH?

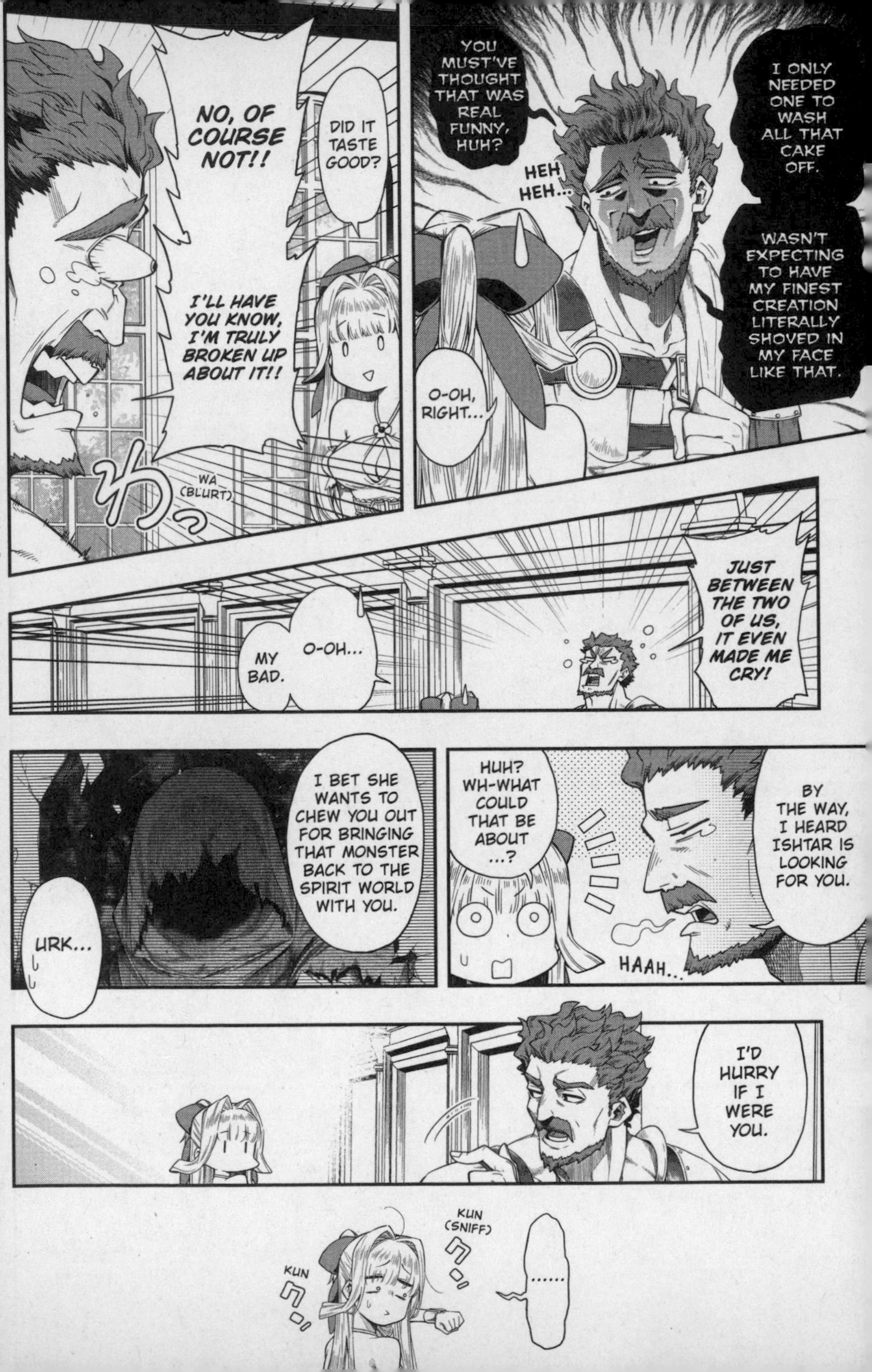
I ONLY NEEDED ONE TO WASH ALL THAT CAKE OFF.
WASN'T EXPECTING TO HAVE MY FINEST CREATION LITERALLY SHOVED IN MY FACE LIKE THAT.
YOU MUST'VE THOUGHT THAT WAS REAL FUNNY, HUH?
HEH HEH...
O-OH, RIGHT...
DID IT TASTE GOOD?
NO, OF COURSE NOT!!
I'LL HAVE YOU KNOW, I'M TRULY BROKEN UP ABOUT IT!!
WA (BLURT)
JUST BETWEEN THE TWO OF US, IT EVEN MADE ME CRY!
O-OH...
MY BAD.
BY THE WAY, I HEARD ISHTAR IS LOOKING FOR YOU.
HAAH...
HUH? WH-WHAT COULD THAT BE ABOUT ...?
I BET SHE WANTS TO CHEW YOU OUT FOR BRINGING THAT MONSTER BACK TO THE SPIRIT WORLD WITH YOU.
URK...
I'D HURRY IF I WERE YOU.
......
KUN (SNIFF)
KUN

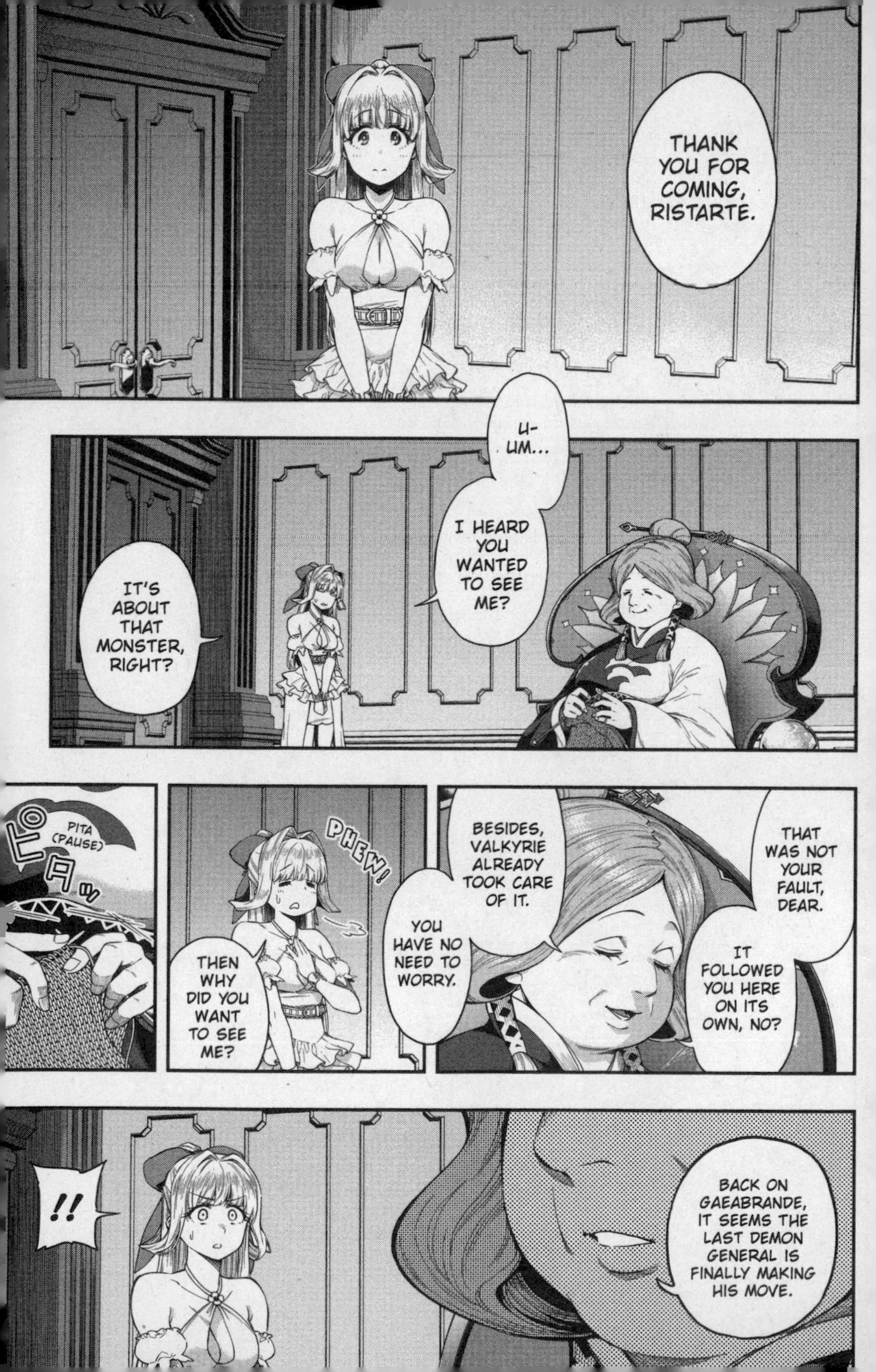
THANK YOU FOR COMING, RISTARTE.
U-UM...
I HEARD YOU WANTED TO SEE ME?
IT'S ABOUT THAT MONSTER, RIGHT?
THAT WAS NOT YOUR FAULT, DEAR.
IT FOLLOWED YOU HERE ON ITS OWN, NO?
BESIDES, VALKYRIE ALREADY TOOK CARE OF IT.
YOU HAVE NO NEED TO WORRY.
PHEW!
THEN WHY DID YOU WANT TO SEE ME?
ピタッ
PITA (PAUSE)
BACK ON GAEABRANDE, IT SEEMS THE LAST DEMON GENERAL IS FINALLY MAKING HIS MOVE.
!!

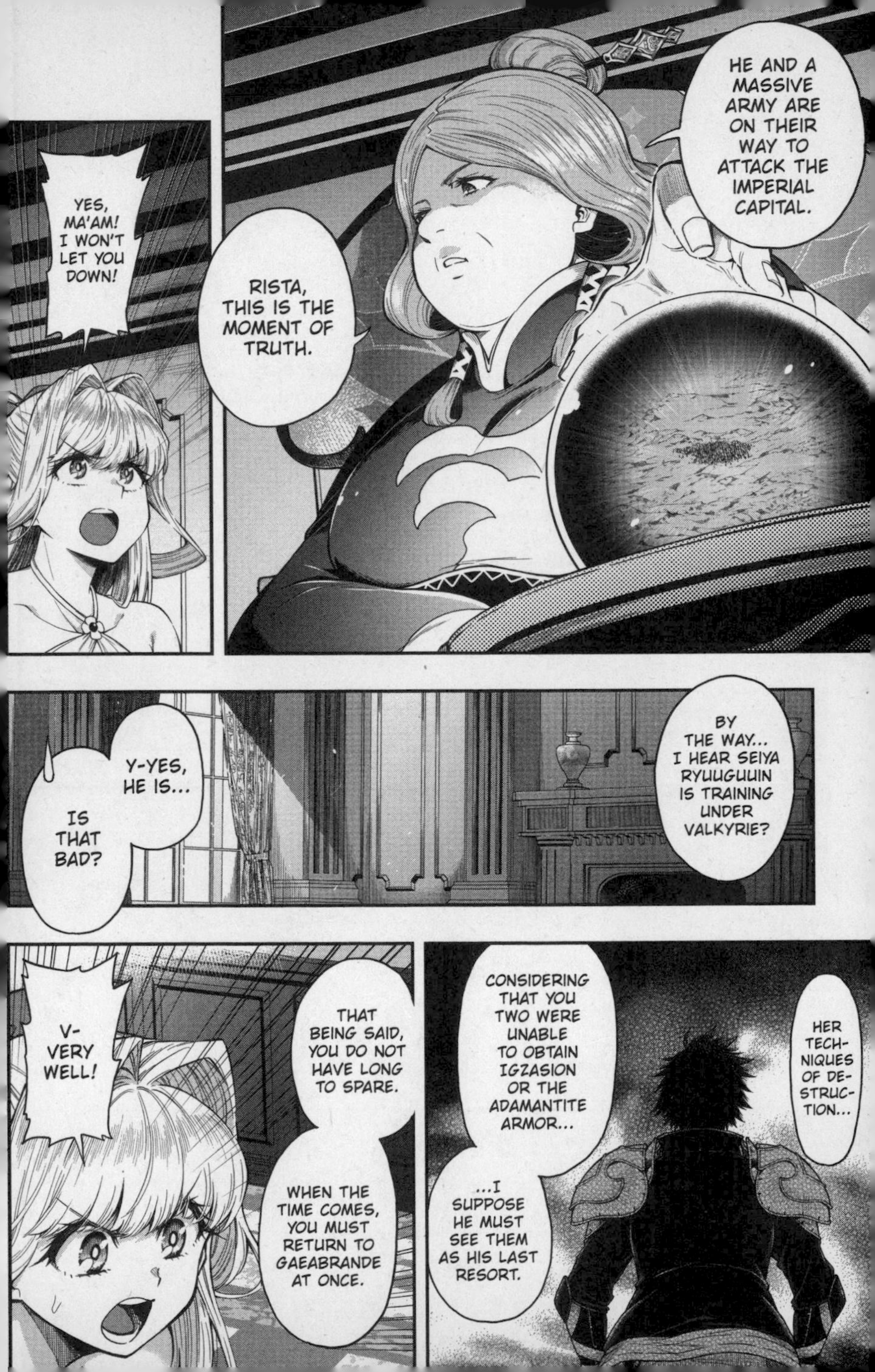
HE AND A MASSIVE ARMY ARE ON THEIR WAY TO ATTACK THE IMPERIAL CAPITAL.
RISTA, THIS IS THE MOMENT OF TRUTH.
YES, MA'AM! I WON'T LET YOU DOWN!
BY THE WAY... I HEAR SEIYA RYUUGUUIN IS TRAINING UNDER VALKYRIE?
Y-YES, HE IS...
IS THAT BAD?
HER TECH-NIQUES OF DE-STRUC-TION...
CONSIDERING THAT YOU TWO WERE UNABLE TO OBTAIN IGZASION OR THE ADAMANTITE ARMOR...
...I SUPPOSE HE MUST SEE THEM AS HIS LAST RESORT.
THAT BEING SAID, YOU DO NOT HAVE LONG TO SPARE.
WHEN THE TIME COMES, YOU MUST RETURN TO GAEABRANDE AT ONCE.
V-VERY WELL!

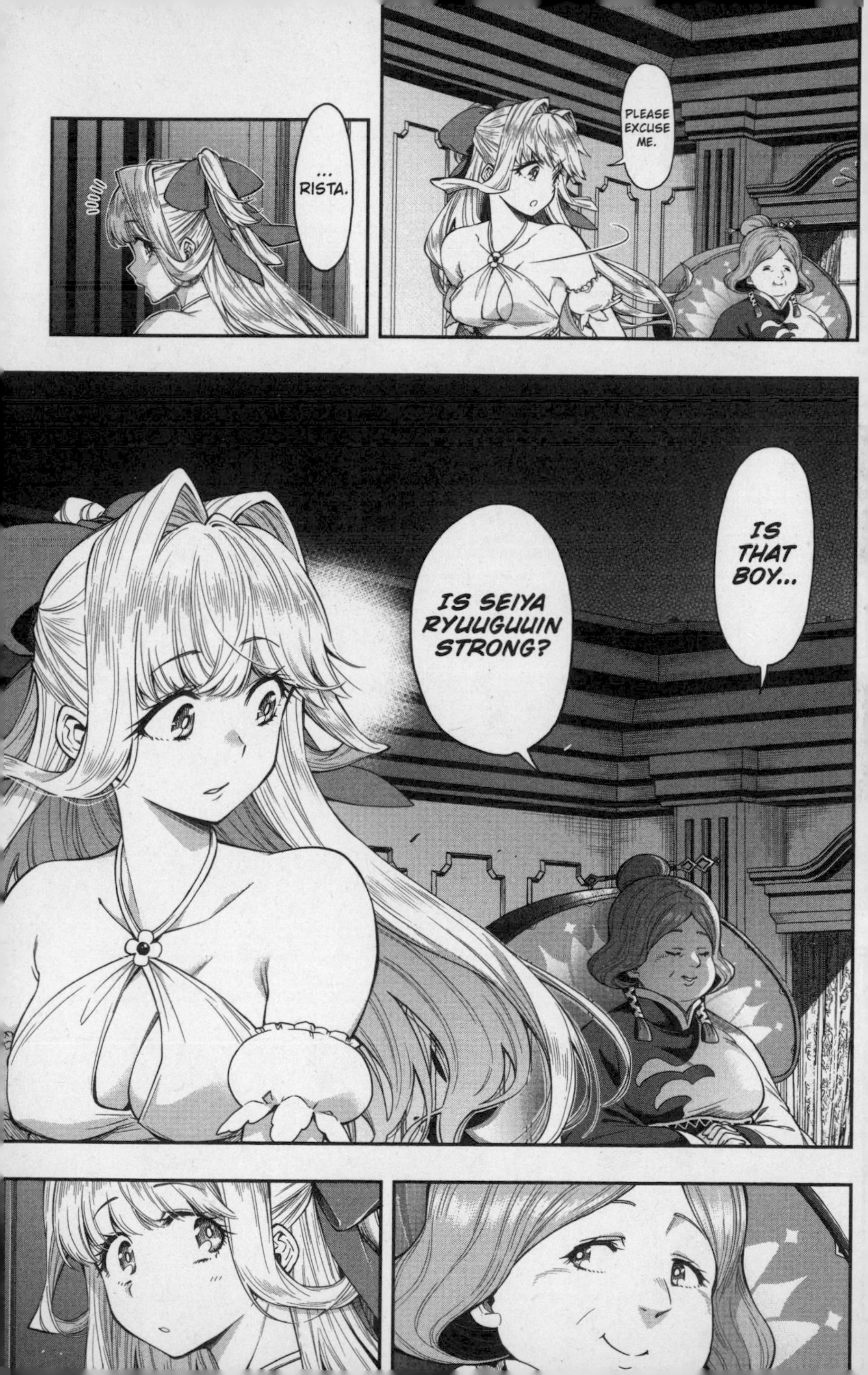
PLEASE EXCUSE ME.
... RISTA.
IS THAT BOY...
IS SEIYA RYUUGUUIN STRONG?

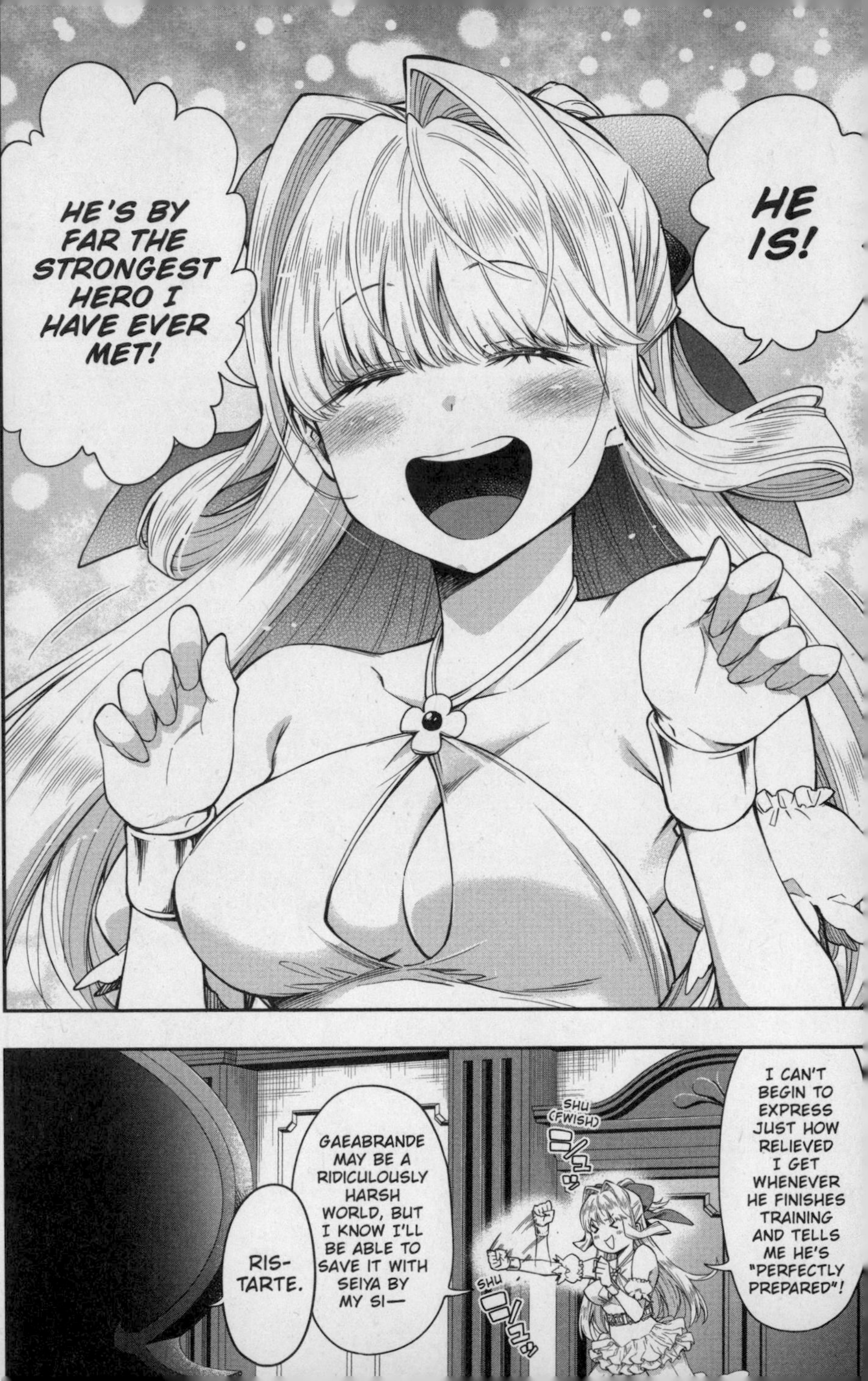
HE IS!
HE'S BY FAR THE STRONGEST HERO I HAVE EVER MET!
I CAN'T BEGIN TO EXPRESS JUST HOW RELIEVED I GET WHENEVER HE FINISHES TRAINING AND TELLS ME HE'S "PERFECTLY PREPARED"!
SHU (FWISH)
SHU
GAEABRANDE MAY BE A RIDICULOUSLY HARSH WORLD, BUT I KNOW I'LL BE ABLE TO SAVE IT WITH SEIYA BY MY SI—
RIS-TARTE.

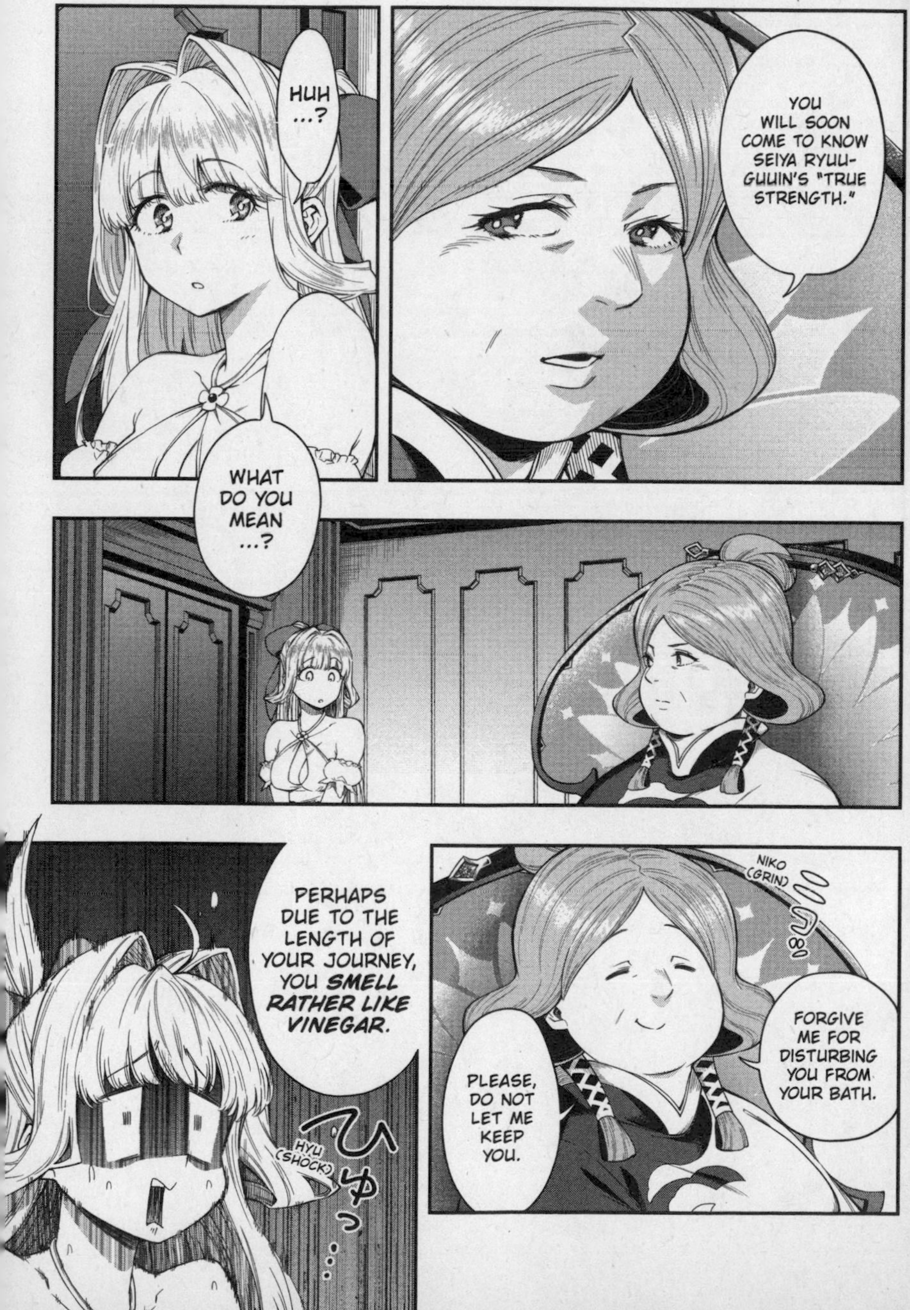
YOU WILL SOON COME TO KNOW SEIYA RYUU-GUUIN'S "TRUE STRENGTH."
HUH ...?
WHAT DO YOU MEAN ...?
NIKO (GRIN)
FORGIVE ME FOR DISTURBING YOU FROM YOUR BATH.
PLEASE, DO NOT LET ME KEEP YOU.
PERHAPS DUE TO THE LENGTH OF YOUR JOURNEY, YOU **SMELL RATHER LIKE VINEGAR.**
HYU (SHOCK)

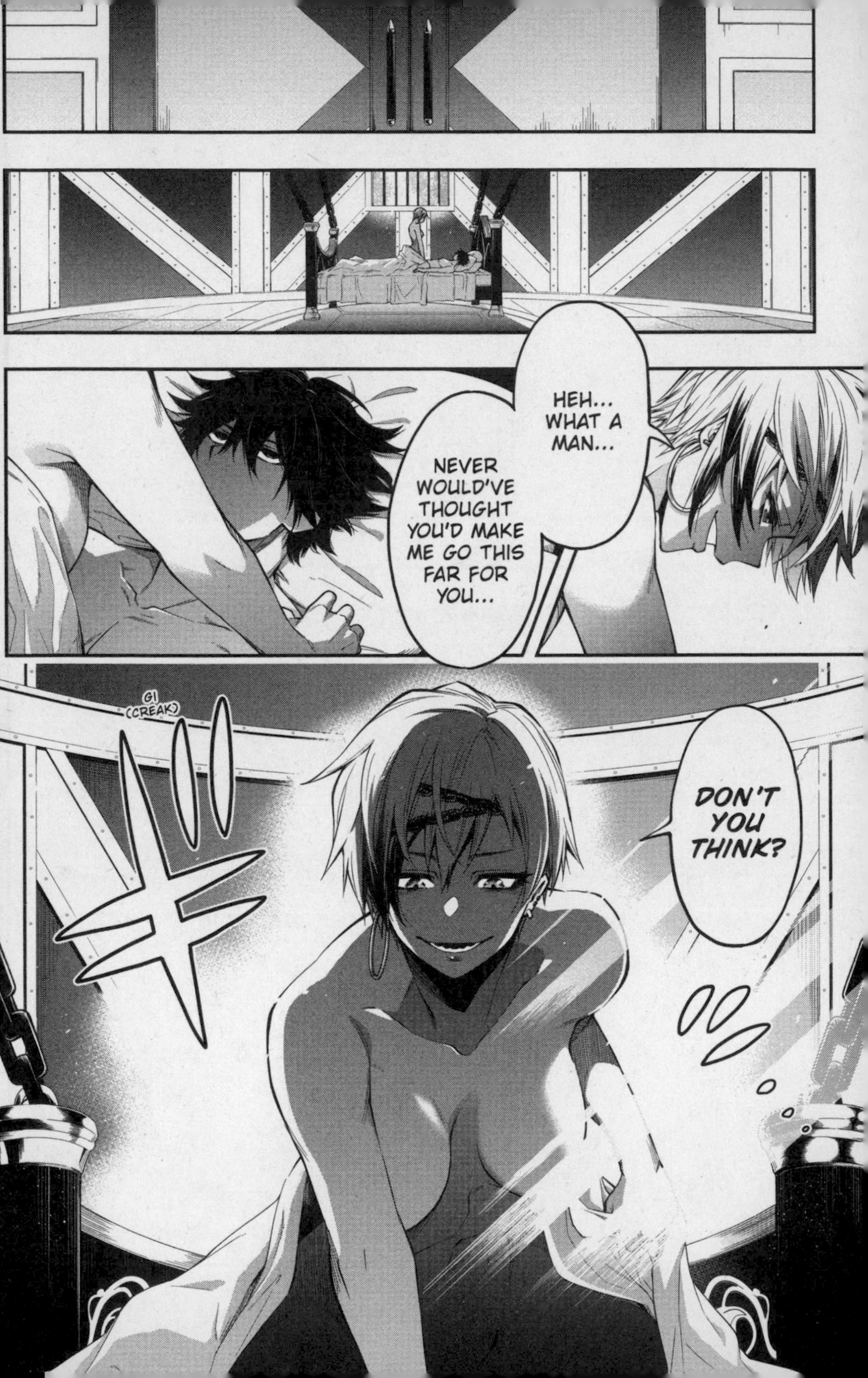
HEH... WHAT A MAN...
NEVER WOULD'VE THOUGHT YOU'D MAKE ME GO THIS FAR FOR YOU...
DON'T YOU THINK?
GI (CREAK)

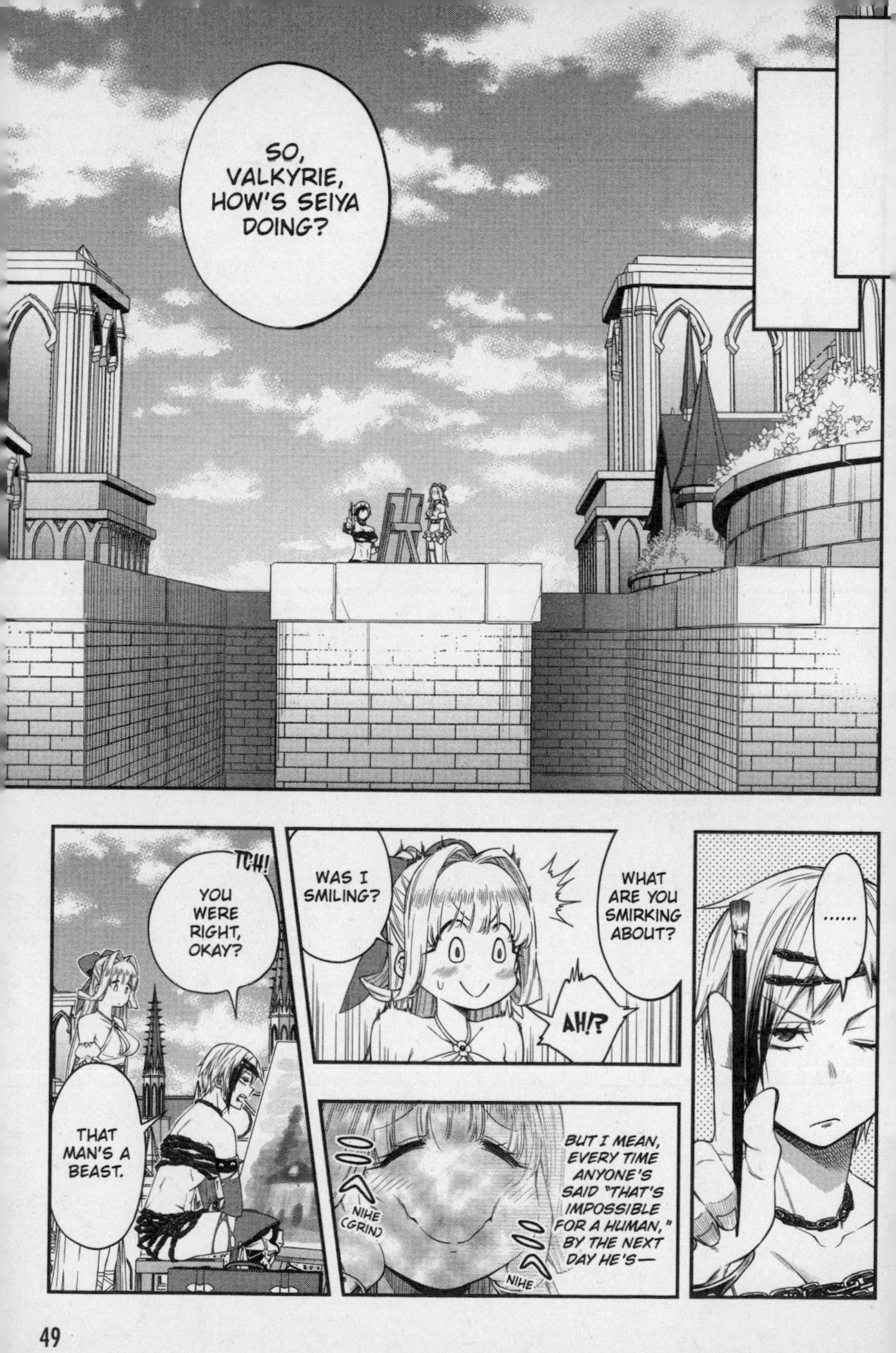
SO, VALKYRIE, HOW'S SEIYA DOING?
......
WHAT ARE YOU SMIRKING ABOUT?
AH!?
WAS I SMILING?
BUT I MEAN, EVERY TIME ANYONE'S SAID "THAT'S IMPOSSIBLE FOR A HUMAN," BY THE NEXT DAY HE'S—
NIHE (GRIN)
NIHE
TCH!
YOU WERE RIGHT, OKAY?
THAT MAN'S A BEAST.

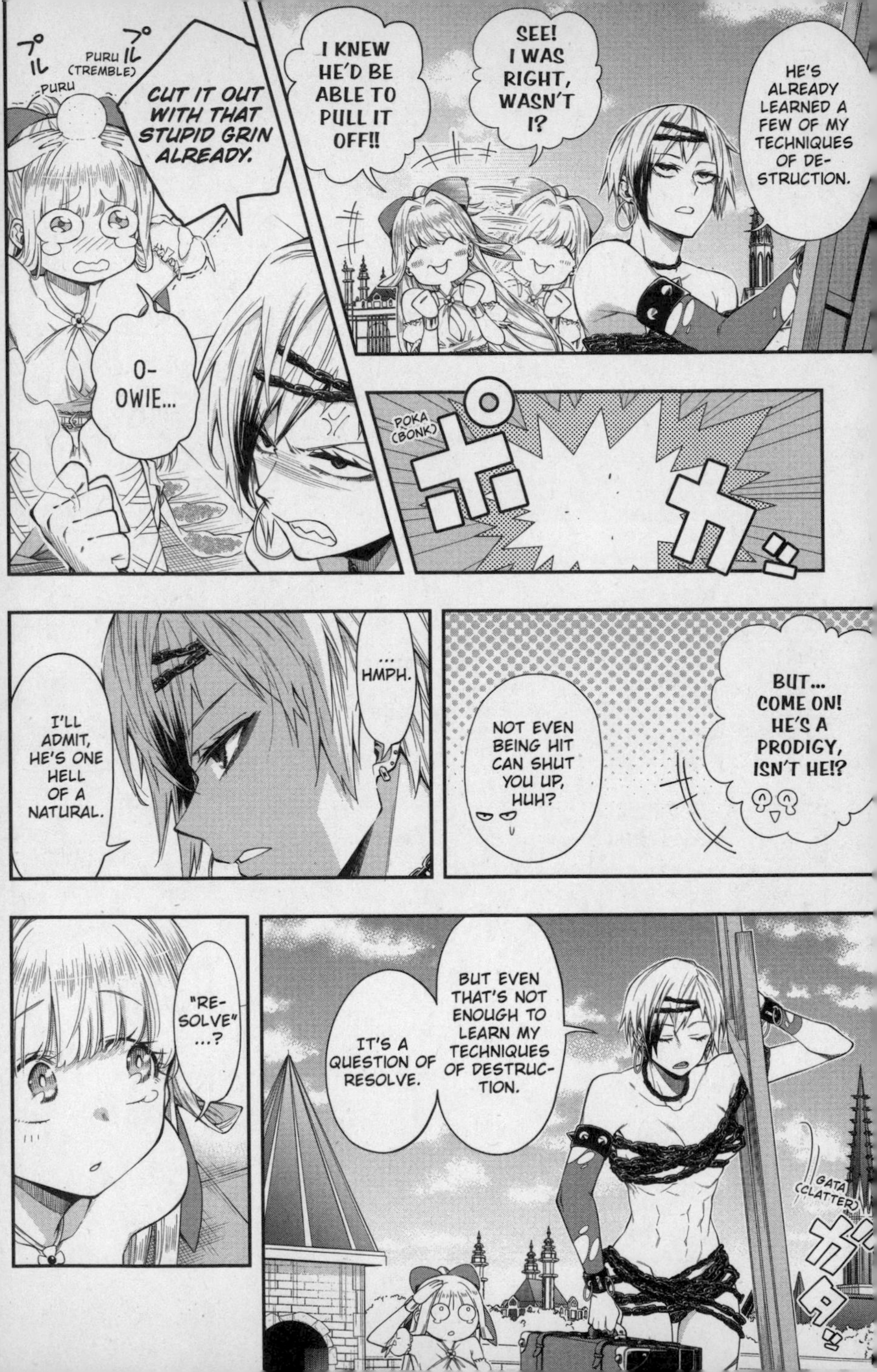
HE'S ALREADY LEARNED A FEW OF MY TECHNIQUES OF DE-STRUCTION.
SEE! I WAS RIGHT, WASN'T I?
I KNEW HE'D BE ABLE TO PULL IT OFF!!
ポカ
POKA (BONK)
プルプル
PURU (TREMBLE)
PURU
CUT IT OUT WITH THAT STUPID GRIN ALREADY.
O-OWIE...
BUT... COME ON! HE'S A PRODIGY, ISN'T HE!?
NOT EVEN BEING HIT CAN SHUT YOU UP, HUH?
... HMPH.
I'LL ADMIT, HE'S ONE HELL OF A NATURAL.
ガタ
GATA (CLATTER)
BUT EVEN THAT'S NOT ENOUGH TO LEARN MY TECHNIQUES OF DESTRUC-TION.
IT'S A QUESTION OF RESOLVE.
"RE-SOLVE" ...?

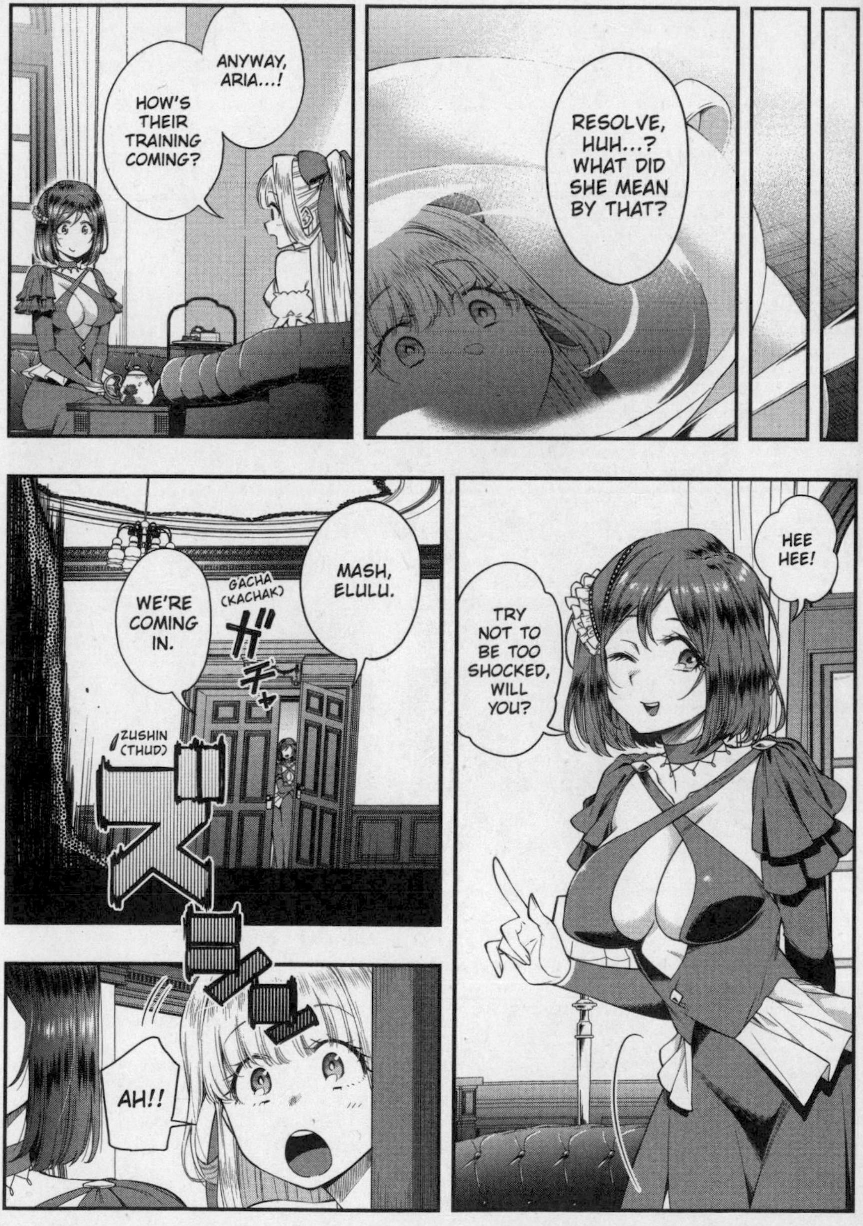
RESOLVE, HUH...? WHAT DID SHE MEAN BY THAT?
ANYWAY, ARIA...!
HOW'S THEIR TRAINING COMING?
HEE HEE!
TRY NOT TO BE TOO SHOCKED, WILL YOU?
MASH, ELULU.
GACHA (KACHAK)
WE'RE COMING IN.
ZUSHIN (THUD)
AH!!

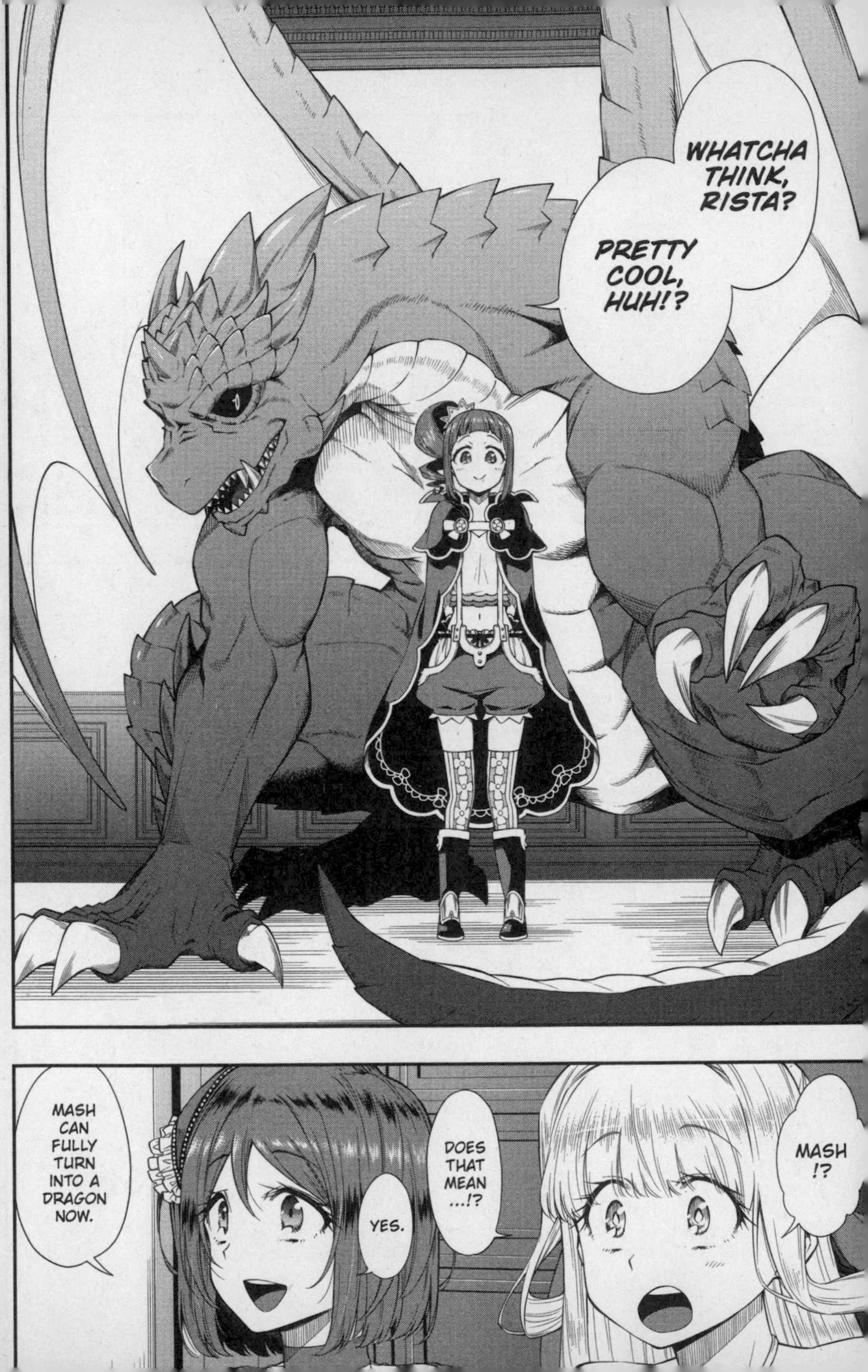
WHATCHA THINK, RISTA?
PRETTY COOL, HUH!?
MASH !?
DOES THAT MEAN ...!?
YES.
MASH CAN FULLY TURN INTO A DRAGON NOW.

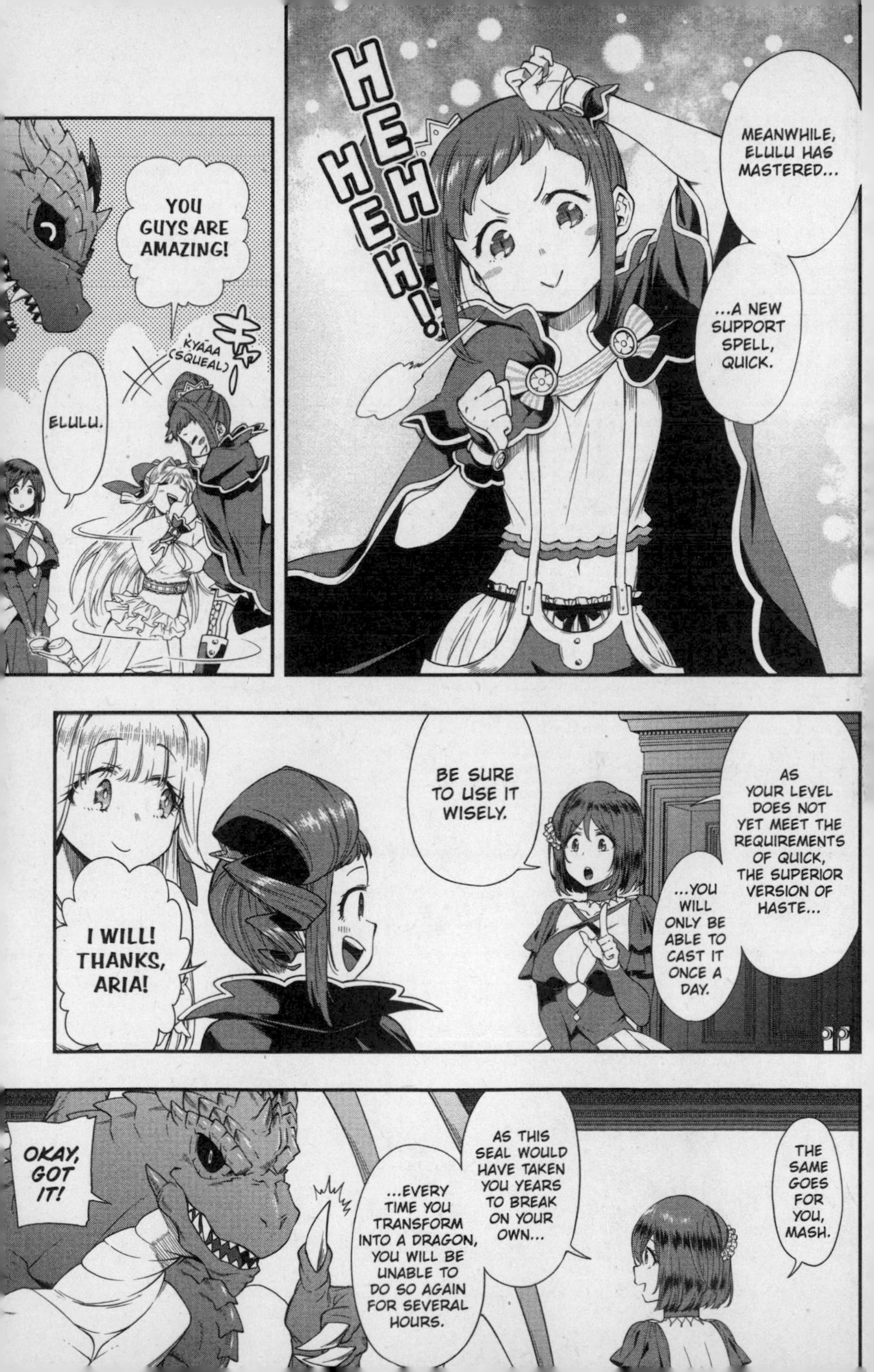
HEHEHEH!
MEANWHILE, ELULU HAS MASTERED...
...A NEW SUPPORT SPELL, QUICK.
YOU GUYS ARE AMAZING!
KYAAA (SQUEAL)
ELULU.
AS YOUR LEVEL DOES NOT YET MEET THE REQUIREMENTS OF QUICK, THE SUPERIOR VERSION OF HASTE...
...YOU WILL ONLY BE ABLE TO CAST IT ONCE A DAY.
BE SURE TO USE IT WISELY.
I WILL! THANKS, ARIA!
THE SAME GOES FOR YOU, MASH.
AS THIS SEAL WOULD HAVE TAKEN YOU YEARS TO BREAK ON YOUR OWN...
...EVERY TIME YOU TRANSFORM INTO A DRAGON, YOU WILL BE UNABLE TO DO SO AGAIN FOR SEVERAL HOURS.
OKAY, GOT IT!

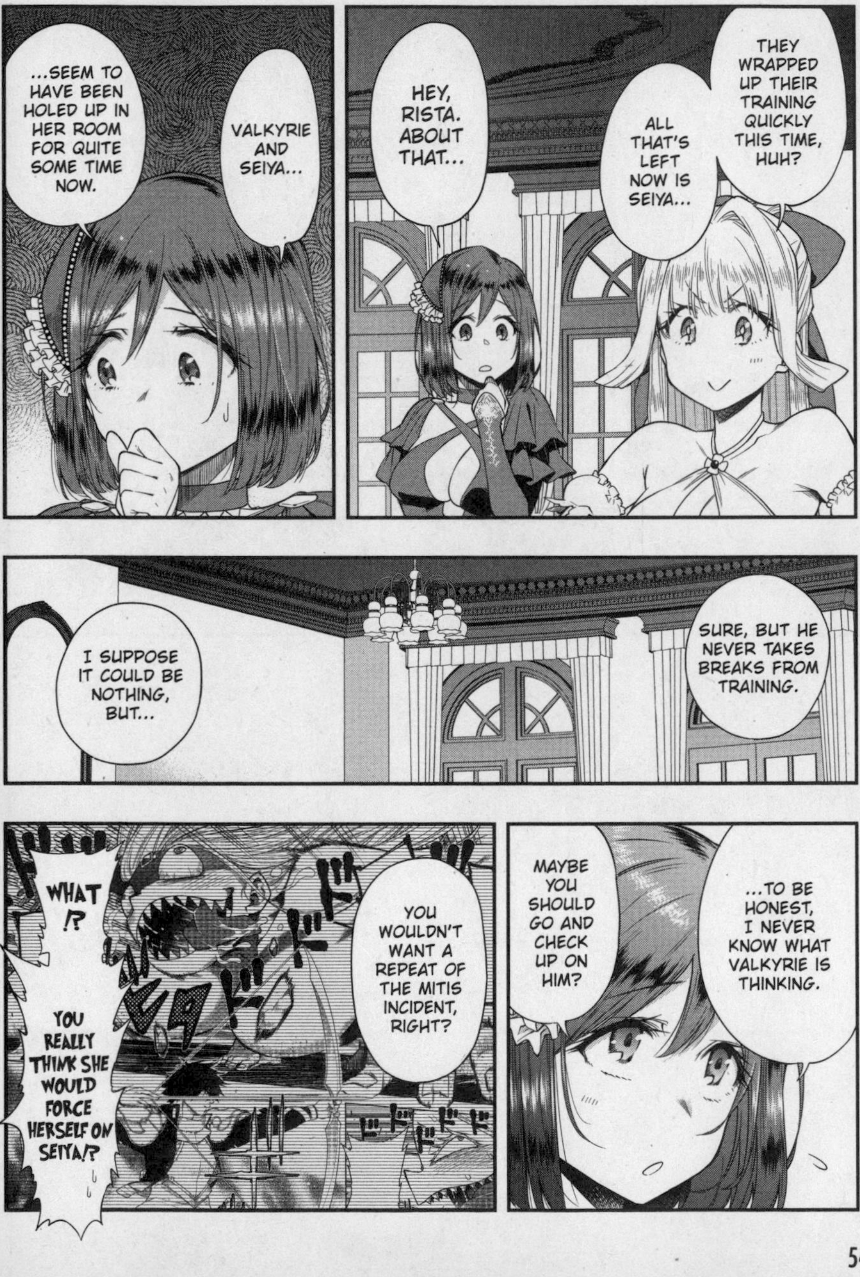
THEY WRAPPED UP THEIR TRAINING QUICKLY THIS TIME, HUH?
ALL THAT'S LEFT NOW IS SEIYA...
HEY, RISTA. ABOUT THAT...
VALKYRIE AND SEIYA...
...SEEM TO HAVE BEEN HOLED UP IN HER ROOM FOR QUITE SOME TIME NOW.
SURE, BUT HE NEVER TAKES BREAKS FROM TRAINING.
I SUPPOSE IT COULD BE NOTHING, BUT...
...TO BE HONEST, I NEVER KNOW WHAT VALKYRIE IS THINKING.
MAYBE YOU SHOULD GO AND CHECK UP ON HIM?
YOU WOULDN'T WANT A REPEAT OF THE MITIS INCIDENT, RIGHT?
WHAT!?
YOU REALLY THINK SHE WOULD FORCE HERSELF ON SEIYA!?

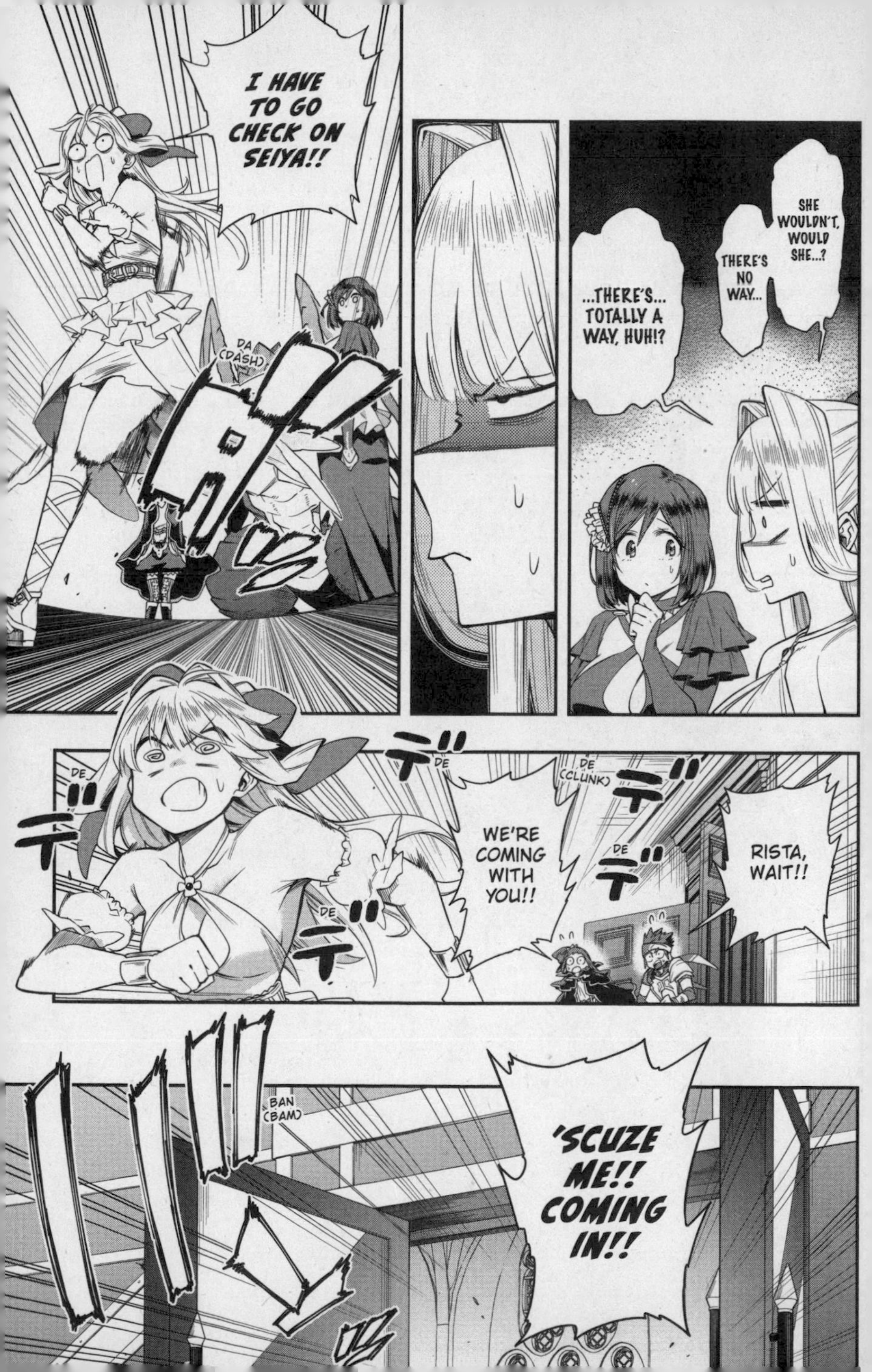
SHE WOULDN'T, WOULD SHE...?
THERE'S NO WAY...
...THERE'S... TOTALLY A WAY, HUH!?
I HAVE TO GO CHECK ON SEIYA!!
DA (DASH)
RISTA, WAIT!!
DE (CLUNK)
DE
DE
WE'RE COMING WITH YOU!!
DE
DE
'SCUZE ME!! COMING IN!!
BAN (BAM)

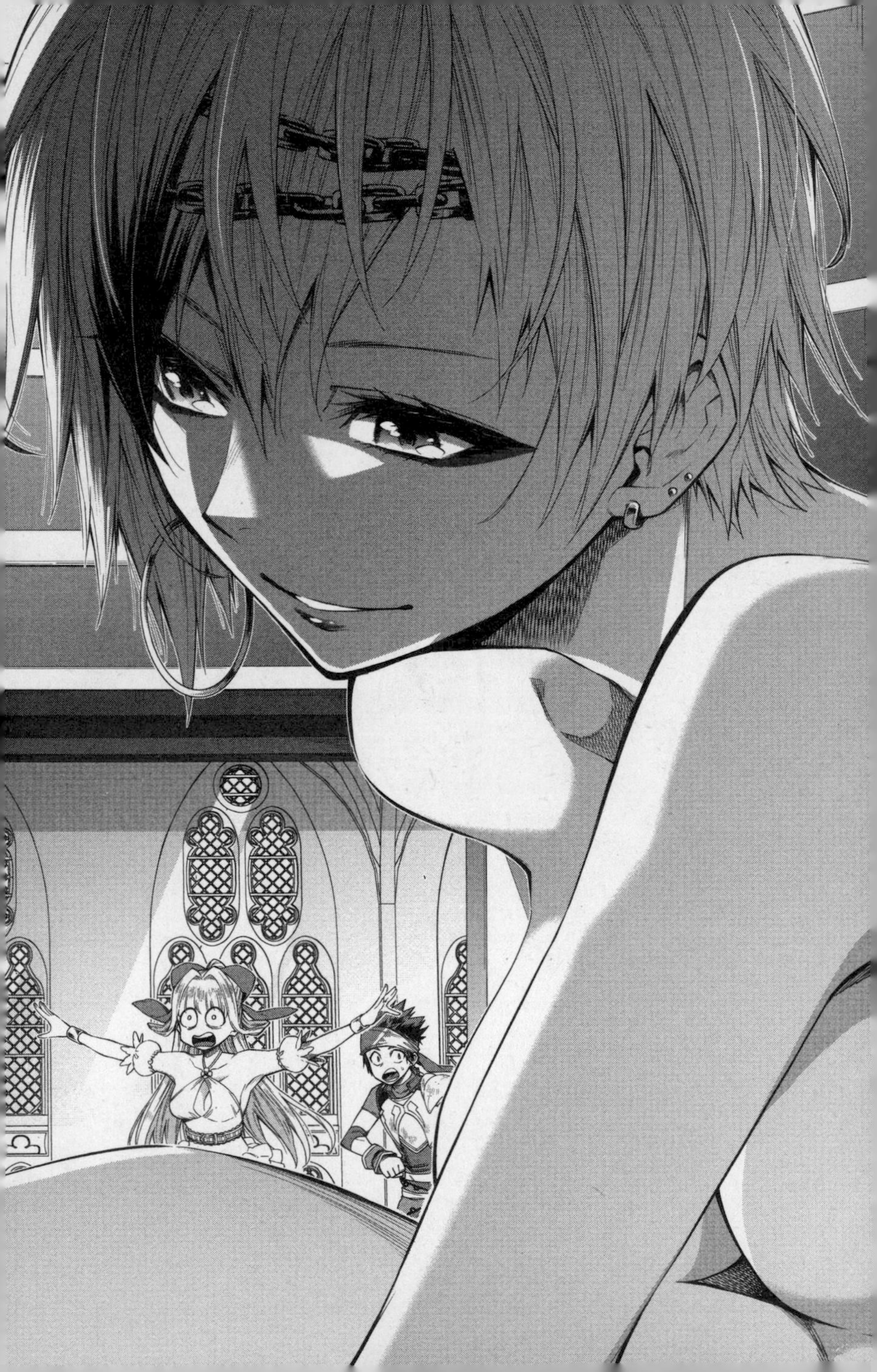

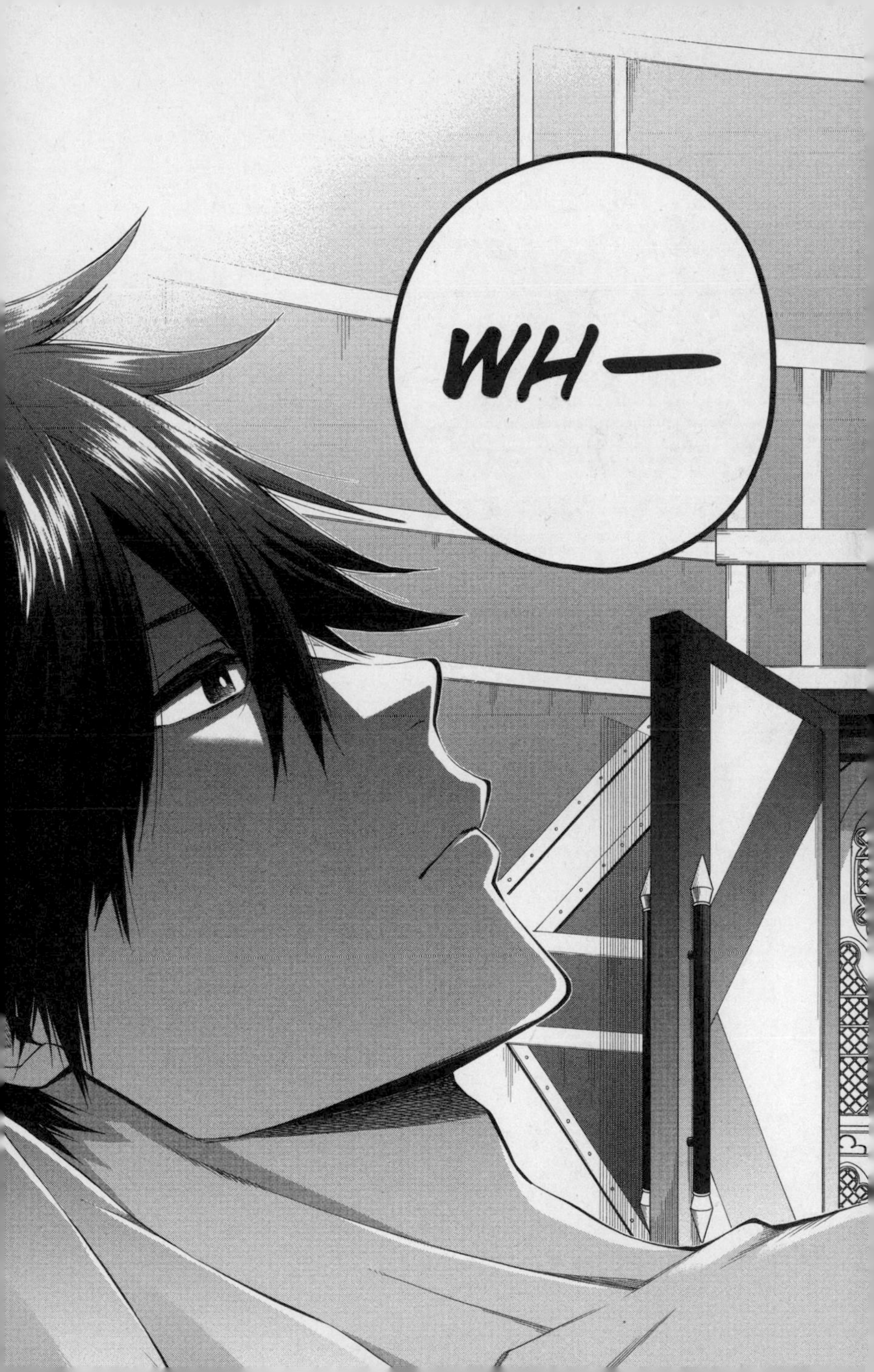
WH—

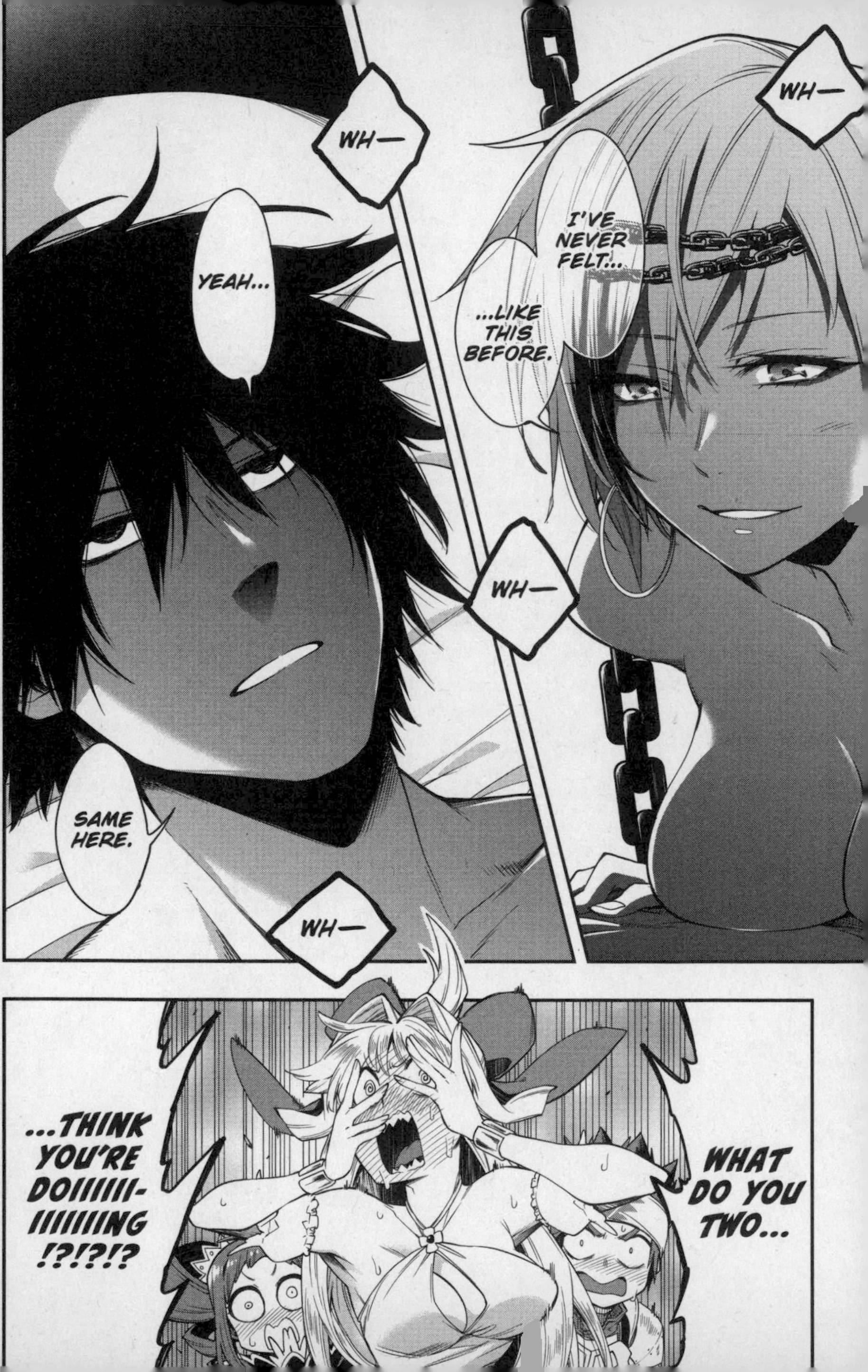
WH—
I'VE NEVER FELT...
...LIKE THIS BEFORE.
WH—
WH—
YEAH...
SAME HERE.
WH—
WHAT DO YOU TWO...
...THINK YOU'RE DOIIIIII-IIIIIIING!?!?!?

THE HERO IS OVERPOWERED BUT
OVERLY CAUTIOUS

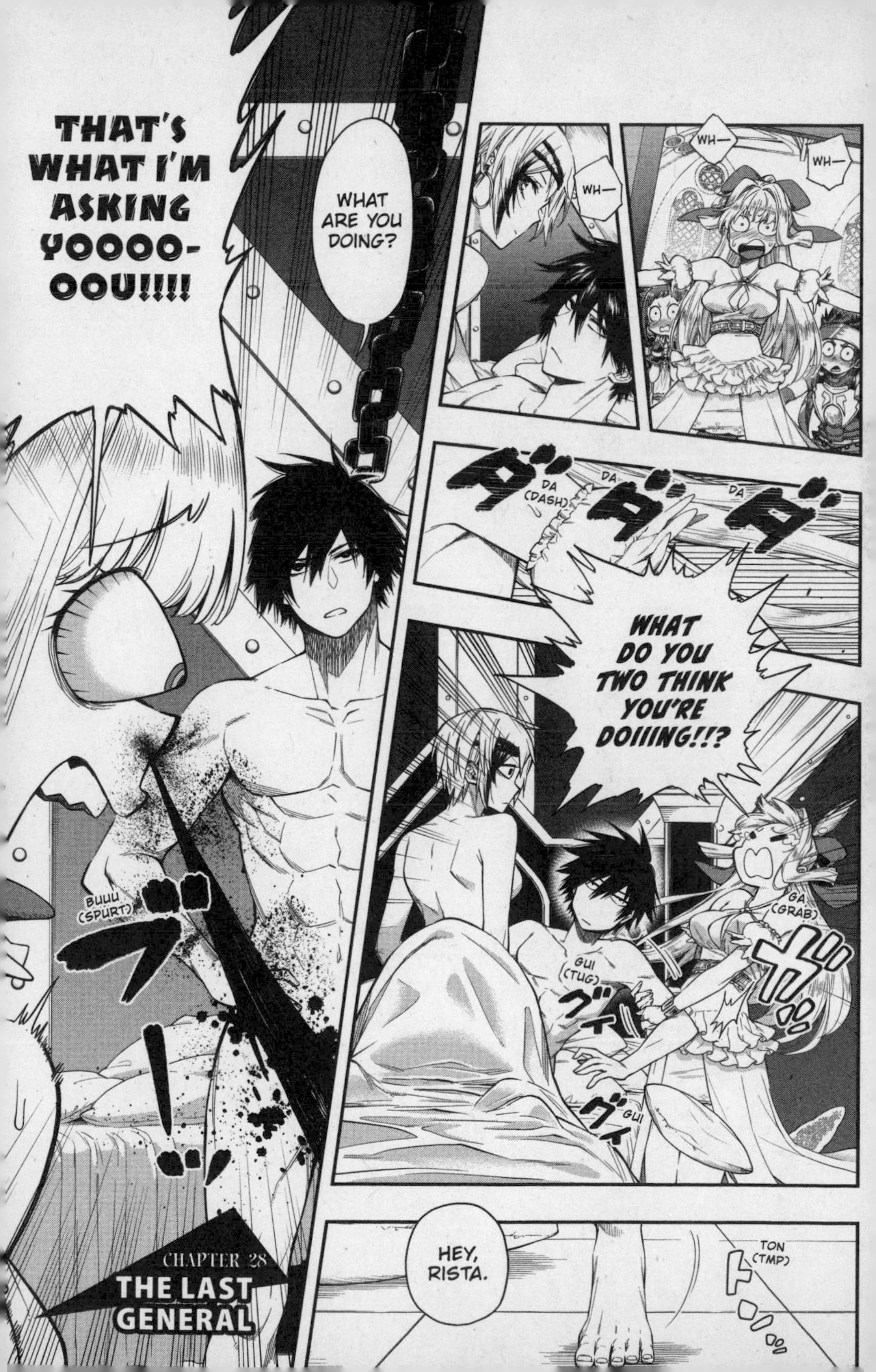
WH—
WH—
WH—
DA
DA (DASH)
DA
WHAT DO YOU TWO THINK YOU'RE DOIIING!!?
GA (GRAB)
GUI (TUG)
GUI
HEY, RISTA.
TON (TMP)
WHAT ARE YOU DOING?
THAT'S WHAT I'M ASKING YOOOO-OOU!!!!
BUUU (SPURT)
CHAPTER 28
THE LAST GENERAL

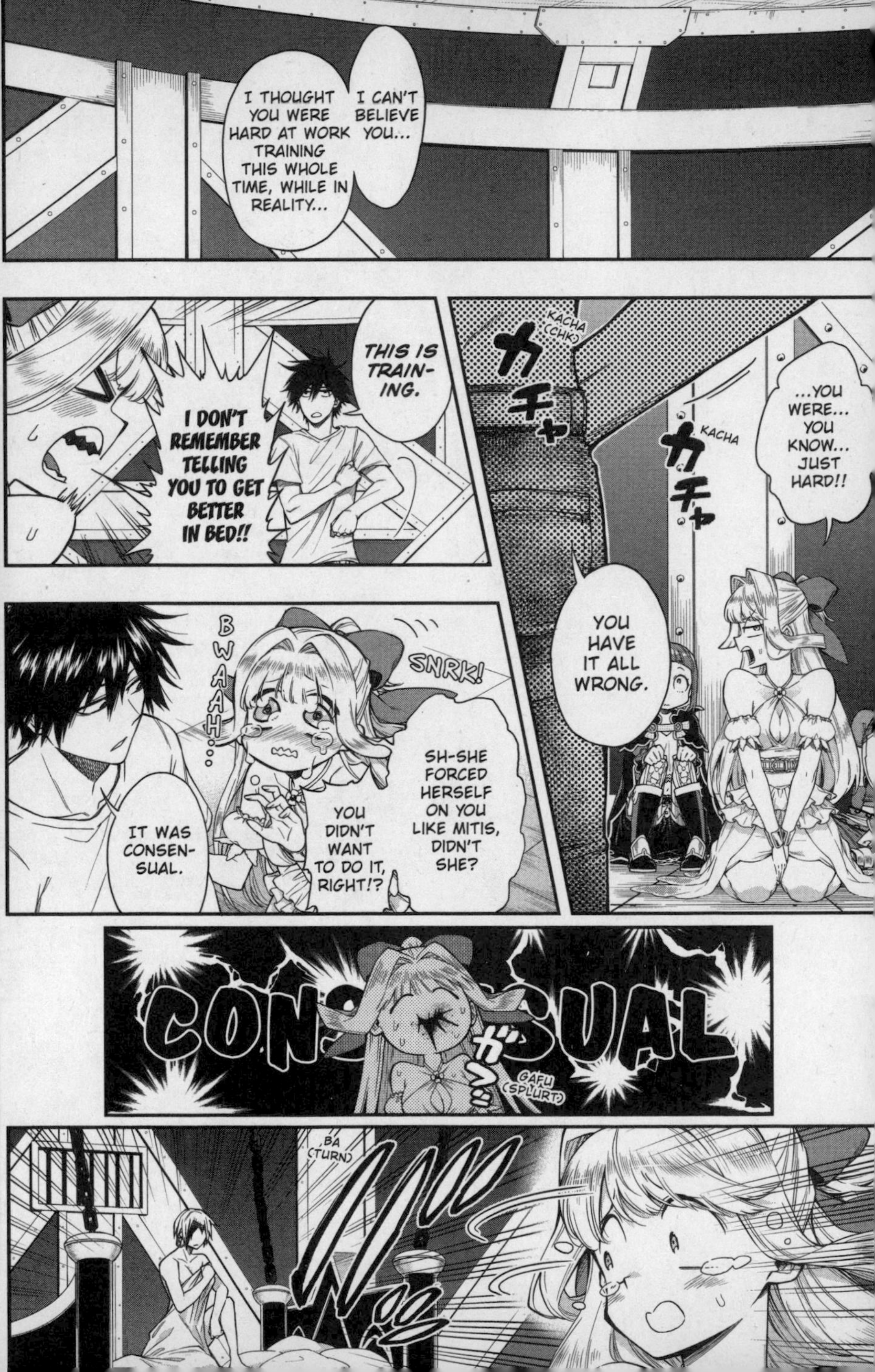

I CAN'T BELIEVE YOU...
I THOUGHT YOU WERE HARD AT WORK TRAINING THIS WHOLE TIME, WHILE IN REALITY...
KACHA (CHK)
KACHA
...YOU WERE... YOU KNOW... JUST HARD!!
YOU HAVE IT ALL WRONG.
THIS IS TRAIN-ING.
I DON'T REMEMBER TELLING YOU TO GET BETTER IN BED!!
SNRK!
BWAAAH...
SH-SHE FORCED HERSELF ON YOU LIKE MITIS, DIDN'T SHE?
YOU DIDN'T WANT TO DO IT, RIGHT!?
IT WAS CONSEN-SUAL.
CON
SUAL
GAFU (SPLURT)
BA (TURN)

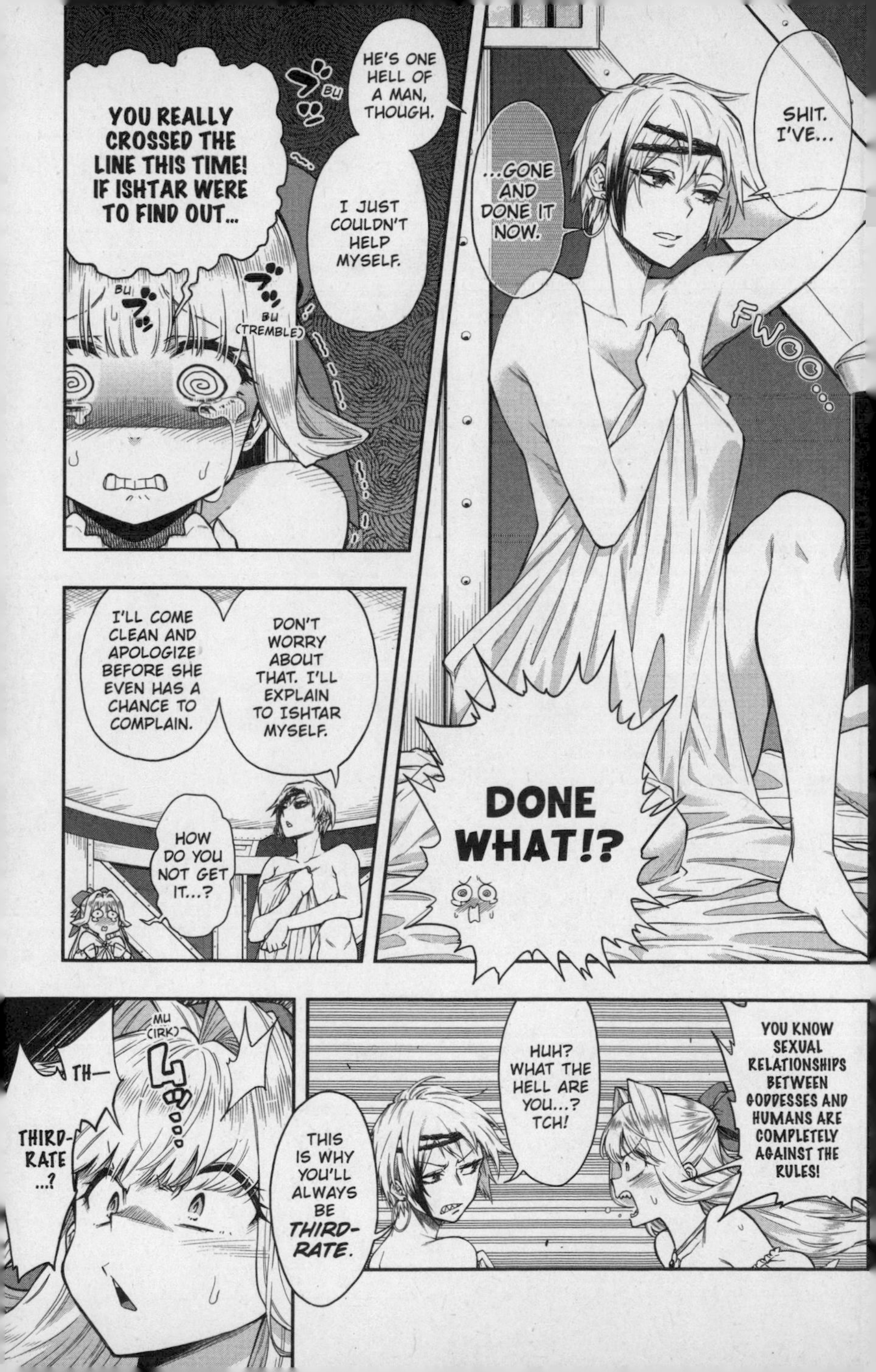
SHIT. I'VE...
...GONE AND DONE IT NOW.
FWOO...
DONE WHAT!?
HE'S ONE HELL OF A MAN, THOUGH.
BU
I JUST COULDN'T HELP MYSELF.
YOU REALLY CROSSED THE LINE THIS TIME! IF ISHTAR WERE TO FIND OUT...
BU
BU (TREMBLE)
DON'T WORRY ABOUT THAT. I'LL EXPLAIN TO ISHTAR MYSELF.
I'LL COME CLEAN AND APOLOGIZE BEFORE SHE EVEN HAS A CHANCE TO COMPLAIN.
HOW DO YOU NOT GET IT...?
YOU KNOW SEXUAL RELATIONSHIPS BETWEEN GODDESSES AND HUMANS ARE COMPLETELY AGAINST THE RULES!
HUH? WHAT THE HELL ARE YOU...? TCH!
THIS IS WHY YOU'LL ALWAYS BE THIRD-RATE.
MU (IRK)
TH—
THIRD-RATE ...?

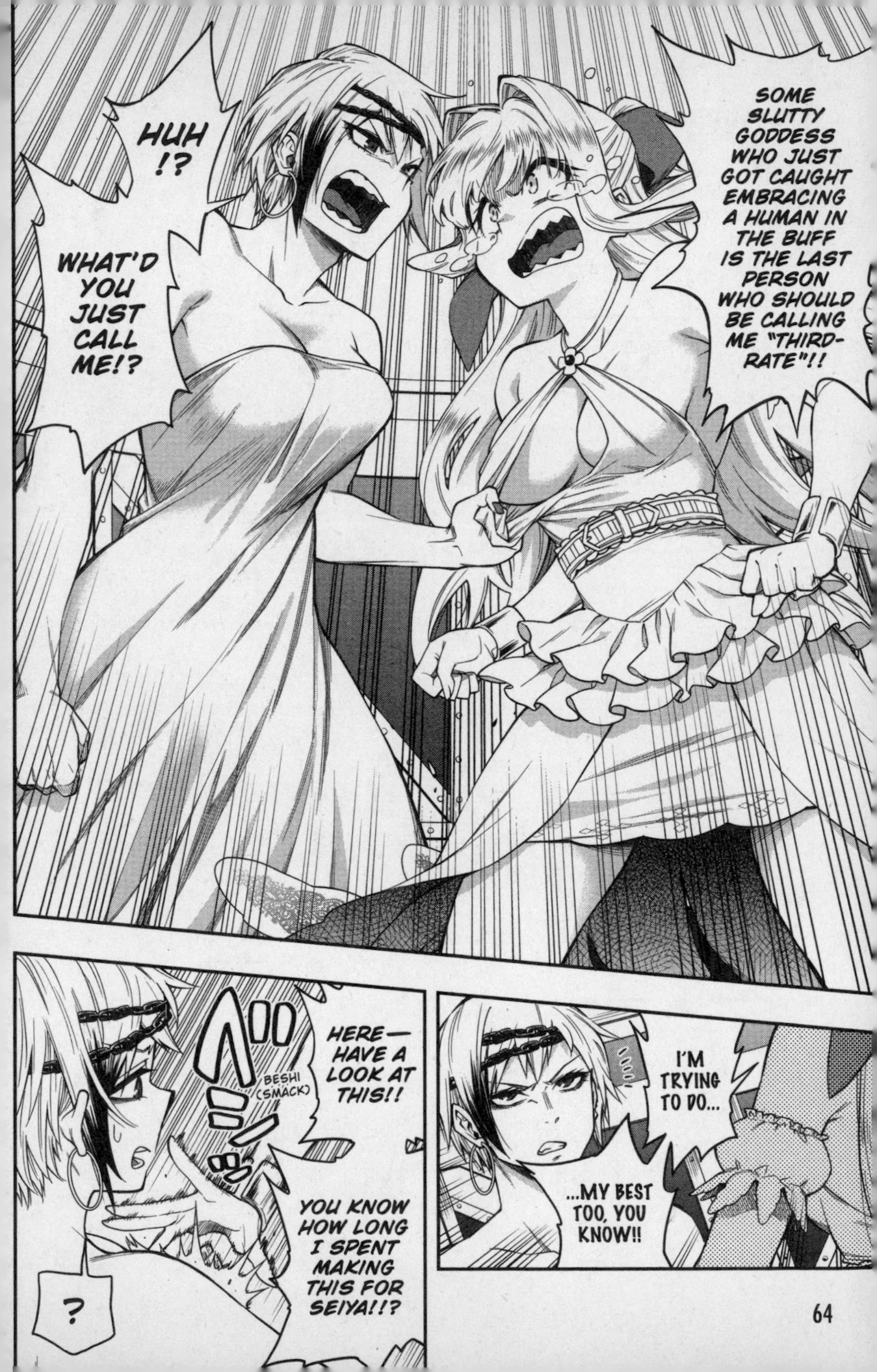
SOME SLUTTY GODDESS WHO JUST GOT CAUGHT EMBRACING A HUMAN IN THE BUFF IS THE LAST PERSON WHO SHOULD BE CALLING ME "THIRD-RATE"!!
HUH!?
WHAT'D YOU JUST CALL ME!?
I'M TRYING TO DO...
...MY BEST TOO, YOU KNOW!!
HERE—HAVE A LOOK AT THIS!!
BESHI (SMACK)
YOU KNOW HOW LONG I SPENT MAKING THIS FOR SEIYA!!?
?

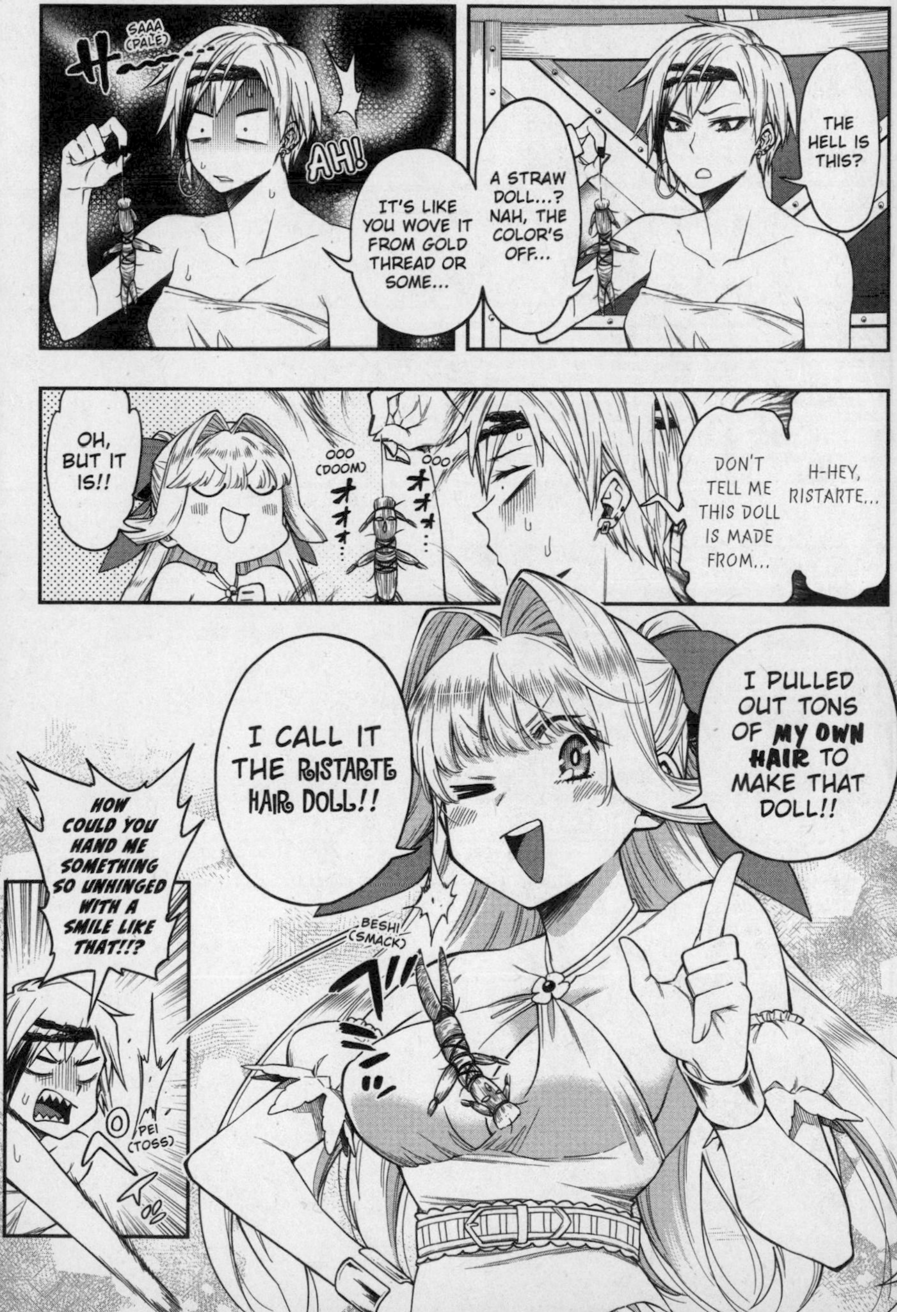
THE HELL IS THIS?
A STRAW DOLL...? NAH, THE COLOR'S OFF...
IT'S LIKE YOU WOVE IT FROM GOLD THREAD OR SOME...
AH!
SAAA (PALE)
H-HEY, RISTARTE...
DON'T TELL ME THIS DOLL IS MADE FROM...
OOO (DOOM)
オオオ...
オオオ...
OH, BUT IT IS!!
I PULLED OUT TONS OF **MY OWN HAIR** TO MAKE THAT DOLL!!
I CALL IT THE RISTARTE HAIR DOLL!!
BESHI (SMACK)
HOW COULD YOU HAND ME SOMETHING SO UNHINGED WITH A SMILE LIKE THAT!!?
PEI (TOSS)

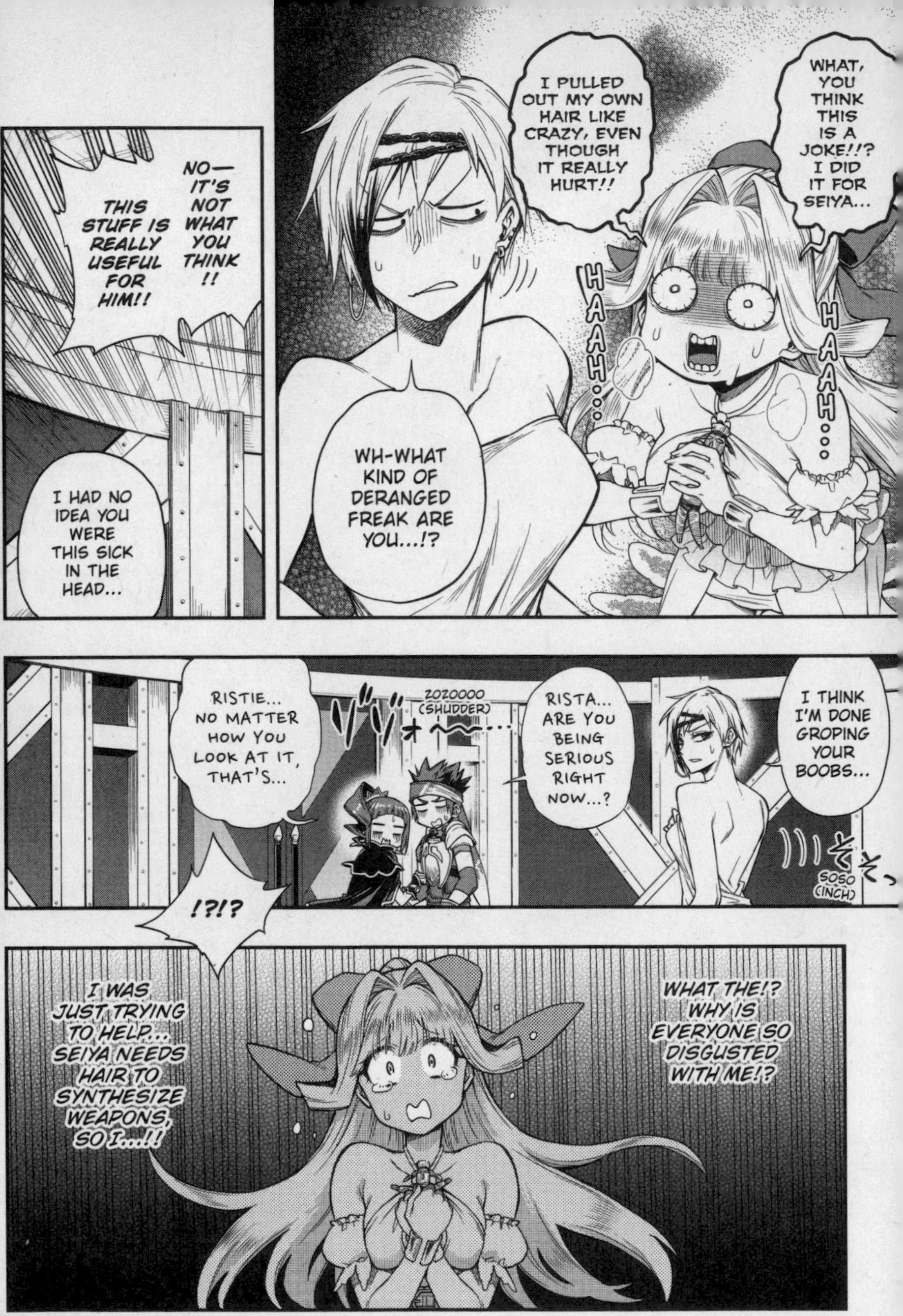
WHAT, YOU THINK THIS IS A JOKE!!? I DID IT FOR SEIYA...
I PULLED OUT MY OWN HAIR LIKE CRAZY, EVEN THOUGH IT REALLY HURT!!
HAAAH...
HAAAH...
WH-WHAT KIND OF DERANGED FREAK ARE YOU...!?
NO— IT'S NOT WHAT YOU THINK!!
THIS STUFF IS REALLY USEFUL FOR HIM!!
I HAD NO IDEA YOU WERE THIS SICK IN THE HEAD...
I THINK I'M DONE GROPING YOUR BOOBS...
SOSO (INCH)
RISTA... ARE YOU BEING SERIOUS RIGHT NOW...?
ZOZOOOO (SHUDDER)
RISTIE... NO MATTER HOW YOU LOOK AT IT, THAT'S...
!?!?
WHAT THE!? WHY IS EVERYONE SO DISGUSTED WITH ME!?
I WAS JUST TRYING TO HELP... SEIYA NEEDS HAIR TO SYNTHESIZE WEAPONS, SO I...!!

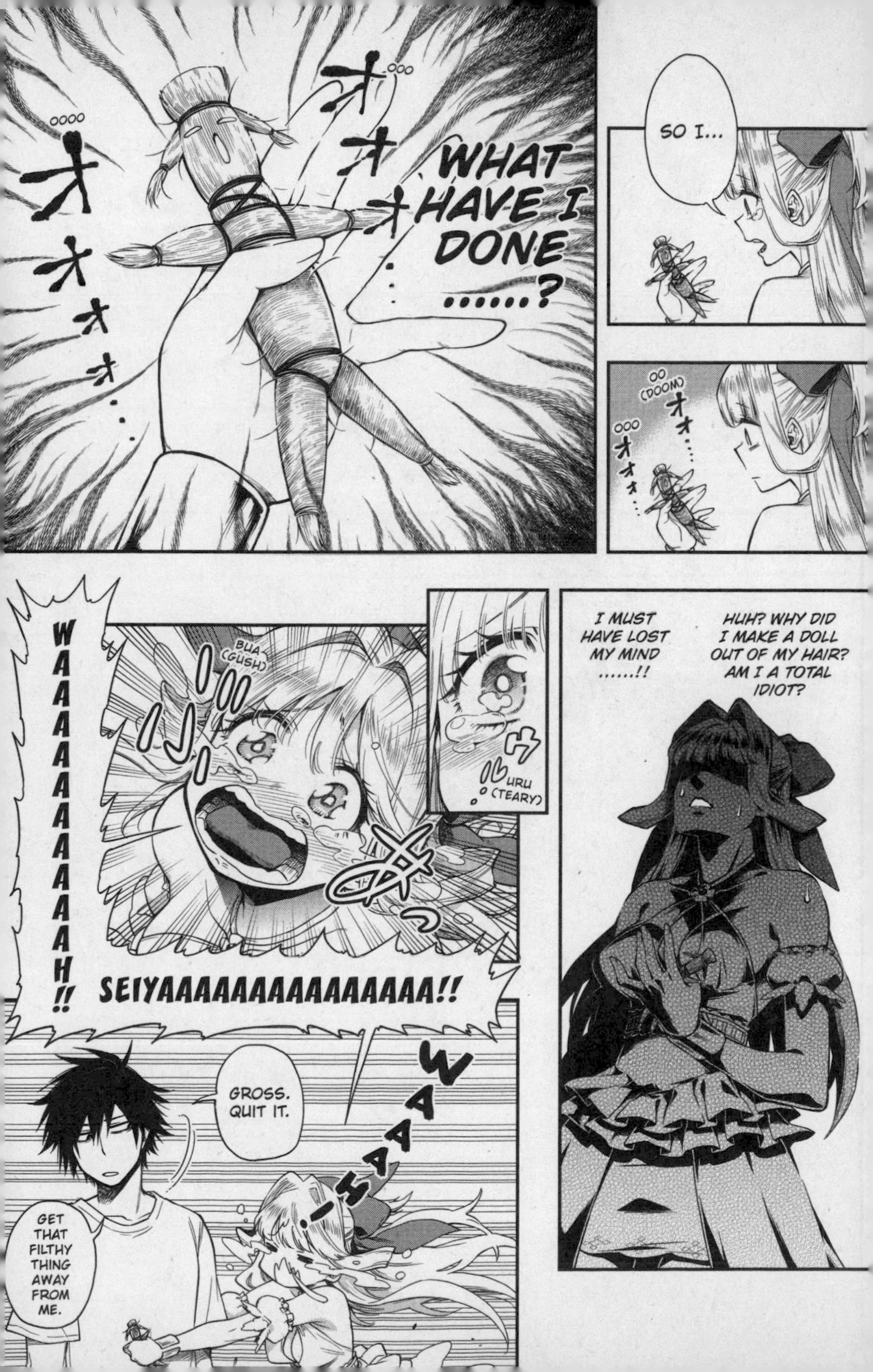
SO I...
OO (DOOM)
OOO
OOOO
OOO
WHAT HAVE I DONE ......?
HUH? WHY DID I MAKE A DOLL OUT OF MY HAIR? AM I A TOTAL IDIOT?
I MUST HAVE LOST MY MIND ......!!
URU (TEARY)
BUA (GUSH)
WAAAAAAAAAAAAH!!
SEIYAAAAAAAAAAAAAAA!!
GROSS. QUIT IT.
GET THAT FILTHY THING AWAY FROM ME.
WAAA

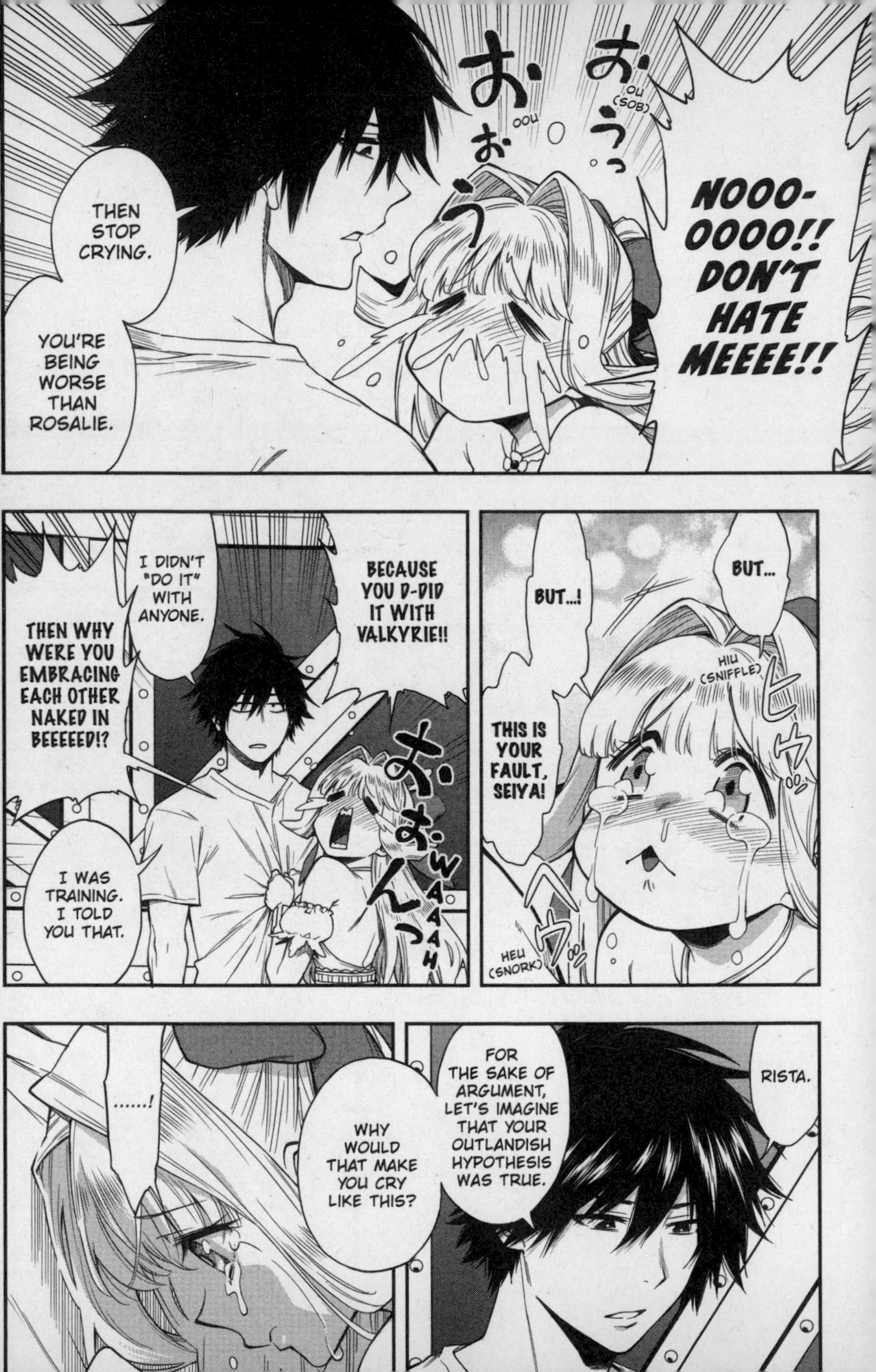
NOOOO-OOOO!! DON'T HATE MEEEE!!
OU (SOB)
OOU
THEN STOP CRYING.
YOU'RE BEING WORSE THAN ROSALIE.
BUT...
BUT...!
HIU (SNIFFLE)
THIS IS YOUR FAULT, SEIYA!
HEU (SNORK)
BECAUSE YOU D-DID IT WITH VALKYRIE!!
I DIDN'T "DO IT" WITH ANYONE.
THEN WHY WERE YOU EMBRACING EACH OTHER NAKED IN BEEEEED!?
WAAAH
I WAS TRAINING. I TOLD YOU THAT.
RISTA.
FOR THE SAKE OF ARGUMENT, LET'S IMAGINE THAT YOUR OUTLANDISH HYPOTHESIS WAS TRUE.
WHY WOULD THAT MAKE YOU CRY LIKE THIS?
......!

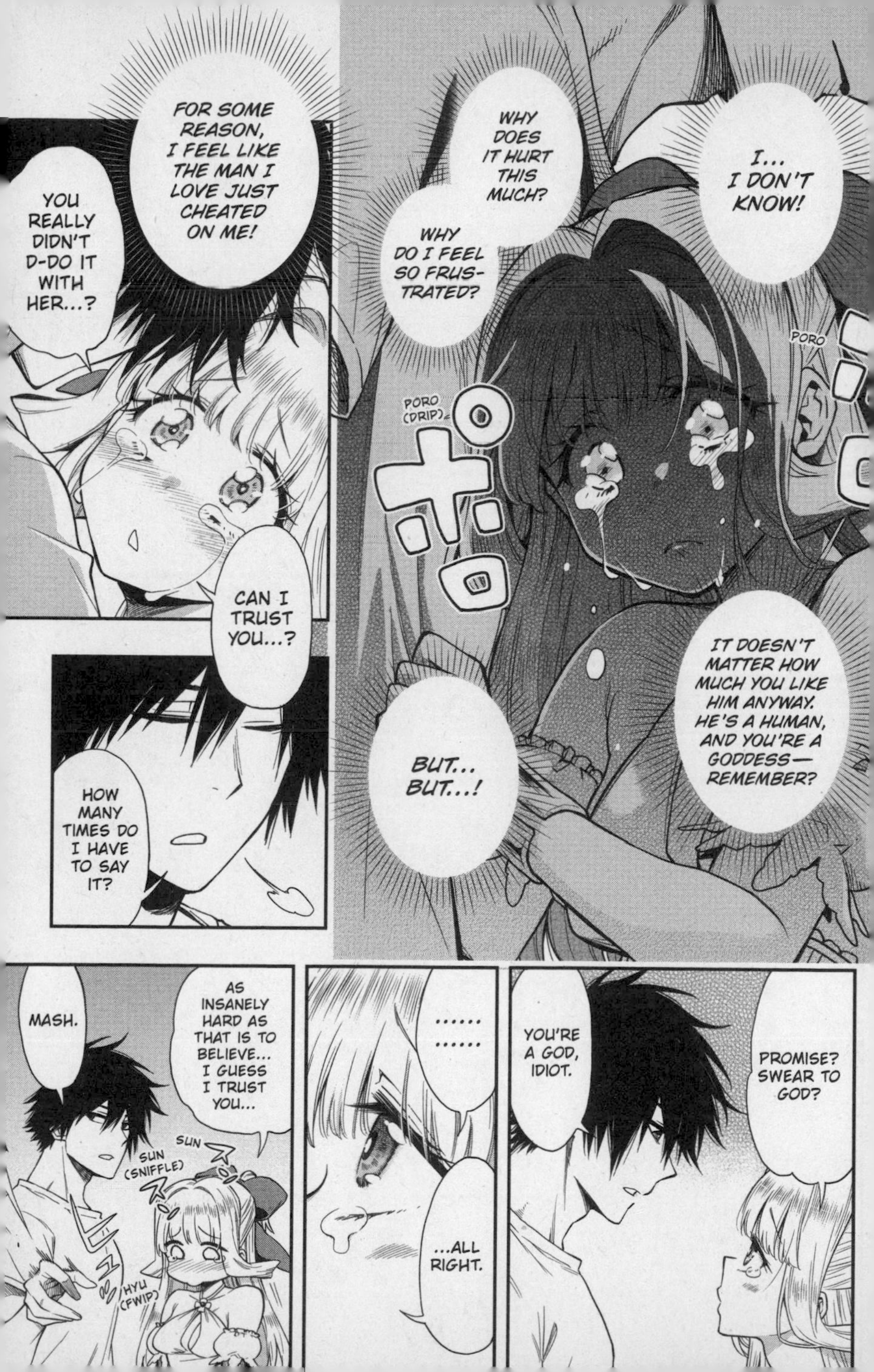
I... I DON'T KNOW!
WHY DOES IT HURT THIS MUCH?
WHY DO I FEEL SO FRUS-TRATED?
PORO
PORO (DRIP)
IT DOESN'T MATTER HOW MUCH YOU LIKE HIM ANYWAY. HE'S A HUMAN, AND YOU'RE A GODDESS—REMEMBER?
BUT... BUT...!
FOR SOME REASON, I FEEL LIKE THE MAN I LOVE JUST CHEATED ON ME!
YOU REALLY DIDN'T D-DO IT WITH HER...?
CAN I TRUST YOU...?
HOW MANY TIMES DO I HAVE TO SAY IT?
PROMISE? SWEAR TO GOD?
YOU'RE A GOD, IDIOT.
......
......
...ALL RIGHT.
AS INSANELY HARD AS THAT IS TO BELIEVE... I GUESS I TRUST YOU...
MASH.
SUN
SUN (SNIFFLE)
HYU (FWIP)

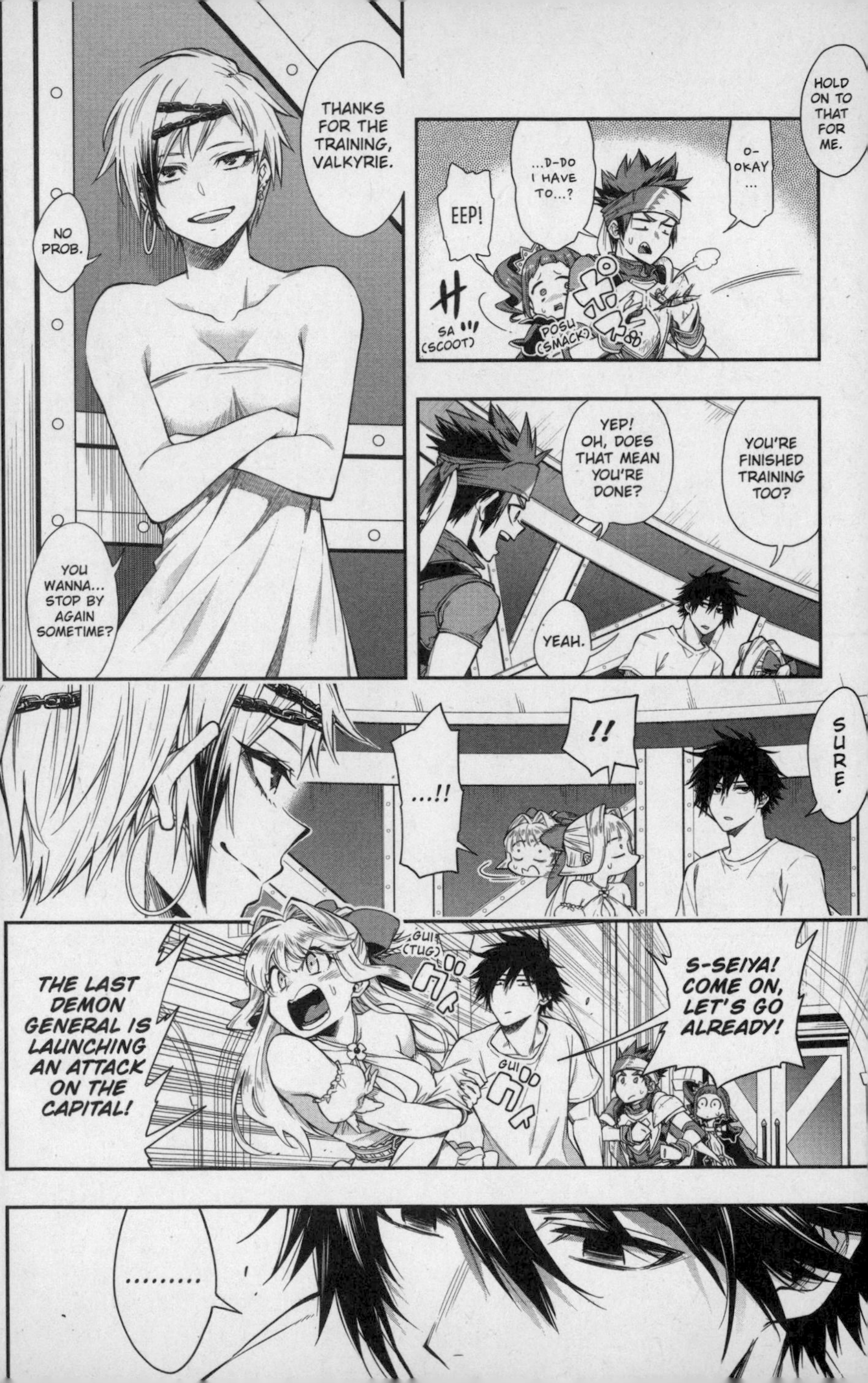
HOLD ON TO THAT FOR ME.
O-OKAY ...
...D-DO I HAVE TO...?
EEP!
POSU (SMACK)
SA (SCOOT)
YOU'RE FINISHED TRAINING TOO?
YEP! OH, DOES THAT MEAN YOU'RE DONE?
YEAH.
THANKS FOR THE TRAINING, VALKYRIE.
NO PROB.
YOU WANNA... STOP BY AGAIN SOMETIME?
SURE.
!!
...!!
S-SEIYA! COME ON, LET'S GO ALREADY!
GUI (TUG)
GUI
THE LAST DEMON GENERAL IS LAUNCHING AN ATTACK ON THE CAPITAL!
....

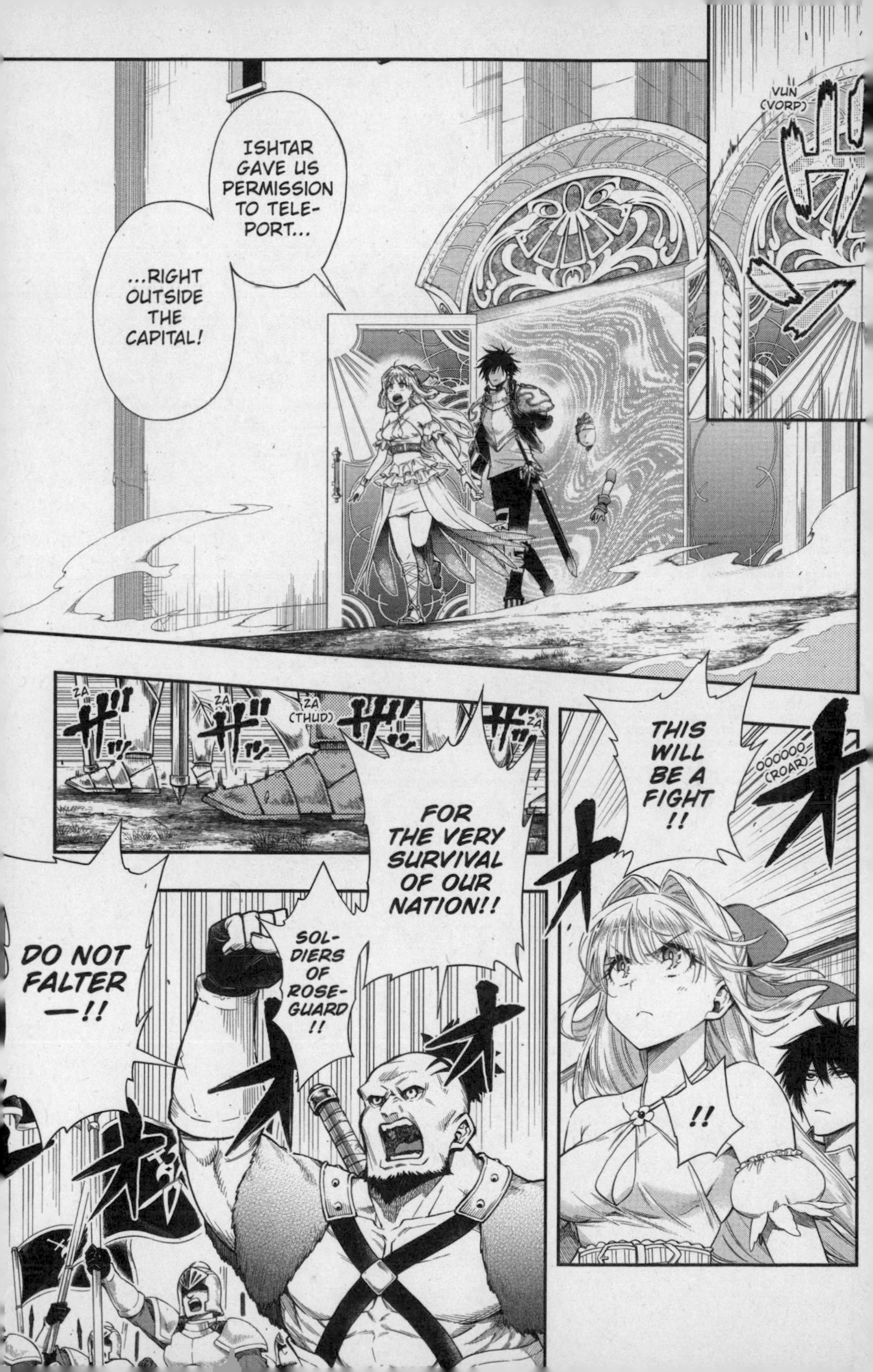
VUN (VORP)
ISHTAR GAVE US PERMISSION TO TELE-PORT...
...RIGHT OUTSIDE THE CAPITAL!
OOOOOO (ROAR)
THIS WILL BE A FIGHT!!
!!
ZA
ZA
ZA (THUD)
ZA
FOR THE VERY SURVIVAL OF OUR NATION!!
SOL-DIERS OF ROSE-GUARD!!
DO NOT FALTER—!!

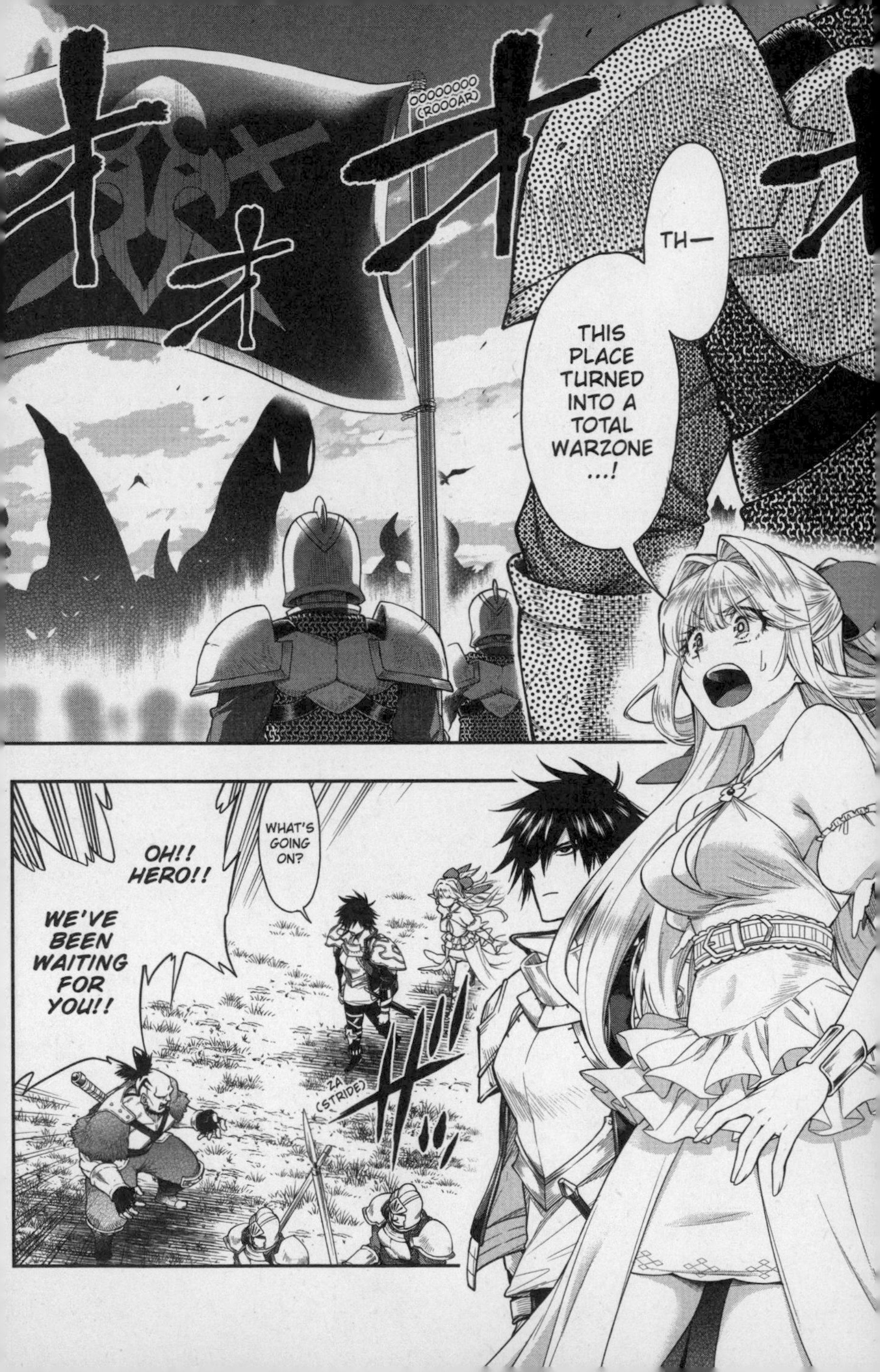
OOOOOOOO
(ROOOAR)
TH—
THIS PLACE TURNED INTO A TOTAL WARZONE ...!
WHAT'S GOING ON?
OH!! HERO!!
WE'VE BEEN WAITING FOR YOU!!
ZA
(STRIDE)

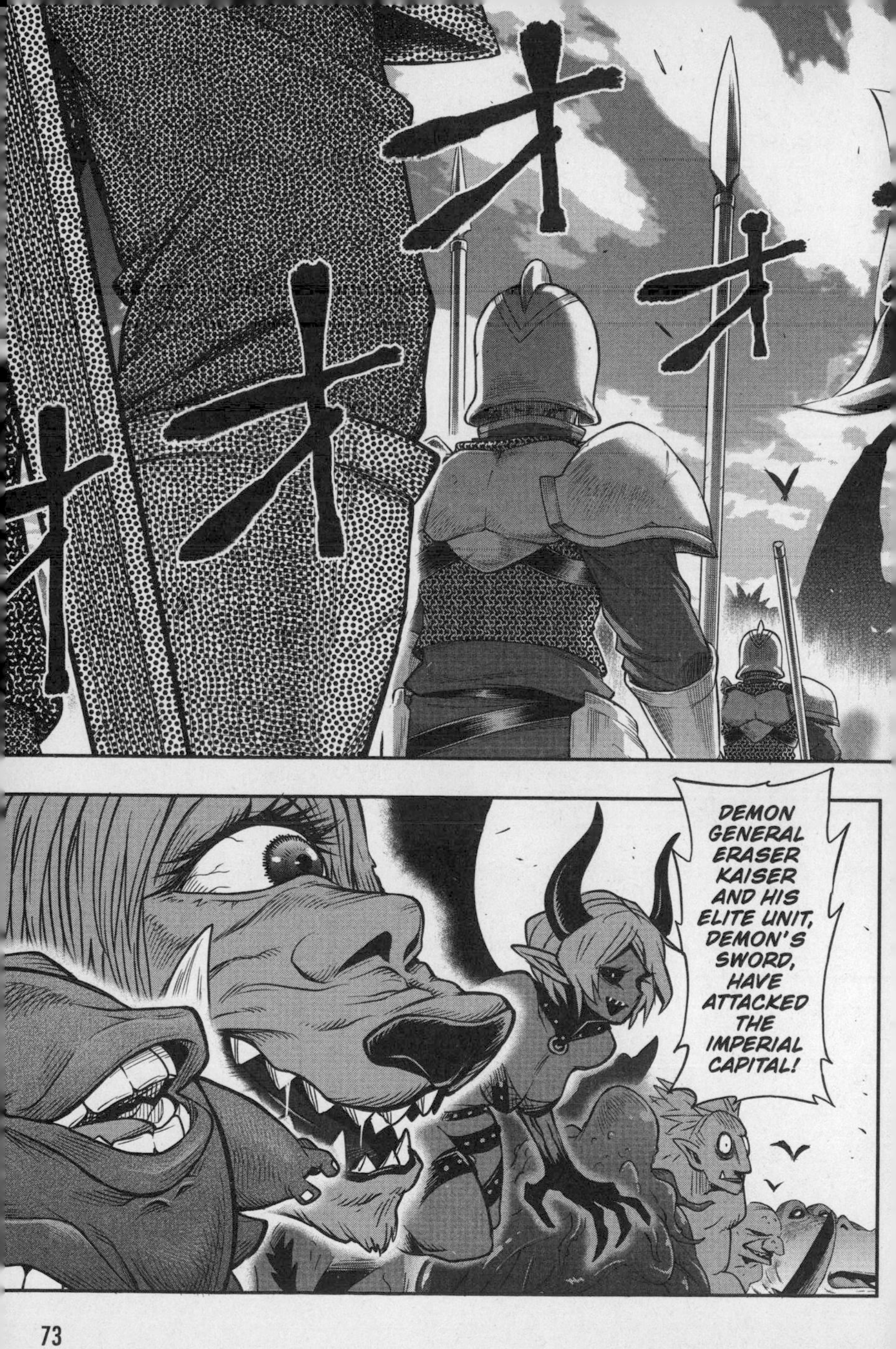

オオオオ
DEMON GENERAL ERASER KAISER AND HIS ELITE UNIT, DEMON'S SWORD, HAVE ATTACKED THE IMPERIAL CAPITAL!

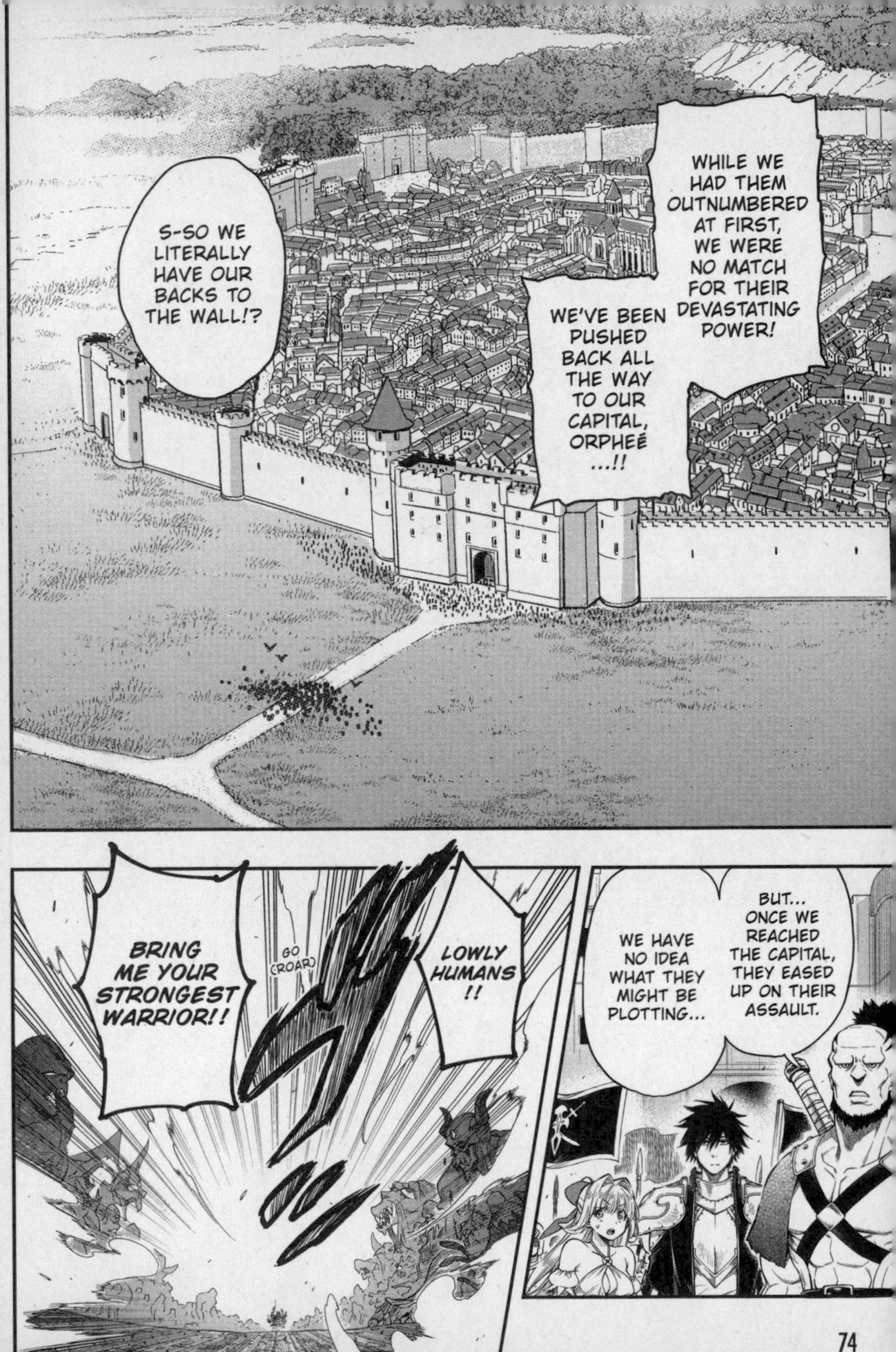
WHILE WE HAD THEM OUTNUMBERED AT FIRST, WE WERE NO MATCH FOR THEIR DEVASTATING POWER!
WE'VE BEEN PUSHED BACK ALL THE WAY TO OUR CAPITAL, ORPHEÉ ...!!
S-SO WE LITERALLY HAVE OUR BACKS TO THE WALL!?
BUT... ONCE WE REACHED THE CAPITAL, THEY EASED UP ON THEIR ASSAULT.
WE HAVE NO IDEA WHAT THEY MIGHT BE PLOTTING...
LOWLY HUMANS !!
GO (ROAR)
BRING ME YOUR STRONGEST WARRIOR!!

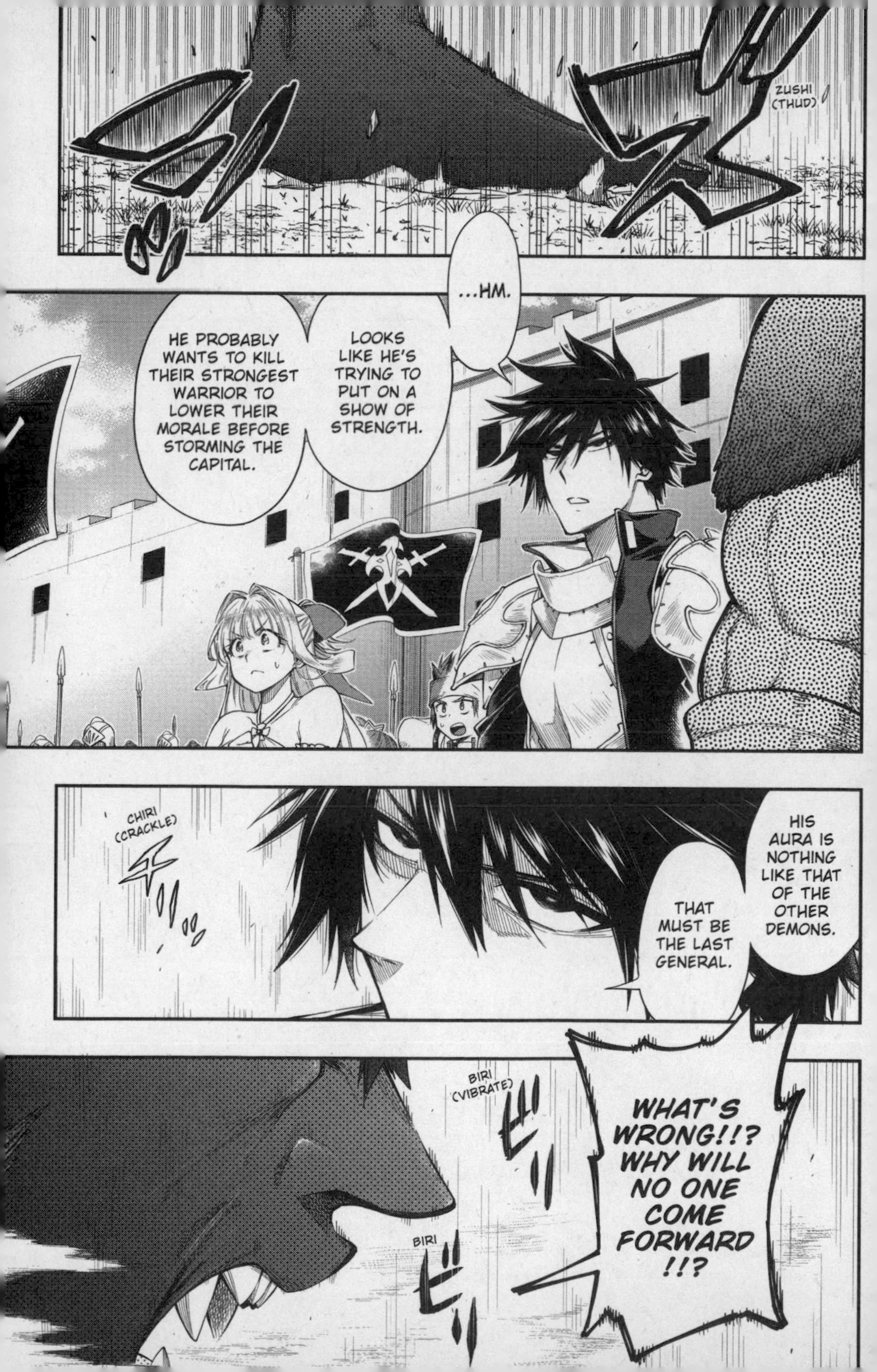
ZUSHI (THUD)
...HM.
LOOKS LIKE HE'S TRYING TO PUT ON A SHOW OF STRENGTH.
HE PROBABLY WANTS TO KILL THEIR STRONGEST WARRIOR TO LOWER THEIR MORALE BEFORE STORMING THE CAPITAL.
HIS AURA IS NOTHING LIKE THAT OF THE OTHER DEMONS.
THAT MUST BE THE LAST GENERAL.
CHIRI (CRACKLE)
WHAT'S WRONG!!? WHY WILL NO ONE COME FORWARD!!?
BIRI (VIBRATE)
BIRI

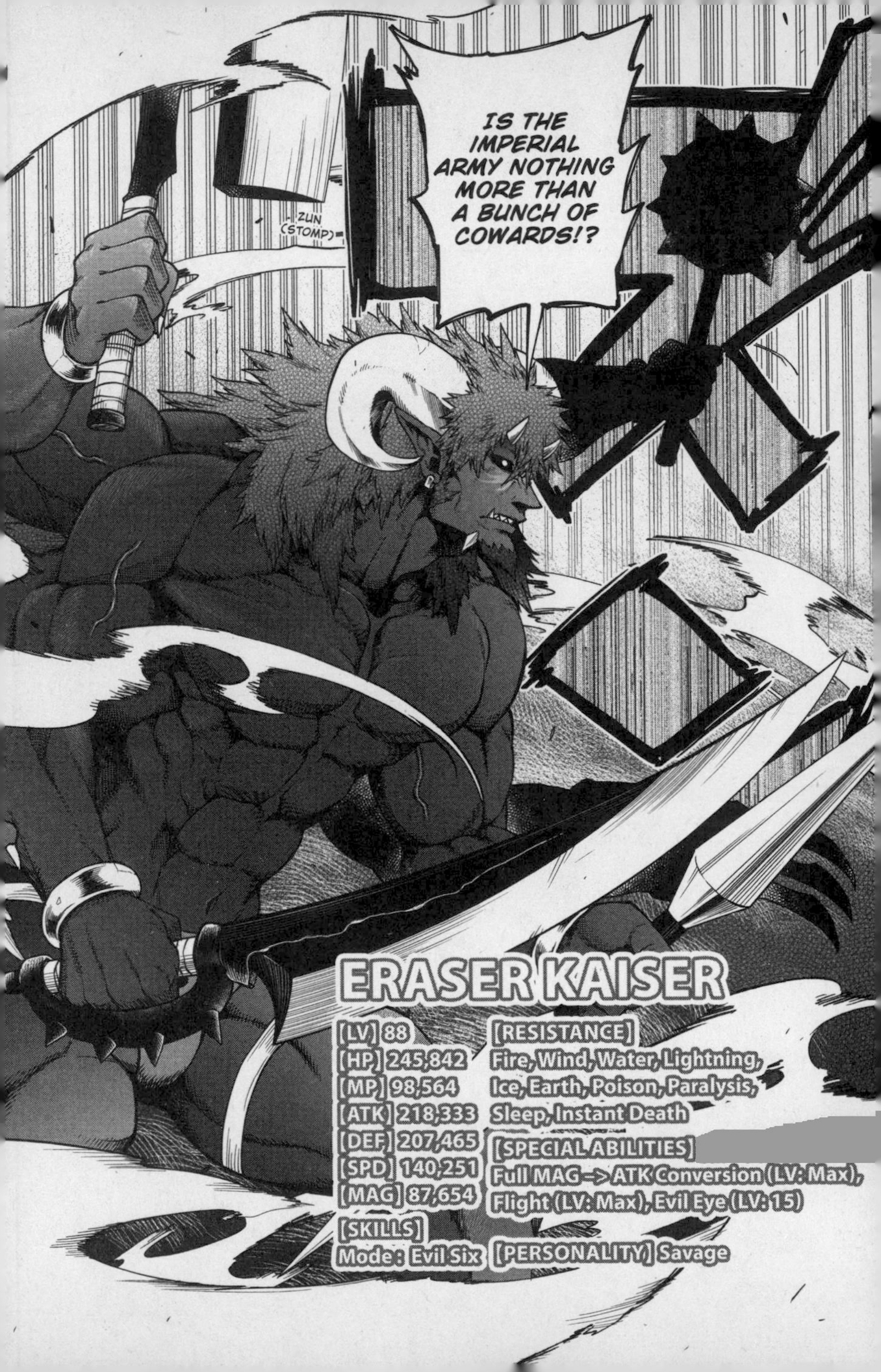
IS THE IMPERIAL ARMY NOTHING MORE THAN A BUNCH OF COWARDS!?
ZUN (STOMP)
ERASER KAISER
[LV] 88
[HP] 245,842
[MP] 98,564
[ATK] 218,333
[DEF] 207,465
[SPD] 140,251
[MAG] 87,654
[SKILLS]
Mode: Evil Six
[RESISTANCE]
Fire, Wind, Water, Lightning, Ice, Earth, Poison, Paralysis, Sleep, Instant Death
[SPECIAL ABILITIES]
Full MAG→ATK Conversion (LV: Max), Flight (LV: Max), Evil Eye (LV: 15)
[PERSONALITY] Savage

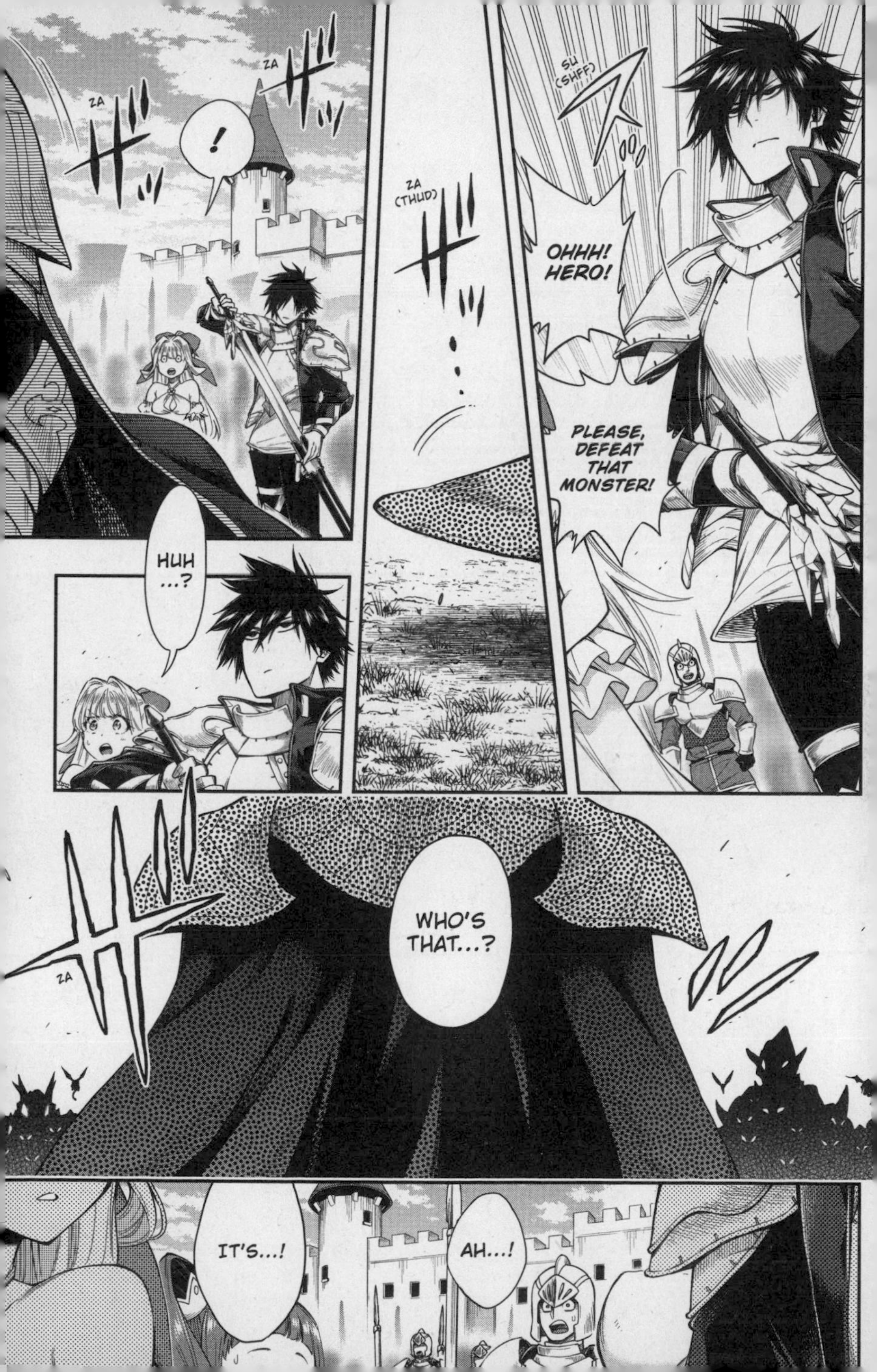
SU (SHFF)
OHHH! HERO!
PLEASE, DEFEAT THAT MONSTER!
ZA (THUD)
...
ZA
ZA
!
HUH ...?
WHO'S THAT...?
ZA
AH...!
IT'S...!

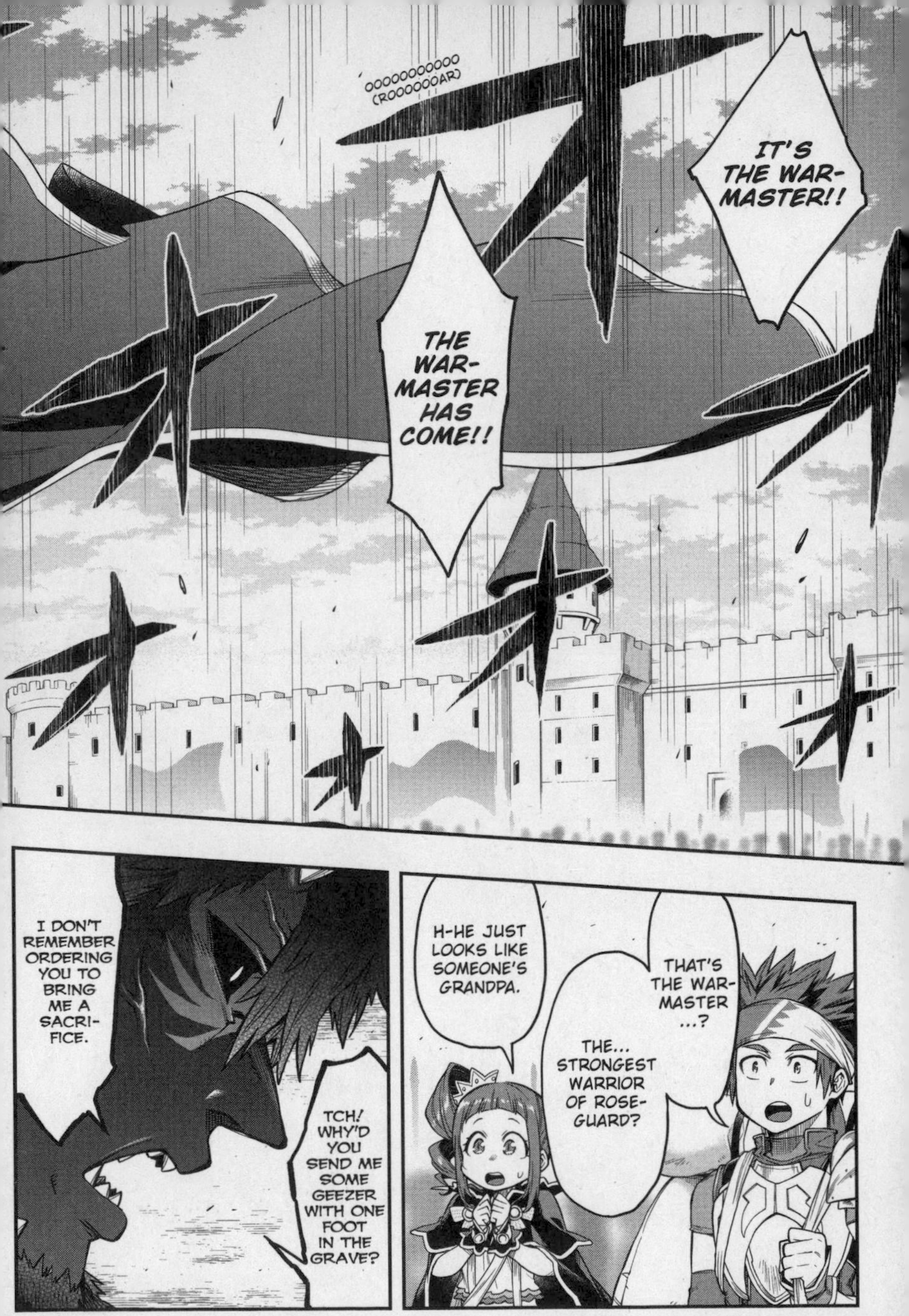
IT'S THE WAR-MASTER!!
THE WAR-MASTER HAS COME!!
OOOOOOOOOOOO (ROOOOOOOAR)
THAT'S THE WAR-MASTER ...?
THE... STRONGEST WARRIOR OF ROSE-GUARD?
H-HE JUST LOOKS LIKE SOMEONE'S GRANDPA.
TCH! WHY'D YOU SEND ME SOME GEEZER WITH ONE FOOT IN THE GRAVE?
I DON'T REMEMBER ORDERING YOU TO BRING ME A SACRIFICE.

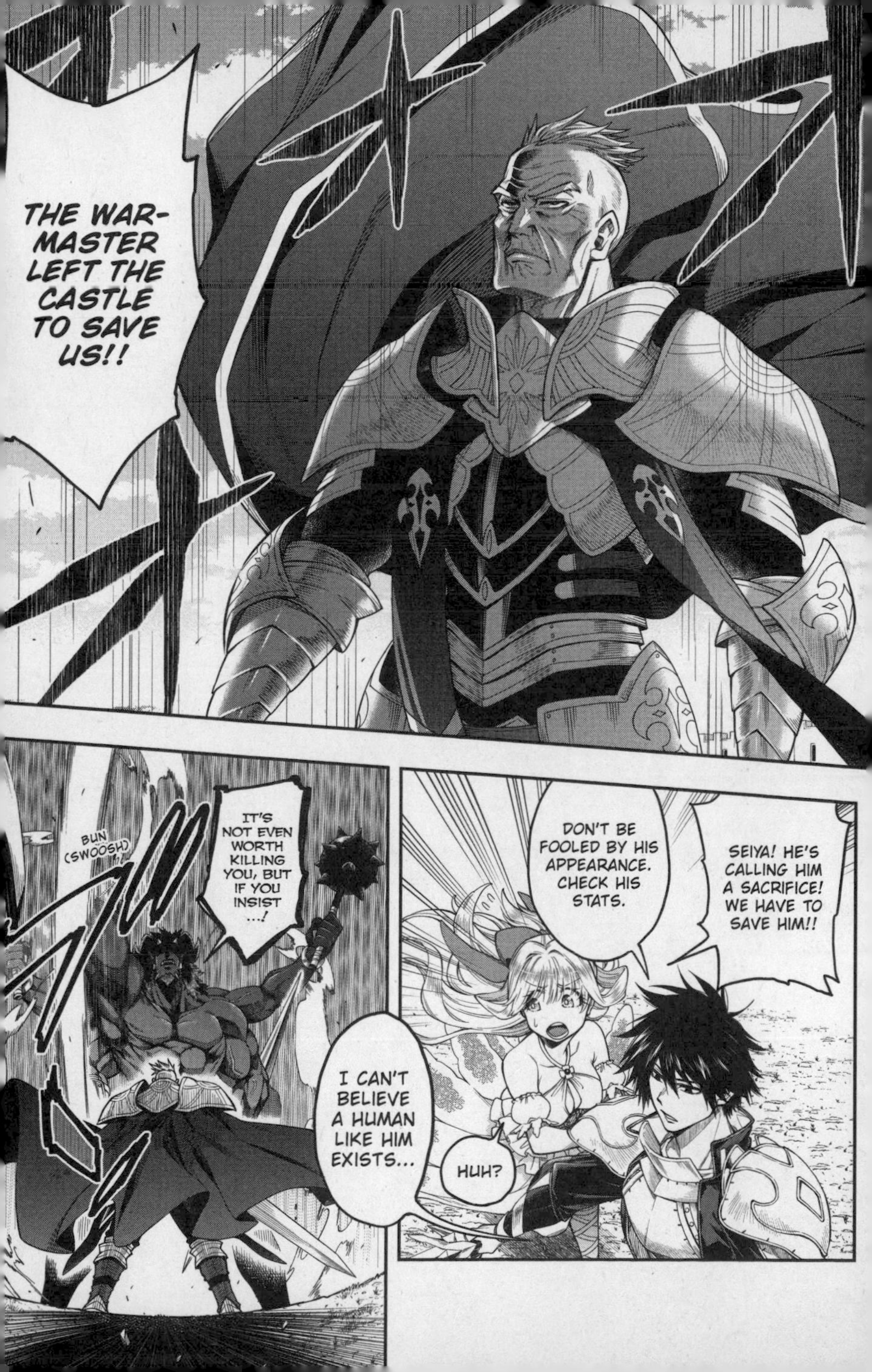
THE WAR-MASTER LEFT THE CASTLE TO SAVE US!!
SEIYA! HE'S CALLING HIM A SACRIFICE! WE HAVE TO SAVE HIM!!
DON'T BE FOOLED BY HIS APPEARANCE. CHECK HIS STATS.
HUH?
I CAN'T BELIEVE A HUMAN LIKE HIM EXISTS...
IT'S NOT EVEN WORTH KILLING YOU, BUT IF YOU INSIST ...!
BUN (SWOOSH)

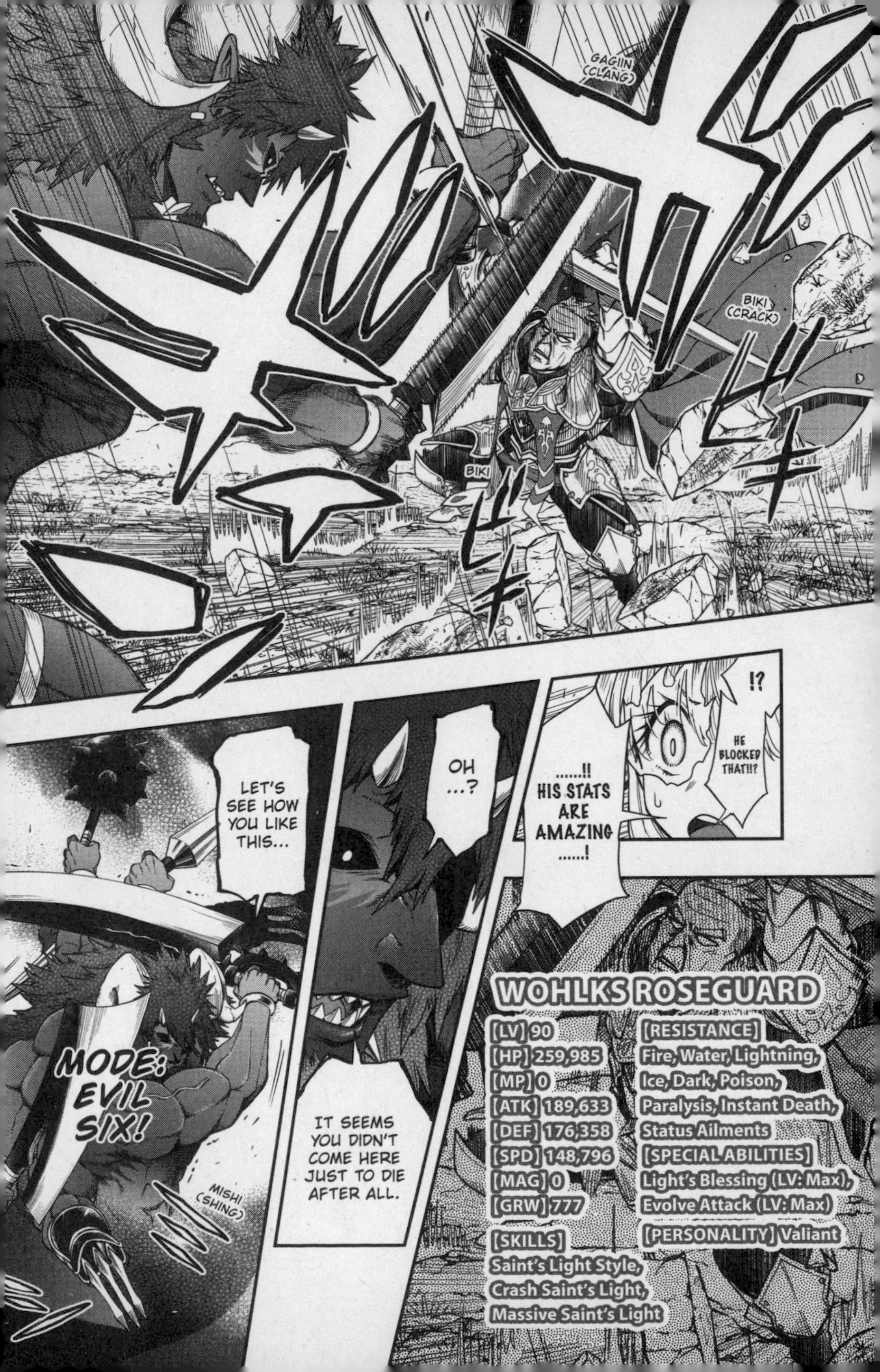
GAGIIN (CLANG)
BIKI (CRACK)
BIKI
!?
HE BLOCKED THAT!!?
......!! HIS STATS ARE AMAZING ......!
WOHLKS ROSEGUARD
[LV] 90
[HP] 259,985
[MP] 0
[ATK] 189,633
[DEF] 176,358
[SPD] 148,796
[MAG] 0
[GRW] 777
[SKILLS]
Saint's Light Style, Crash Saint's Light, Massive Saint's Light
[RESISTANCE]
Fire, Water, Lightning, Ice, Dark, Poison, Paralysis, Instant Death, Status Ailments
[SPECIAL ABILITIES]
Light's Blessing (LV: Max), Evolve Attack (LV: Max)
[PERSONALITY] Valiant
OH ...?
IT SEEMS YOU DIDN'T COME HERE JUST TO DIE AFTER ALL.
LET'S SEE HOW YOU LIKE THIS...
...
MODE: EVIL SIX!
MISHI (SHING)

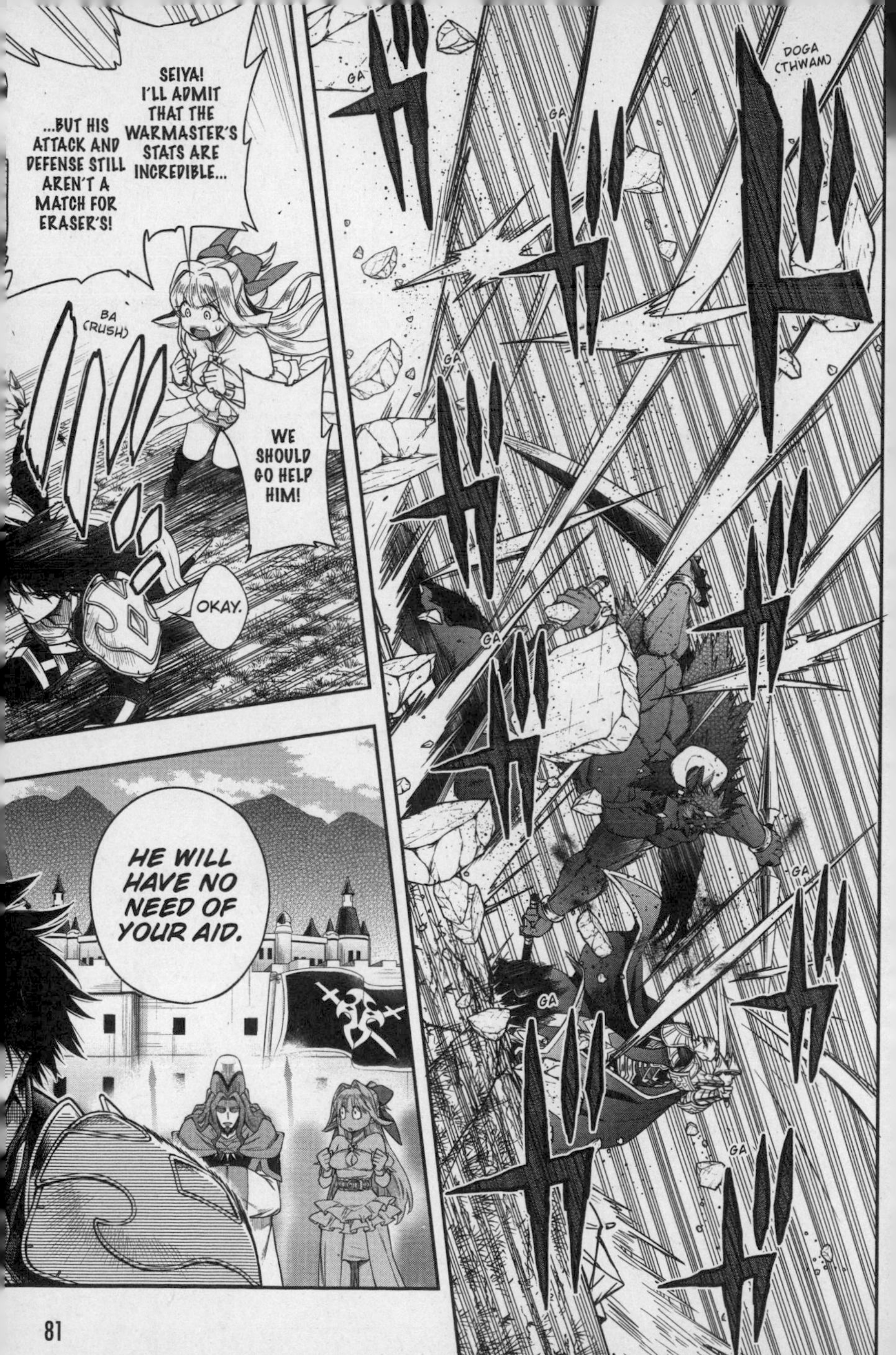
DOGA (THWAM)
GA
GA
GA
GA
GA
GA
GA
GA
SEIYA! I'LL ADMIT THAT THE WARMASTER'S STATS ARE INCREDIBLE...
...BUT HIS ATTACK AND DEFENSE STILL AREN'T A MATCH FOR ERASER'S!
WE SHOULD GO HELP HIM!
BA (RUSH)
OKAY.
HE WILL HAVE NO NEED OF YOUR AID.

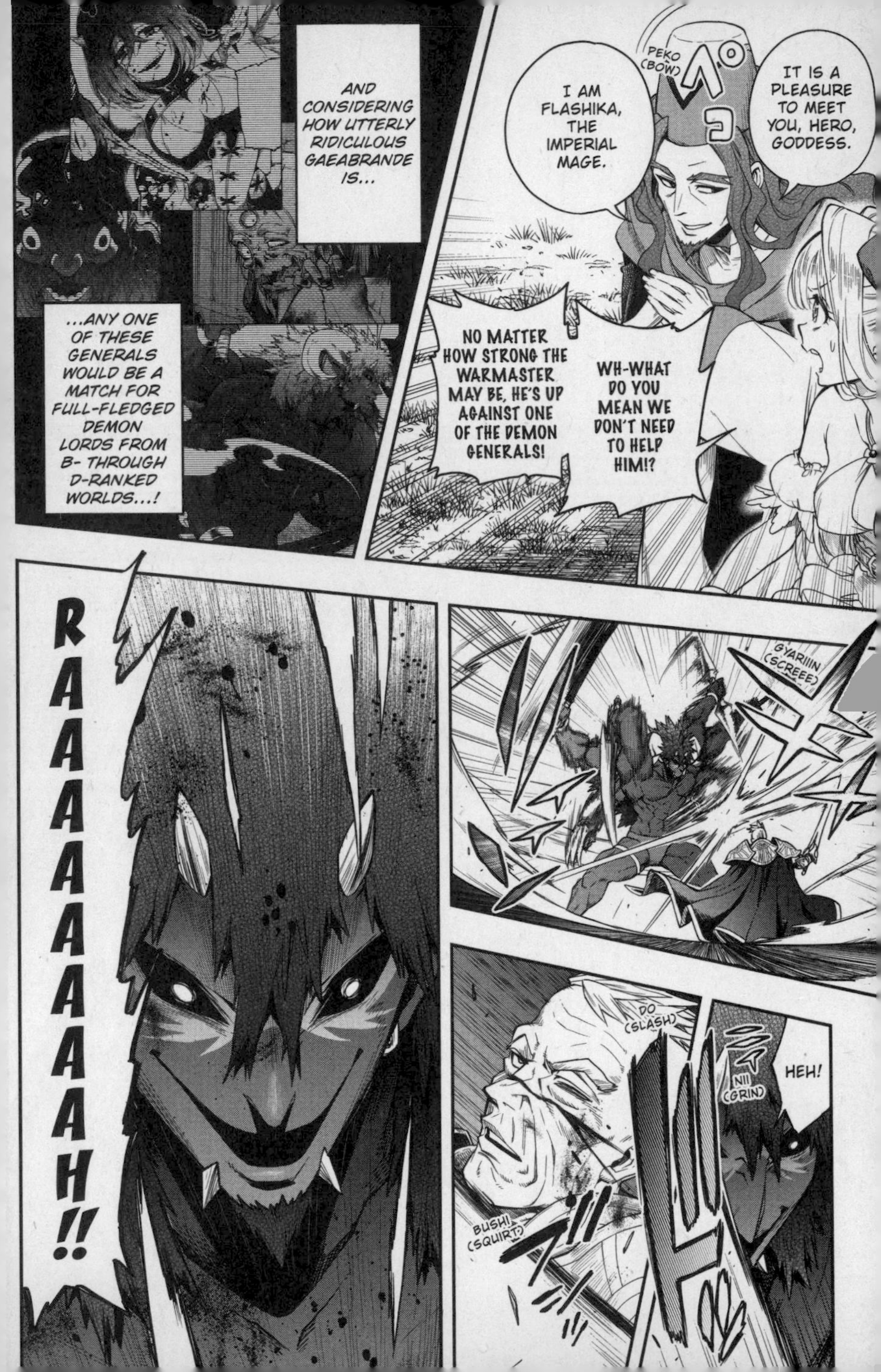
IT IS A PLEASURE TO MEET YOU, HERO, GODDESS.
PEKO (BOW)
I AM FLASHIKA, THE IMPERIAL MAGE.
WH-WHAT DO YOU MEAN WE DON'T NEED TO HELP HIM!?
NO MATTER HOW STRONG THE WARMASTER MAY BE, HE'S UP AGAINST ONE OF THE DEMON GENERALS!
AND CONSIDERING HOW UTTERLY RIDICULOUS GAEABRANDE IS...
...ANY ONE OF THESE GENERALS WOULD BE A MATCH FOR FULL-FLEDGED DEMON LORDS FROM B- THROUGH D-RANKED WORLDS...!
GYARIIIN (SCREEE)
HEH!
NII (GRIN)
DO (SLASH)
BUSHI (SQUIRT)
RAAAAAAAAAH!!

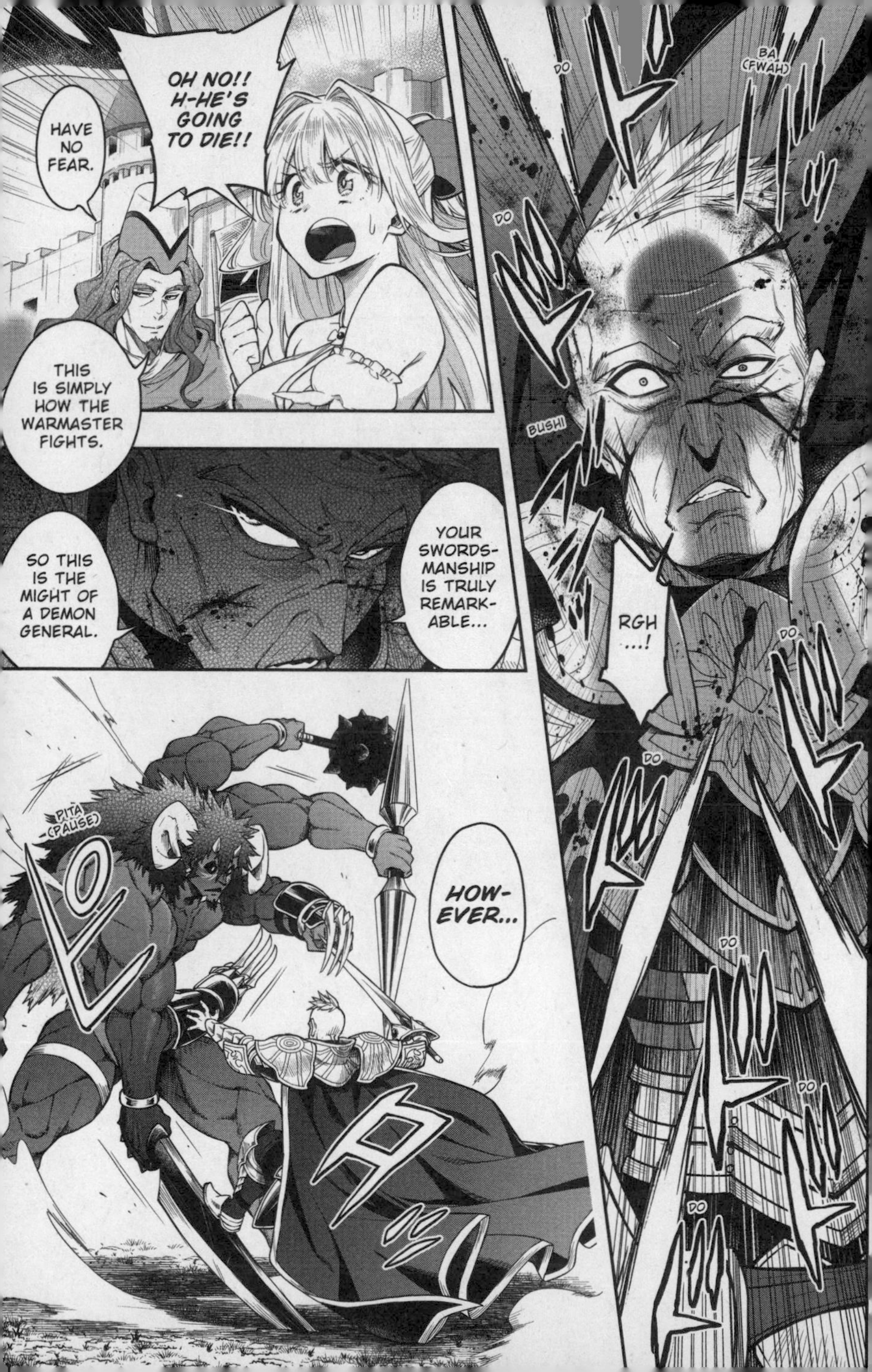
DO
BA (FWAH)
DO
BUSHI
RGH ...!
DO
DO
DO
DO
DO
OH NO!! H-HE'S GOING TO DIE!!
HAVE NO FEAR.
THIS IS SIMPLY HOW THE WARMASTER FIGHTS.
YOUR SWORDS-MANSHIP IS TRULY REMARK-ABLE...
SO THIS IS THE MIGHT OF A DEMON GENERAL.
HOW-EVER...
PITA (PAUSE)

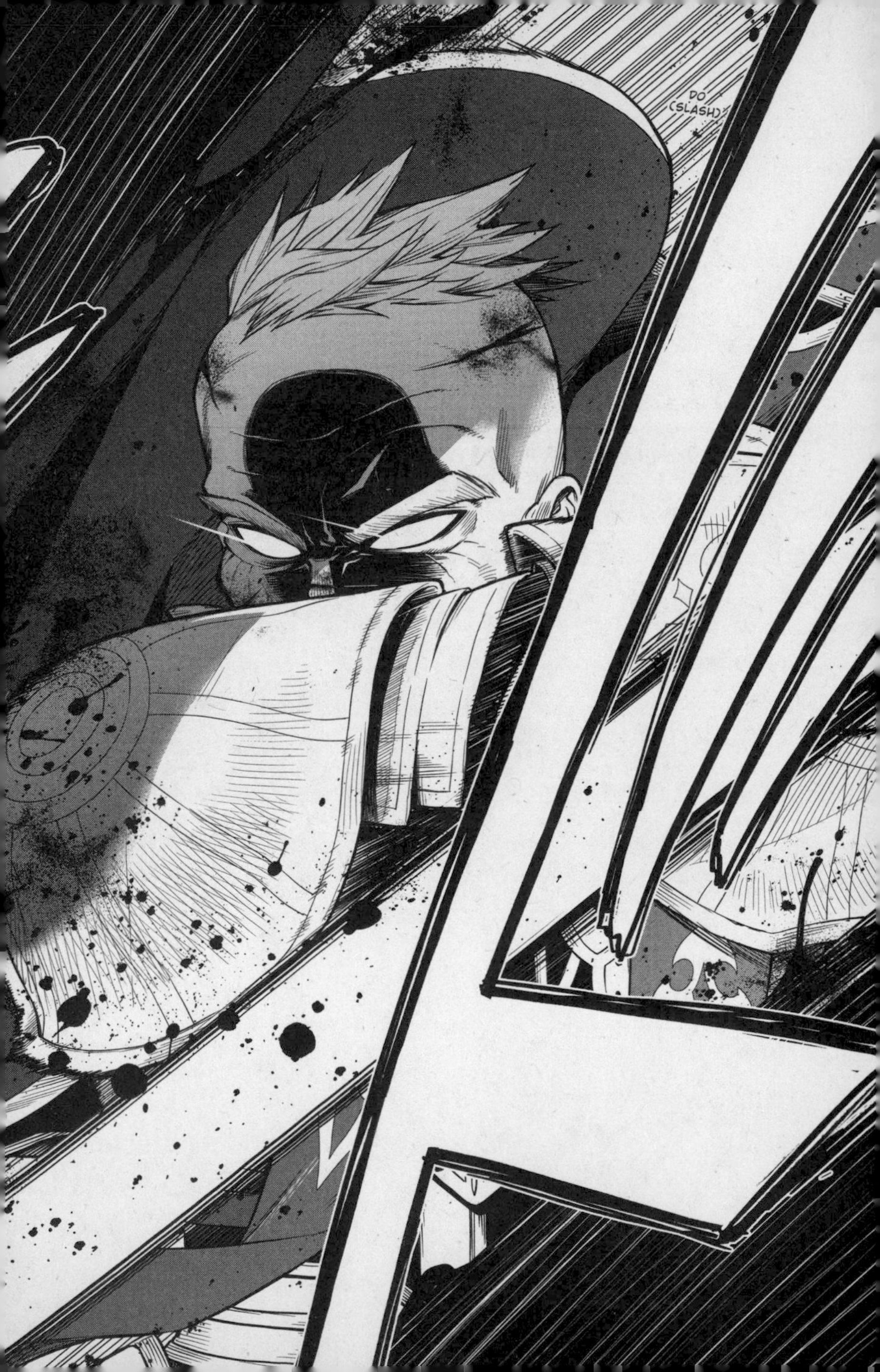
DO
(SLASH)

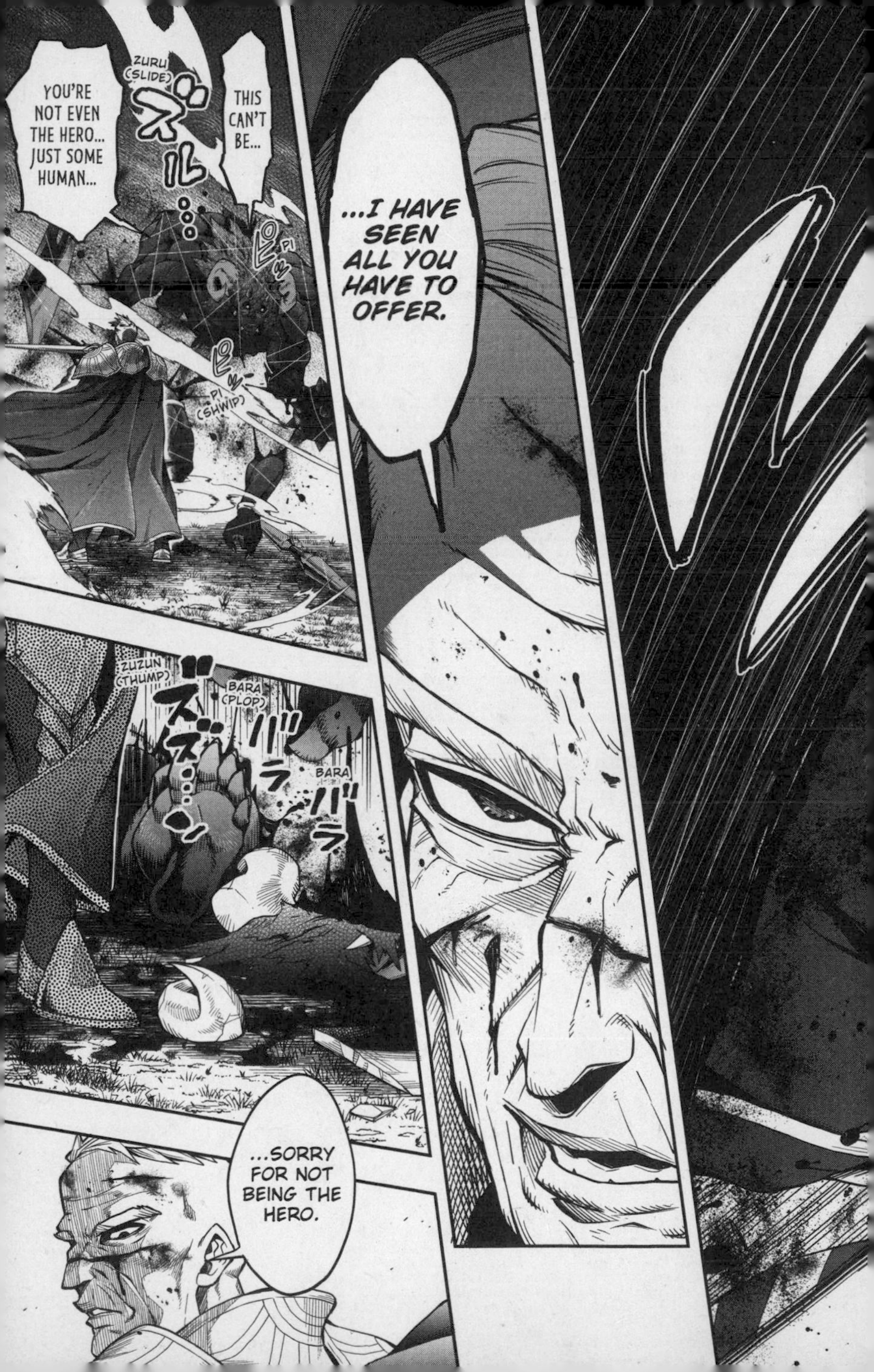
...I HAVE SEEN ALL YOU HAVE TO OFFER.
THIS CAN'T BE...
ZURU (SLIDE)
YOU'RE NOT EVEN THE HERO... JUST SOME HUMAN...
PI
PI (SHWIP)
ZUZUN (THUMP)
BARA (PLOP)
BARA
...SORRY FOR NOT BEING THE HERO.

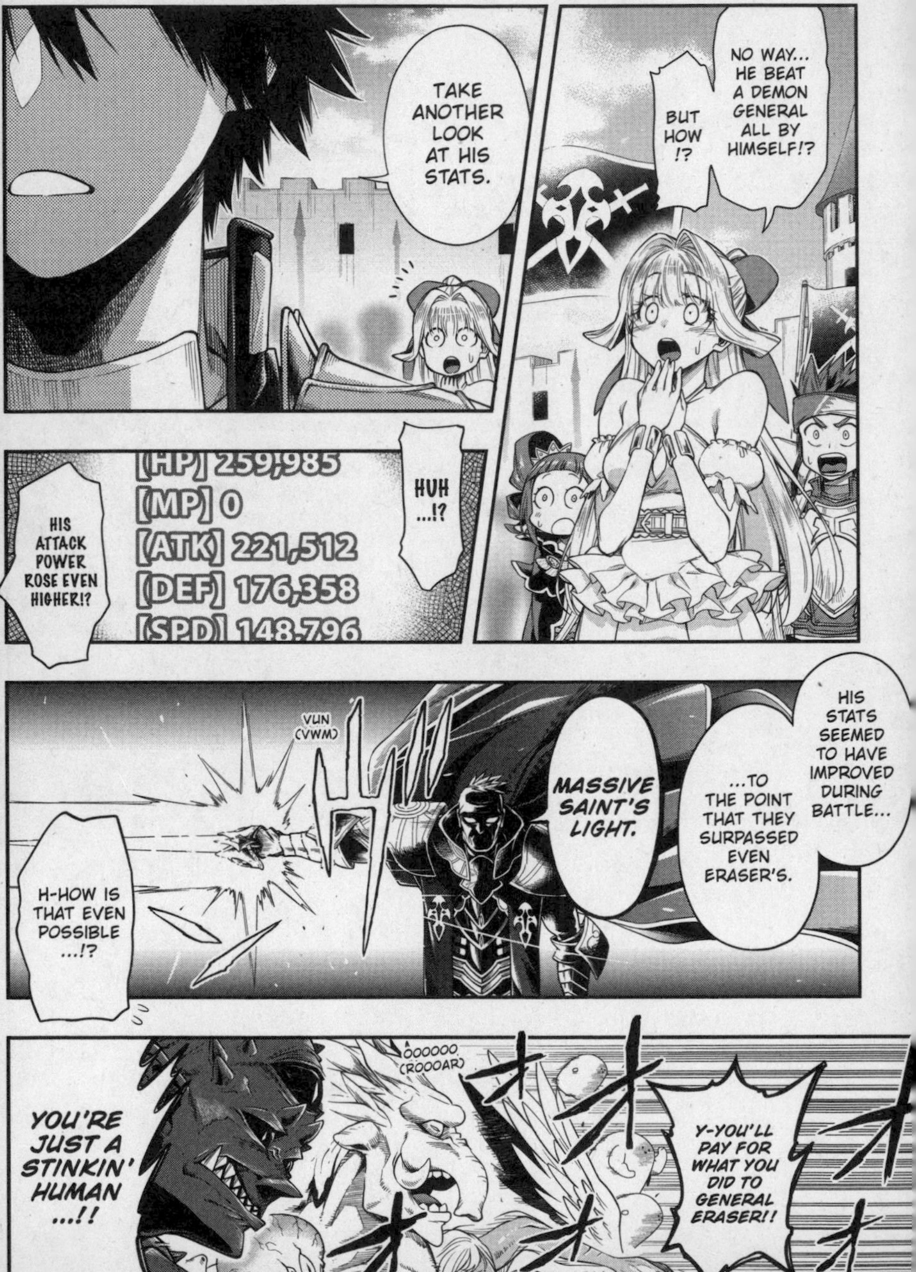
NO WAY... HE BEAT A DEMON GENERAL ALL BY HIMSELF!?
BUT HOW!?
TAKE ANOTHER LOOK AT HIS STATS.
HUH ...!?
[HP] 259,985
[MP] 0
[ATK] 221,512
[DEF] 176,358
[SPD] 148,796
HIS ATTACK POWER ROSE EVEN HIGHER!?
HIS STATS SEEMED TO HAVE IMPROVED DURING BATTLE...
...TO THE POINT THAT THEY SURPASSED EVEN ERASER'S.
MASSIVE SAINT'S LIGHT.
VUN (VWM)
H-HOW IS THAT EVEN POSSIBLE ...!?
OOOOOO (ROOOAR)
Y-YOU'LL PAY FOR WHAT YOU DID TO GENERAL ERASER!!
YOU'RE JUST A STINKIN' HUMAN ...!!

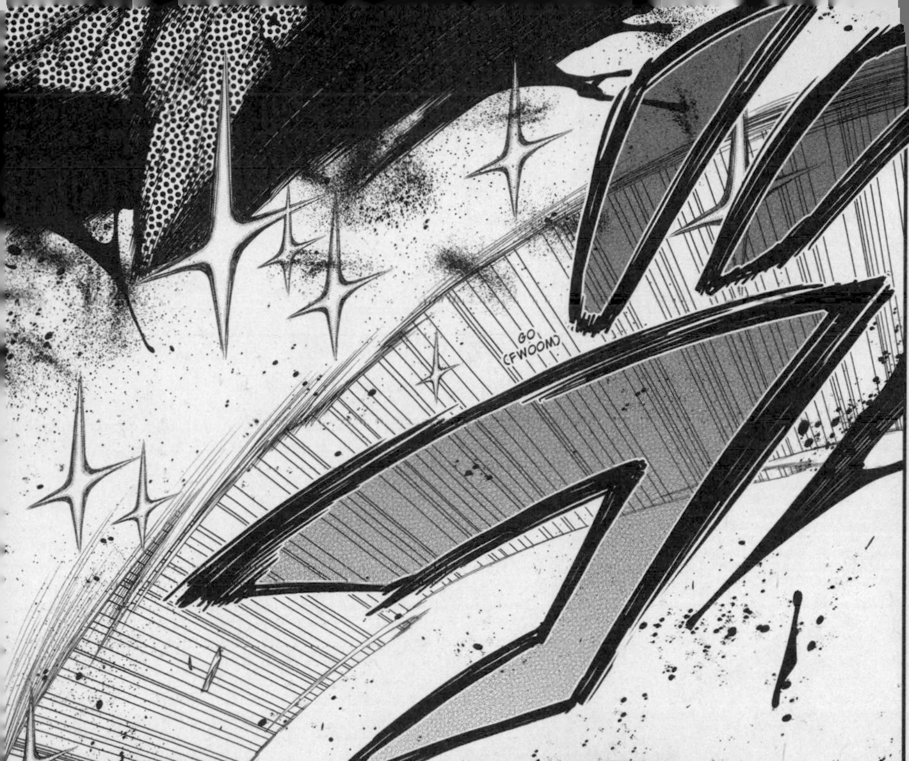
GO
(FWOOM)
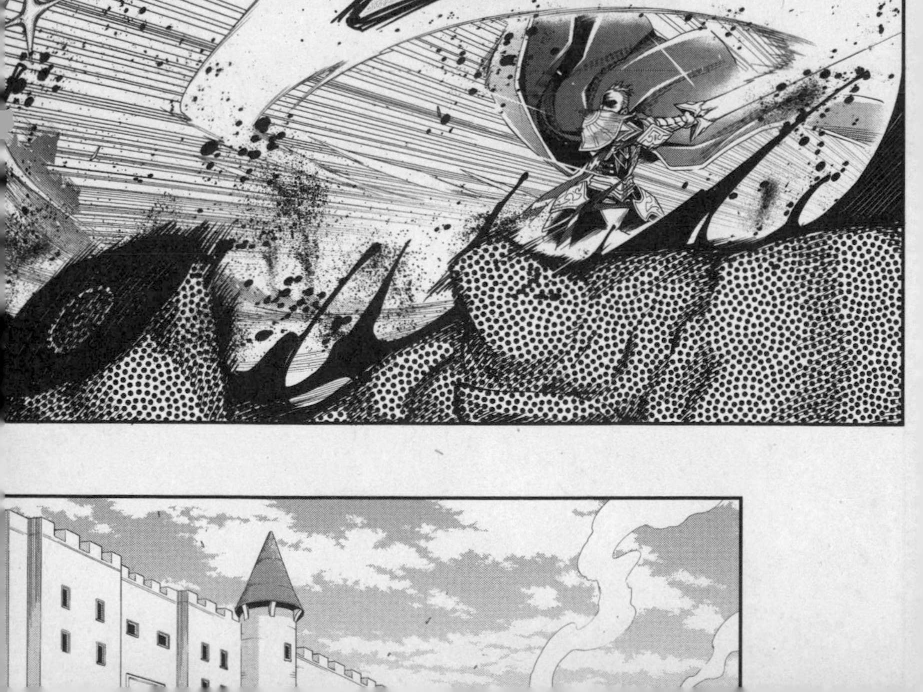

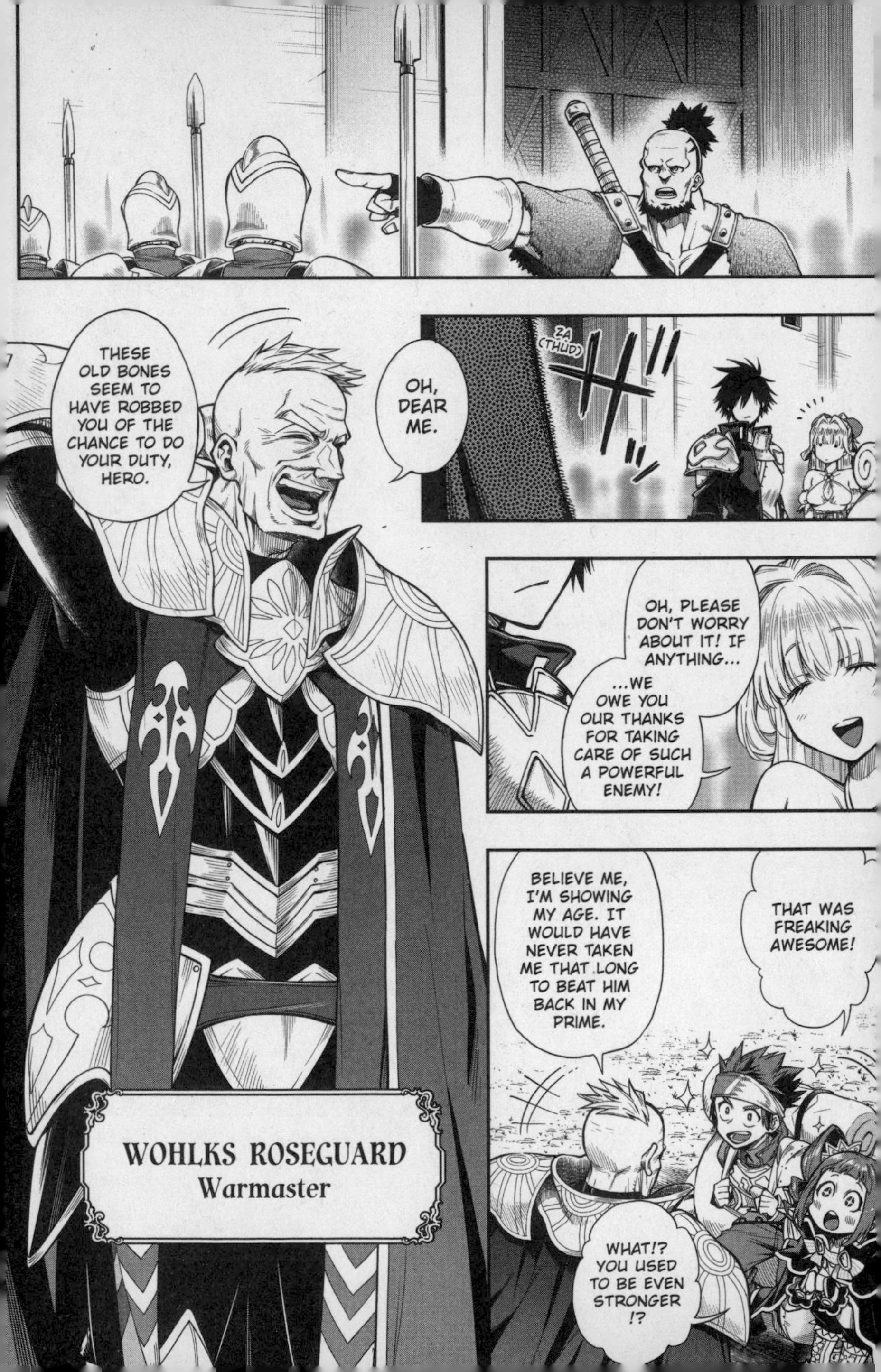
ZA (THUD)
OH, PLEASE DON'T WORRY ABOUT IT! IF ANYTHING...
...WE OWE YOU OUR THANKS FOR TAKING CARE OF SUCH A POWERFUL ENEMY!
THAT WAS FREAKING AWESOME!
BELIEVE ME, I'M SHOWING MY AGE. IT WOULD HAVE NEVER TAKEN ME THAT LONG TO BEAT HIM BACK IN MY PRIME.
WHAT!? YOU USED TO BE EVEN STRONGER !?
OH, DEAR ME.
THESE OLD BONES SEEM TO HAVE ROBBED YOU OF THE CHANCE TO DO YOUR DUTY, HERO.
WOHLKS ROSEGUARD
Warmaster

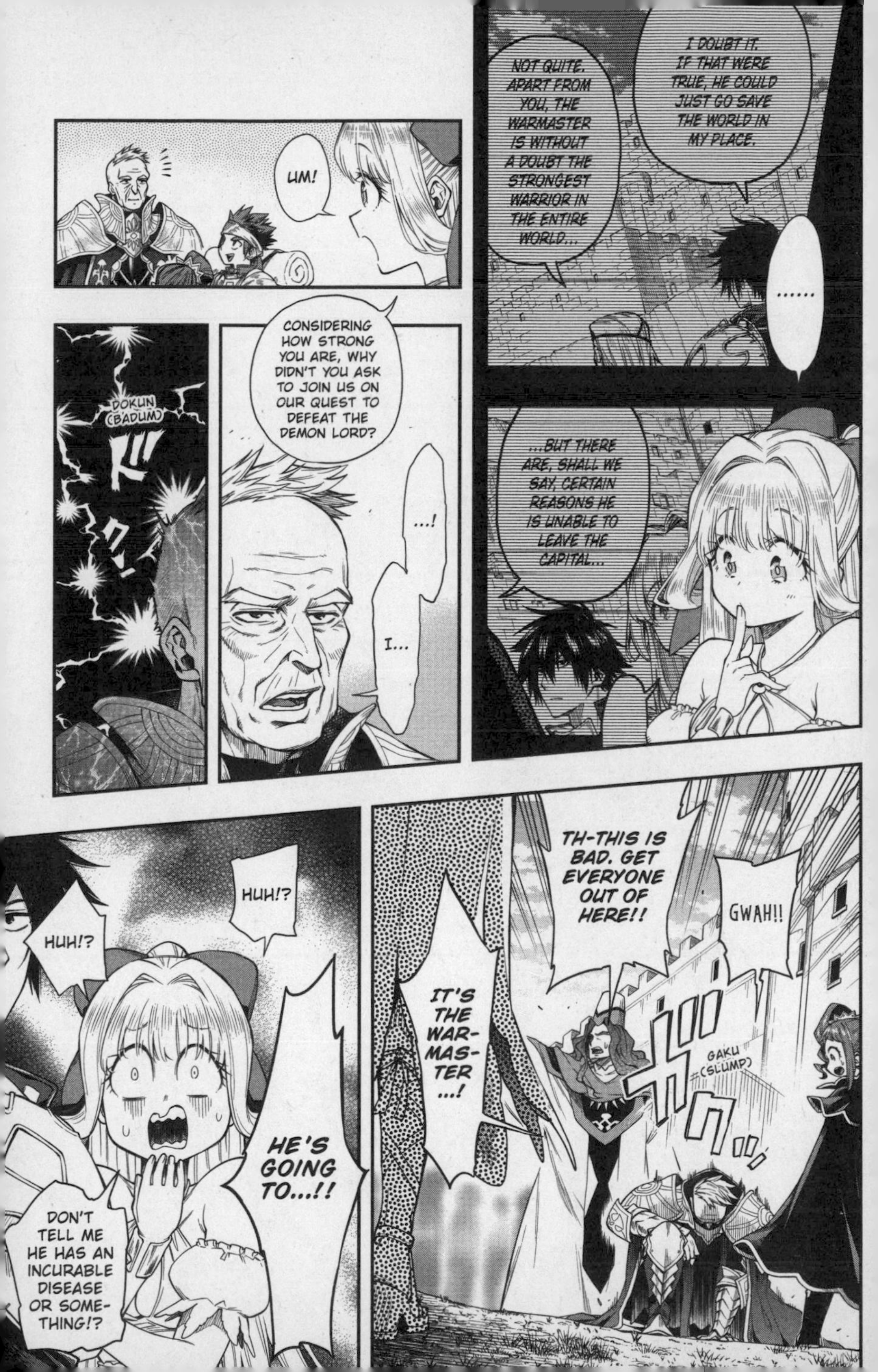
I DOUBT IT. IF THAT WERE TRUE, HE COULD JUST GO SAVE THE WORLD IN MY PLACE.
NOT QUITE. APART FROM YOU, THE WARMASTER IS WITHOUT A DOUBT THE STRONGEST WARRIOR IN THE ENTIRE WORLD...
......
...BUT THERE ARE, SHALL WE SAY, CERTAIN REASONS HE IS UNABLE TO LEAVE THE CAPITAL...
UM!
CONSIDERING HOW STRONG YOU ARE, WHY DIDN'T YOU ASK TO JOIN US ON OUR QUEST TO DEFEAT THE DEMON LORD?
...!
I...
DOKUN (BADUM)
GWAH!!
TH-THIS IS BAD. GET EVERYONE OUT OF HERE!!
IT'S THE WAR-MAS-TER...!
GAKU (SLUMP)
HUH!?
HUH!?
HE'S GOING TO...!!
DON'T TELL ME HE HAS AN INCURABLE DISEASE OR SOME-THING!?

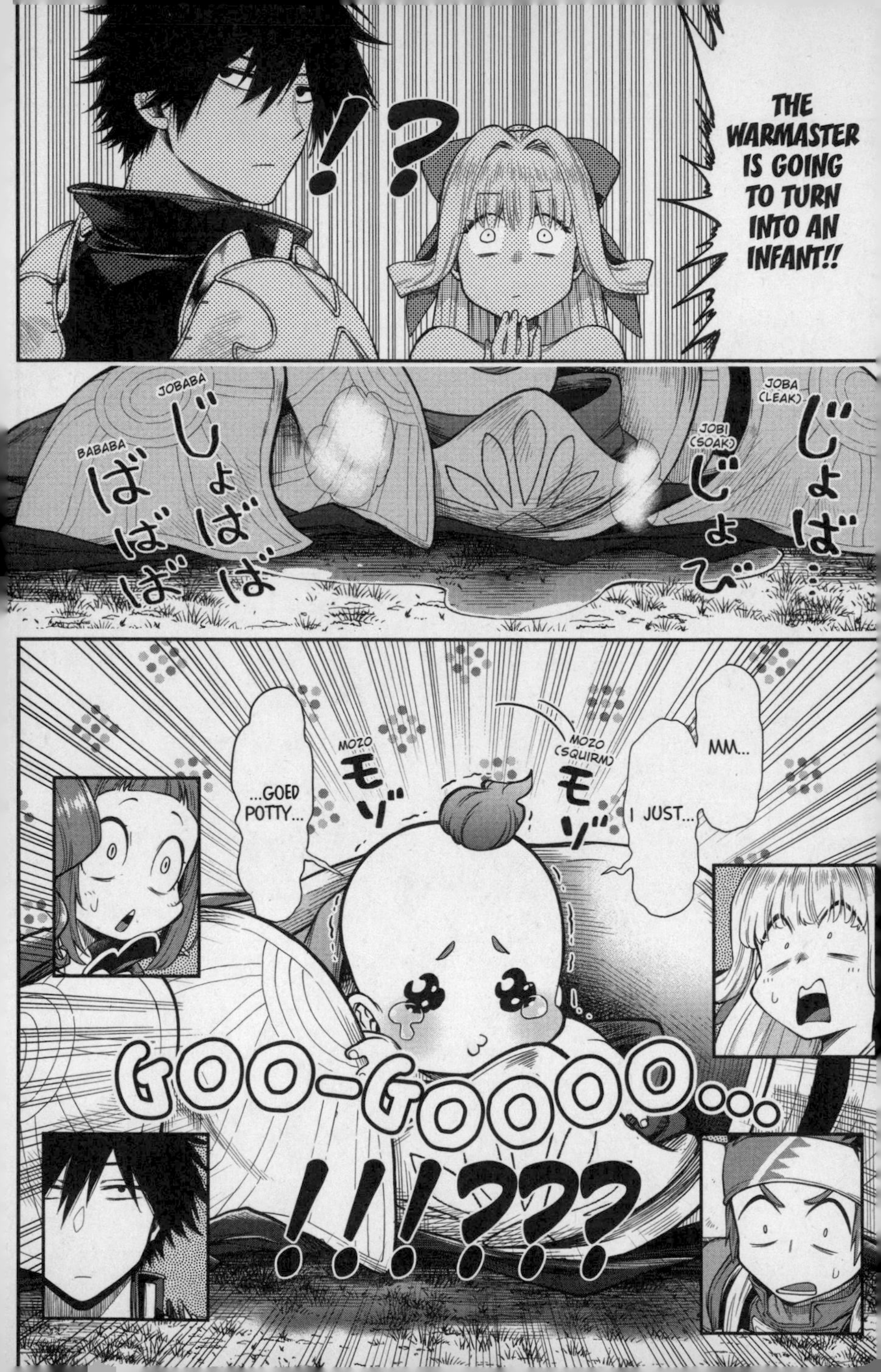
THE WARMASTER IS GOING TO TURN INTO AN INFANT!!
!?
じょばっ JOBA (LEAK)
じょび JOBI (SOAK)
じょばばば JOBABA
ばばば BABABA
MM... I JUST...
モゾ MOZO (SQUIRM)
モゾ MOZO
...GOED POTTY...
GOO-GOOOOO...
!!!???

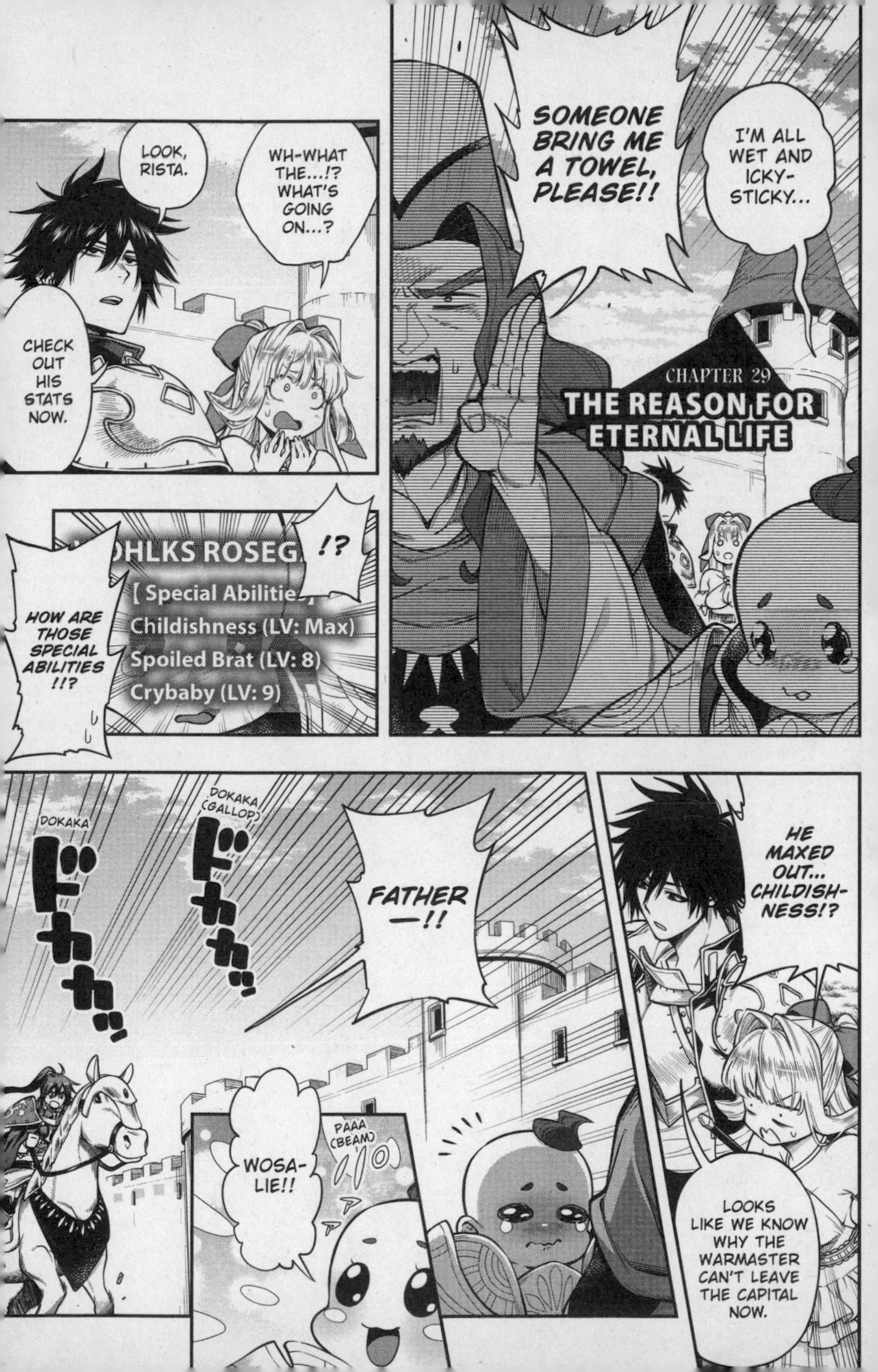
I'M ALL WET AND ICKY-STICKY...
SOMEONE BRING ME A TOWEL, PLEASE!!
CHAPTER 29
THE REASON FOR ETERNAL LIFE
WH-WHAT THE...!? WHAT'S GOING ON...?
LOOK, RISTA.
CHECK OUT HIS STATS NOW.
!?
OHLKS ROSEG
[Special Abilitie
Childishness (LV: Max)
Spoiled Brat (LV: 8)
Crybaby (LV: 9)
HOW ARE THOSE SPECIAL ABILITIES!!?
HE MAXED OUT... CHILDISHNESS!?
LOOKS LIKE WE KNOW WHY THE WARMASTER CAN'T LEAVE THE CAPITAL NOW.
FATHER—!!
PAAA (BEAM)
WOSA-LIE!!
DOKAKA (GALLOP)
DOKAKA

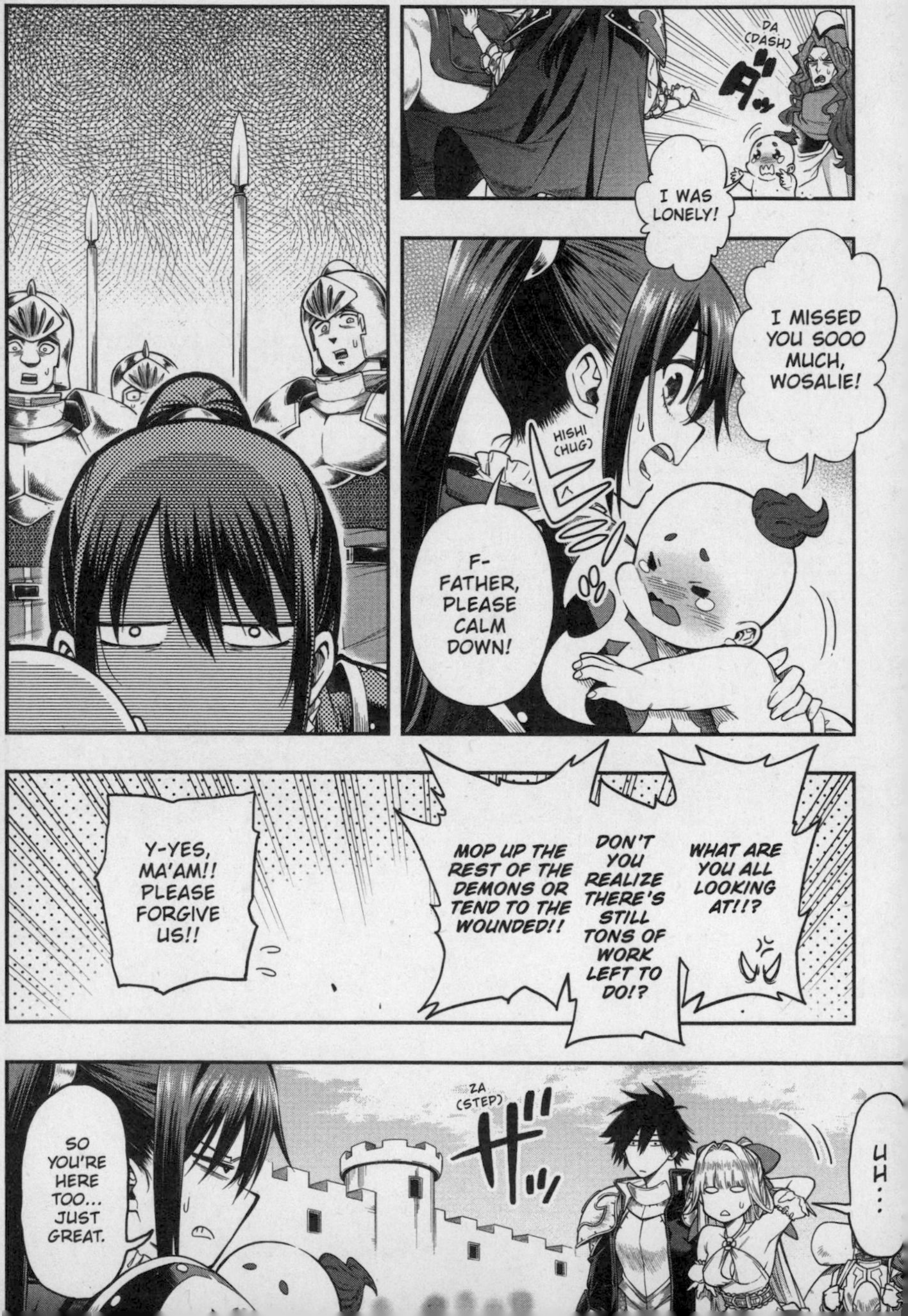
DA (DASH)
I WAS LONELY!
I MISSED YOU SOOO MUCH, WOSALIE!
HISHI (HUG)
F-FATHER, PLEASE CALM DOWN!
WHAT ARE YOU ALL LOOKING AT!!?
DON'T YOU REALIZE THERE'S STILL TONS OF WORK LEFT TO DO!?
MOP UP THE REST OF THE DEMONS OR TEND TO THE WOUNDED!!
Y-YES, MA'AM!! PLEASE FORGIVE US!!
UH...
ZA (STEP)
SO YOU'RE HERE TOO... JUST GREAT.

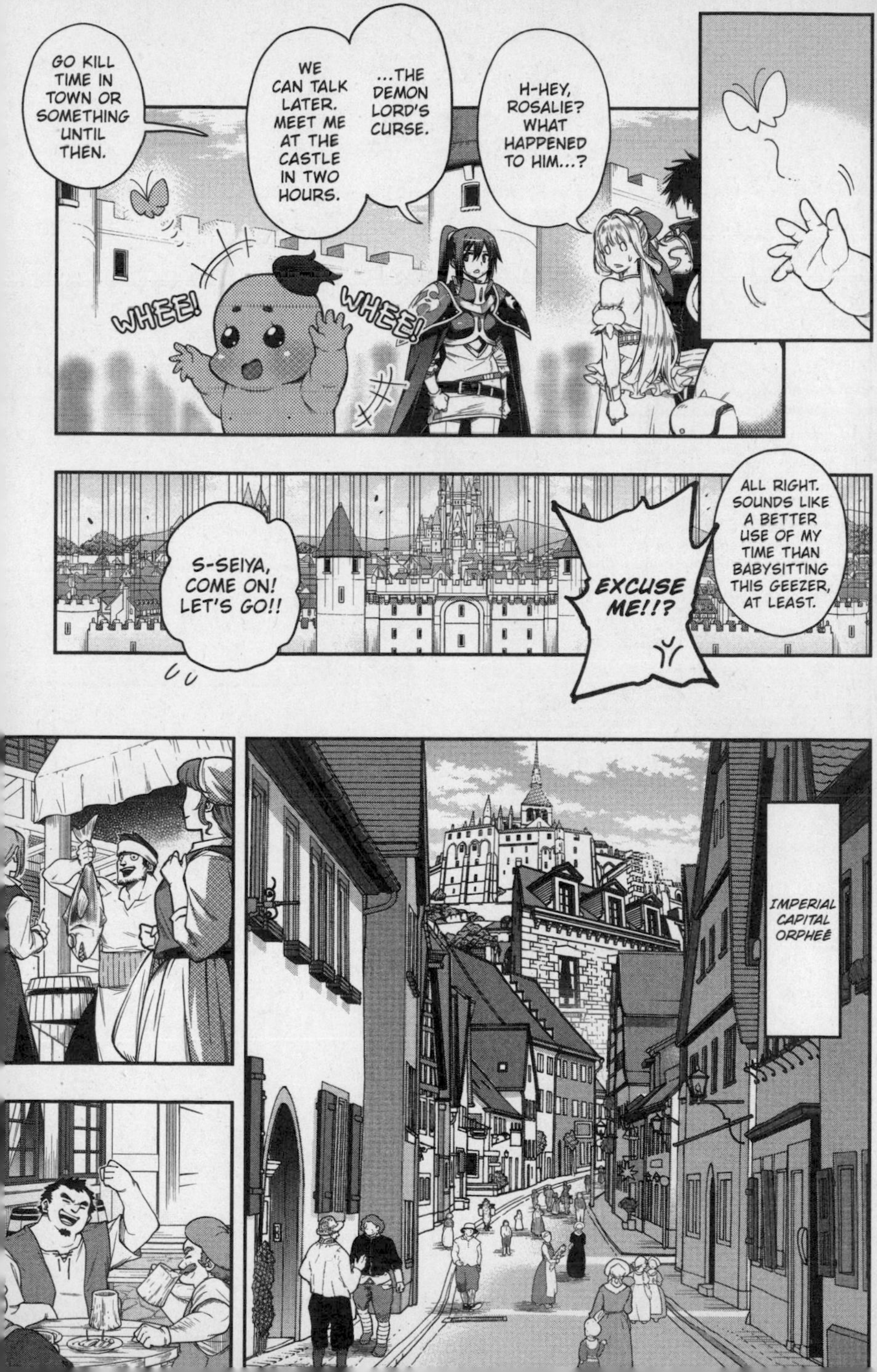
H-HEY, ROSALIE? WHAT HAPPENED TO HIM...?
...THE DEMON LORD'S CURSE.
WE CAN TALK LATER. MEET ME AT THE CASTLE IN TWO HOURS.
GO KILL TIME IN TOWN OR SOMETHING UNTIL THEN.
WHEE!
WHEE!
ALL RIGHT. SOUNDS LIKE A BETTER USE OF MY TIME THAN BABYSITTING THIS GEEZER, AT LEAST.
EXCUSE ME!!?
S-SEIYA, COME ON! LET'S GO!!
IMPERIAL CAPITAL ORPHEÉ

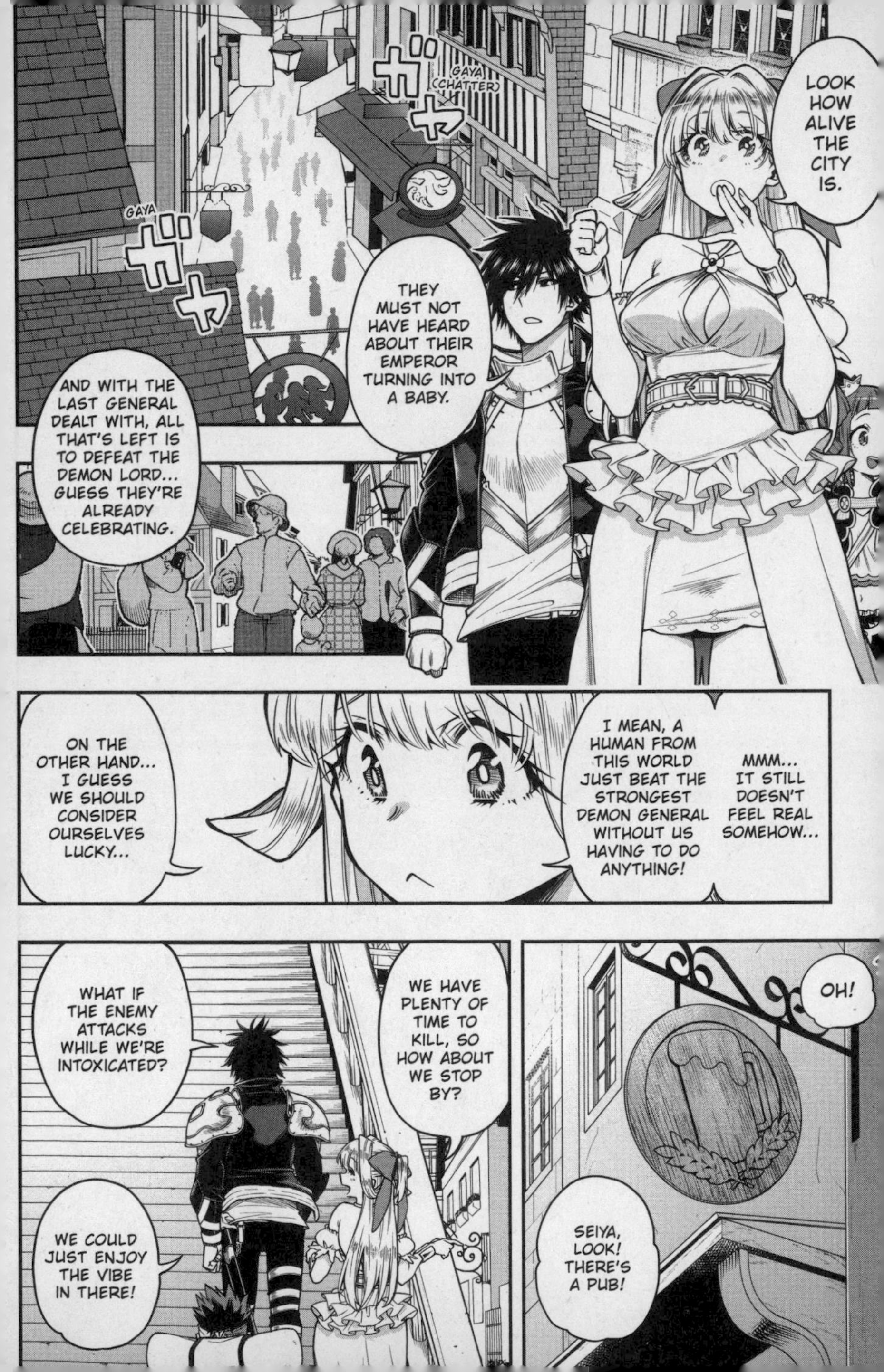

LOOK HOW ALIVE THE CITY IS.
GAYA (CHATTER)
THEY MUST NOT HAVE HEARD ABOUT THEIR EMPEROR TURNING INTO A BABY.
GAYA
AND WITH THE LAST GENERAL DEALT WITH, ALL THAT'S LEFT IS TO DEFEAT THE DEMON LORD... GUESS THEY'RE ALREADY CELEBRATING.
MMM... IT STILL DOESN'T FEEL REAL SOMEHOW...
I MEAN, A HUMAN FROM THIS WORLD JUST BEAT THE STRONGEST DEMON GENERAL WITHOUT US HAVING TO DO ANYTHING!
ON THE OTHER HAND... I GUESS WE SHOULD CONSIDER OURSELVES LUCKY...
OH!
SEIYA, LOOK! THERE'S A PUB!
WE HAVE PLENTY OF TIME TO KILL, SO HOW ABOUT WE STOP BY?
WHAT IF THE ENEMY ATTACKS WHILE WE'RE INTOXICATED?
WE COULD JUST ENJOY THE VIBE IN THERE!

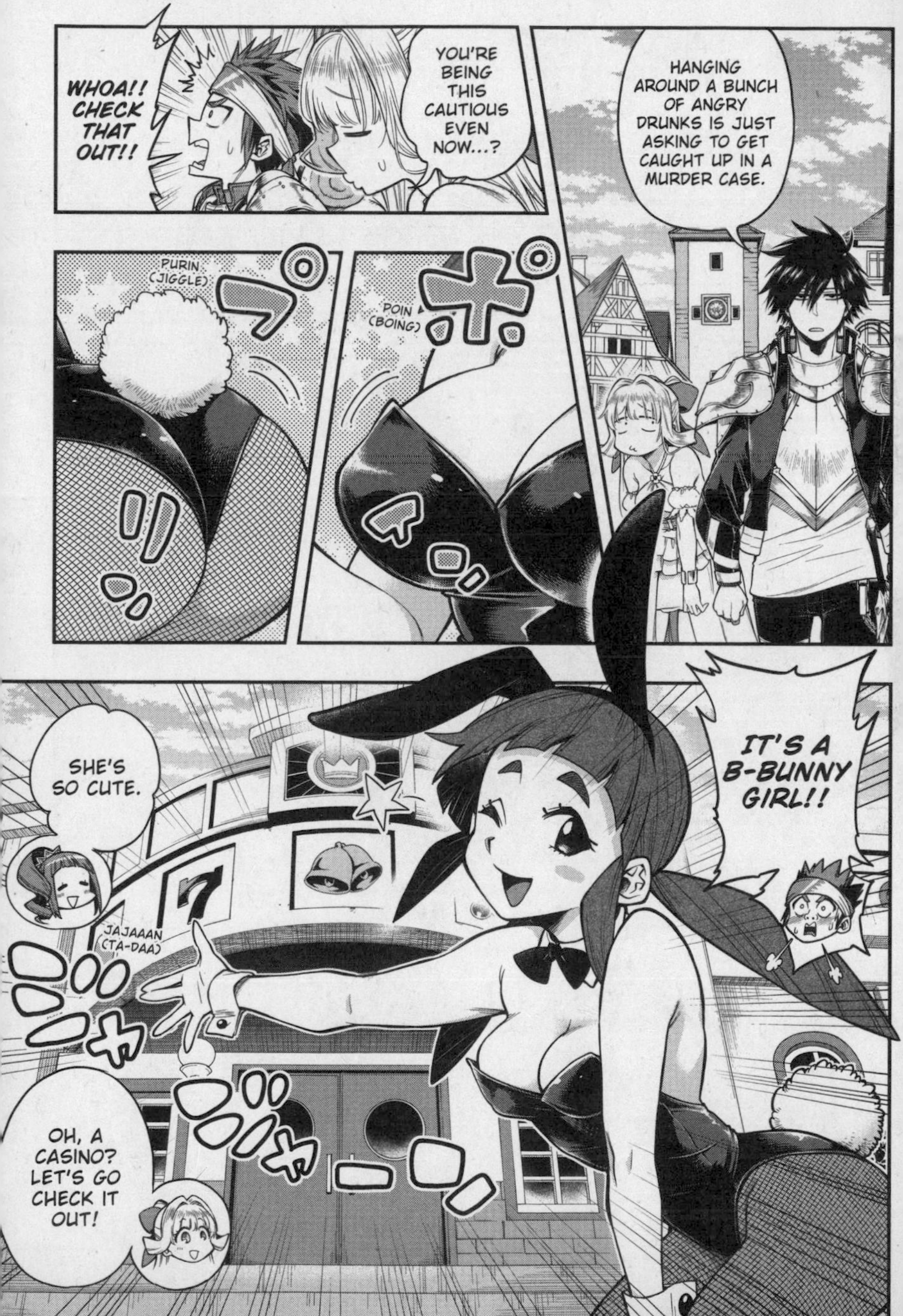
HANGING AROUND A BUNCH OF ANGRY DRUNKS IS JUST ASKING TO GET CAUGHT UP IN A MURDER CASE.
YOU'RE BEING THIS CAUTIOUS EVEN NOW...?
WHOA!! CHECK THAT OUT!!
POIN (BOING)
PURIN (JIGGLE)
IT'S A B-BUNNY GIRL!!
SHE'S SO CUTE.
JAJAAAN (TA-DAA)
OH, A CASINO? LET'S GO CHECK IT OUT!

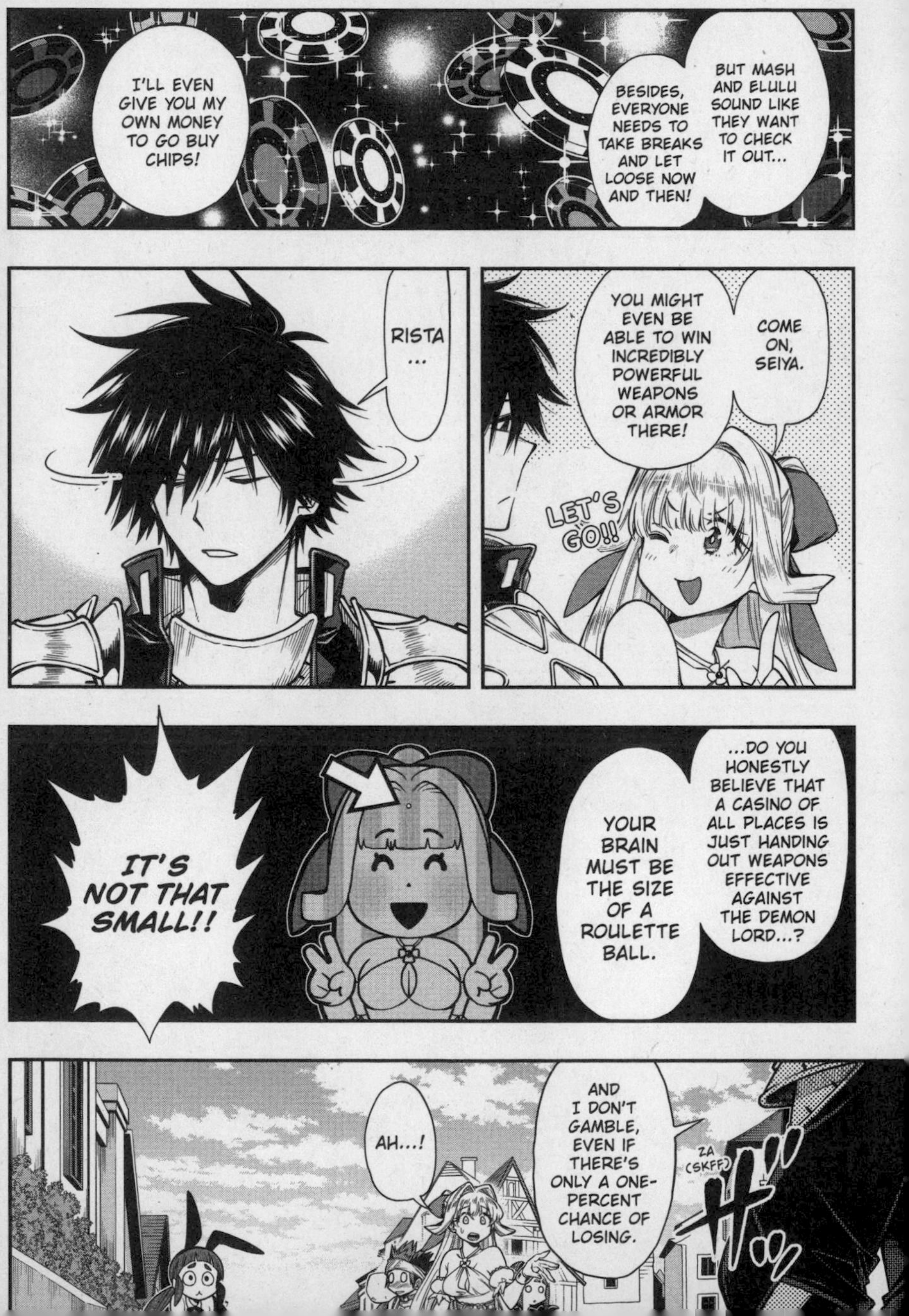
BUT MASH AND ELULU SOUND LIKE THEY WANT TO CHECK IT OUT...
BESIDES, EVERYONE NEEDS TO TAKE BREAKS AND LET LOOSE NOW AND THEN!
I'LL EVEN GIVE YOU MY OWN MONEY TO GO BUY CHIPS!
COME ON, SEIYA.
YOU MIGHT EVEN BE ABLE TO WIN INCREDIBLY POWERFUL WEAPONS OR ARMOR THERE!
LET'S GO!!
RISTA...
...DO YOU HONESTLY BELIEVE THAT A CASINO OF ALL PLACES IS JUST HANDING OUT WEAPONS EFFECTIVE AGAINST THE DEMON LORD...?
YOUR BRAIN MUST BE THE SIZE OF A ROULETTE BALL.
IT'S NOT THAT SMALL!!
AND I DON'T GAMBLE, EVEN IF THERE'S ONLY A ONE-PERCENT CHANCE OF LOSING.
ZA (SKFF)
AH...!

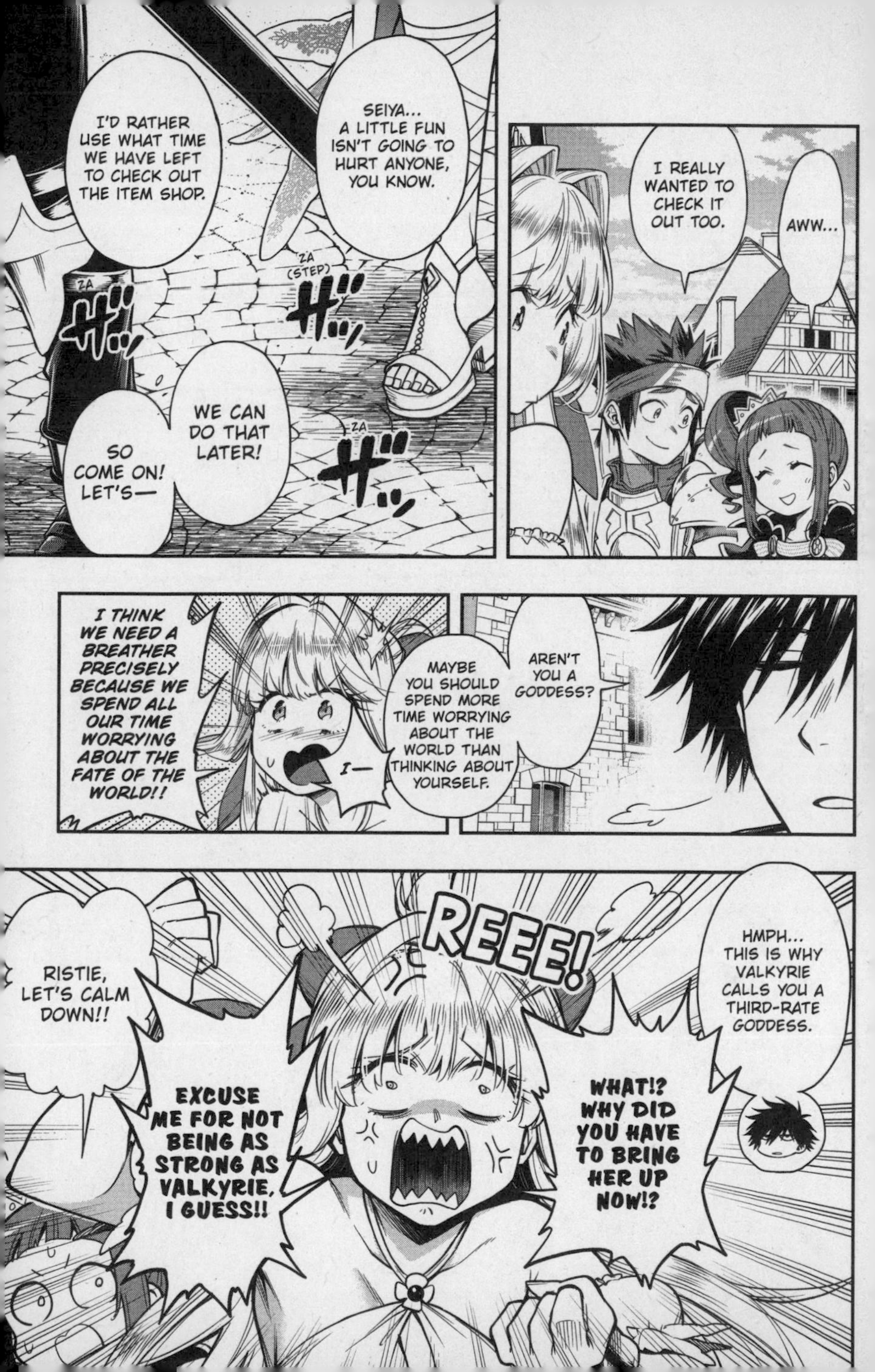
AWW...
I REALLY WANTED TO CHECK IT OUT TOO.
SEIYA... A LITTLE FUN ISN'T GOING TO HURT ANYONE, YOU KNOW.
I'D RATHER USE WHAT TIME WE HAVE LEFT TO CHECK OUT THE ITEM SHOP.
ZA (STEP)
ZA
WE CAN DO THAT LATER!
ZA
SO COME ON! LET'S—
AREN'T YOU A GODDESS?
MAYBE YOU SHOULD SPEND MORE TIME WORRYING ABOUT THE WORLD THAN THINKING ABOUT YOURSELF.
I—
I THINK WE NEED A BREATHER PRECISELY BECAUSE WE SPEND ALL OUR TIME WORRYING ABOUT THE FATE OF THE WORLD!!
HMPH... THIS IS WHY VALKYRIE CALLS YOU A THIRD-RATE GODDESS.
REEE!
WHAT!? WHY DID YOU HAVE TO BRING HER UP NOW!?
EXCUSE ME FOR NOT BEING AS STRONG AS VALKYRIE, I GUESS!!
RISTIE, LET'S CALM DOWN!!

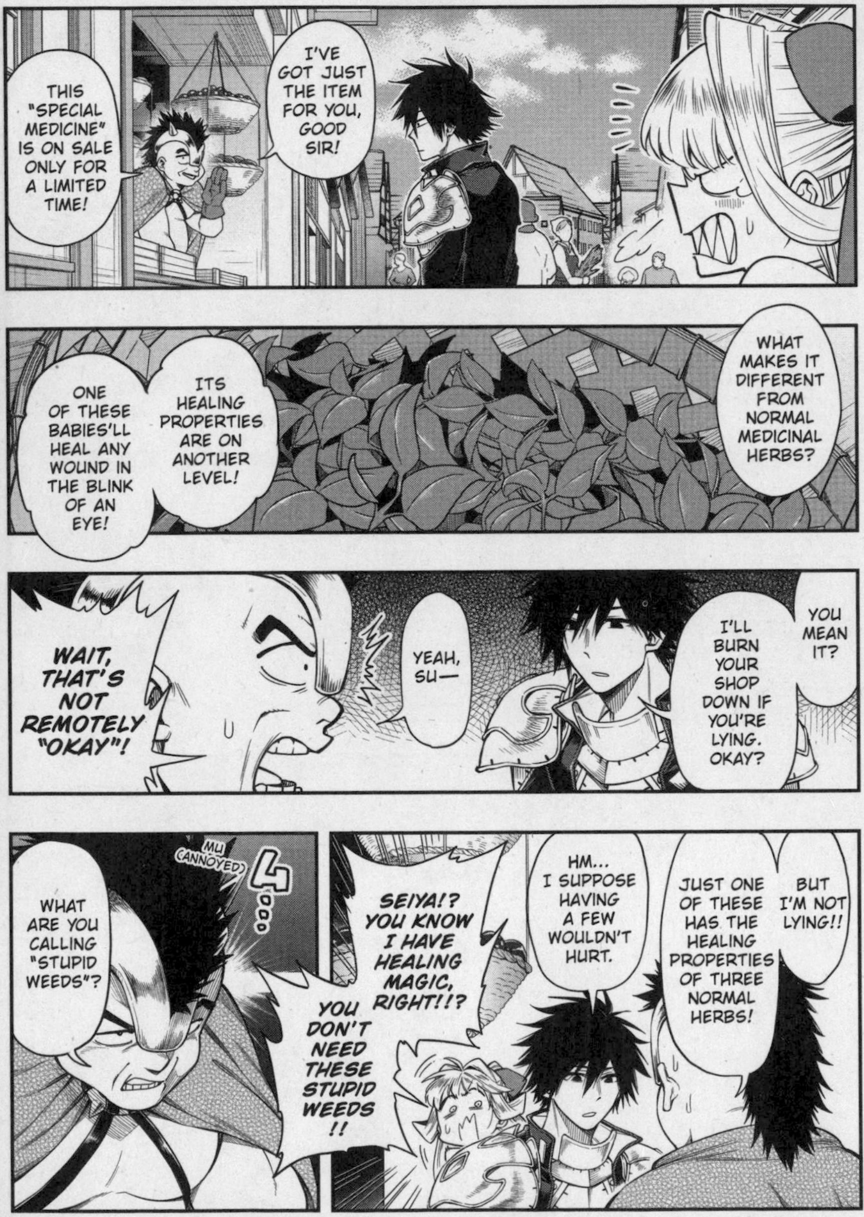
I'VE GOT JUST THE ITEM FOR YOU, GOOD SIR!
THIS "SPECIAL MEDICINE" IS ON SALE ONLY FOR A LIMITED TIME!
WHAT MAKES IT DIFFERENT FROM NORMAL MEDICINAL HERBS?
ITS HEALING PROPERTIES ARE ON ANOTHER LEVEL!
ONE OF THESE BABIES'LL HEAL ANY WOUND IN THE BLINK OF AN EYE!
YOU MEAN IT?
I'LL BURN YOUR SHOP DOWN IF YOU'RE LYING. OKAY?
YEAH, SU—
WAIT, THAT'S NOT REMOTELY "OKAY"!
BUT I'M NOT LYING!!
JUST ONE OF THESE HAS THE HEALING PROPERTIES OF THREE NORMAL HERBS!
HM... I SUPPOSE HAVING A FEW WOULDN'T HURT.
SEIYA!? YOU KNOW I HAVE HEALING MAGIC, RIGHT!!?
YOU DON'T NEED THESE STUPID WEEDS!!
MU (ANNOYED)
WHAT ARE YOU CALLING "STUPID WEEDS"?

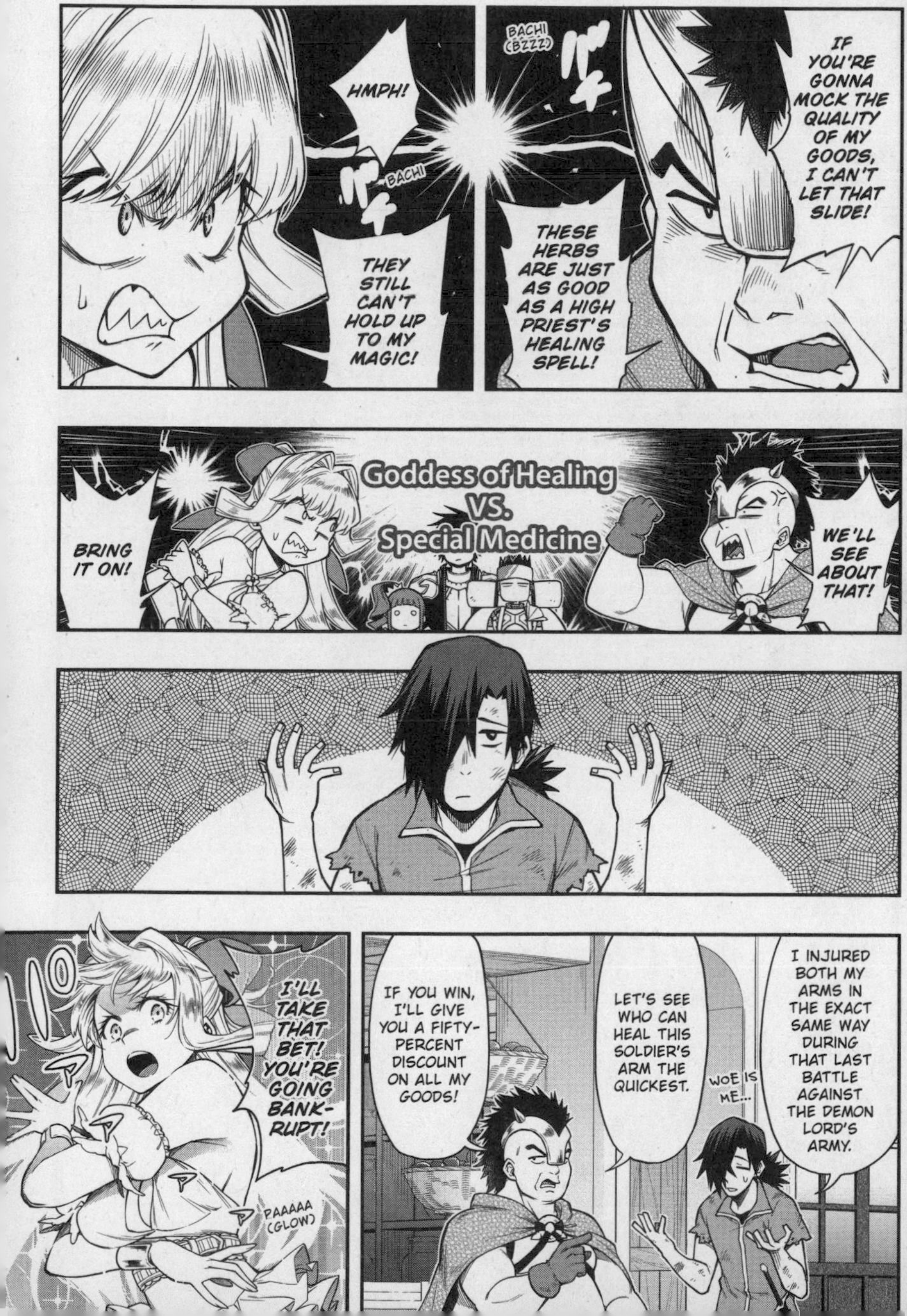
IF YOU'RE GONNA MOCK THE QUALITY OF MY GOODS, I CAN'T LET THAT SLIDE!
BACHI (BZZZ)
THESE HERBS ARE JUST AS GOOD AS A HIGH PRIEST'S HEALING SPELL!
HMPH!
BACHI
THEY STILL CAN'T HOLD UP TO MY MAGIC!
WE'LL SEE ABOUT THAT!
Goddess of Healing VS. Special Medicine
BRING IT ON!
I INJURED BOTH MY ARMS IN THE EXACT SAME WAY DURING THAT LAST BATTLE AGAINST THE DEMON LORD'S ARMY.
WOE IS ME...
LET'S SEE WHO CAN HEAL THIS SOLDIER'S ARM THE QUICKEST.
IF YOU WIN, I'LL GIVE YOU A FIFTY-PERCENT DISCOUNT ON ALL MY GOODS!
I'LL TAKE THAT BET! YOU'RE GOING BANK-RUPT!
PAAAAA (GLOW)

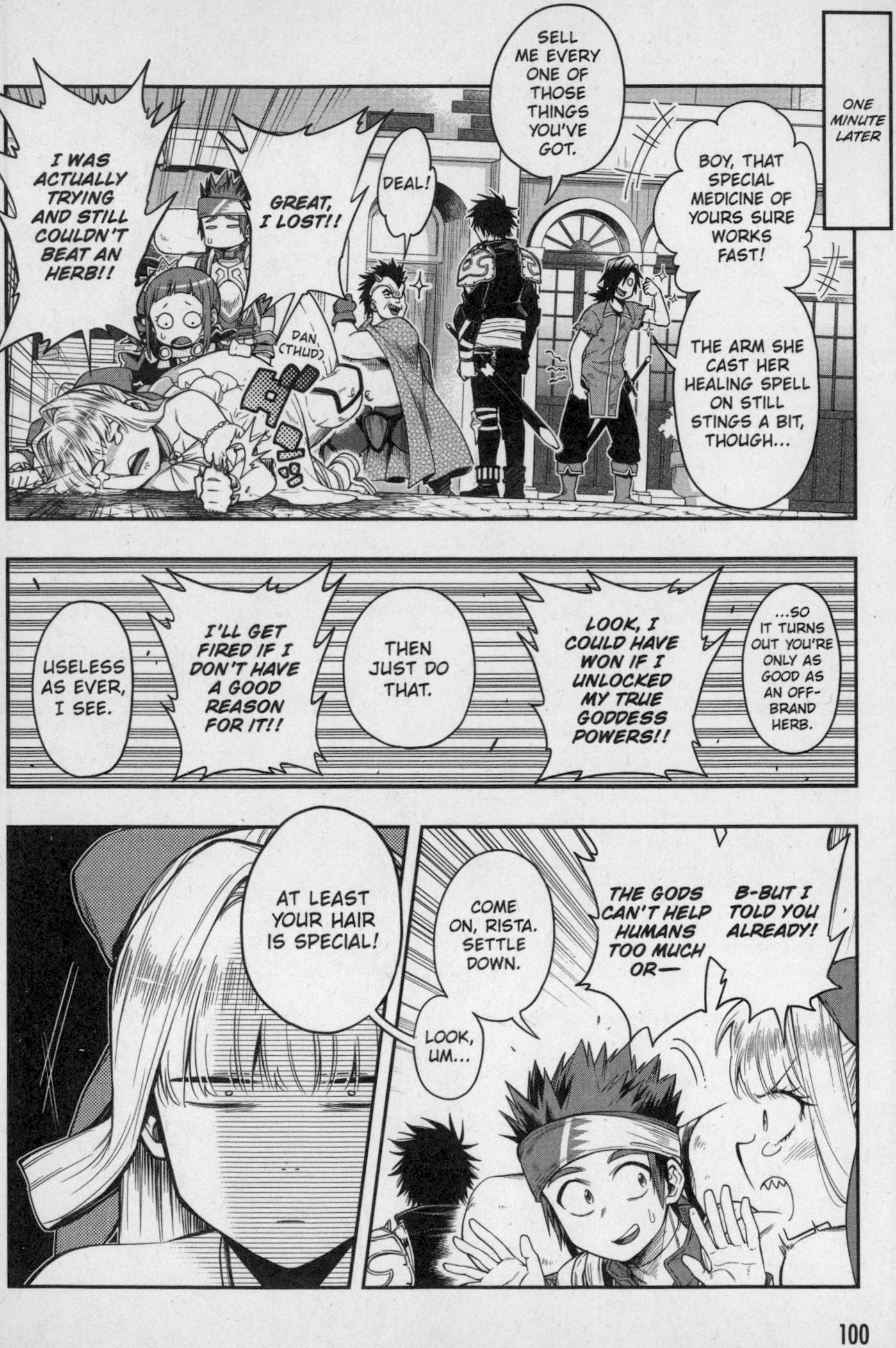
ONE MINUTE LATER
BOY, THAT SPECIAL MEDICINE OF YOURS SURE WORKS FAST!
THE ARM SHE CAST HER HEALING SPELL ON STILL STINGS A BIT, THOUGH...
SELL ME EVERY ONE OF THOSE THINGS YOU'VE GOT.
DEAL!
GREAT, I LOST!!
I WAS ACTUALLY TRYING AND STILL COULDN'T BEAT AN HERB!!
DAN (THUD)
...SO IT TURNS OUT YOU'RE ONLY AS GOOD AS AN OFF-BRAND HERB.
LOOK, I COULD HAVE WON IF I UNLOCKED MY TRUE GODDESS POWERS!!
THEN JUST DO THAT.
I'LL GET FIRED IF I DON'T HAVE A GOOD REASON FOR IT!!
USELESS AS EVER, I SEE.
B-BUT I TOLD YOU ALREADY!
THE GODS CAN'T HELP HUMANS TOO MUCH OR—
COME ON, RISTA. SETTLE DOWN.
LOOK, UM...
AT LEAST YOUR HAIR IS SPECIAL!

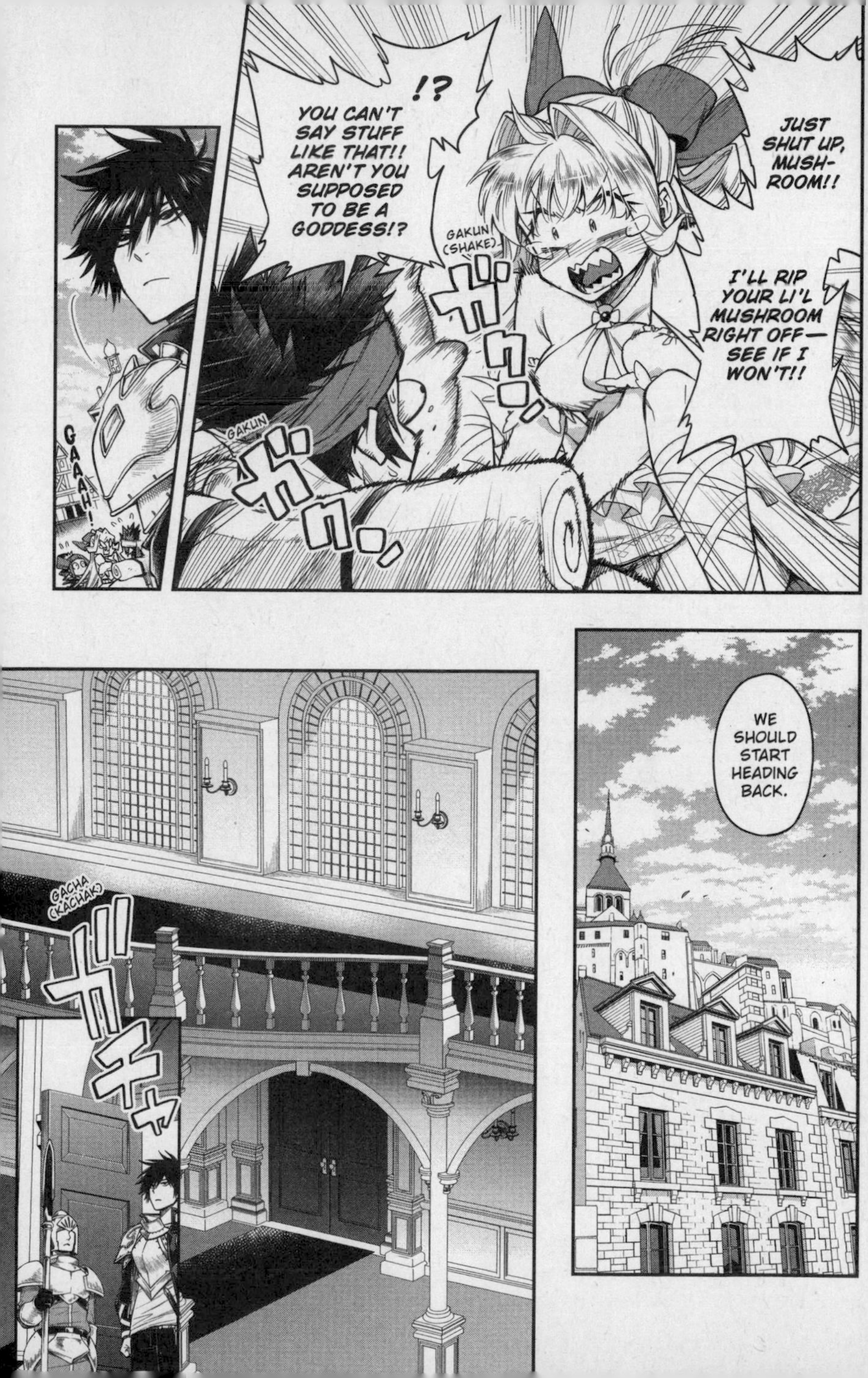
JUST SHUT UP, MUSH-ROOM!!
I'LL RIP YOUR LI'L MUSHROOM RIGHT OFF—SEE IF I WON'T!!
!?
YOU CAN'T SAY STUFF LIKE THAT!! AREN'T YOU SUPPOSED TO BE A GODDESS!?
GAKUN (SHAKE)
GAKUN
GAAAH!
WE SHOULD START HEADING BACK.
GACHA (KACHAK)

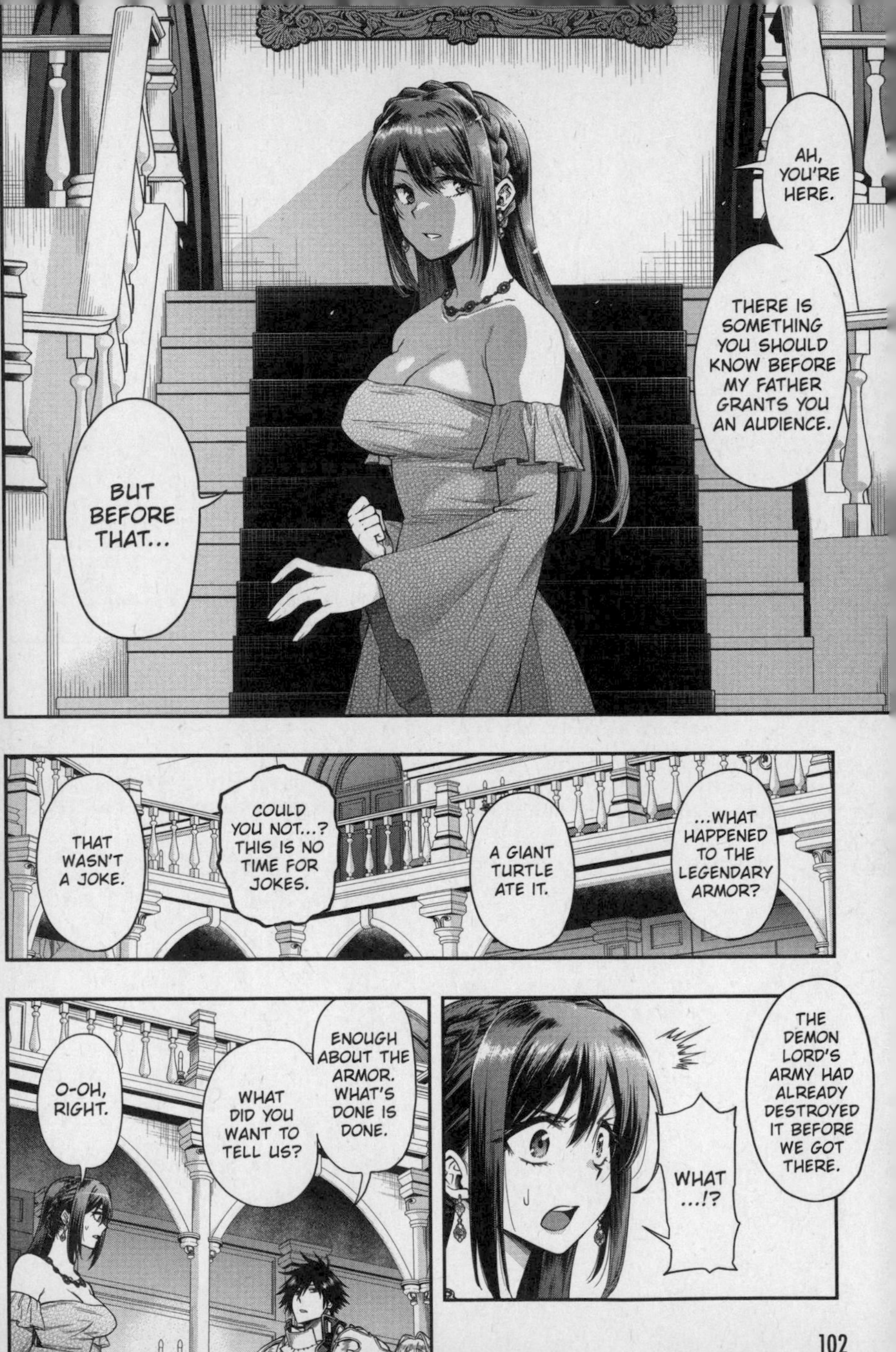
AH, YOU'RE HERE.
THERE IS SOMETHING YOU SHOULD KNOW BEFORE MY FATHER GRANTS YOU AN AUDIENCE.
BUT BEFORE THAT...
...WHAT HAPPENED TO THE LEGENDARY ARMOR?
A GIANT TURTLE ATE IT.
COULD YOU NOT...? THIS IS NO TIME FOR JOKES.
THAT WASN'T A JOKE.
THE DEMON LORD'S ARMY HAD ALREADY DESTROYED IT BEFORE WE GOT THERE.
WHAT ...!?
ENOUGH ABOUT THE ARMOR. WHAT'S DONE IS DONE.
WHAT DID YOU WANT TO TELL US?
O-OH, RIGHT.

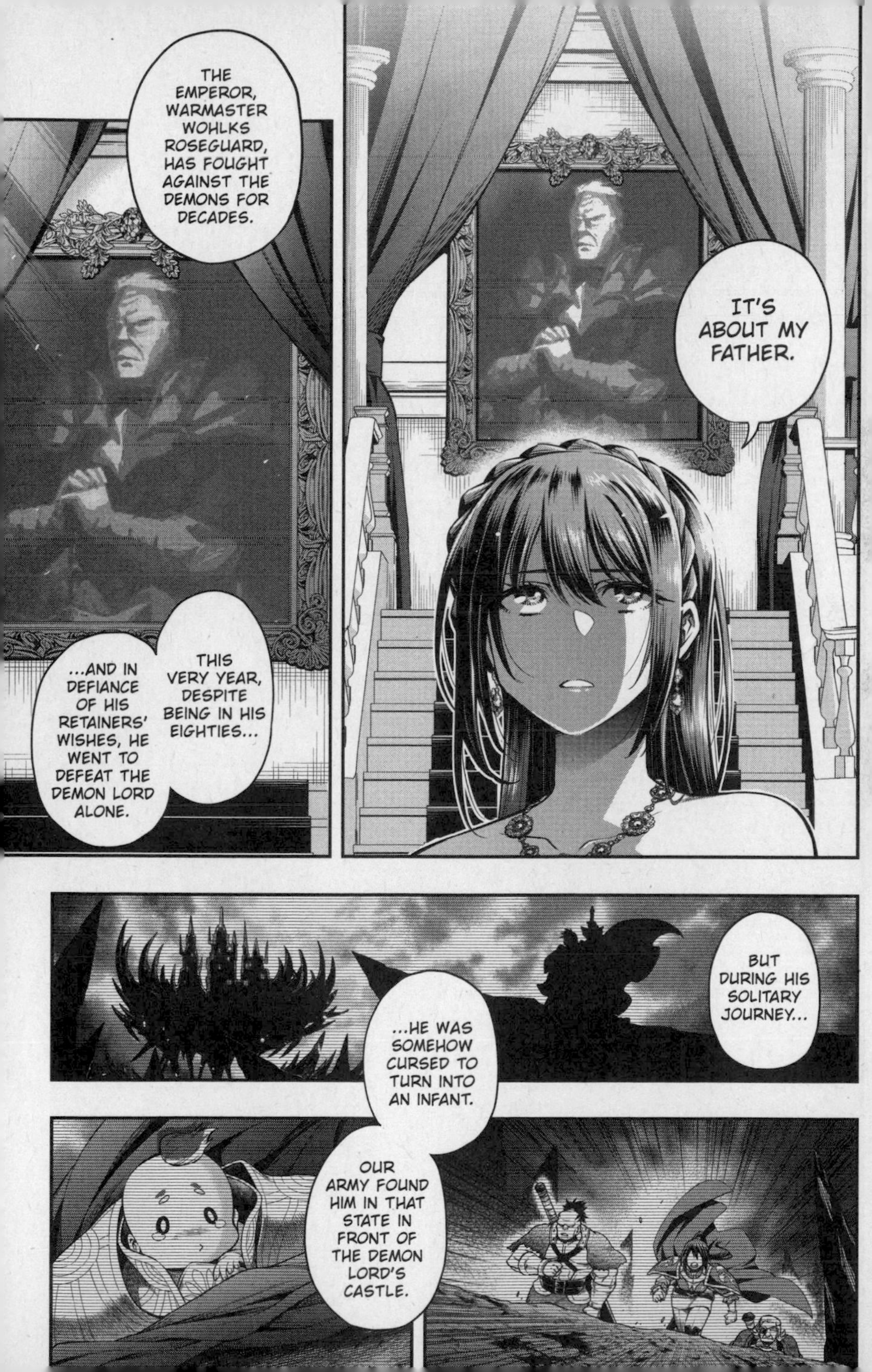
IT'S ABOUT MY FATHER.
THE EMPEROR, WARMASTER WOHLKS ROSEGUARD, HAS FOUGHT AGAINST THE DEMONS FOR DECADES.
THIS VERY YEAR, DESPITE BEING IN HIS EIGHTIES...
...AND IN DEFIANCE OF HIS RETAINERS' WISHES, HE WENT TO DEFEAT THE DEMON LORD ALONE.
BUT DURING HIS SOLITARY JOURNEY...
...HE WAS SOMEHOW CURSED TO TURN INTO AN INFANT.
OUR ARMY FOUND HIM IN THAT STATE IN FRONT OF THE DEMON LORD'S CASTLE.

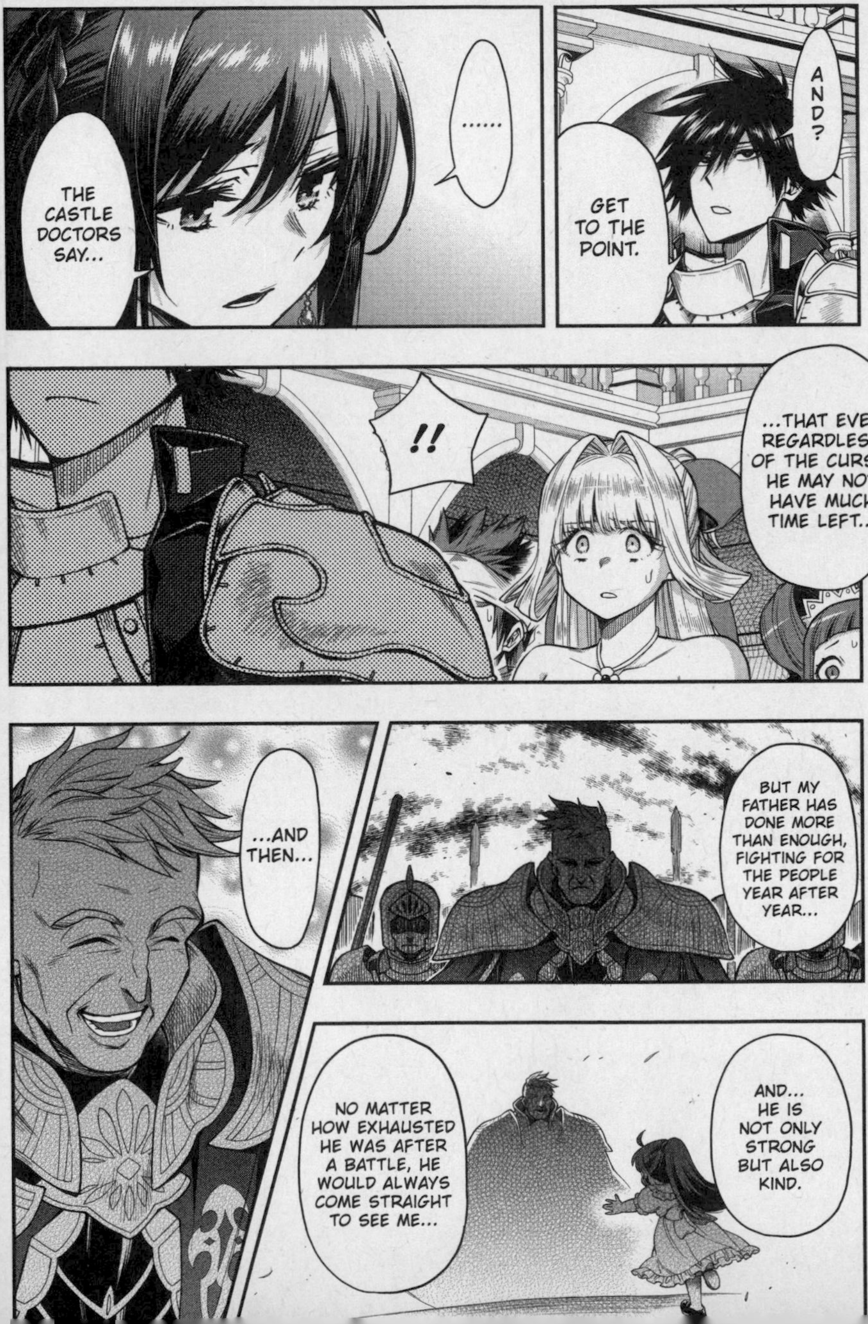
AND?
GET TO THE POINT.
......
THE CASTLE DOCTORS SAY...
...THAT EVEN REGARDLESS OF THE CURSE, HE MAY NOT HAVE MUCH TIME LEFT...
!!
BUT MY FATHER HAS DONE MORE THAN ENOUGH, FIGHTING FOR THE PEOPLE YEAR AFTER YEAR...
AND... HE IS NOT ONLY STRONG BUT ALSO KIND.
NO MATTER HOW EXHAUSTED HE WAS AFTER A BATTLE, HE WOULD ALWAYS COME STRAIGHT TO SEE ME...
...AND THEN...

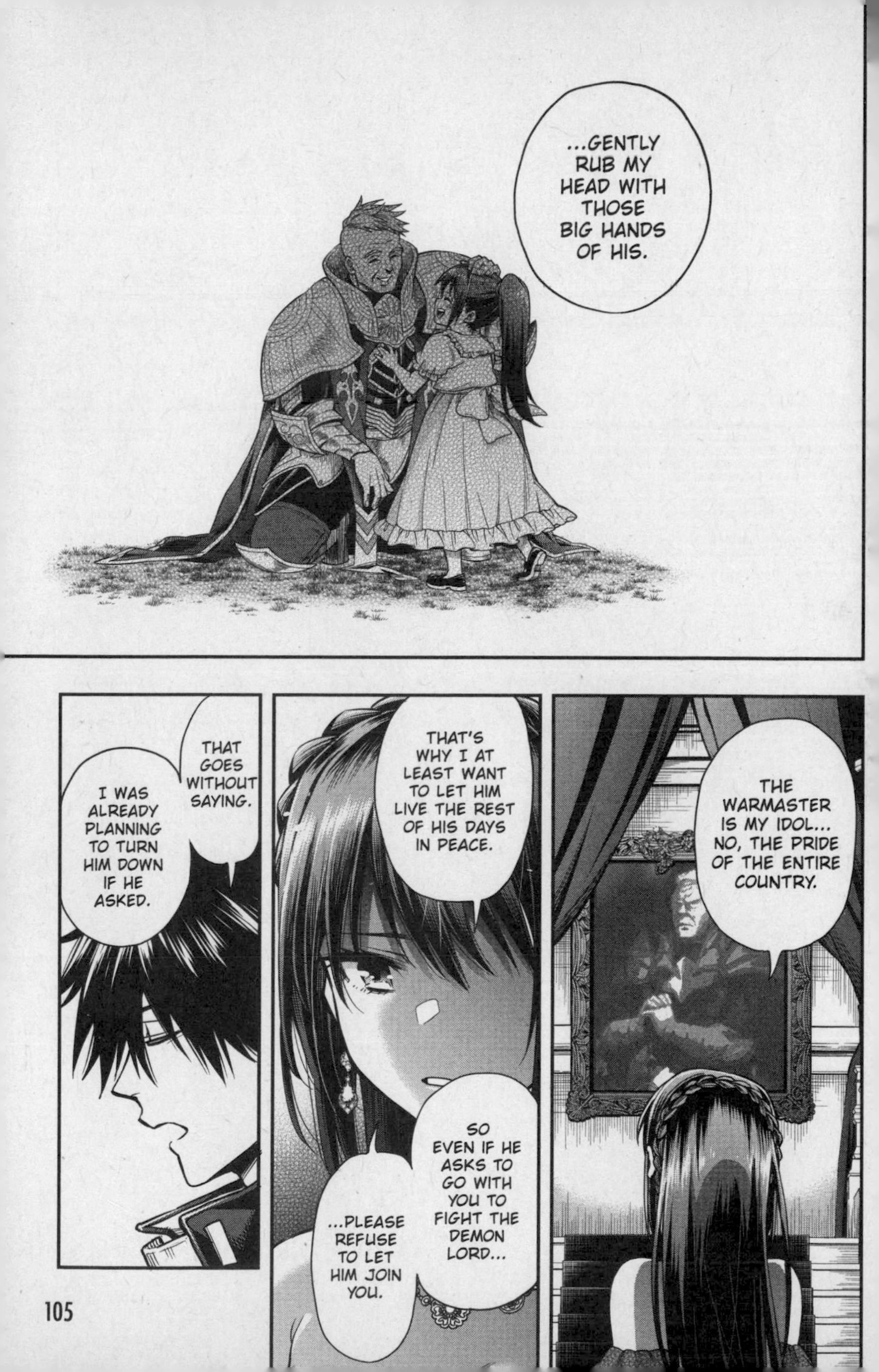
...GENTLY RUB MY HEAD WITH THOSE BIG HANDS OF HIS.
THE WARMASTER IS MY IDOL... NO, THE PRIDE OF THE ENTIRE COUNTRY.
THAT'S WHY I AT LEAST WANT TO LET HIM LIVE THE REST OF HIS DAYS IN PEACE.
SO EVEN IF HE ASKS TO GO WITH YOU TO FIGHT THE DEMON LORD...
...PLEASE REFUSE TO LET HIM JOIN YOU.
THAT GOES WITHOUT SAYING.
I WAS ALREADY PLANNING TO TURN HIM DOWN IF HE ASKED.

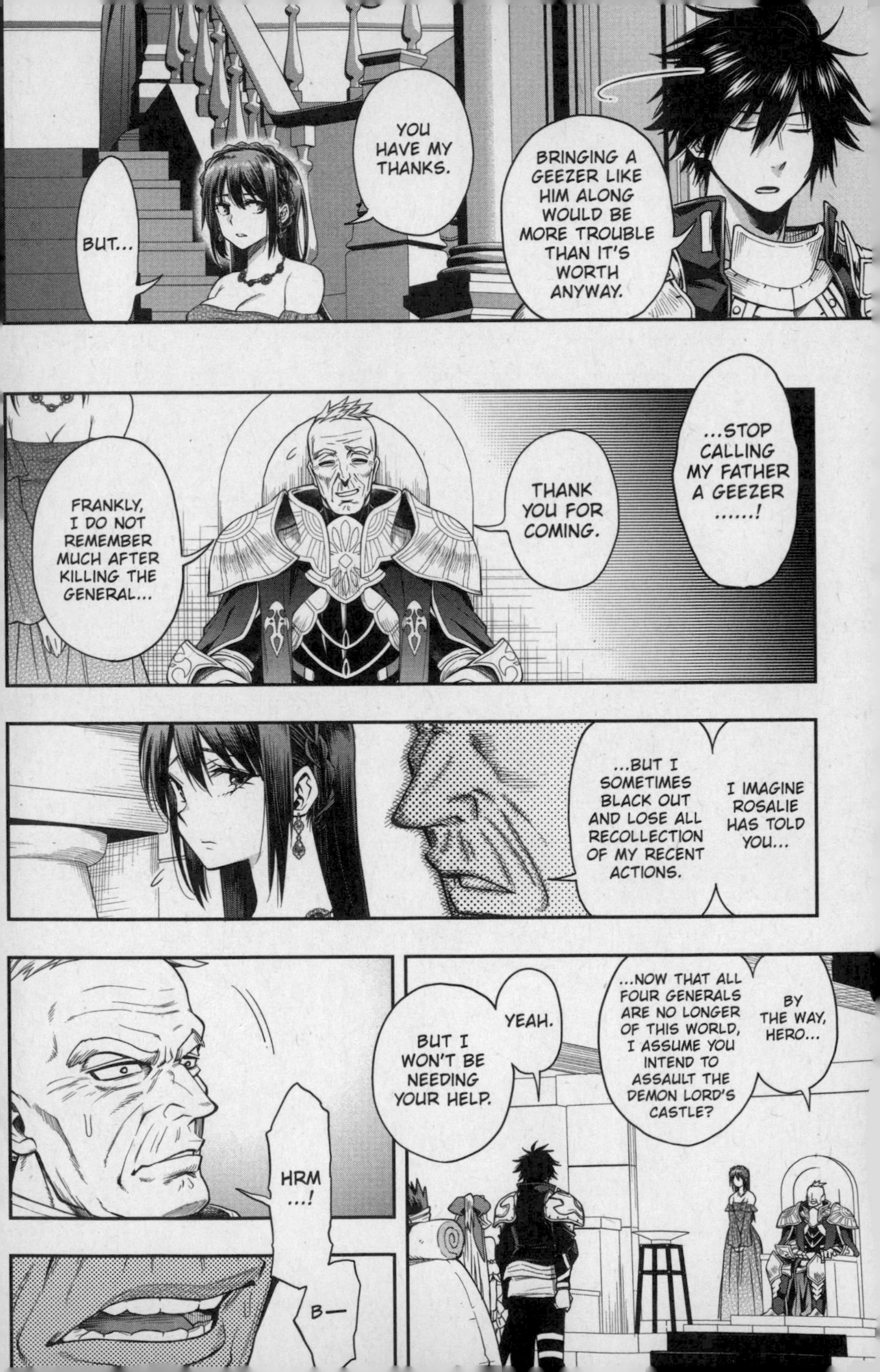
BRINGING A GEEZER LIKE HIM ALONG WOULD BE MORE TROUBLE THAN IT'S WORTH ANYWAY.
YOU HAVE MY THANKS.
BUT...
...STOP CALLING MY FATHER A GEEZER ......!
THANK YOU FOR COMING.
FRANKLY, I DO NOT REMEMBER MUCH AFTER KILLING THE GENERAL...
I IMAGINE ROSALIE HAS TOLD YOU...
...BUT I SOMETIMES BLACK OUT AND LOSE ALL RECOLLECTION OF MY RECENT ACTIONS.
BY THE WAY, HERO...
...NOW THAT ALL FOUR GENERALS ARE NO LONGER OF THIS WORLD, I ASSUME YOU INTEND TO ASSAULT THE DEMON LORD'S CASTLE?
YEAH.
BUT I WON'T BE NEEDING YOUR HELP.
HRM ...!
B—

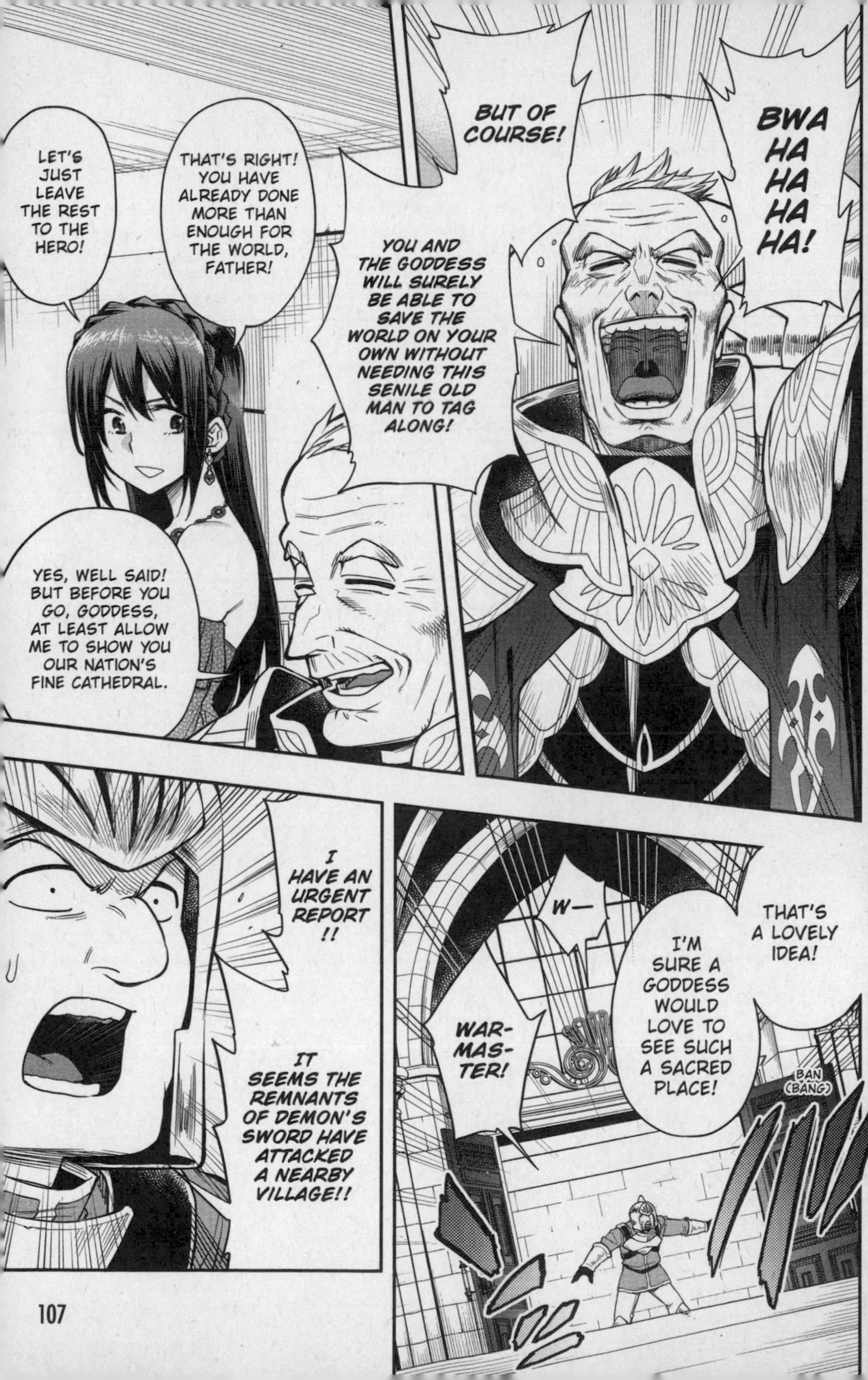
BWA HA HA HA HA!
BUT OF COURSE!
YOU AND THE GODDESS WILL SURELY BE ABLE TO SAVE THE WORLD ON YOUR OWN WITHOUT NEEDING THIS SENILE OLD MAN TO TAG ALONG!
THAT'S RIGHT! YOU HAVE ALREADY DONE MORE THAN ENOUGH FOR THE WORLD, FATHER!
LET'S JUST LEAVE THE REST TO THE HERO!
YES, WELL SAID! BUT BEFORE YOU GO, GODDESS, AT LEAST ALLOW ME TO SHOW YOU OUR NATION'S FINE CATHEDRAL.
THAT'S A LOVELY IDEA!
I'M SURE A GODDESS WOULD LOVE TO SEE SUCH A SACRED PLACE!
BAN (BANG)
W—
WAR-MAS-TER!
I HAVE AN URGENT REPORT!!
IT SEEMS THE REMNANTS OF DEMON'S SWORD HAVE ATTACKED A NEARBY VILLAGE!!

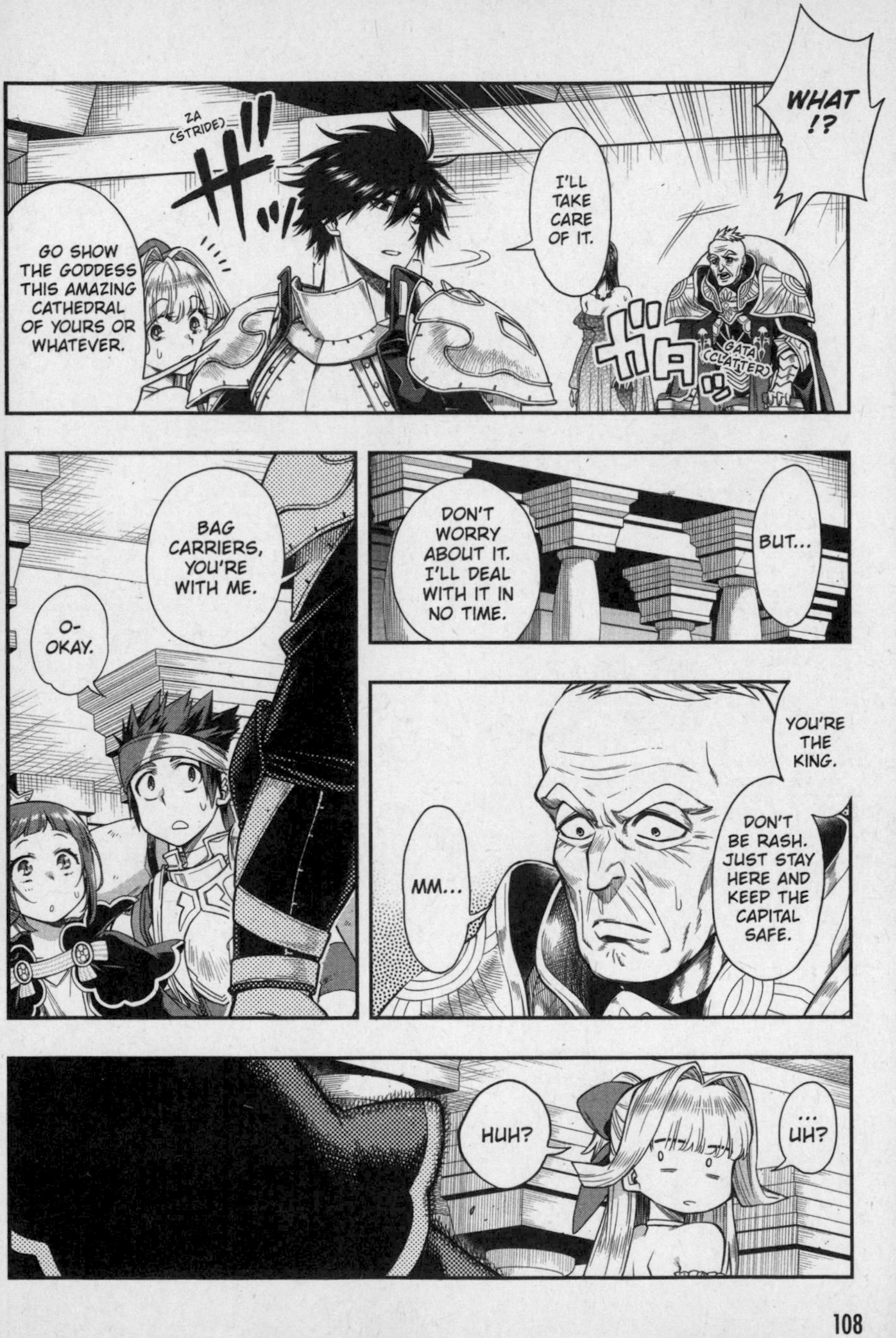
WHAT!?
GATA (CLATTER)
I'LL TAKE CARE OF IT.
ZA (STRIDE)
GO SHOW THE GODDESS THIS AMAZING CATHEDRAL OF YOURS OR WHATEVER.
BUT...
DON'T WORRY ABOUT IT. I'LL DEAL WITH IT IN NO TIME.
YOU'RE THE KING.
DON'T BE RASH. JUST STAY HERE AND KEEP THE CAPITAL SAFE.
MM...
BAG CARRIERS, YOU'RE WITH ME.
O-OKAY.
...UH?
HUH?

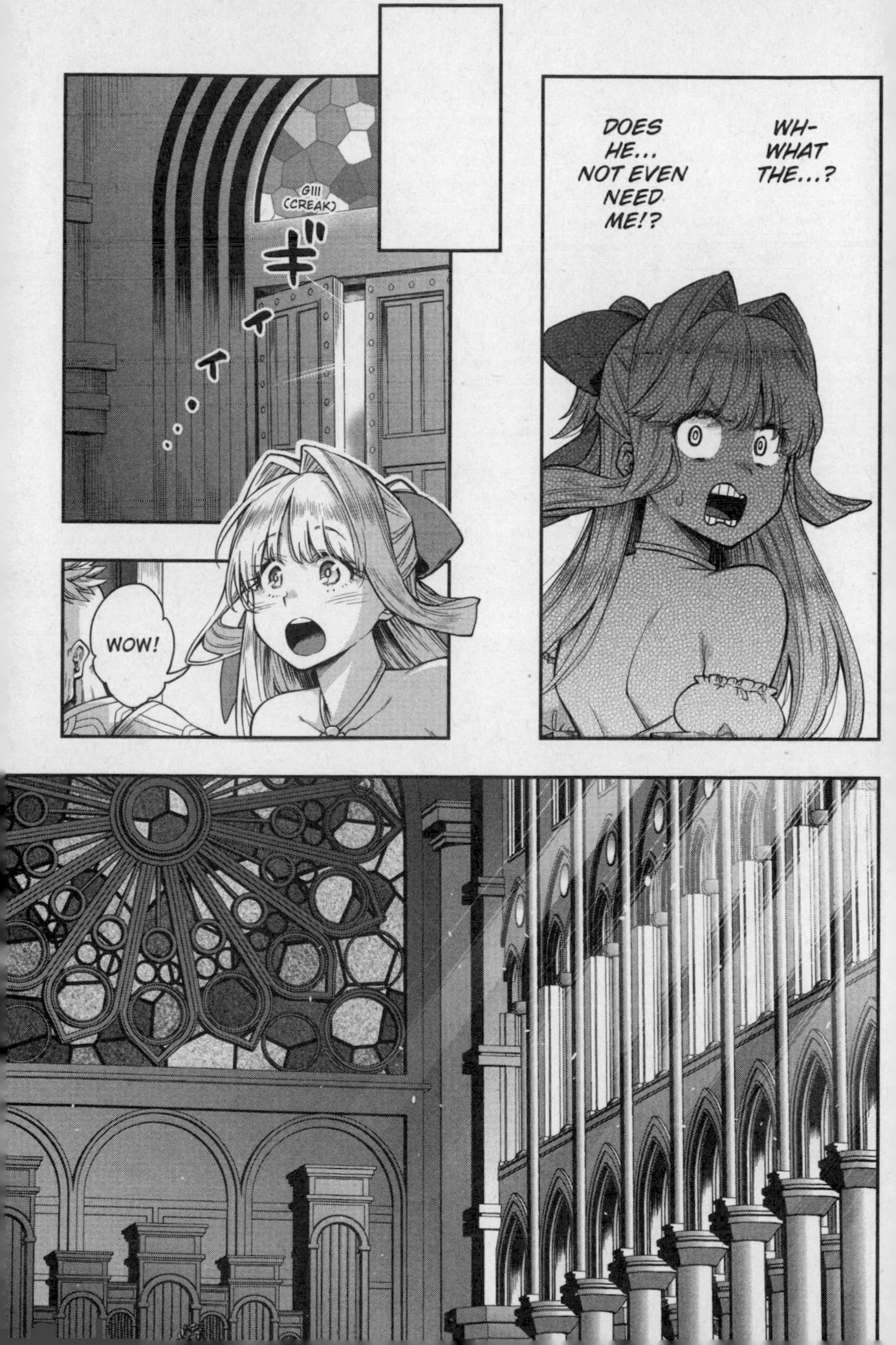
WH- WHAT THE...?
DOES HE... NOT EVEN NEED ME!?
GIII (CREAK)
ギイイ
WOW!

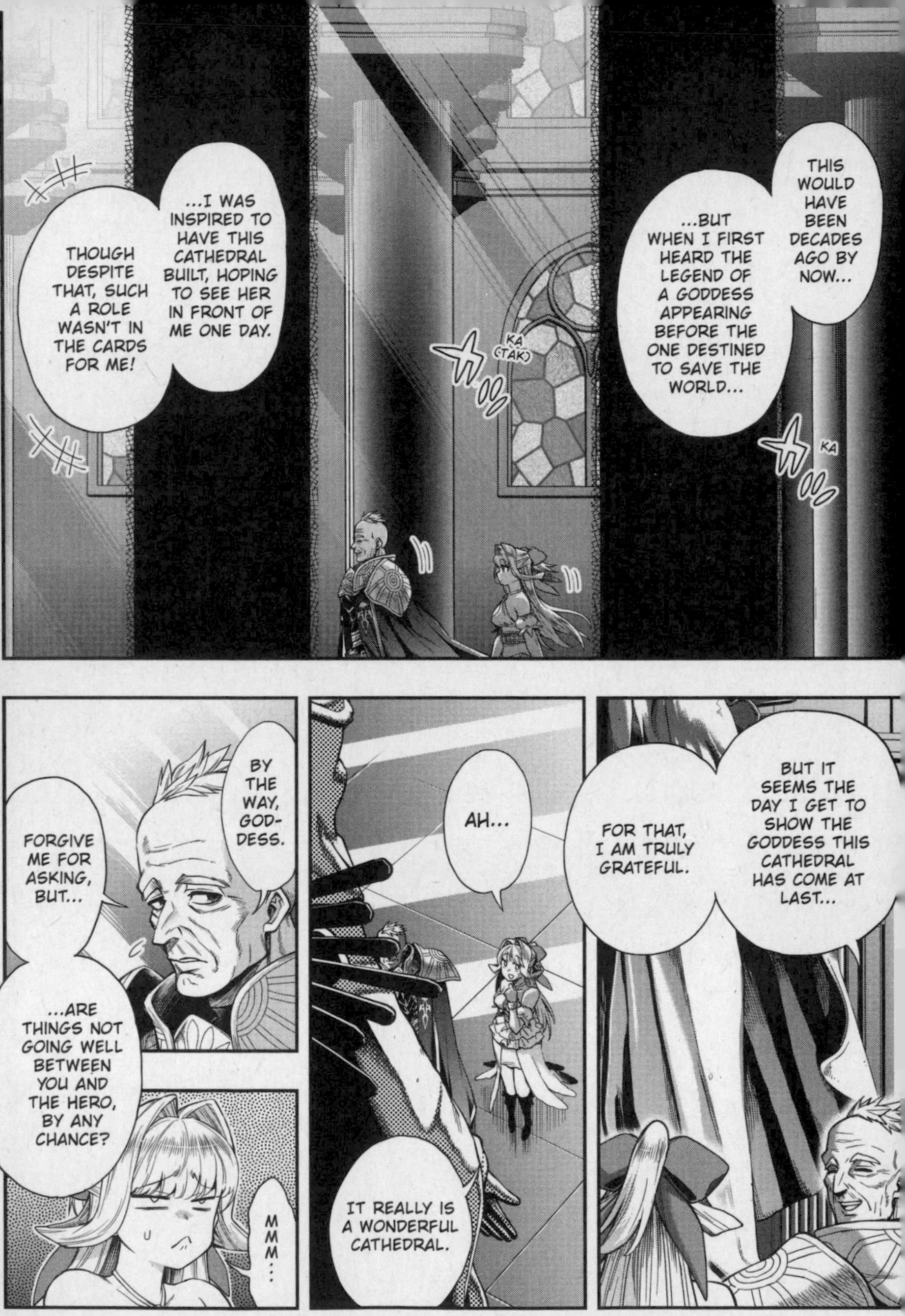
THIS WOULD HAVE BEEN DECADES AGO BY NOW...
KA
...BUT WHEN I FIRST HEARD THE LEGEND OF A GODDESS APPEARING BEFORE THE ONE DESTINED TO SAVE THE WORLD...
KA (TAK)
...I WAS INSPIRED TO HAVE THIS CATHEDRAL BUILT, HOPING TO SEE HER IN FRONT OF ME ONE DAY.
THOUGH DESPITE THAT, SUCH A ROLE WASN'T IN THE CARDS FOR ME!
BUT IT SEEMS THE DAY I GET TO SHOW THE GODDESS THIS CATHEDRAL HAS COME AT LAST...
FOR THAT, I AM TRULY GRATEFUL.
AH...
IT REALLY IS A WONDERFUL CATHEDRAL.
BY THE WAY, GOD-DESS.
FORGIVE ME FOR ASKING, BUT...
...ARE THINGS NOT GOING WELL BETWEEN YOU AND THE HERO, BY ANY CHANCE?
MMM...

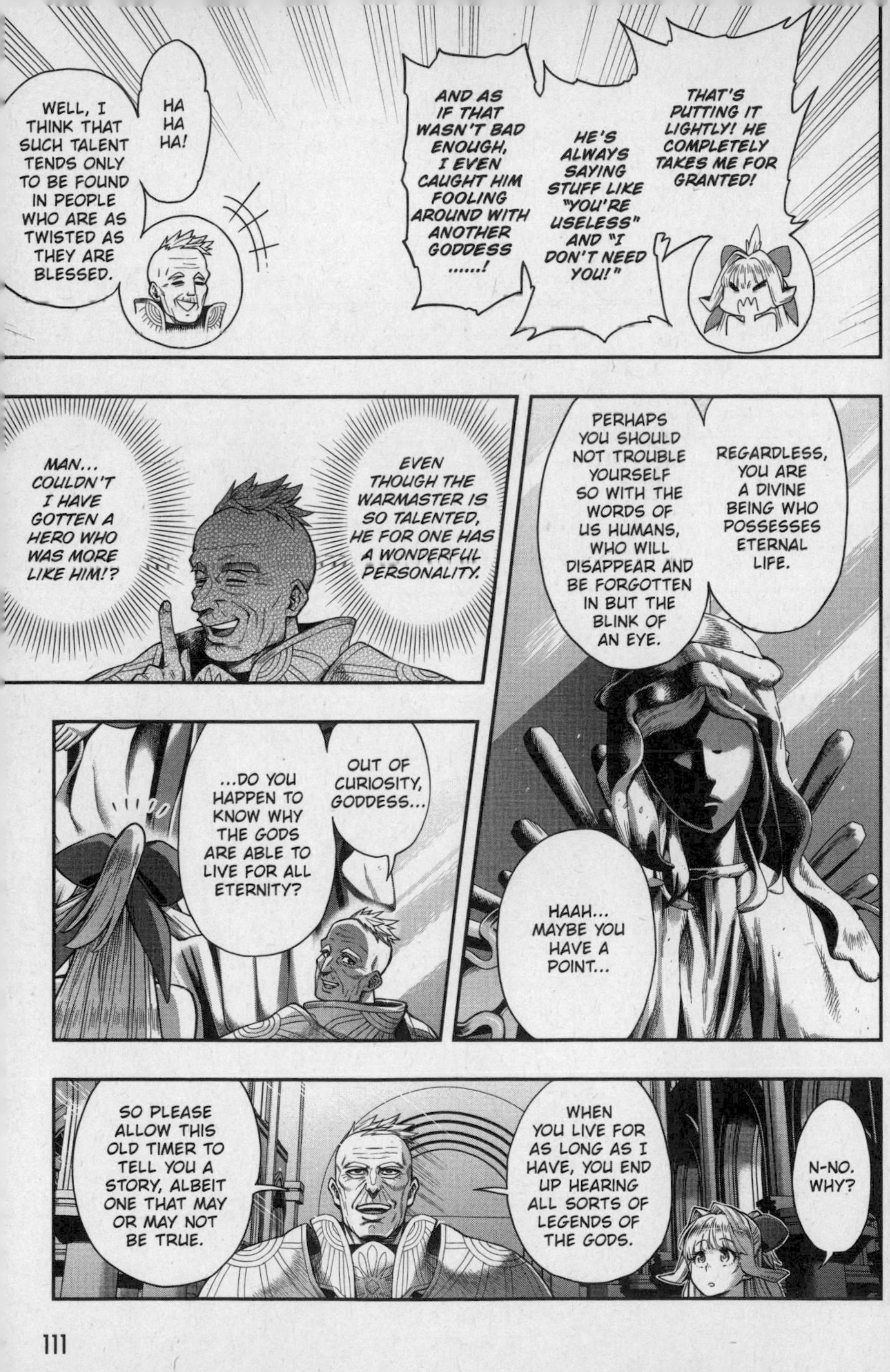
THAT'S PUTTING IT LIGHTLY! HE COMPLETELY TAKES ME FOR GRANTED!
HE'S ALWAYS SAYING STUFF LIKE "YOU'RE USELESS" AND "I DON'T NEED YOU!"
AND AS IF THAT WASN'T BAD ENOUGH, I EVEN CAUGHT HIM FOOLING AROUND WITH ANOTHER GODDESS ......!
HA HA HA!
WELL, I THINK THAT SUCH TALENT TENDS ONLY TO BE FOUND IN PEOPLE WHO ARE AS TWISTED AS THEY ARE BLESSED.
REGARDLESS, YOU ARE A DIVINE BEING WHO POSSESSES ETERNAL LIFE.
PERHAPS YOU SHOULD NOT TROUBLE YOURSELF SO WITH THE WORDS OF US HUMANS, WHO WILL DISAPPEAR AND BE FORGOTTEN IN BUT THE BLINK OF AN EYE.
HAAH... MAYBE YOU HAVE A POINT...
EVEN THOUGH THE WARMASTER IS SO TALENTED, HE FOR ONE HAS A WONDERFUL PERSONALITY.
MAN... COULDN'T I HAVE GOTTEN A HERO WHO WAS MORE LIKE HIM!?
OUT OF CURIOSITY, GODDESS...
...DO YOU HAPPEN TO KNOW WHY THE GODS ARE ABLE TO LIVE FOR ALL ETERNITY?
N-NO. WHY?
WHEN YOU LIVE FOR AS LONG AS I HAVE, YOU END UP HEARING ALL SORTS OF LEGENDS OF THE GODS.
SO PLEASE ALLOW THIS OLD TIMER TO TELL YOU A STORY, ALBEIT ONE THAT MAY OR MAY NOT BE TRUE.

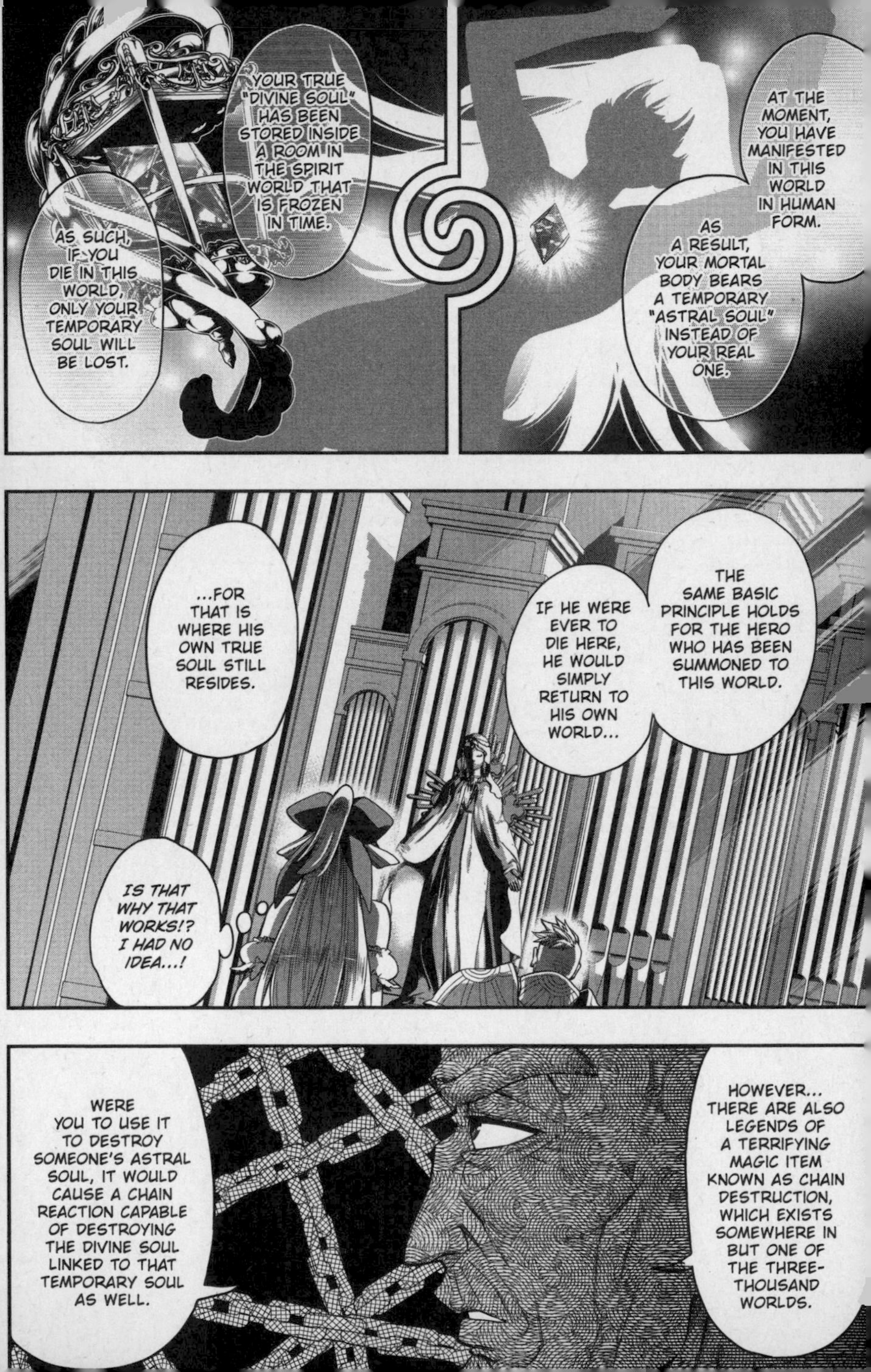
AT THE MOMENT, YOU HAVE MANIFESTED IN THIS WORLD IN HUMAN FORM.
AS A RESULT, YOUR MORTAL BODY BEARS A TEMPORARY "ASTRAL SOUL" INSTEAD OF YOUR REAL ONE.
YOUR TRUE "DIVINE SOUL" HAS BEEN STORED INSIDE A ROOM IN THE SPIRIT WORLD THAT IS FROZEN IN TIME.
AS SUCH, IF YOU DIE IN THIS WORLD, ONLY YOUR TEMPORARY SOUL WILL BE LOST.
THE SAME BASIC PRINCIPLE HOLDS FOR THE HERO WHO HAS BEEN SUMMONED TO THIS WORLD.
IF HE WERE EVER TO DIE HERE, HE WOULD SIMPLY RETURN TO HIS OWN WORLD...
...FOR THAT IS WHERE HIS OWN TRUE SOUL STILL RESIDES.
IS THAT WHY THAT WORKS!? I HAD NO IDEA...!
HOWEVER... THERE ARE ALSO LEGENDS OF A TERRIFYING MAGIC ITEM KNOWN AS CHAIN DESTRUCTION, WHICH EXISTS SOMEWHERE IN BUT ONE OF THE THREE-THOUSAND WORLDS.
WERE YOU TO USE IT TO DESTROY SOMEONE'S ASTRAL SOUL, IT WOULD CAUSE A CHAIN REACTION CAPABLE OF DESTROYING THE DIVINE SOUL LINKED TO THAT TEMPORARY SOUL AS WELL.

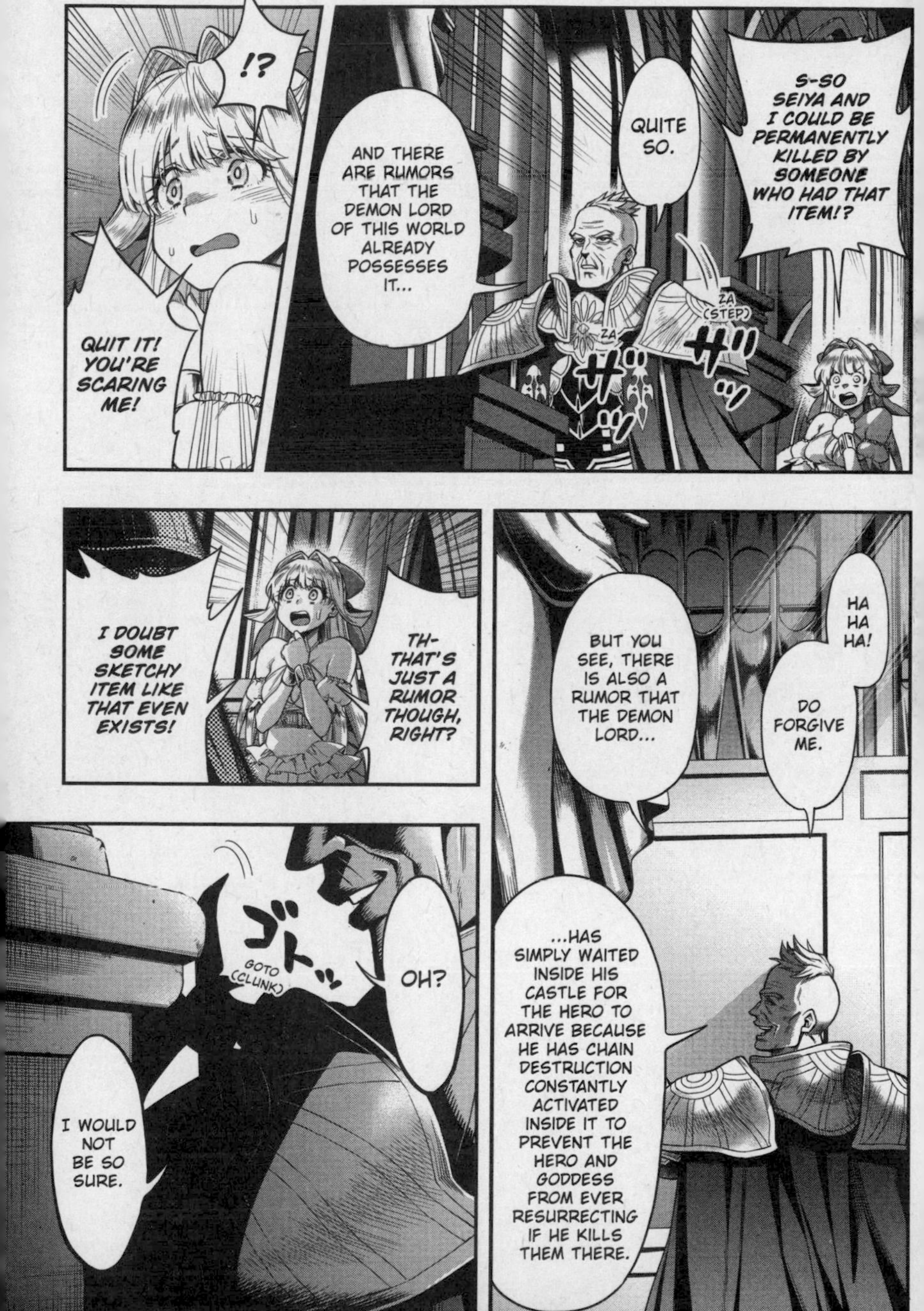
S-SO SEIYA AND I COULD BE PERMANENTLY KILLED BY SOMEONE WHO HAD THAT ITEM!?
QUITE SO.
AND THERE ARE RUMORS THAT THE DEMON LORD OF THIS WORLD ALREADY POSSESSES IT...
ザッ
ZA (STEP)
ザッ
ZA
!?
QUIT IT! YOU'RE SCARING ME!
HA HA HA!
DO FORGIVE ME.
BUT YOU SEE, THERE IS ALSO A RUMOR THAT THE DEMON LORD...
...HAS SIMPLY WAITED INSIDE HIS CASTLE FOR THE HERO TO ARRIVE BECAUSE HE HAS CHAIN DESTRUCTION CONSTANTLY ACTIVATED INSIDE IT TO PREVENT THE HERO AND GODDESS FROM EVER RESURRECTING IF HE KILLS THEM THERE.
TH-THAT'S JUST A RUMOR THOUGH, RIGHT?
I DOUBT SOME SKETCHY ITEM LIKE THAT EVEN EXISTS!
OH?
ゴトッ
GOTO (CLUNK)
I WOULD NOT BE SO SURE.

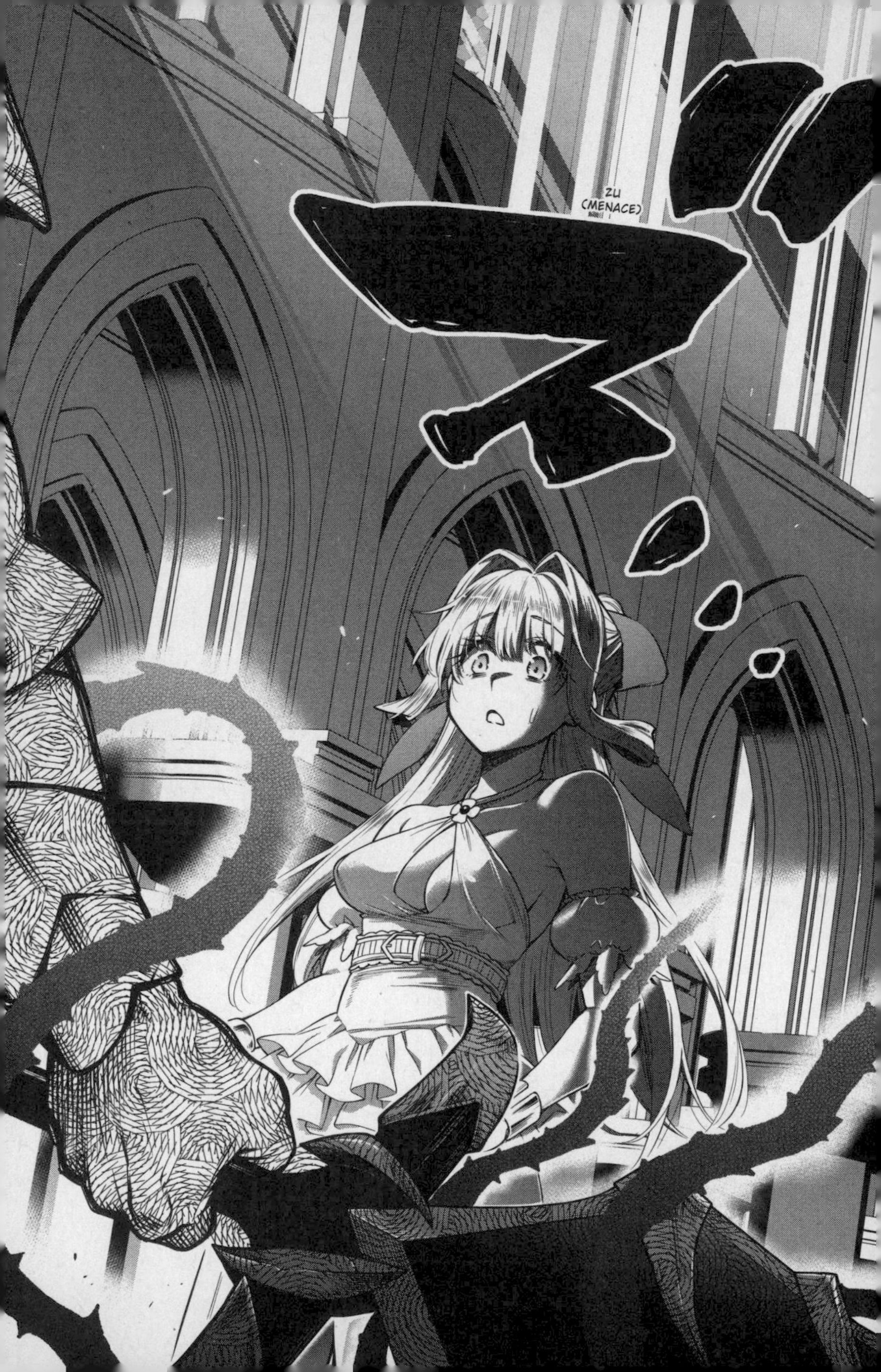
ZU
(MENACE)

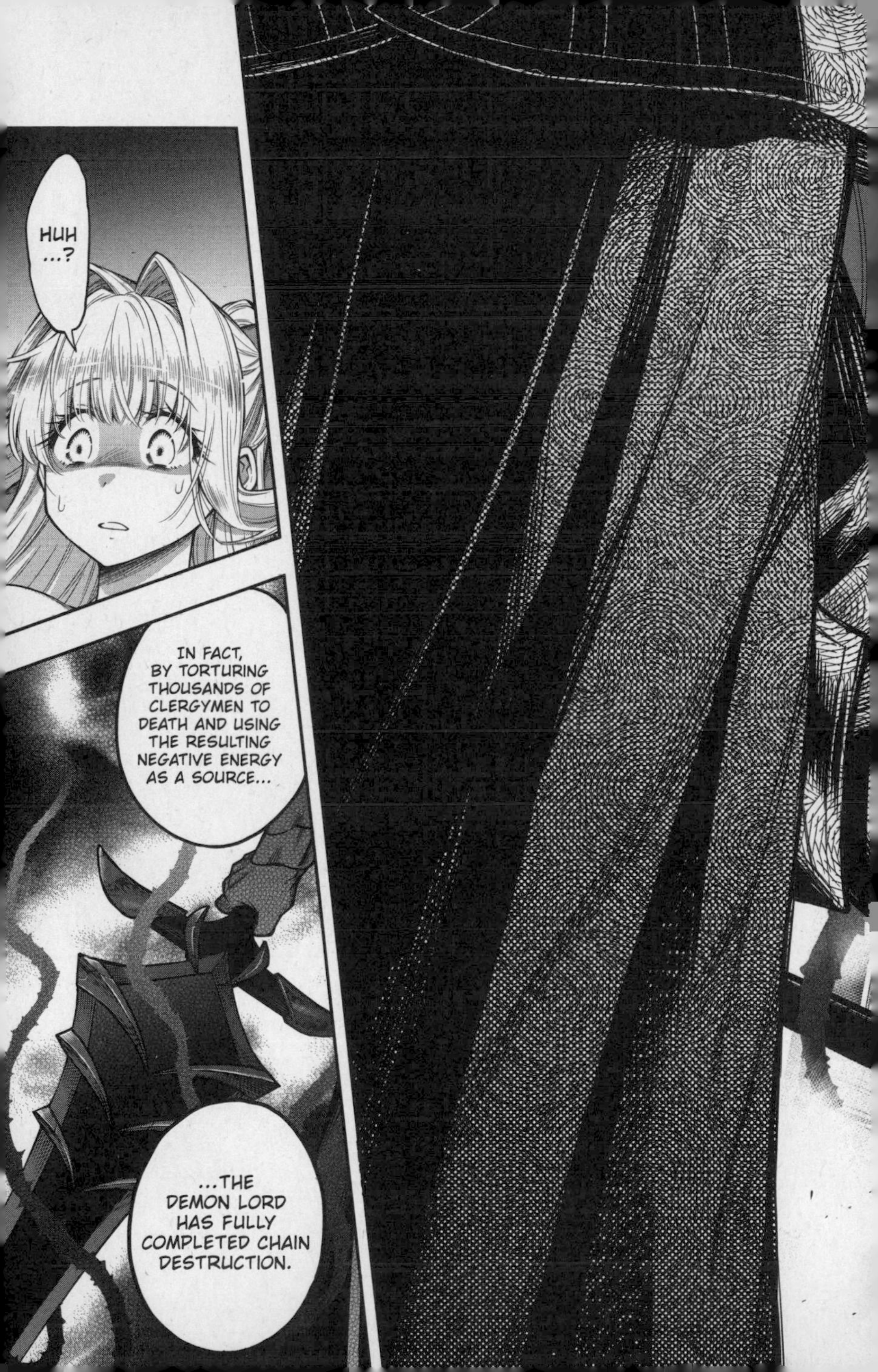
HUH ...?
IN FACT, BY TORTURING THOUSANDS OF CLERGYMEN TO DEATH AND USING THE RESULTING NEGATIVE ENERGY AS A SOURCE...
...THE DEMON LORD HAS FULLY COMPLETED CHAIN DESTRUCTION.

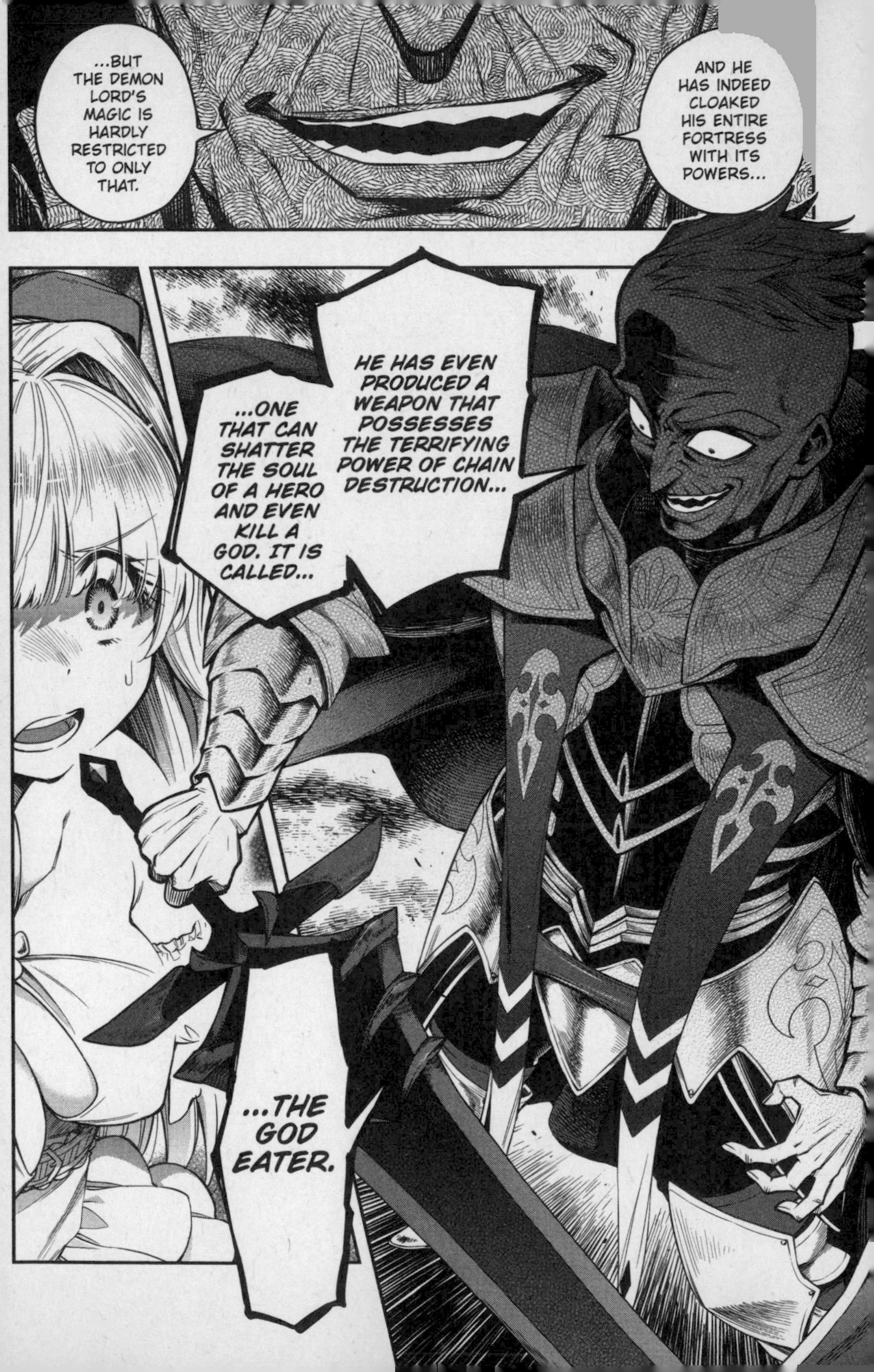
AND HE HAS INDEED CLOAKED HIS ENTIRE FORTRESS WITH ITS POWERS...
...BUT THE DEMON LORD'S MAGIC IS HARDLY RESTRICTED TO ONLY THAT.
HE HAS EVEN PRODUCED A WEAPON THAT POSSESSES THE TERRIFYING POWER OF CHAIN DESTRUCTION...
...ONE THAT CAN SHATTER THE SOUL OF A HERO AND EVEN KILL A GOD. IT IS CALLED...
...THE GOD EATER.

THE HERO IS OVERPOWERED BUT OVERLY CAUTIOUS

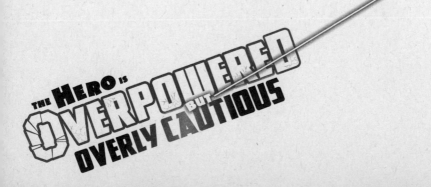

THE HERO IS OVERPOWERED BUT
OVERLY CAUTIOUS

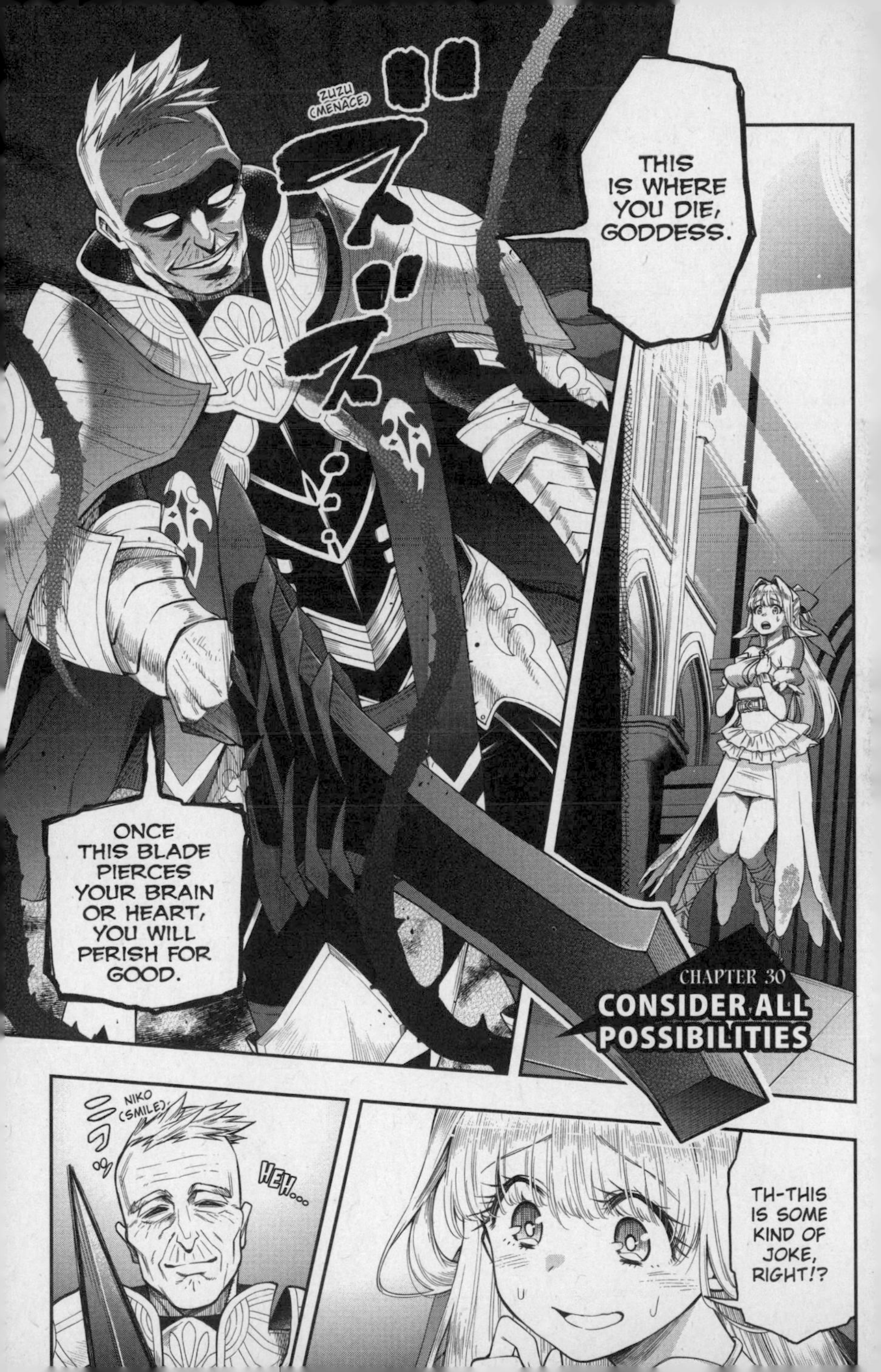
THIS IS WHERE YOU DIE, GODDESS.
ZUZU (MENACE)
CHAPTER 30
CONSIDER ALL POSSIBILITIES
ONCE THIS BLADE PIERCES YOUR BRAIN OR HEART, YOU WILL PERISH FOR GOOD.
TH-THIS IS SOME KIND OF JOKE, RIGHT!?
NIKO (SMILE)
HEH...

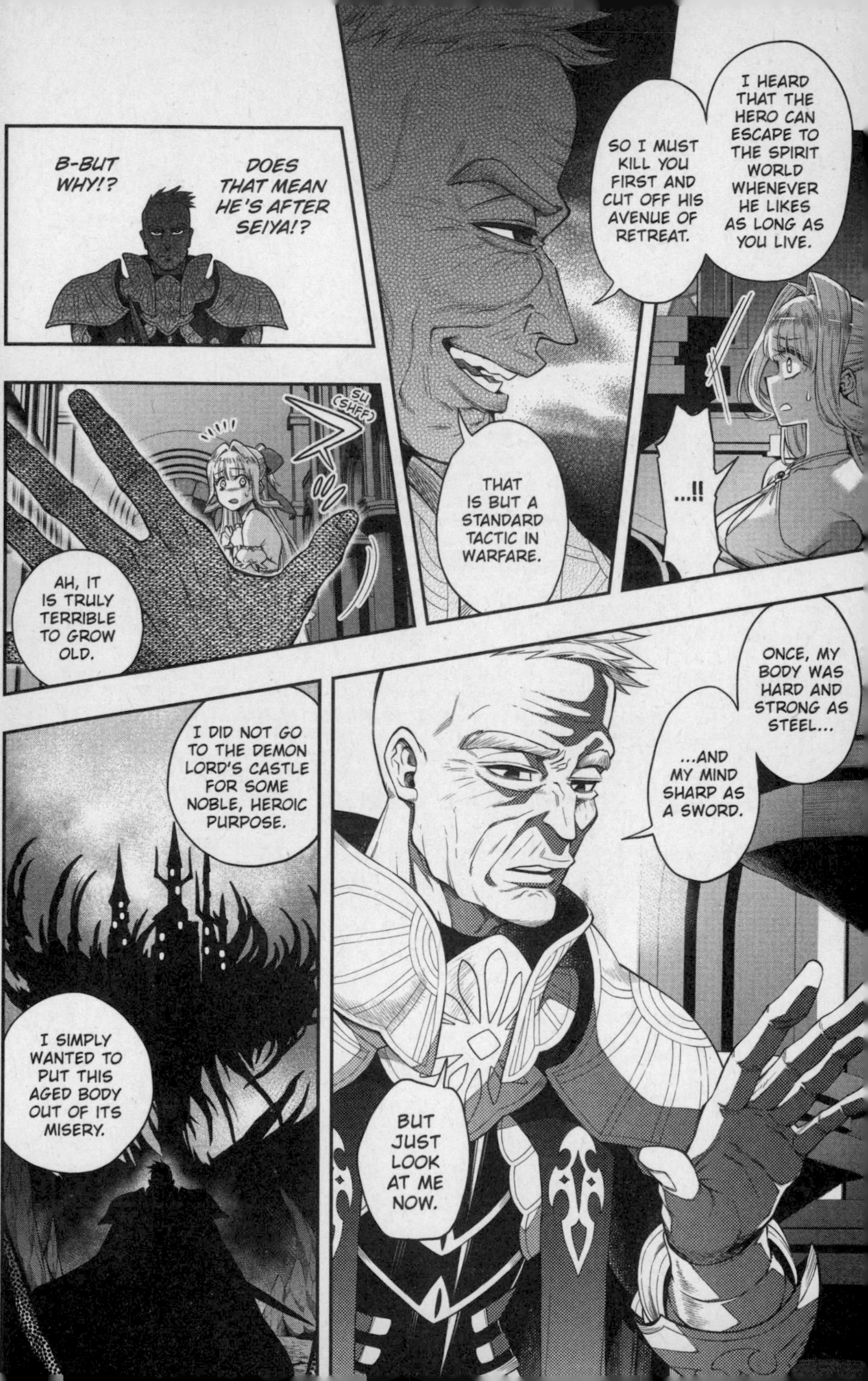
I HEARD THAT THE HERO CAN ESCAPE TO THE SPIRIT WORLD WHENEVER HE LIKES AS LONG AS YOU LIVE.
SO I MUST KILL YOU FIRST AND CUT OFF HIS AVENUE OF RETREAT.
...!!
THAT IS BUT A STANDARD TACTIC IN WARFARE.
DOES THAT MEAN HE'S AFTER SEIYA!?
B-BUT WHY!?
SU (SHFF)
AH, IT IS TRULY TERRIBLE TO GROW OLD.
ONCE, MY BODY WAS HARD AND STRONG AS STEEL...
...AND MY MIND SHARP AS A SWORD.
BUT JUST LOOK AT ME NOW.
I DID NOT GO TO THE DEMON LORD'S CASTLE FOR SOME NOBLE, HEROIC PURPOSE.
I SIMPLY WANTED TO PUT THIS AGED BODY OUT OF ITS MISERY.

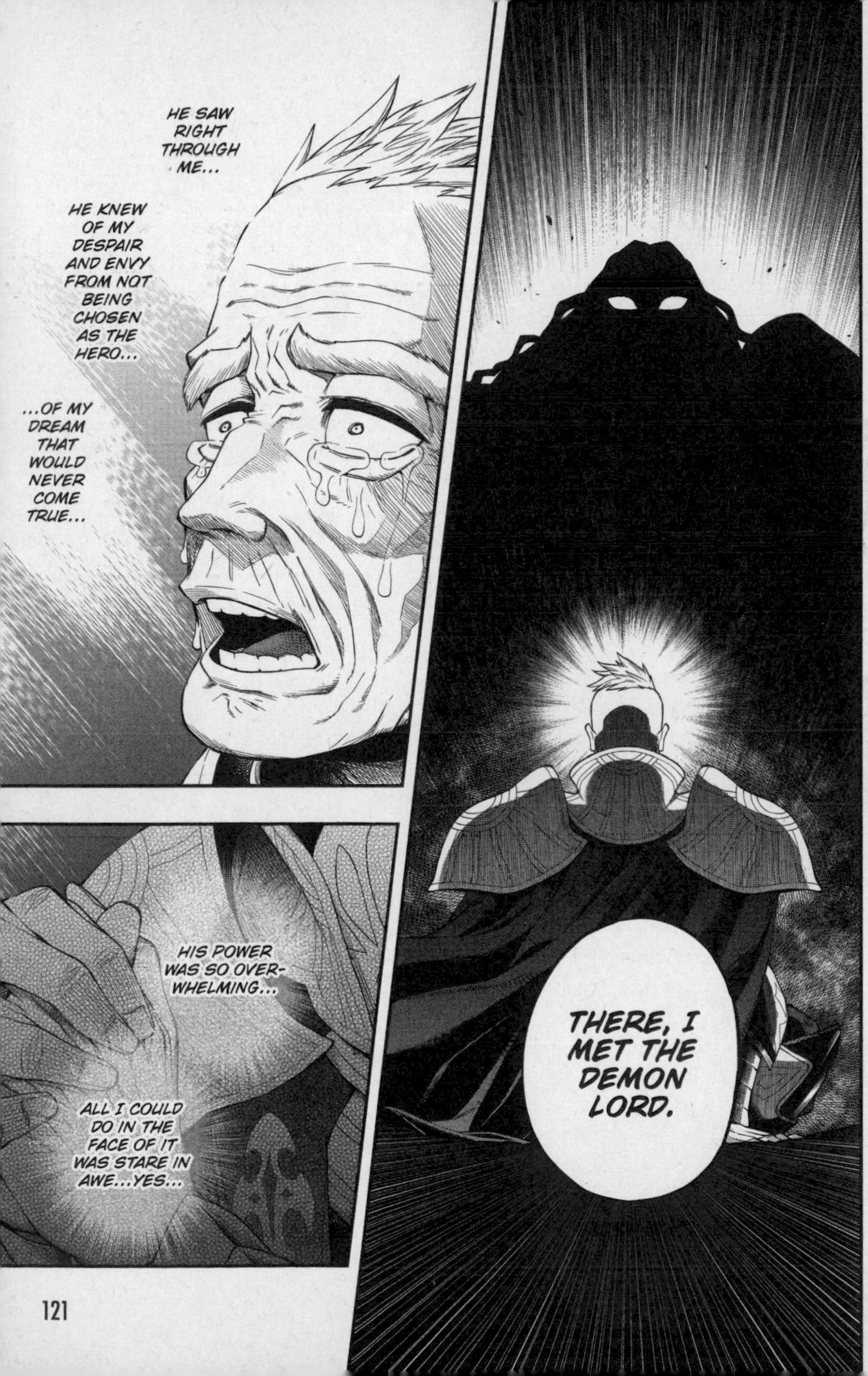
THERE, I MET THE DEMON LORD.
HE SAW RIGHT THROUGH ME...
HE KNEW OF MY DESPAIR AND ENVY FROM NOT BEING CHOSEN AS THE HERO...
...OF MY DREAM THAT WOULD NEVER COME TRUE...
HIS POWER WAS SO OVER-WHELMING...
ALL I COULD DO IN THE FACE OF IT WAS STARE IN AWE...YES...

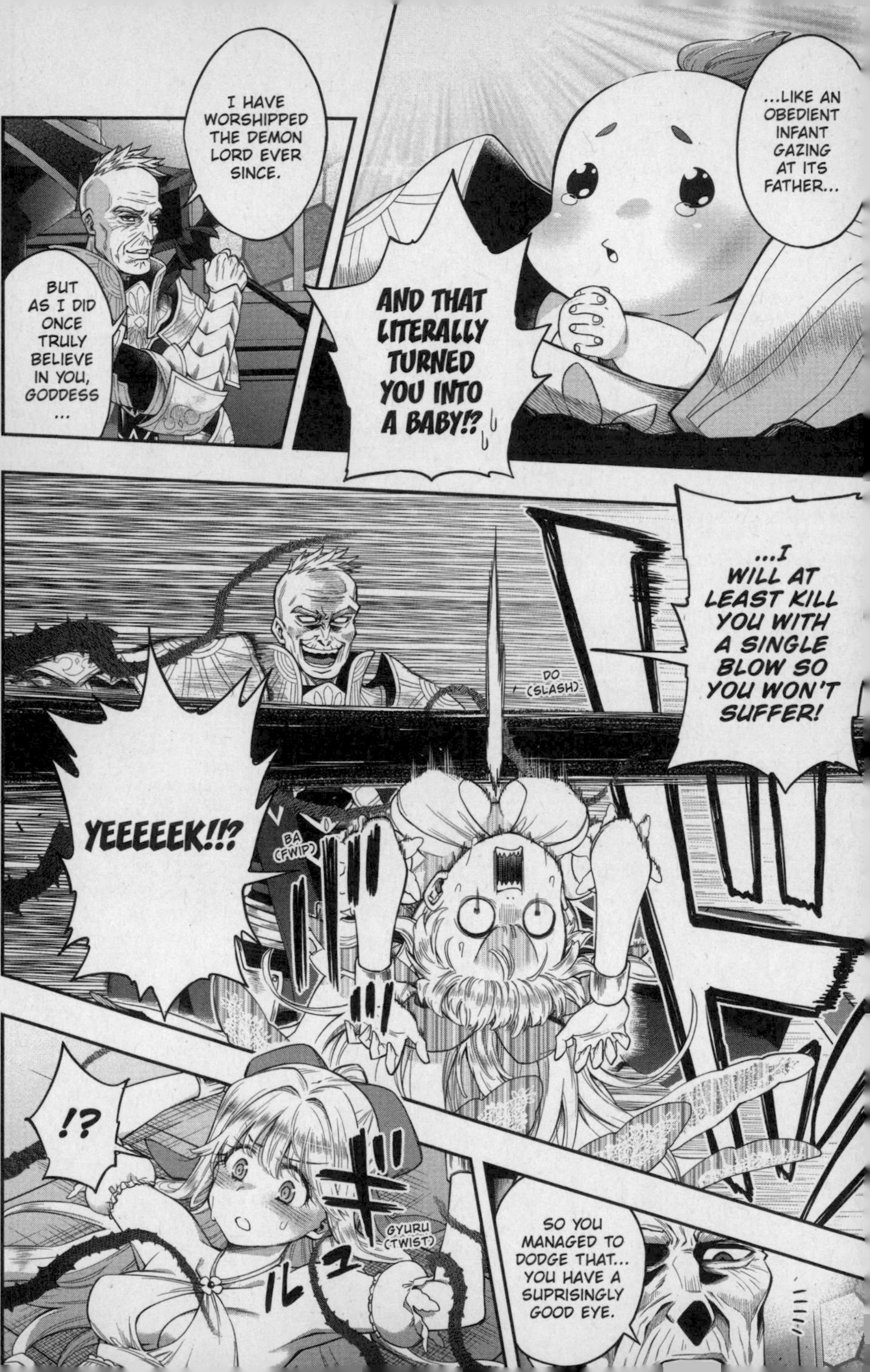
...LIKE AN OBEDIENT INFANT GAZING AT ITS FATHER...
AND THAT LITERALLY TURNED YOU INTO A BABY!?
I HAVE WORSHIPPED THE DEMON LORD EVER SINCE.
BUT AS I DID ONCE TRULY BELIEVE IN YOU, GODDESS...
...I WILL AT LEAST KILL YOU WITH A SINGLE BLOW SO YOU WON'T SUFFER!
DO (SLASH)
YEEEEEK!!?
BA (FWIP)
SO YOU MANAGED TO DODGE THAT... YOU HAVE A SUPRISINGLY GOOD EYE.
!?
GYURU (TWIST)

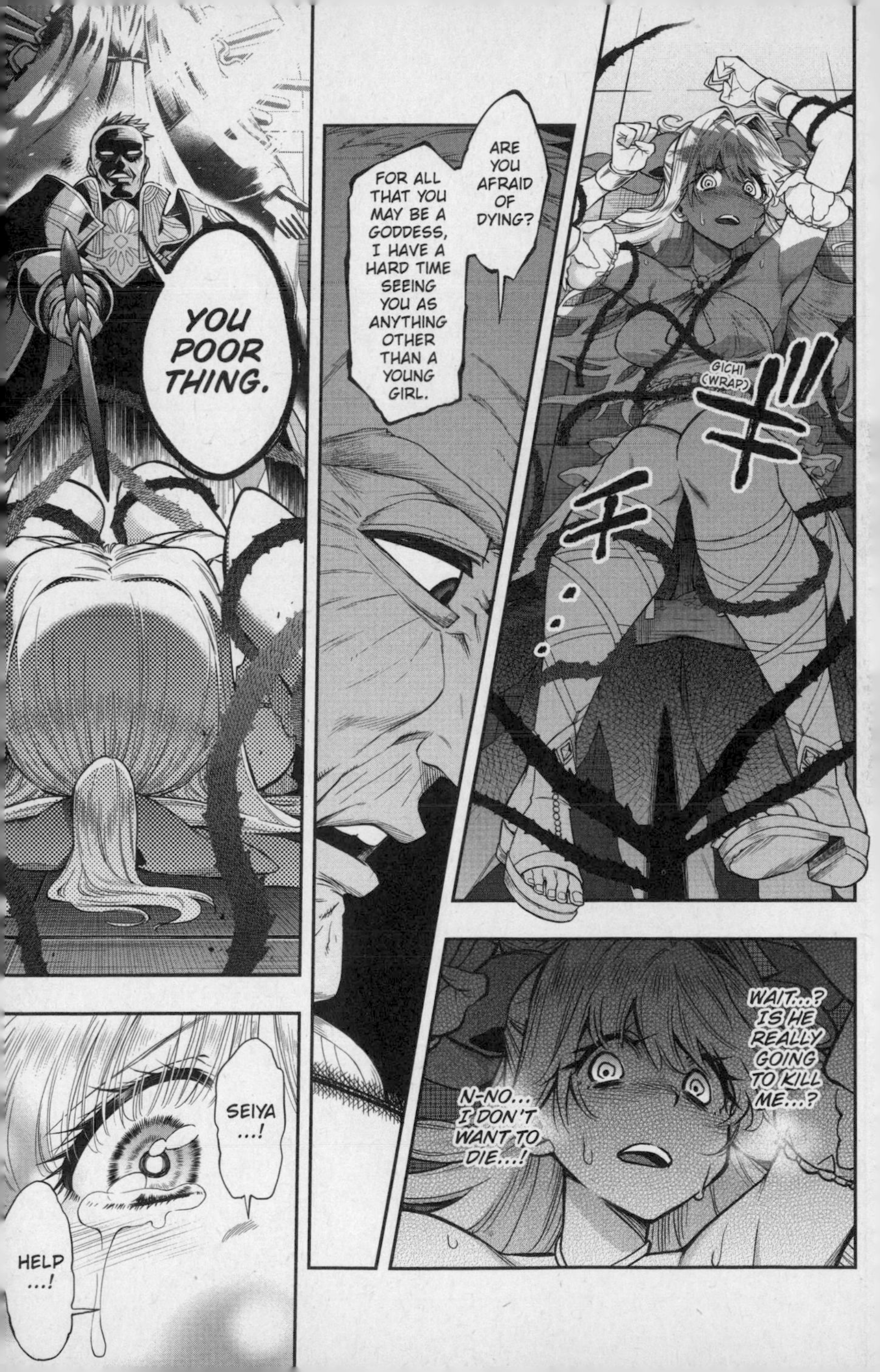
GICHI (WRAP)
WAIT...? IS HE REALLY GOING TO KILL ME...?
N-NO... I DON'T WANT TO DIE...!
ARE YOU AFRAID OF DYING?
FOR ALL THAT YOU MAY BE A GODDESS, I HAVE A HARD TIME SEEING YOU AS ANYTHING OTHER THAN A YOUNG GIRL.
YOU POOR THING.
SEIYA ...!
HELP ...!

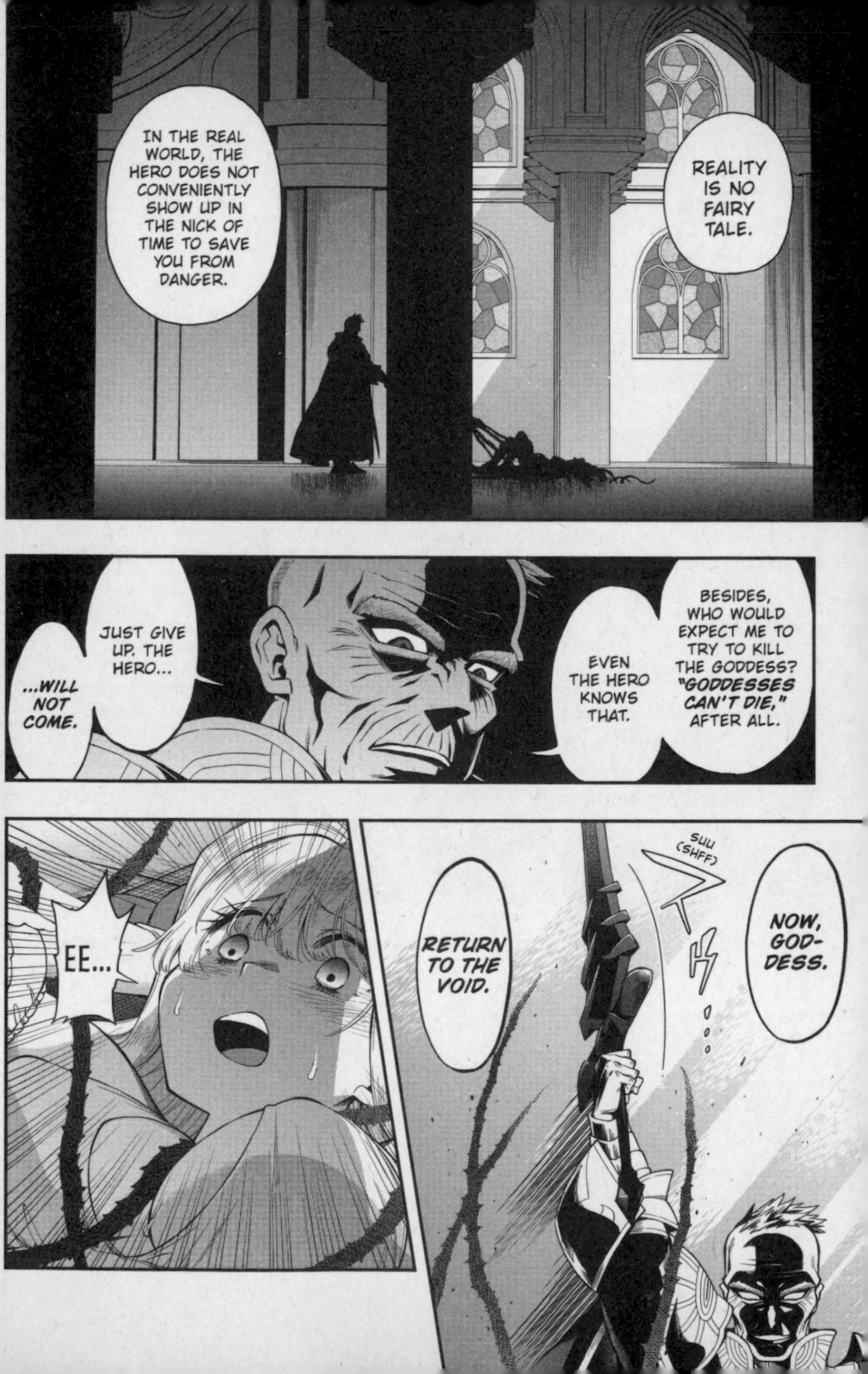
REALITY IS NO FAIRY TALE.
IN THE REAL WORLD, THE HERO DOES NOT CONVENIENTLY SHOW UP IN THE NICK OF TIME TO SAVE YOU FROM DANGER.
BESIDES, WHO WOULD EXPECT ME TO TRY TO KILL THE GODDESS? "GODDESSES CAN'T DIE," AFTER ALL.
EVEN THE HERO KNOWS THAT.
JUST GIVE UP. THE HERO...
...WILL NOT COME.
SUU (SHFF)
NOW, GOD-DESS.
RETURN TO THE VOID.
EE...

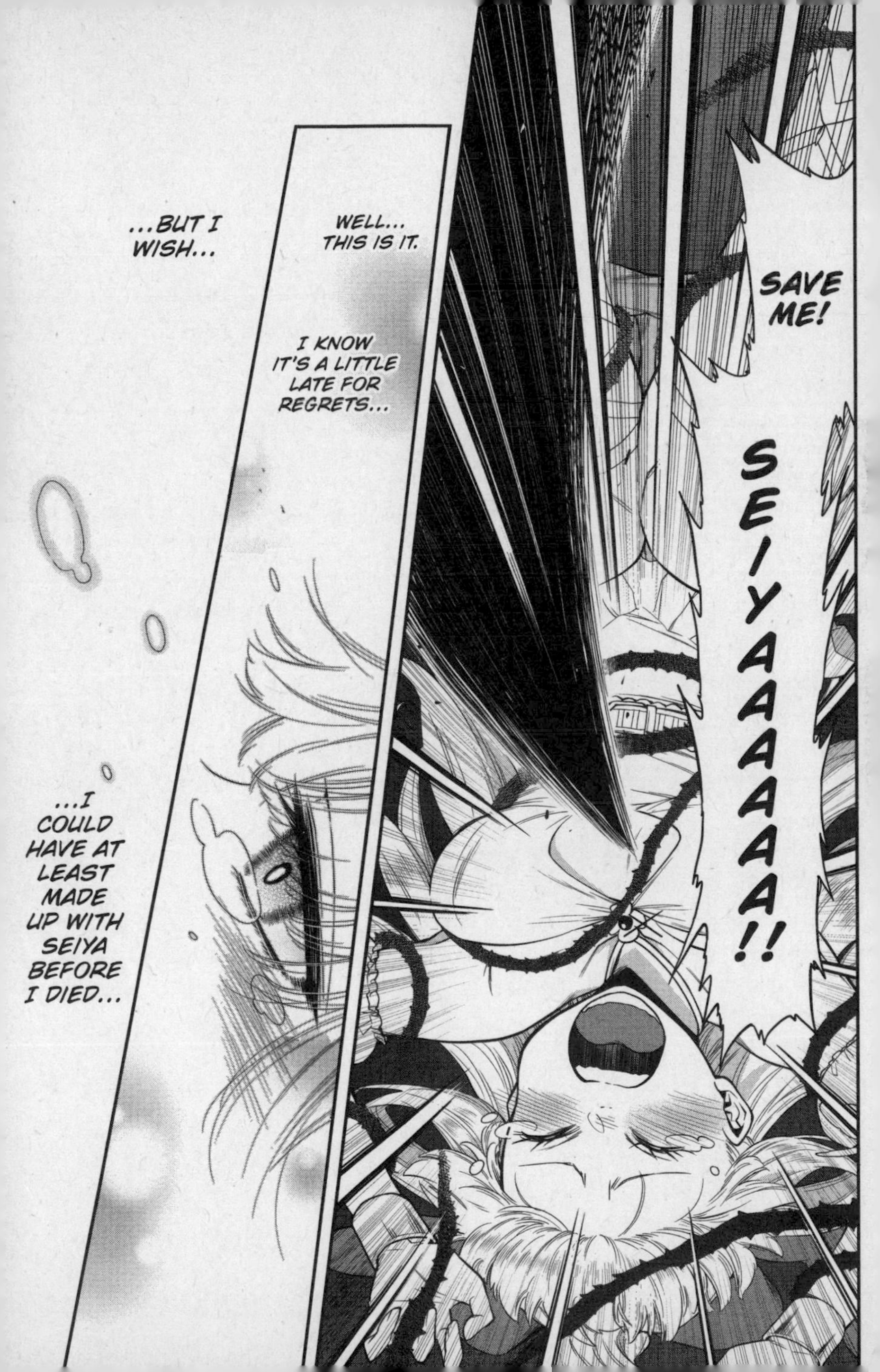
SAVE ME!
SEIYAAAAAA!!
WELL... THIS IS IT.
I KNOW IT'S A LITTLE LATE FOR REGRETS...
...BUT I WISH...
...I COULD HAVE AT LEAST MADE UP WITH SEIYA BEFORE I DIED...

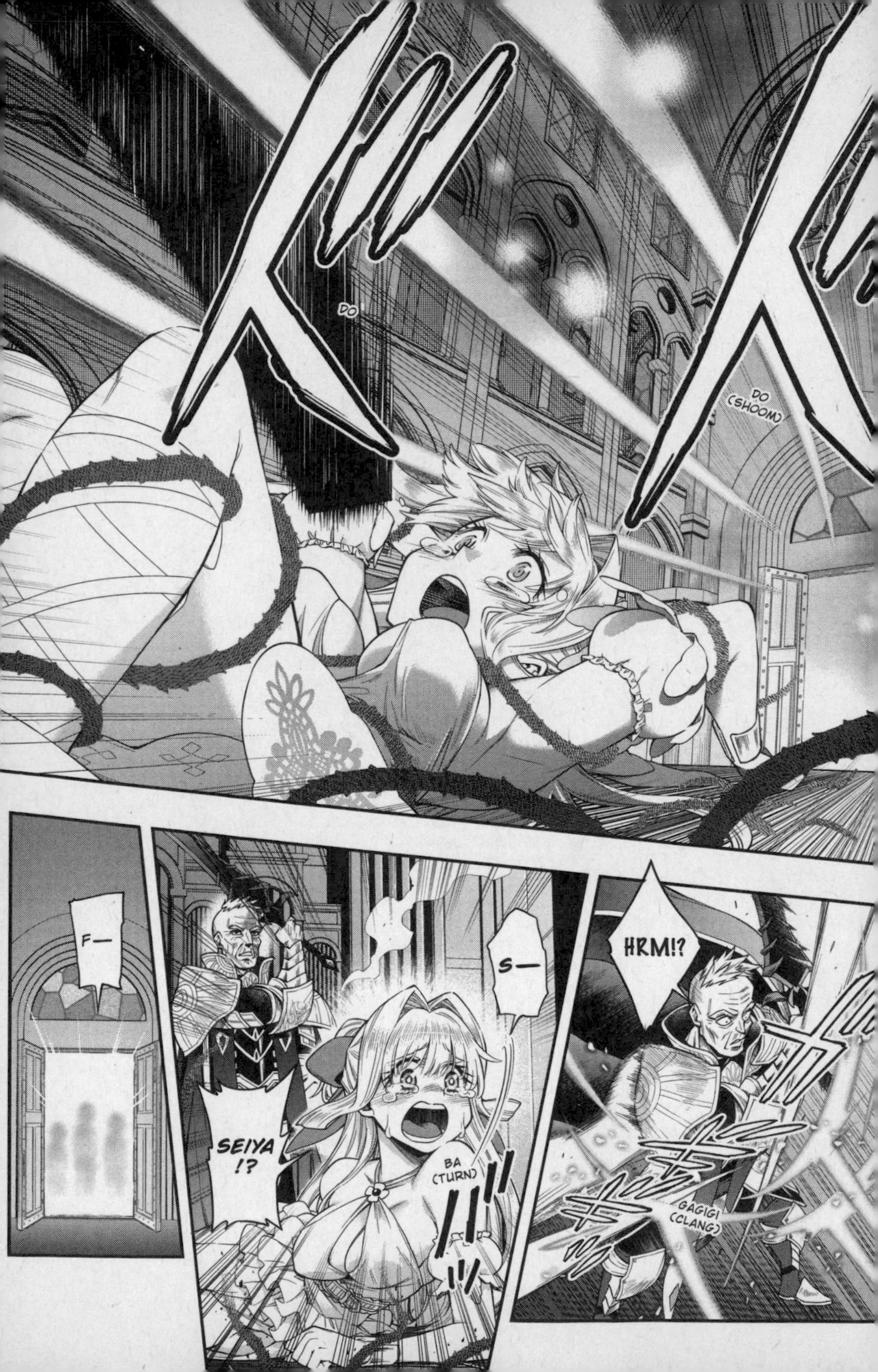
DO (SHOOM)
DO
HRM!?
GAGIGI (CLANG)
S—
SEIYA !?
BA (TURN)
F—

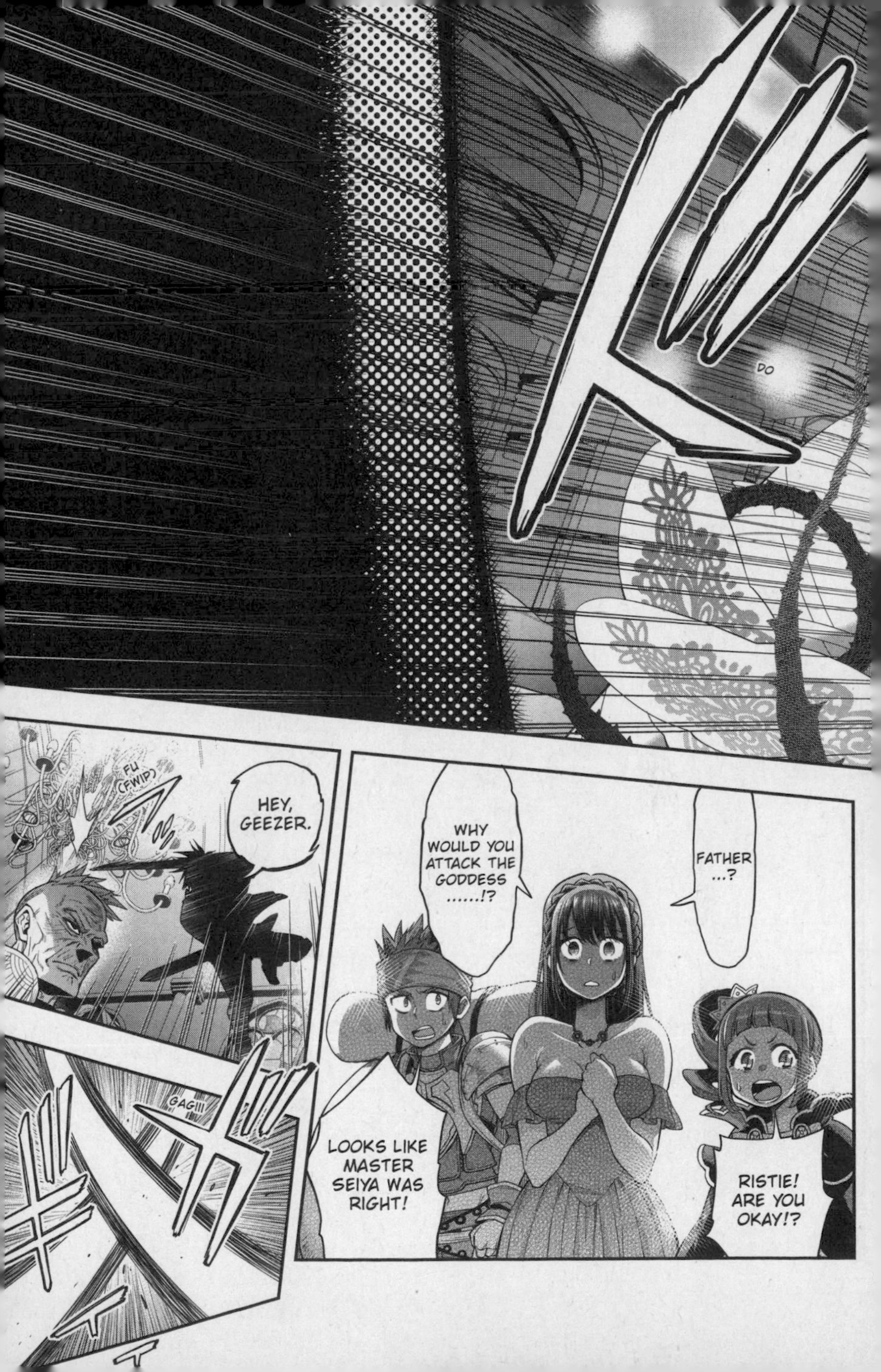
DO
FATHER ...?
WHY WOULD YOU ATTACK THE GODDESS ......!?
RISTIE! ARE YOU OKAY!?
LOOKS LIKE MASTER SEIYA WAS RIGHT!
HEY, GEEZER.
FU (FWIP)
GAG

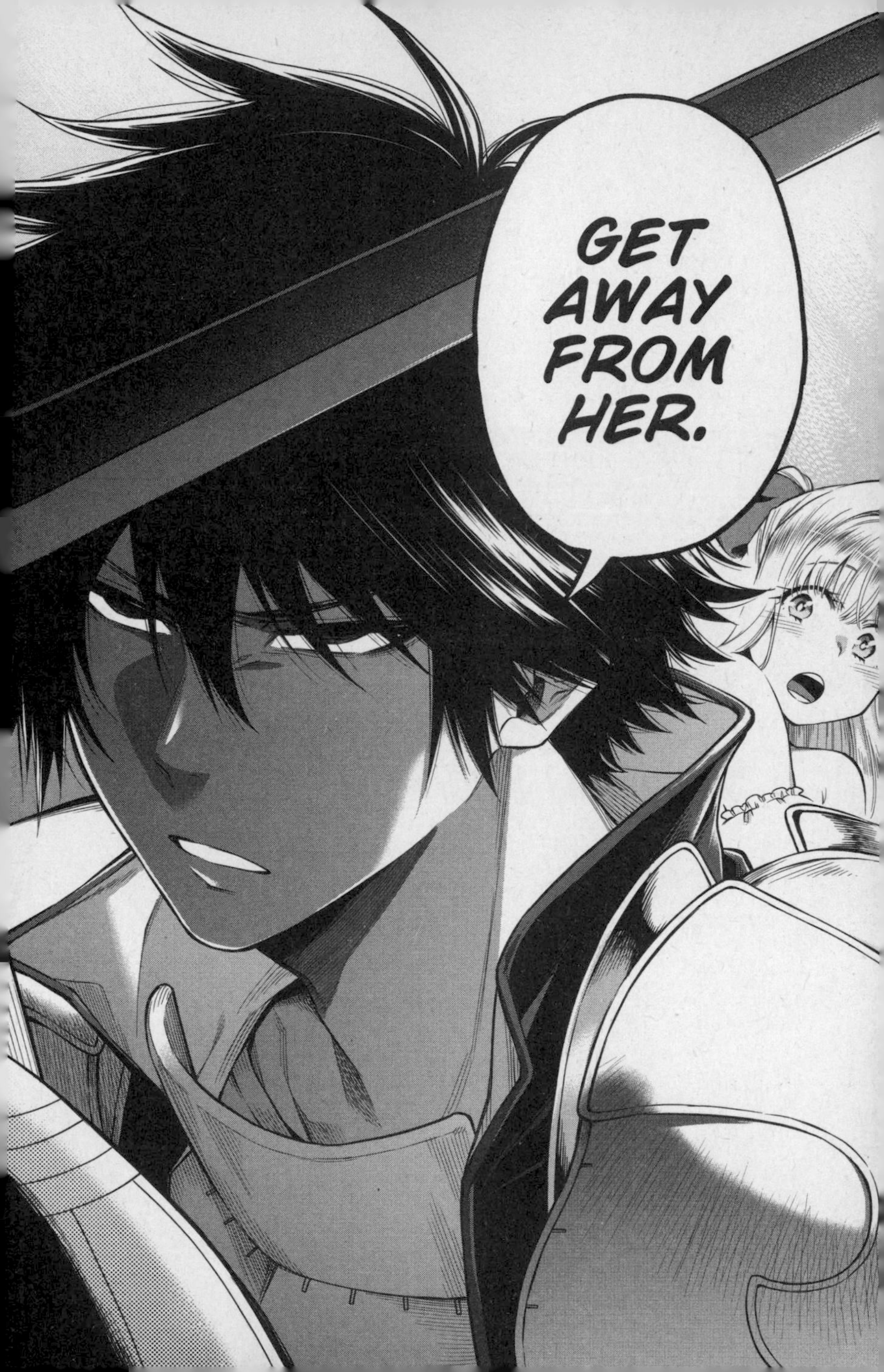
GET AWAY FROM HER.

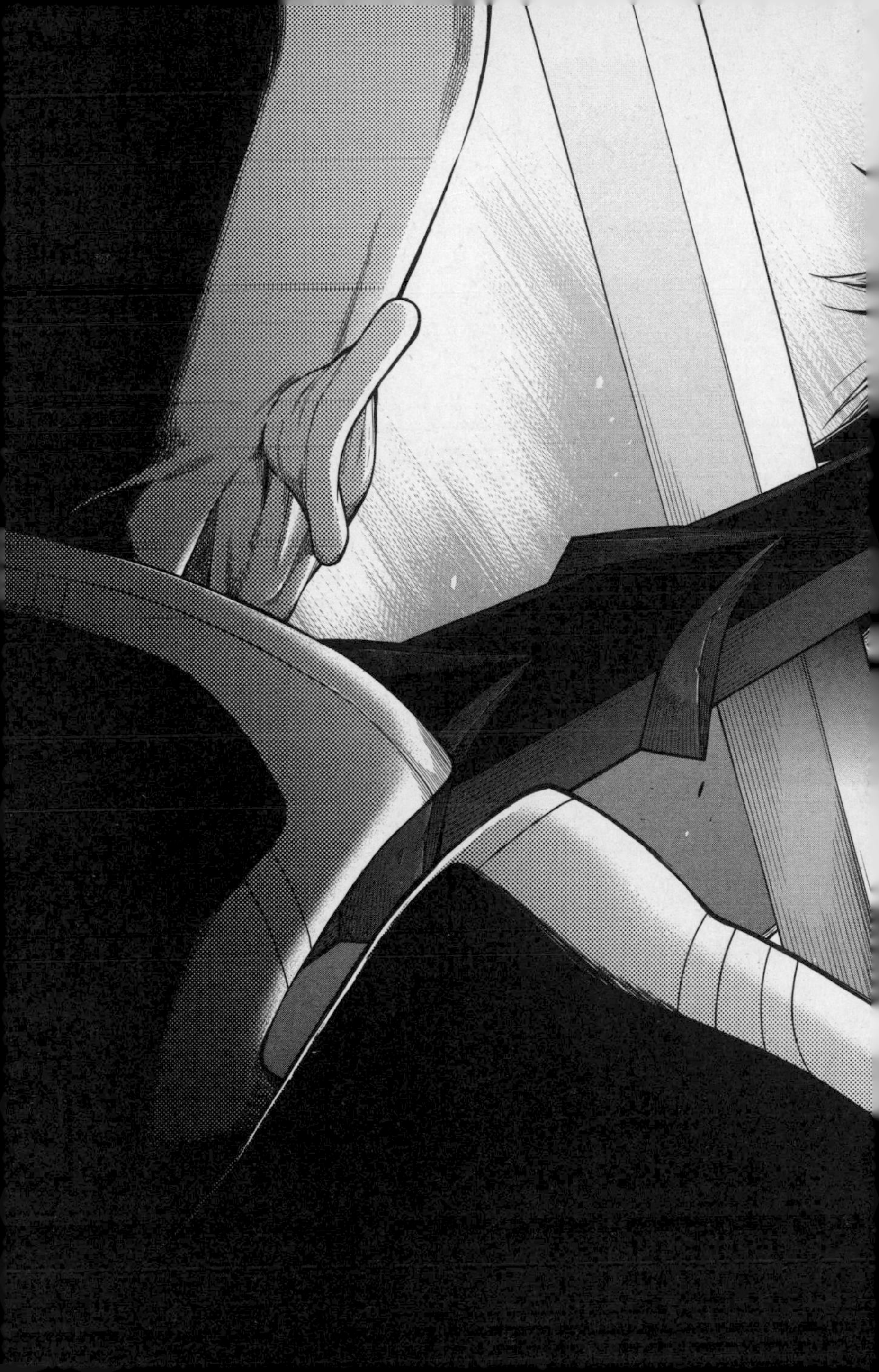

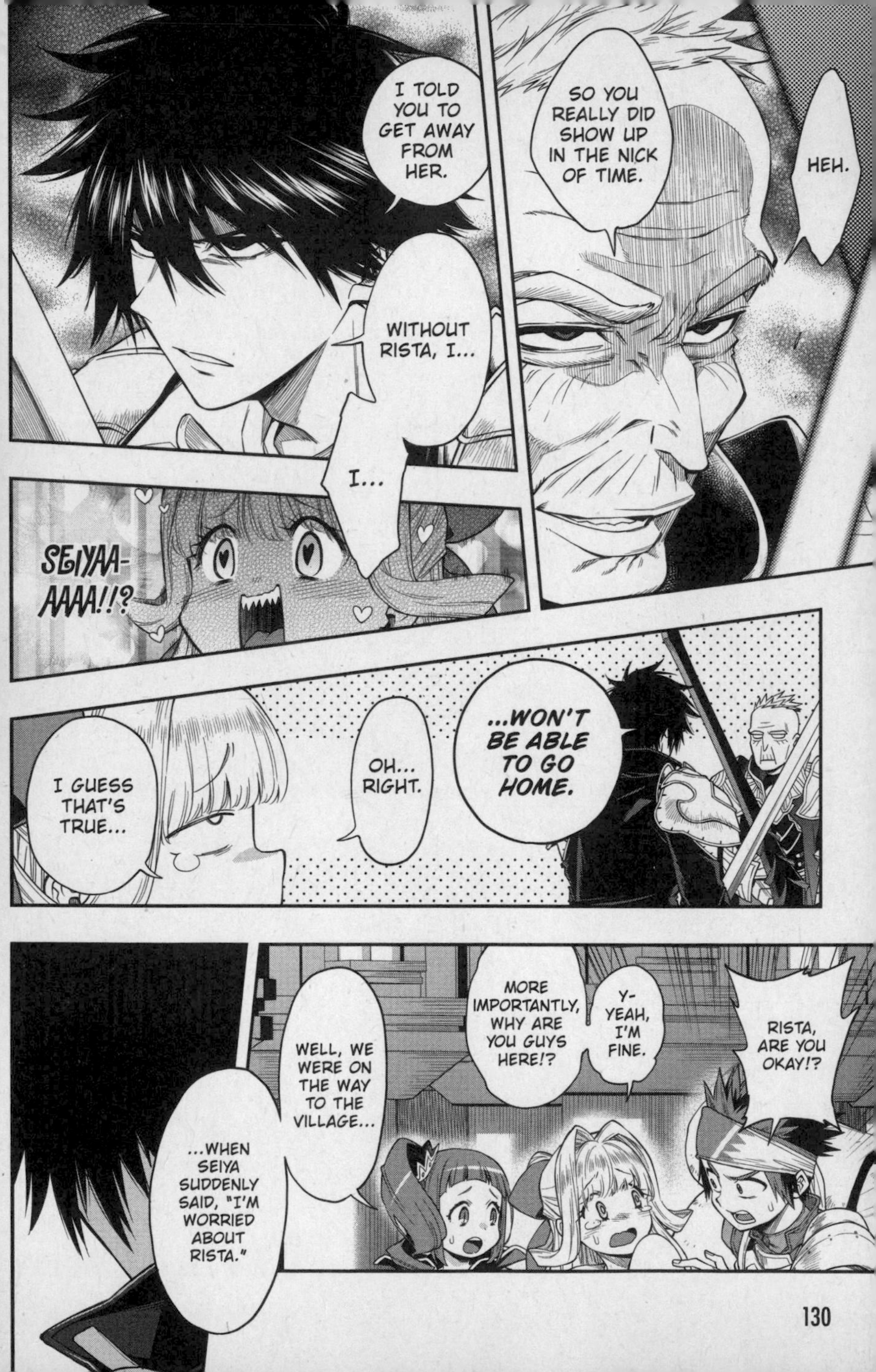
HEH.
SO YOU REALLY DID SHOW UP IN THE NICK OF TIME.
I TOLD YOU TO GET AWAY FROM HER.
WITHOUT RISTA, I...
I...
SEIYAA-AAAA!!?
...WON'T BE ABLE TO GO HOME.
OH... RIGHT.
I GUESS THAT'S TRUE...
RISTA, ARE YOU OKAY!?
Y-YEAH, I'M FINE.
MORE IMPORTANTLY, WHY ARE YOU GUYS HERE!?
WELL, WE WERE ON THE WAY TO THE VILLAGE...
...WHEN SEIYA SUDDENLY SAID, "I'M WORRIED ABOUT RISTA."

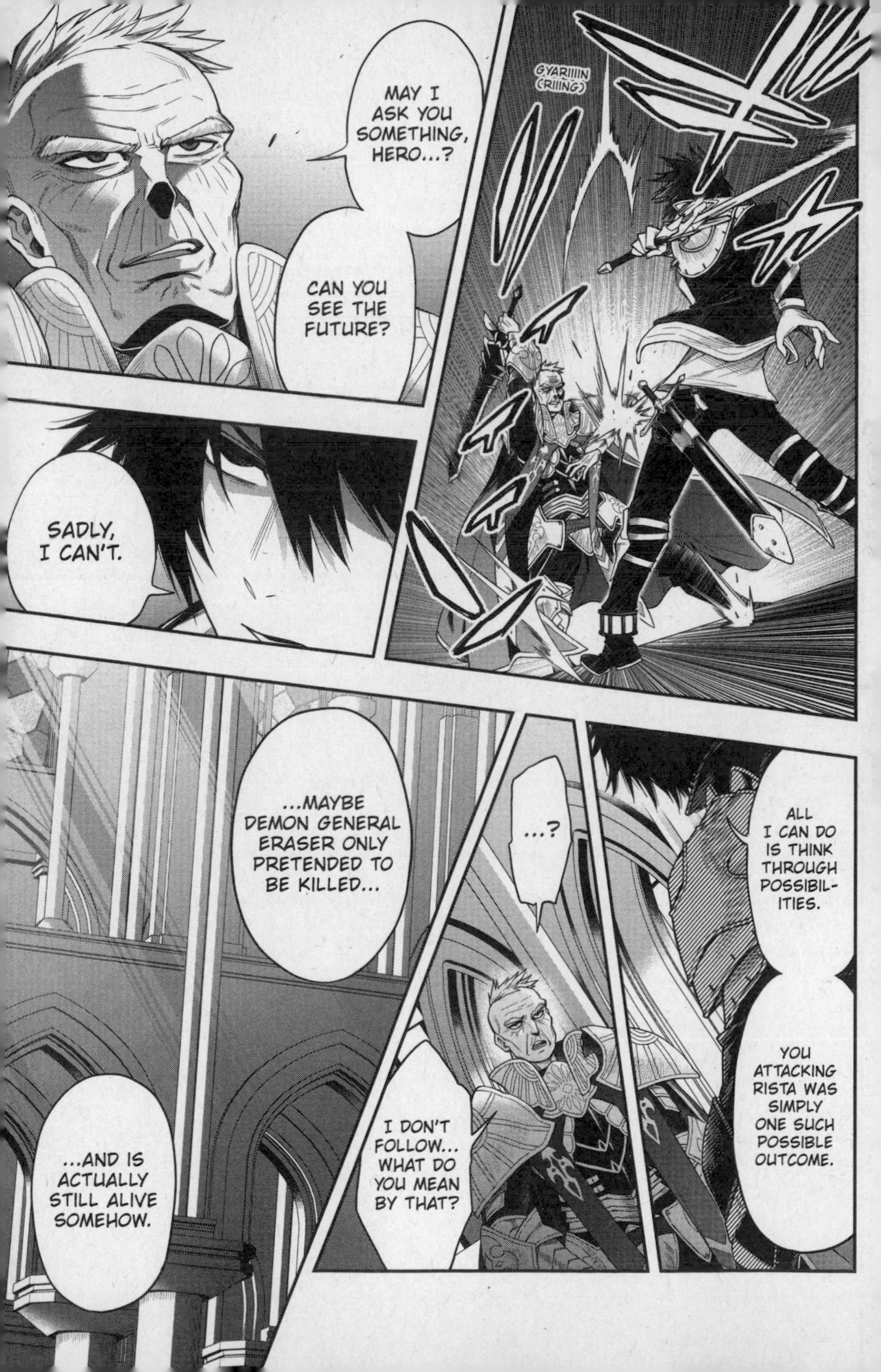
GYARIIIN (RIIING)
MAY I ASK YOU SOMETHING, HERO...?
CAN YOU SEE THE FUTURE?
SADLY, I CAN'T.
ALL I CAN DO IS THINK THROUGH POSSIBIL-ITIES.
YOU ATTACKING RISTA WAS SIMPLY ONE SUCH POSSIBLE OUTCOME.
...?
I DON'T FOLLOW... WHAT DO YOU MEAN BY THAT?
...MAYBE DEMON GENERAL ERASER ONLY PRETENDED TO BE KILLED...
...AND IS ACTUALLY STILL ALIVE SOMEHOW.

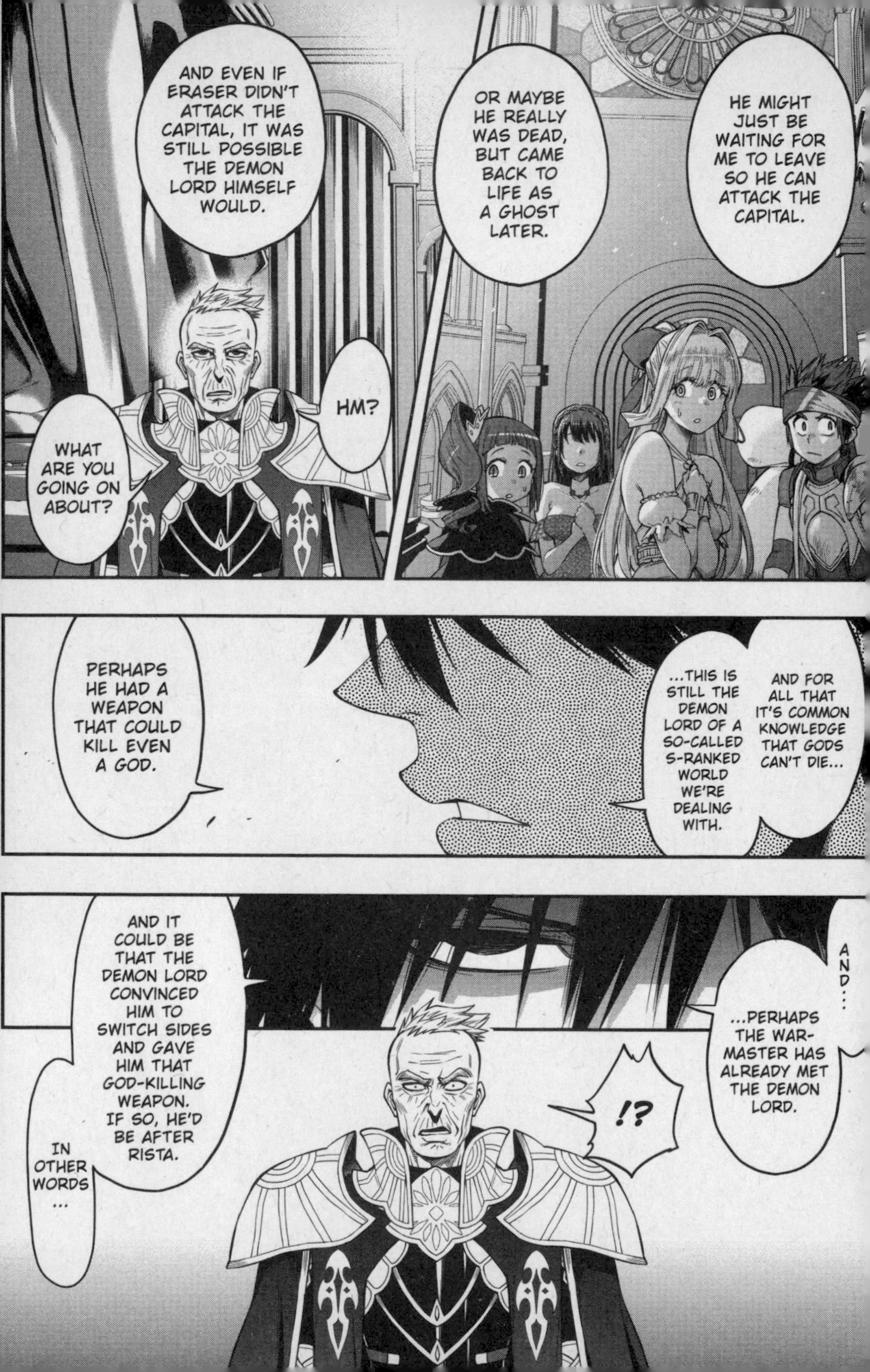
HE MIGHT JUST BE WAITING FOR ME TO LEAVE SO HE CAN ATTACK THE CAPITAL.
OR MAYBE HE REALLY WAS DEAD, BUT CAME BACK TO LIFE AS A GHOST LATER.
AND EVEN IF ERASER DIDN'T ATTACK THE CAPITAL, IT WAS STILL POSSIBLE THE DEMON LORD HIMSELF WOULD.
HM?
WHAT ARE YOU GOING ON ABOUT?
AND FOR ALL THAT IT'S COMMON KNOWLEDGE THAT GODS CAN'T DIE...
...THIS IS STILL THE DEMON LORD OF A SO-CALLED S-RANKED WORLD WE'RE DEALING WITH.
PERHAPS HE HAD A WEAPON THAT COULD KILL EVEN A GOD.
AND...
...PERHAPS THE WAR-MASTER HAS ALREADY MET THE DEMON LORD.
!?
AND IT COULD BE THAT THE DEMON LORD CONVINCED HIM TO SWITCH SIDES AND GAVE HIM THAT GOD-KILLING WEAPON. IF SO, HE'D BE AFTER RISTA.
IN OTHER WORDS...

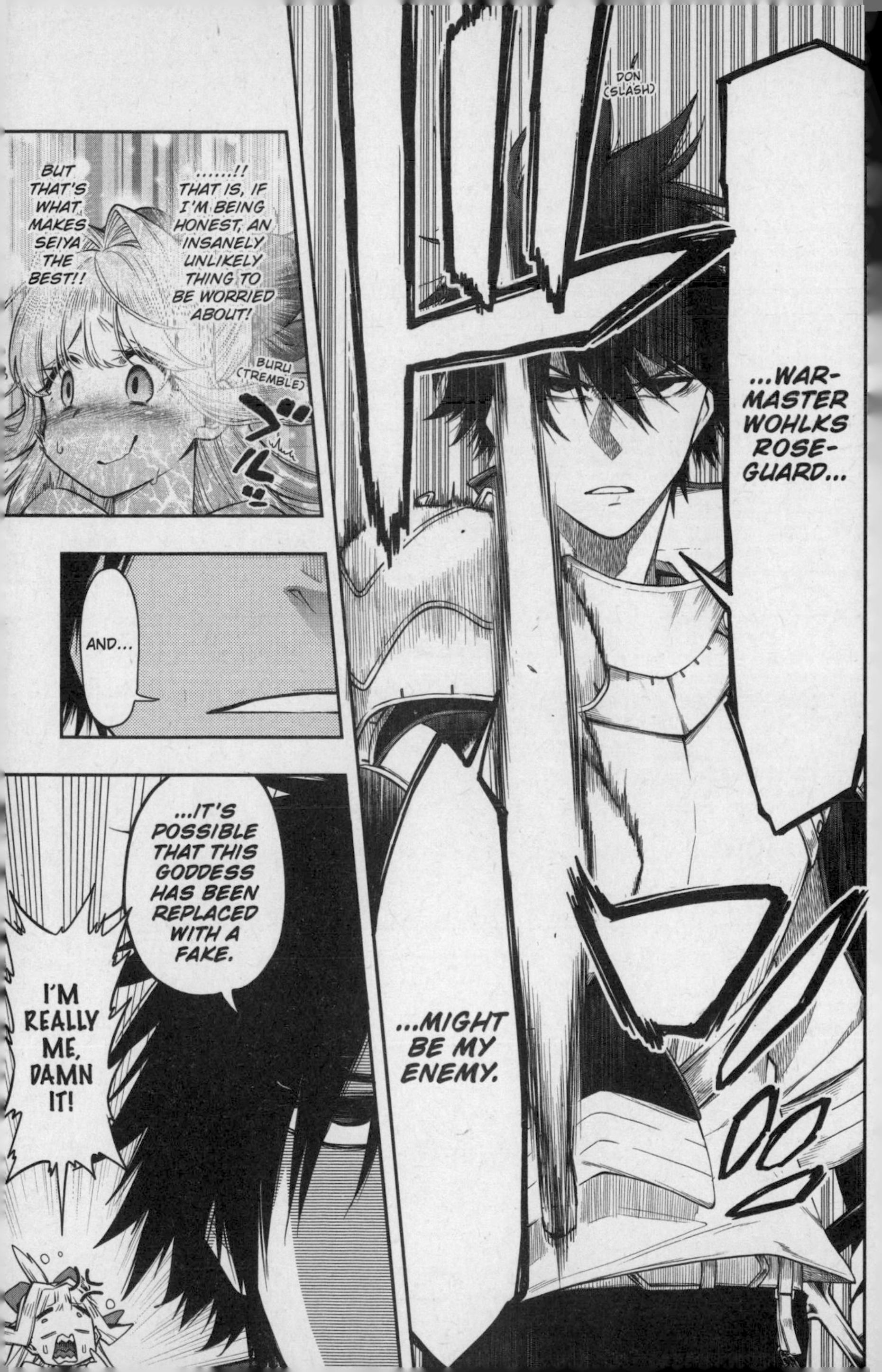
DON (SLASH)
...WAR-MASTER WOHLKS ROSE-GUARD...
...MIGHT BE MY ENEMY.
......!! THAT IS, IF I'M BEING HONEST, AN INSANELY UNLIKELY THING TO BE WORRIED ABOUT!
BUT THAT'S WHAT MAKES SEIYA THE BEST!!
BURU (TREMBLE)
AND...
...IT'S POSSIBLE THAT THIS GODDESS HAS BEEN REPLACED WITH A FAKE.
I'M REALLY ME, DAMN IT!

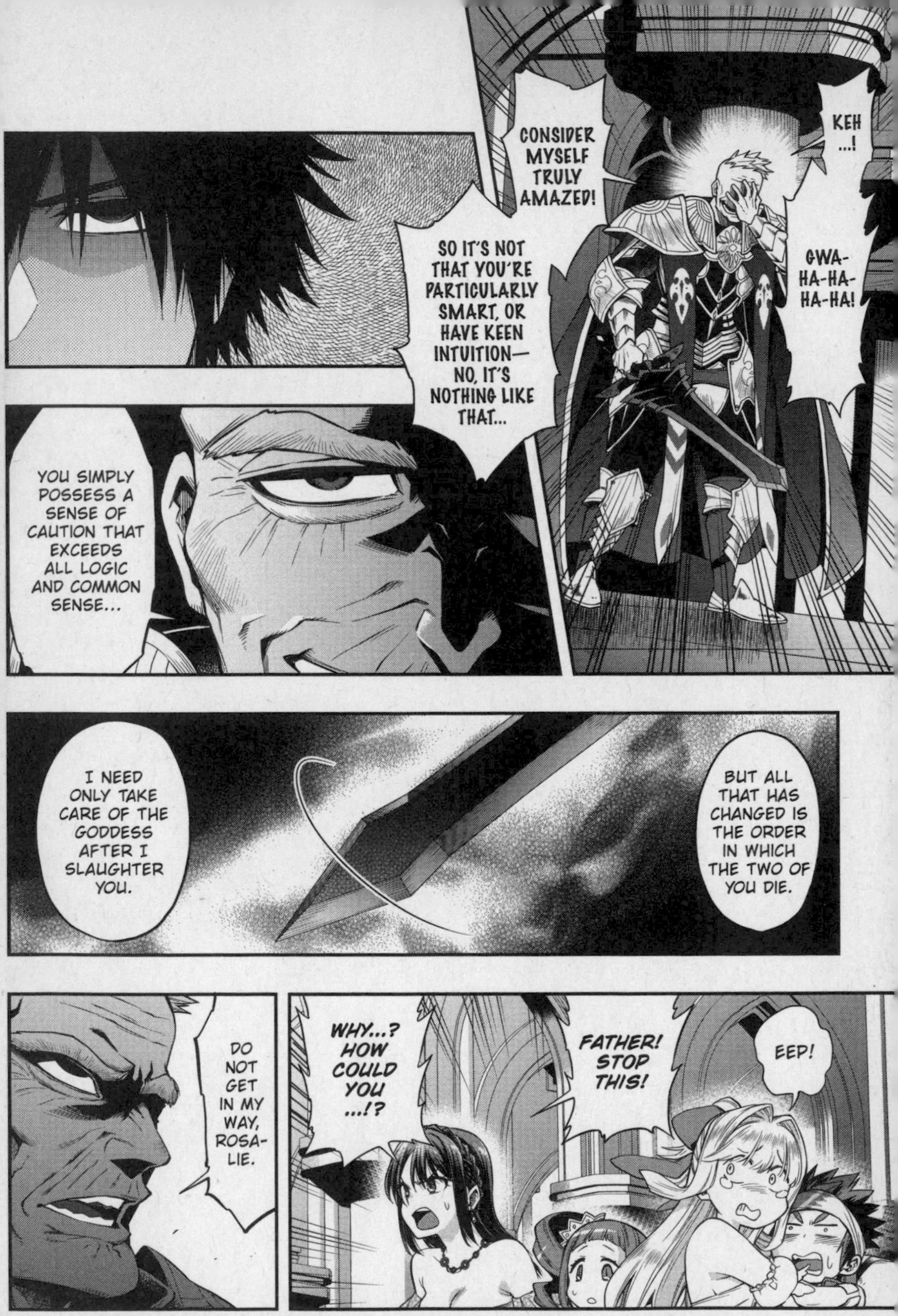
KEH ...!
CONSIDER MYSELF TRULY AMAZED!
GWA-HA-HA-HA-HA!
SO IT'S NOT THAT YOU'RE PARTICULARLY SMART, OR HAVE KEEN INTUITION— NO, IT'S NOTHING LIKE THAT...
YOU SIMPLY POSSESS A SENSE OF CAUTION THAT EXCEEDS ALL LOGIC AND COMMON SENSE...
BUT ALL THAT HAS CHANGED IS THE ORDER IN WHICH THE TWO OF YOU DIE.
I NEED ONLY TAKE CARE OF THE GODDESS AFTER I SLAUGHTER YOU.
EEP!
FATHER! STOP THIS!
WHY...? HOW COULD YOU ...!?
DO NOT GET IN MY WAY, ROSALIE.

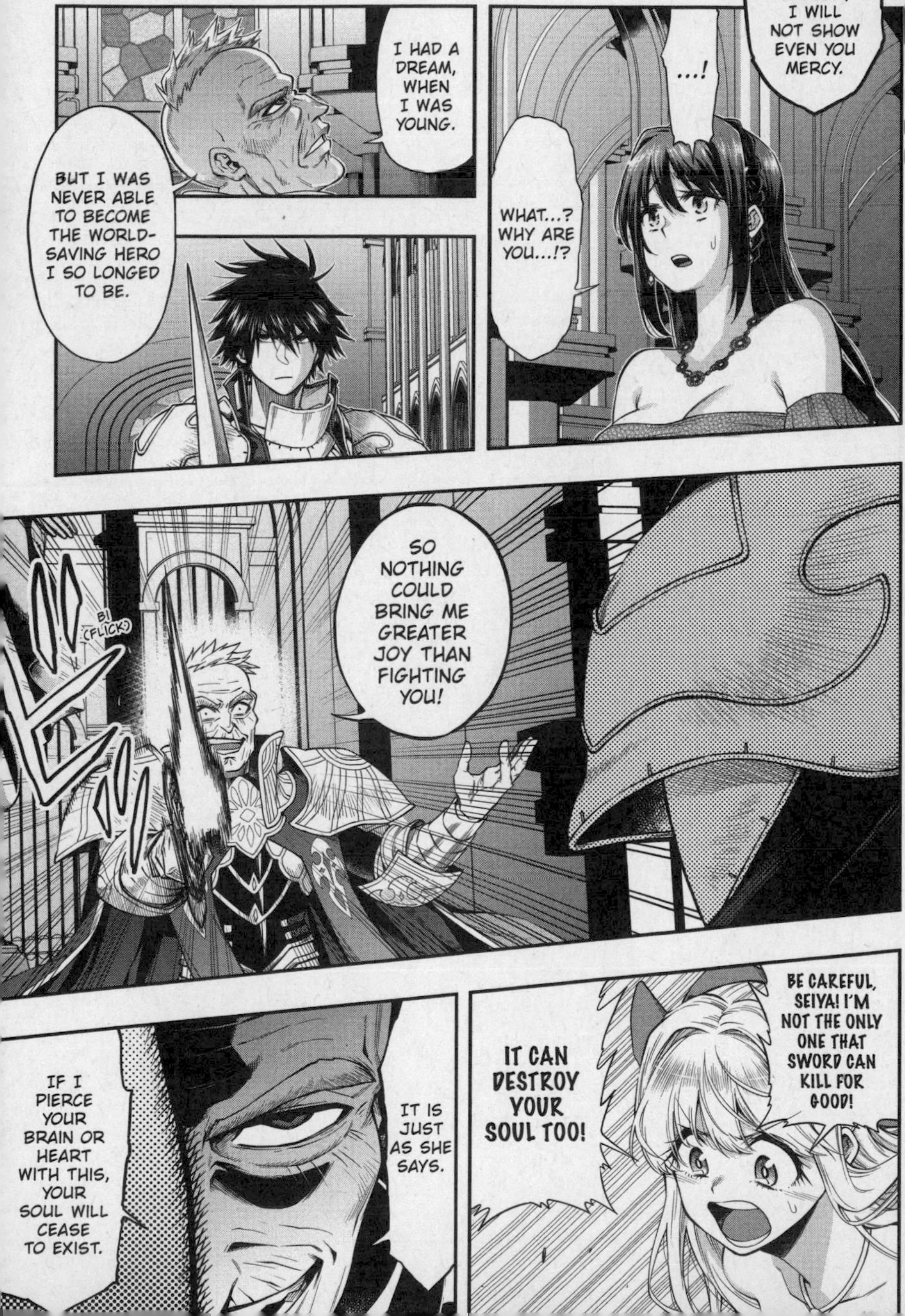
IF YOU COME ANY CLOSER, I WILL NOT SHOW EVEN YOU MERCY.
...!
WHAT...? WHY ARE YOU...!?
I HAD A DREAM, WHEN I WAS YOUNG.
BUT I WAS NEVER ABLE TO BECOME THE WORLD-SAVING HERO I SO LONGED TO BE.
SO NOTHING COULD BRING ME GREATER JOY THAN FIGHTING YOU!
BI (FLICK)
BE CAREFUL, SEIYA! I'M NOT THE ONLY ONE THAT SWORD CAN KILL FOR GOOD!
IT CAN DESTROY YOUR SOUL TOO!
IT IS JUST AS SHE SAYS.
IF I PIERCE YOUR BRAIN OR HEART WITH THIS, YOUR SOUL WILL CEASE TO EXIST.

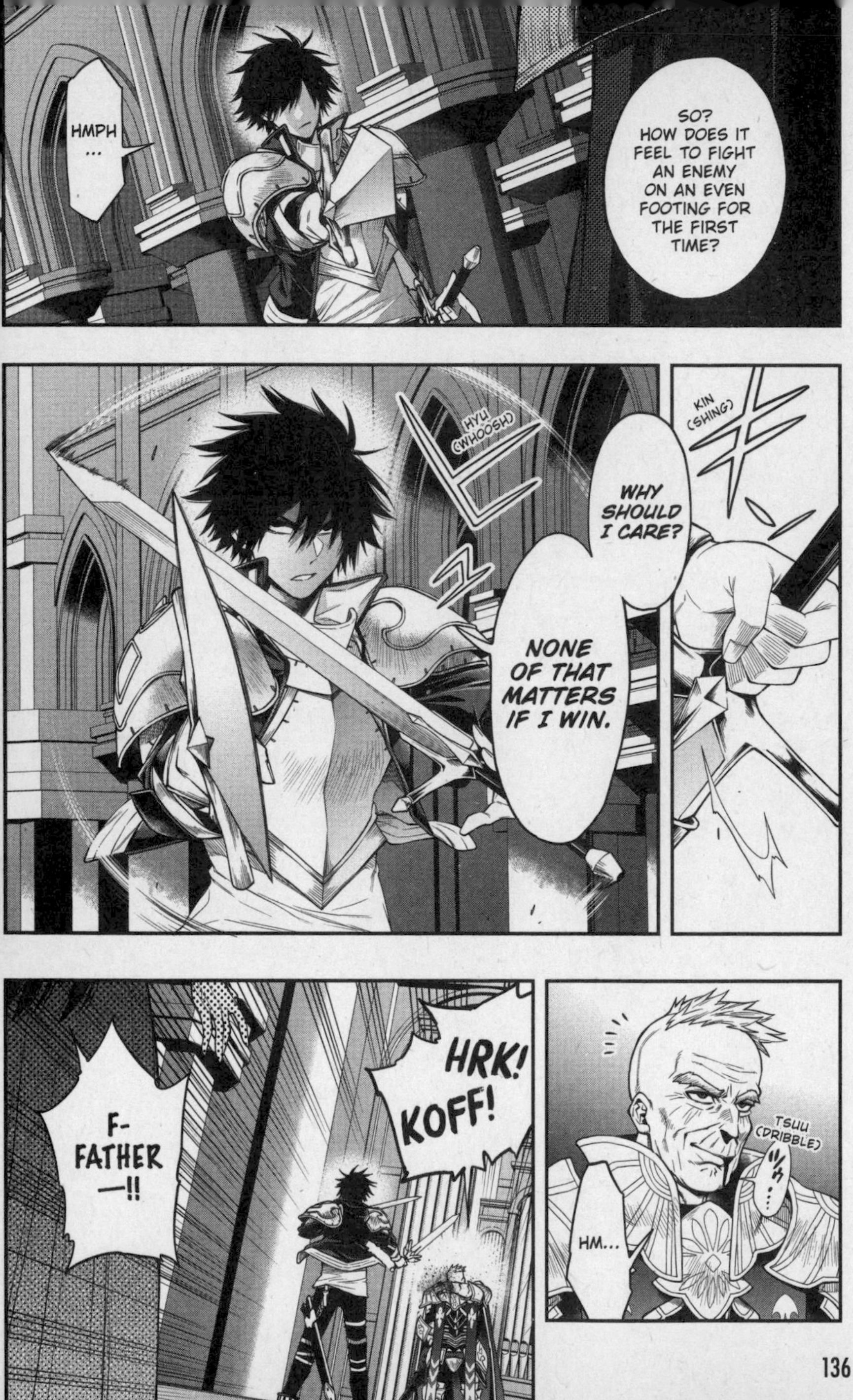
SO? HOW DOES IT FEEL TO FIGHT AN ENEMY ON AN EVEN FOOTING FOR THE FIRST TIME?
HMPH ...
KIN (SHING)
HYU (WHOOSH)
WHY SHOULD I CARE?
NONE OF THAT MATTERS IF I WIN.
TSUU (DRIBBLE)
HM...
HRK! KOFF!
F-FATHER—!!

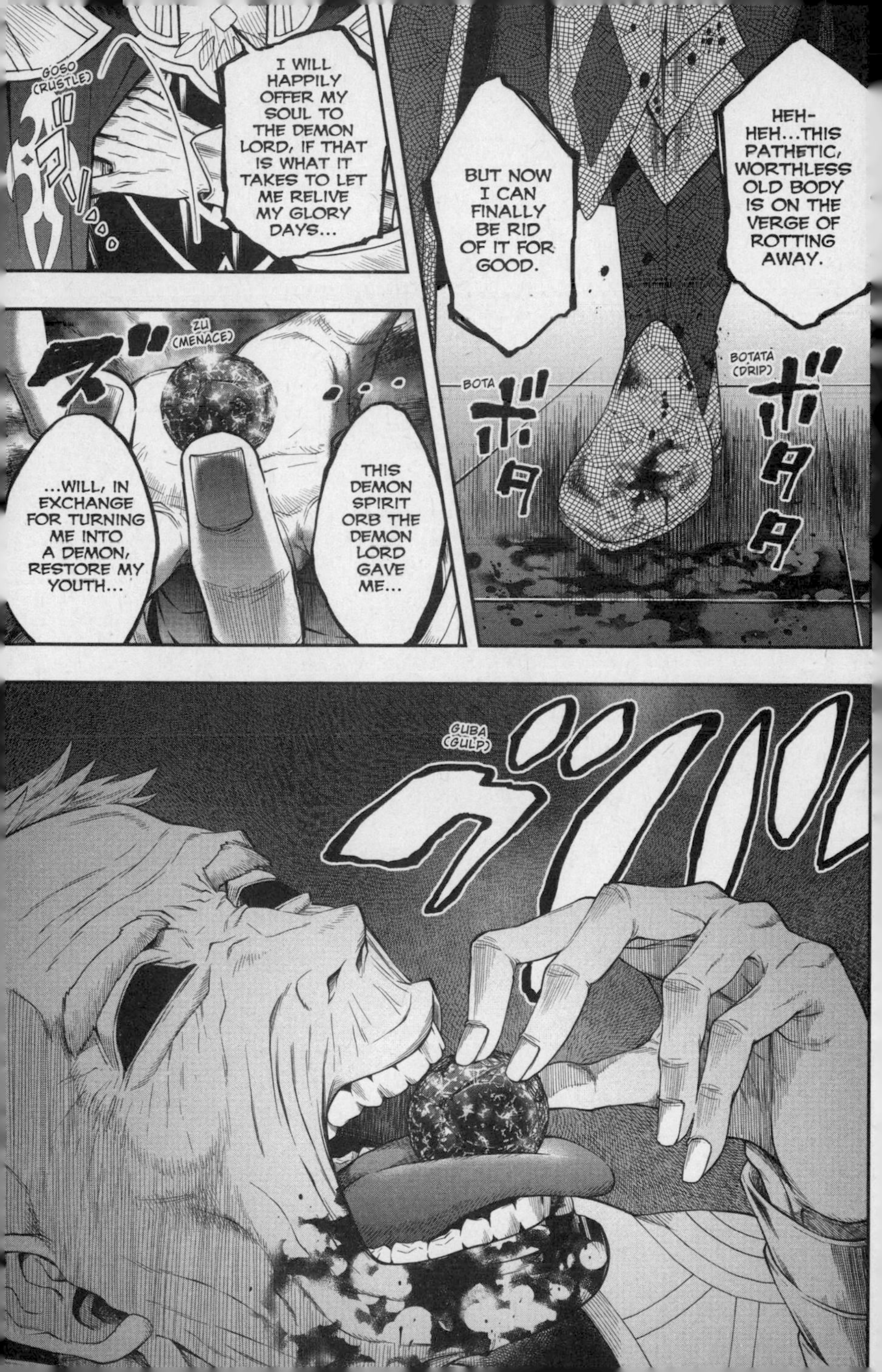
HEH-HEH…THIS PATHETIC, WORTHLESS OLD BODY IS ON THE VERGE OF ROTTING AWAY.
BUT NOW I CAN FINALLY BE RID OF IT FOR GOOD.
BOTATA (DRIP)
BOTA
GOSO (RUSTLE)
I WILL HAPPILY OFFER MY SOUL TO THE DEMON LORD, IF THAT IS WHAT IT TAKES TO LET ME RELIVE MY GLORY DAYS…
ZU (MENACE)
THIS DEMON SPIRIT ORB THE DEMON LORD GAVE ME…
…WILL, IN EXCHANGE FOR TURNING ME INTO A DEMON, RESTORE MY YOUTH…
GUBA (GULP)

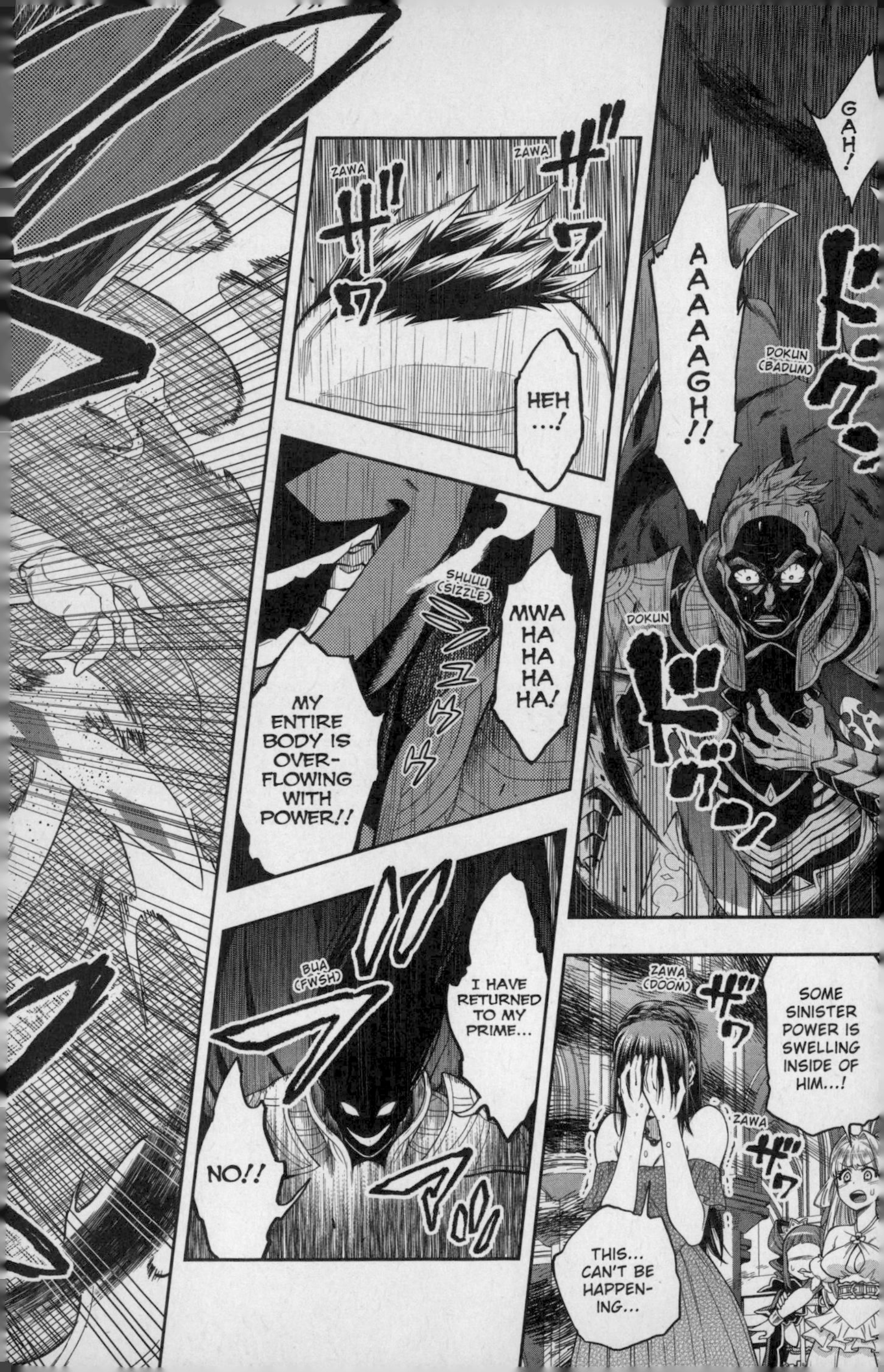
GAH!
DOKUN (BADUM)
AAAAAAGH!!
DOKUN
ZAWA
ZAWA
HEH ...!
SHUUU (SIZZLE)
MWA HA HA HA HA!
MY ENTIRE BODY IS OVER-FLOWING WITH POWER!!
BUA (FWSH)
I HAVE RETURNED TO MY PRIME...
NO!!
ZAWA (DOOM)
SOME SINISTER POWER IS SWELLING INSIDE OF HIM...!
ZAWA
THIS... CAN'T BE HAPPEN-ING...

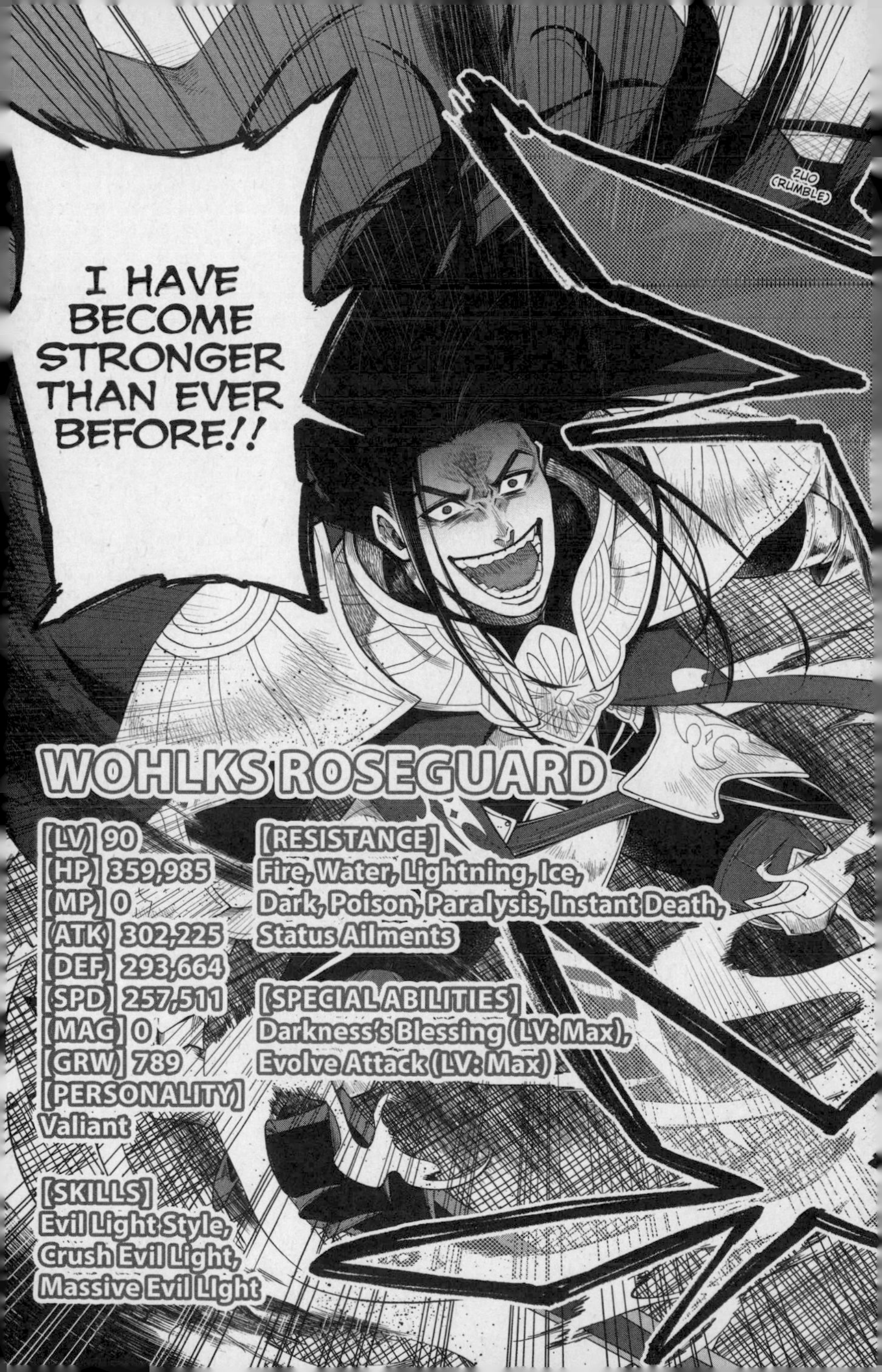
ZUO (RUMBLE)
I HAVE BECOME STRONGER THAN EVER BEFORE!!
WOHLKS ROSEGUARD
[LV] 90
[HP] 359,985
[MP] 0
[ATK] 302,225
[DEF] 293,664
[SPD] 257,511
[MAG] 0
[GRW] 789
[PERSONALITY]
Valiant
[SKILLS]
Evil Light Style, Crush Evil Light, Massive Evil Light
[RESISTANCE]
Fire, Water, Lightning, Ice, Dark, Poison, Paralysis, Instant Death, Status Ailments
[SPECIAL ABILITIES]
Darkness's Blessing (LV: Max), Evolve Attack (LV: Max)

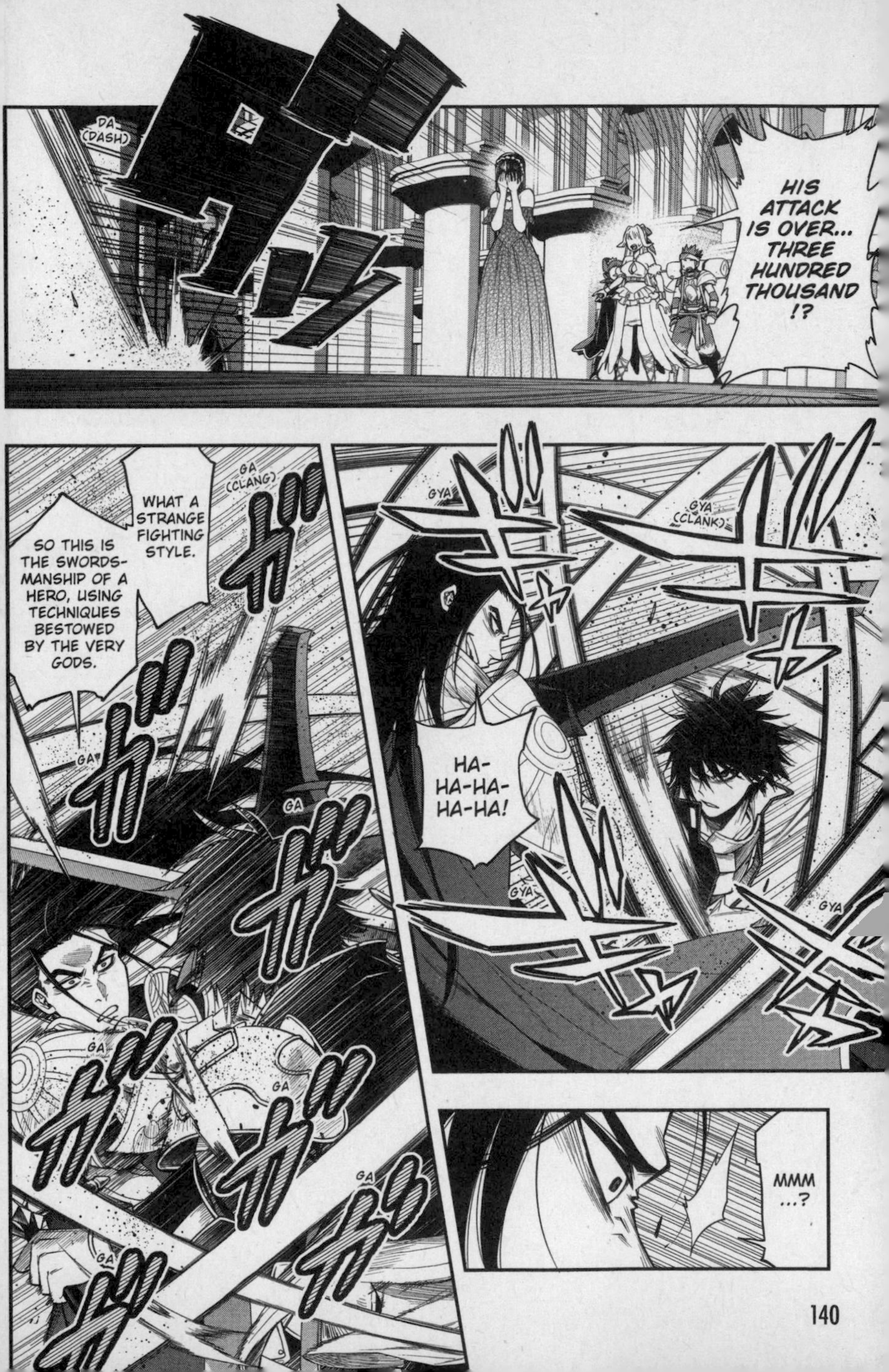
HIS ATTACK IS OVER... THREE HUNDRED THOUSAND!?
DA (DASH)
GYA (CLANK)
GYA
HA-HA-HA-HA-HA!
GYA
GYA
MMM ...?
WHAT A STRANGE FIGHTING STYLE.
GA (CLANG)
SO THIS IS THE SWORDSMANSHIP OF A HERO, USING TECHNIQUES BESTOWED BY THE VERY GODS.
GA
GA
GA
GA
GA
GA

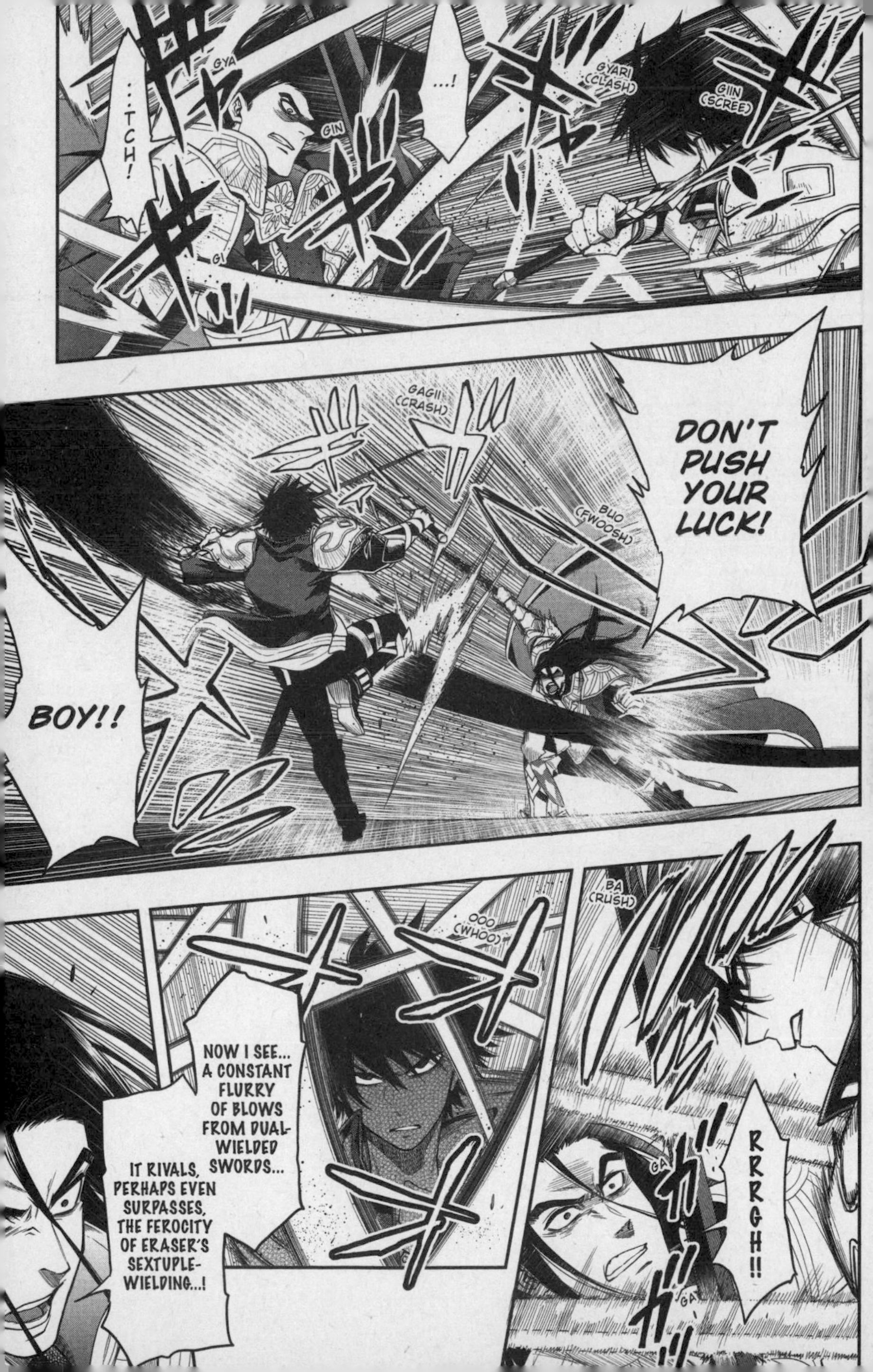
GIIN (SCREE)
GYARI (CLASH)
...!
GIN
GYA
...TCH!
GI
DON'T PUSH YOUR LUCK!
BUO (FWOOSH)
GAGII (CRASH)
BOY!!
BA (RUSH)
RRRGH!!
GA
GA
OOO (WHOO)
NOW I SEE... A CONSTANT FLURRY OF BLOWS FROM DUAL-WIELDED SWORDS...
IT RIVALS, PERHAPS EVEN SURPASSES, THE FEROCITY OF ERASER'S SEXTUPLE-WIELDING...!

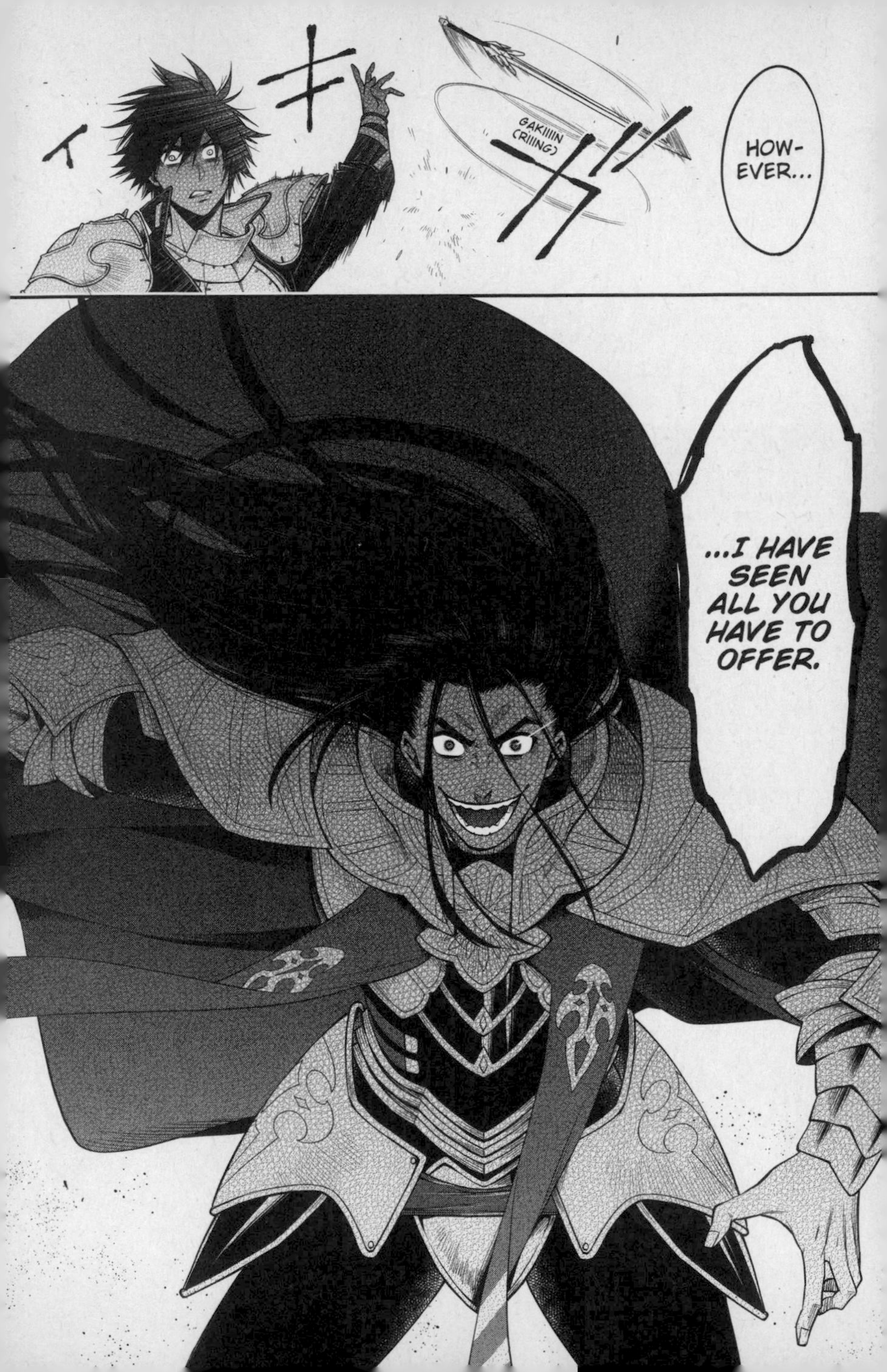
HOW-EVER...
GAKIIIIN (RIIING)
...I HAVE SEEN ALL YOU HAVE TO OFFER.

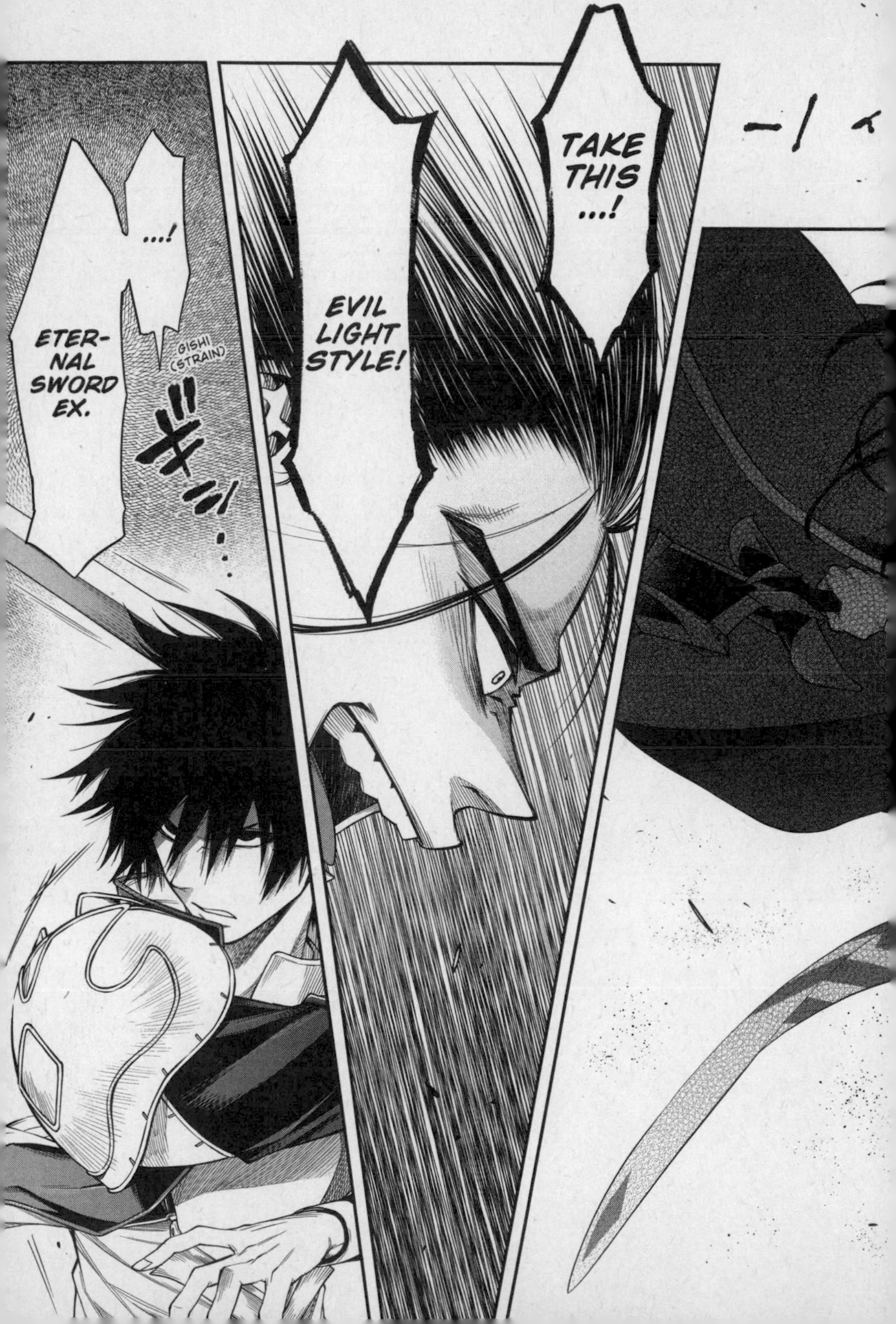
TAKE THIS ...!
EVIL LIGHT STYLE!
...!
ETER-NAL SWORD EX.
GISHI (STRAIN)

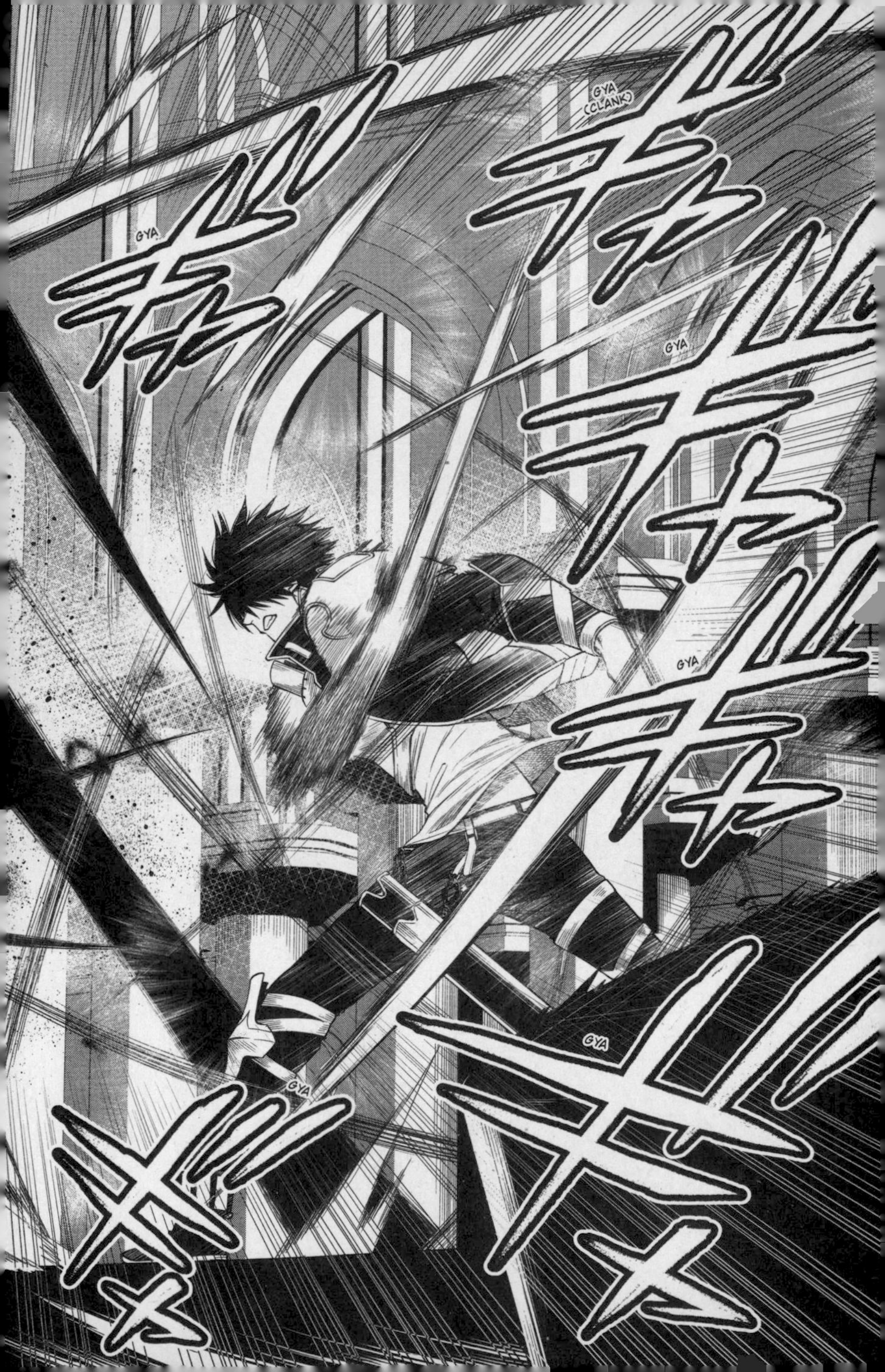
GYA
(CLANK)
GYA
GYA
GYA
GYA
GYA

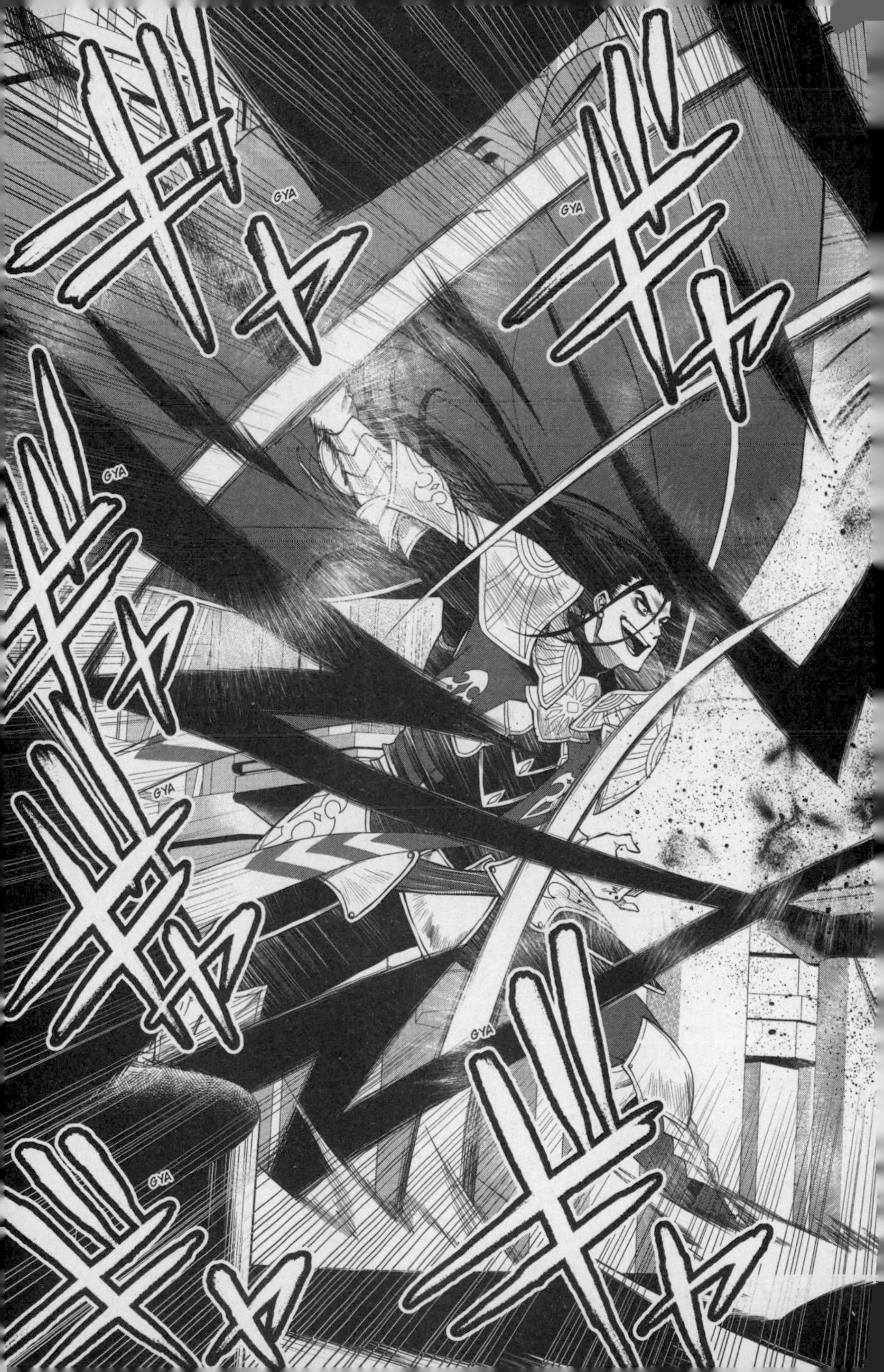
GYA
GYA
GYA
GYA
GYA
GYA

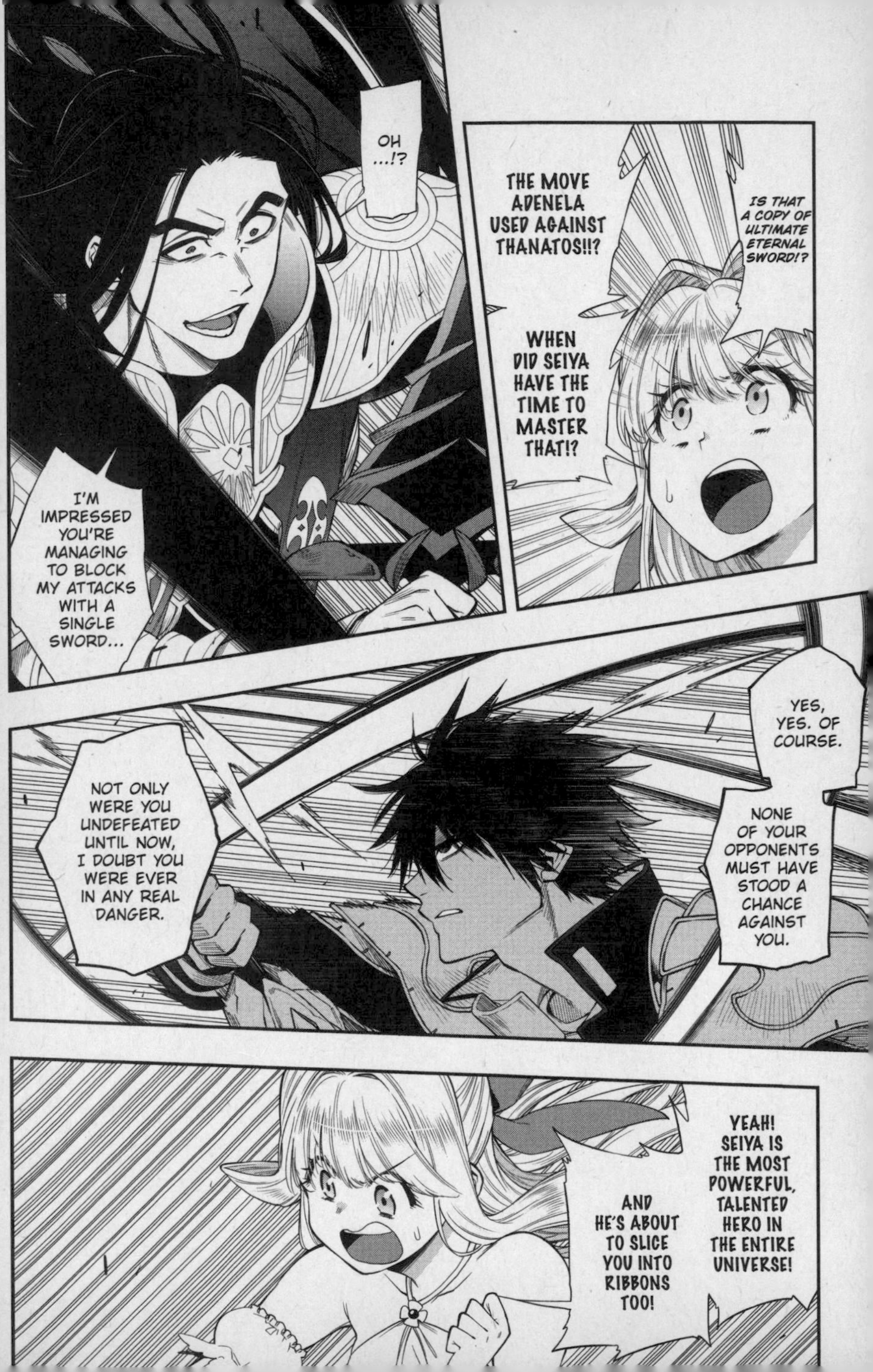
IS THAT A COPY OF ULTIMATE ETERNAL SWORD!?
THE MOVE ADENELA USED AGAINST THANATOS!!?
WHEN DID SEIYA HAVE THE TIME TO MASTER THAT!?
OH ...!?
I'M IMPRESSED YOU'RE MANAGING TO BLOCK MY ATTACKS WITH A SINGLE SWORD...
YES, YES. OF COURSE.
NONE OF YOUR OPPONENTS MUST HAVE STOOD A CHANCE AGAINST YOU.
NOT ONLY WERE YOU UNDEFEATED UNTIL NOW, I DOUBT YOU WERE EVER IN ANY REAL DANGER.
YEAH! SEIYA IS THE MOST POWERFUL, TALENTED HERO IN THE ENTIRE UNIVERSE!
AND HE'S ABOUT TO SLICE YOU INTO RIBBONS TOO!

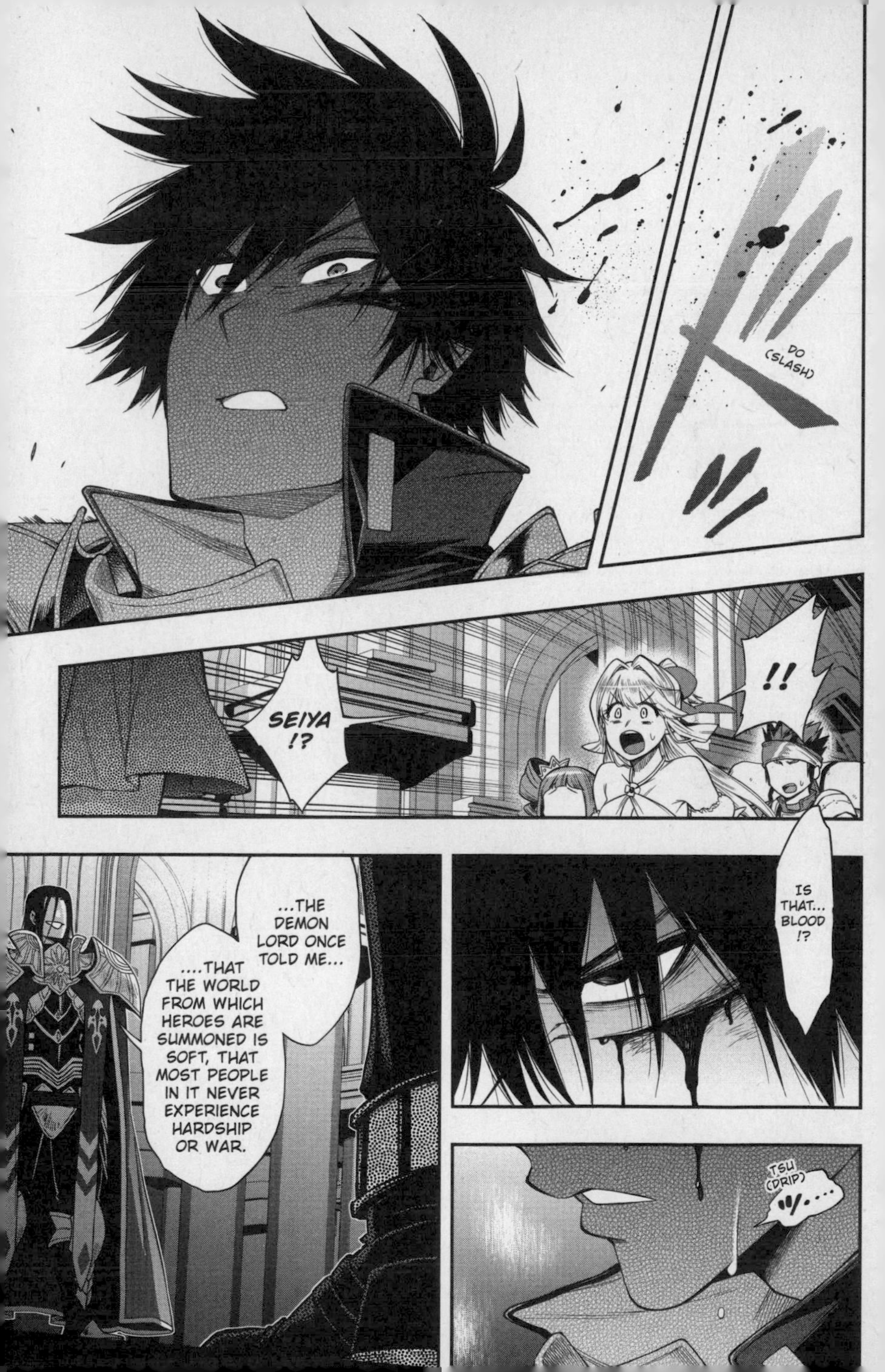
DO (SLASH)
!!
SEIYA !?
IS THAT... BLOOD !?
TSU (DRIP)
...
...THE DEMON LORD ONCE TOLD ME...
....THAT THE WORLD FROM WHICH HEROES ARE SUMMONED IS SOFT, THAT MOST PEOPLE IN IT NEVER EXPERIENCE HARDSHIP OR WAR.

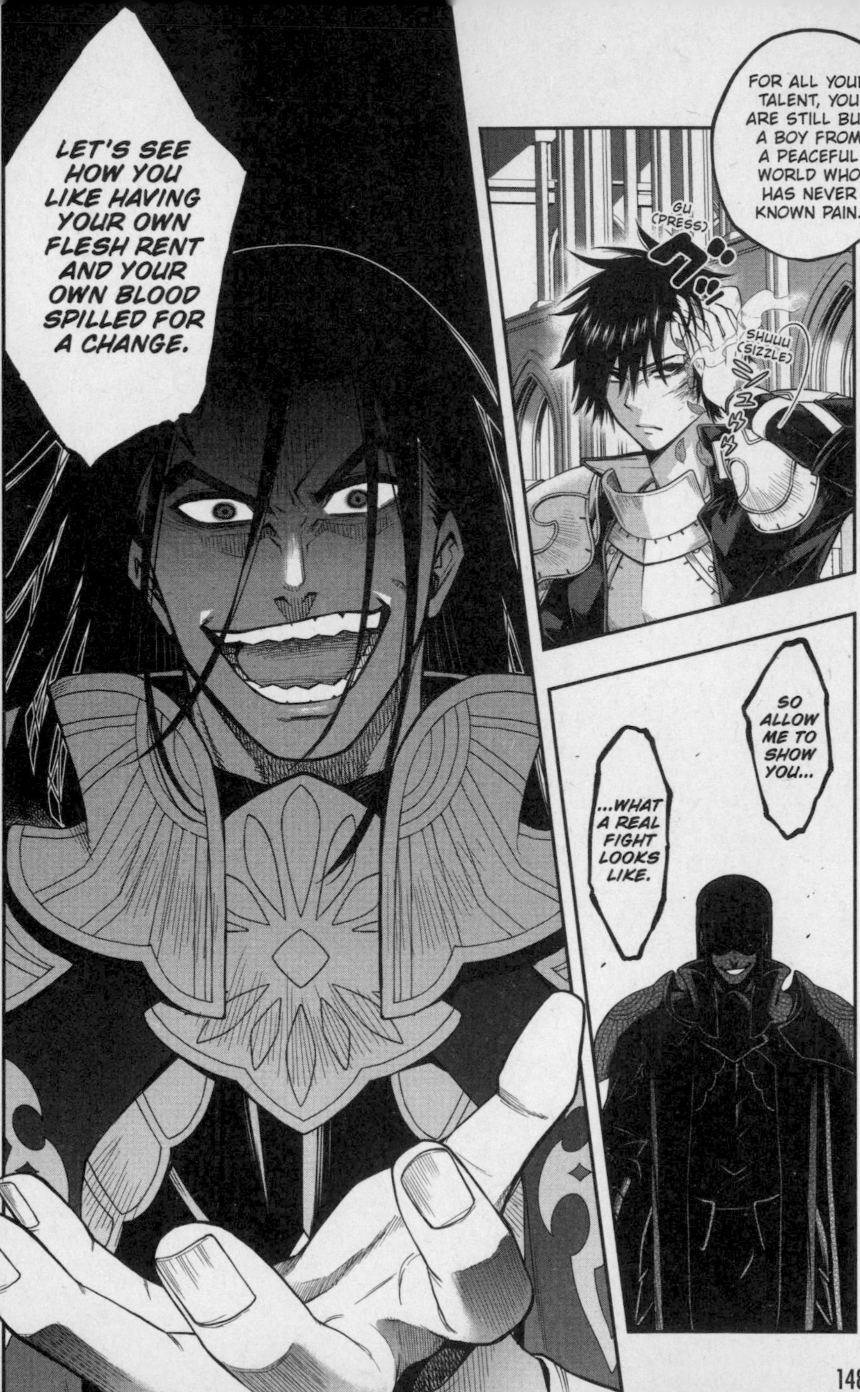
FOR ALL YOUR TALENT, YOU ARE STILL BUT A BOY FROM A PEACEFUL WORLD WHO HAS NEVER KNOWN PAIN.
GU (PRESS)
SHUUU (SIZZLE)
SO ALLOW ME TO SHOW YOU...
...WHAT A REAL FIGHT LOOKS LIKE.
LET'S SEE HOW YOU LIKE HAVING YOUR OWN FLESH RENT AND YOUR OWN BLOOD SPILLED FOR A CHANGE.

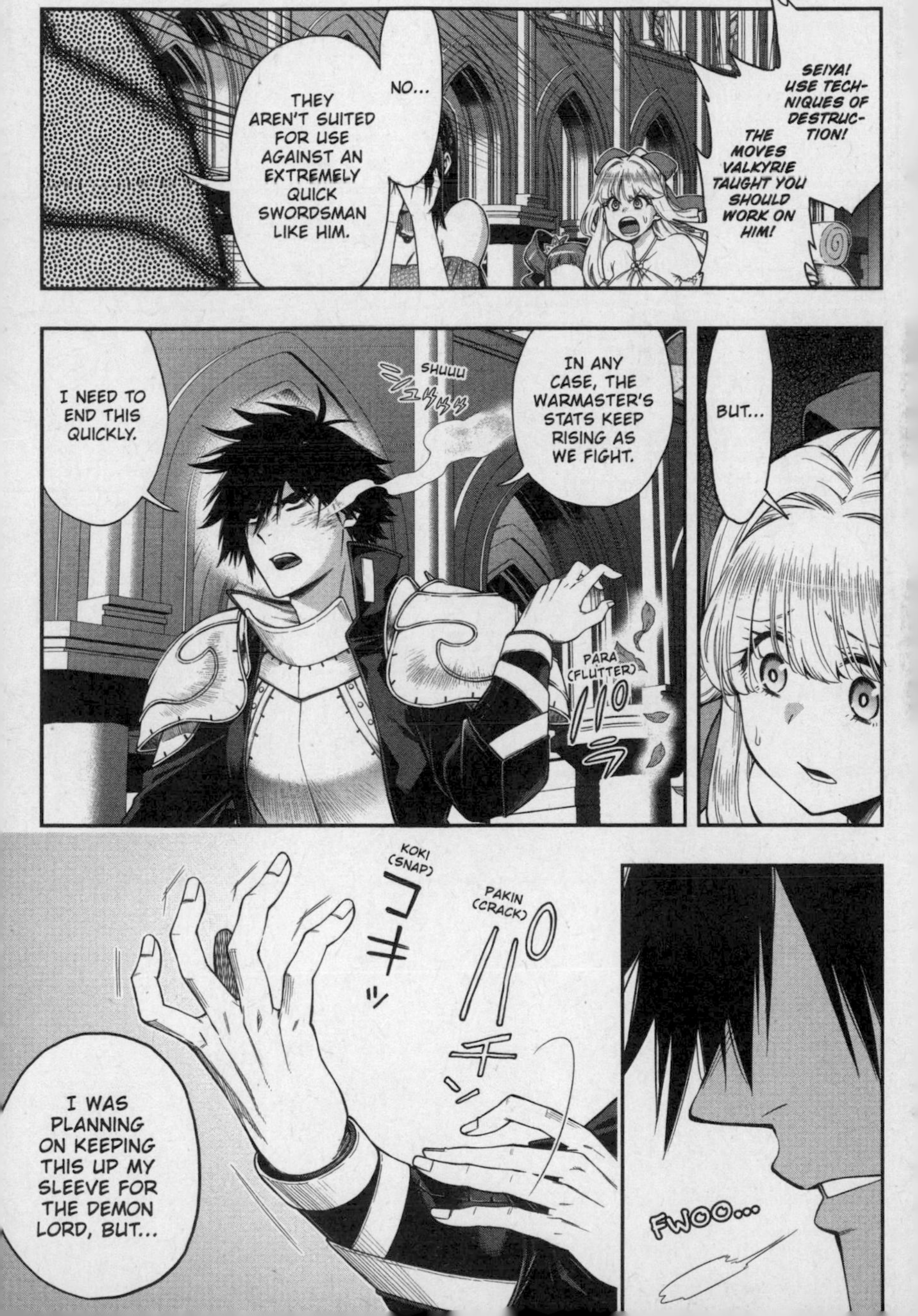
SEIYA! USE TECH-NIQUES OF DESTRUC-TION!
THE MOVES VALKYRIE TAUGHT YOU SHOULD WORK ON HIM!
NO...
THEY AREN'T SUITED FOR USE AGAINST AN EXTREMELY QUICK SWORDSMAN LIKE HIM.
BUT...
IN ANY CASE, THE WARMASTER'S STATS KEEP RISING AS WE FIGHT.
SHUUU
I NEED TO END THIS QUICKLY.
PARA (FLUTTER)
FWOO...
KOKI (SNAP)
PAKIN (CRACK)
I WAS PLANNING ON KEEPING THIS UP MY SLEEVE FOR THE DEMON LORD, BUT...

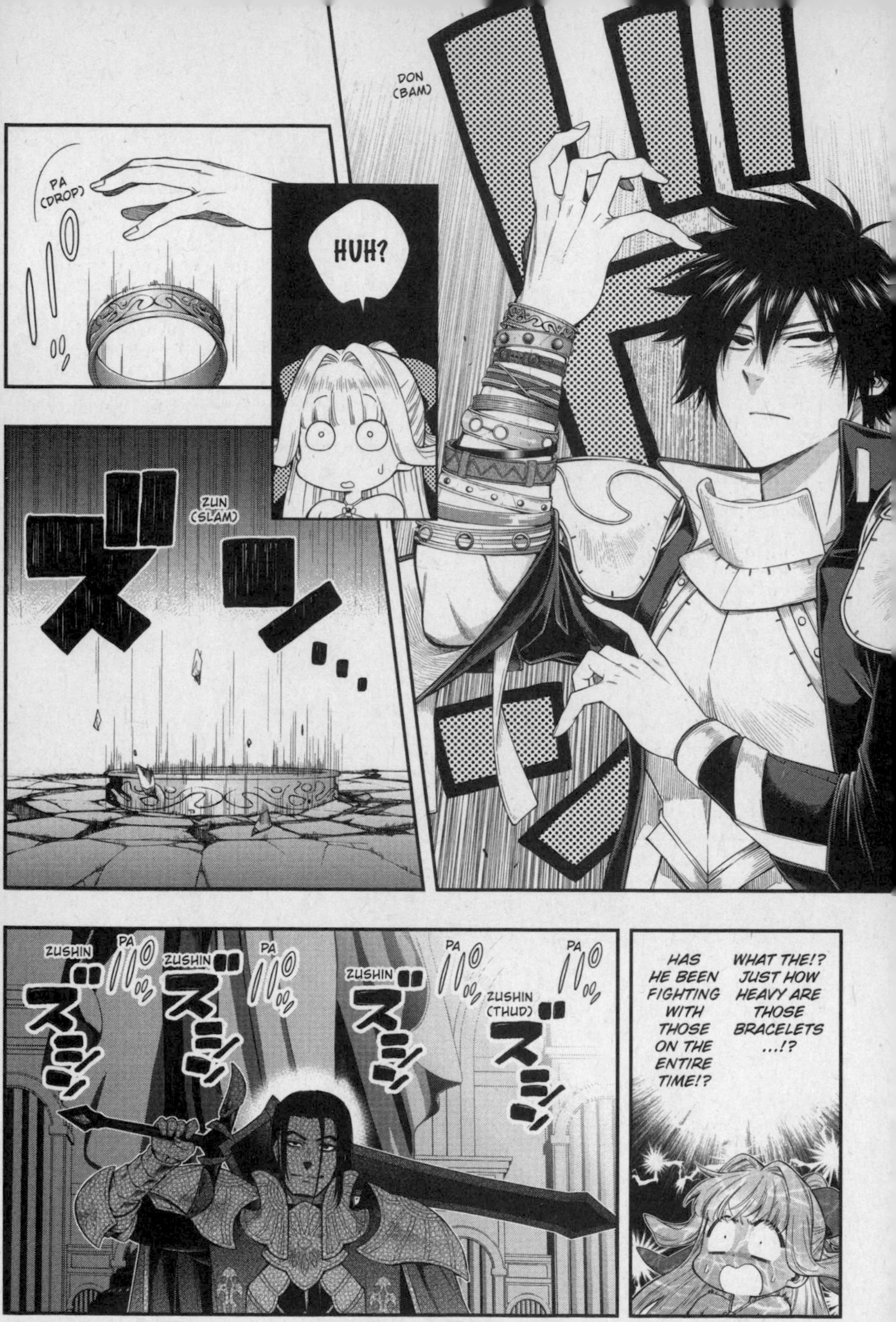
DON (BAM)
HUH?
PA (DROP)
ZUN (SLAM)
WHAT THE!? JUST HOW HEAVY ARE THOSE BRACELETS ...!?
HAS HE BEEN FIGHTING WITH THOSE ON THE ENTIRE TIME!?
PA
ZUSHIN (THUD)
PA
ZUSHIN
PA
ZUSHIN
PA
ZUSHIN

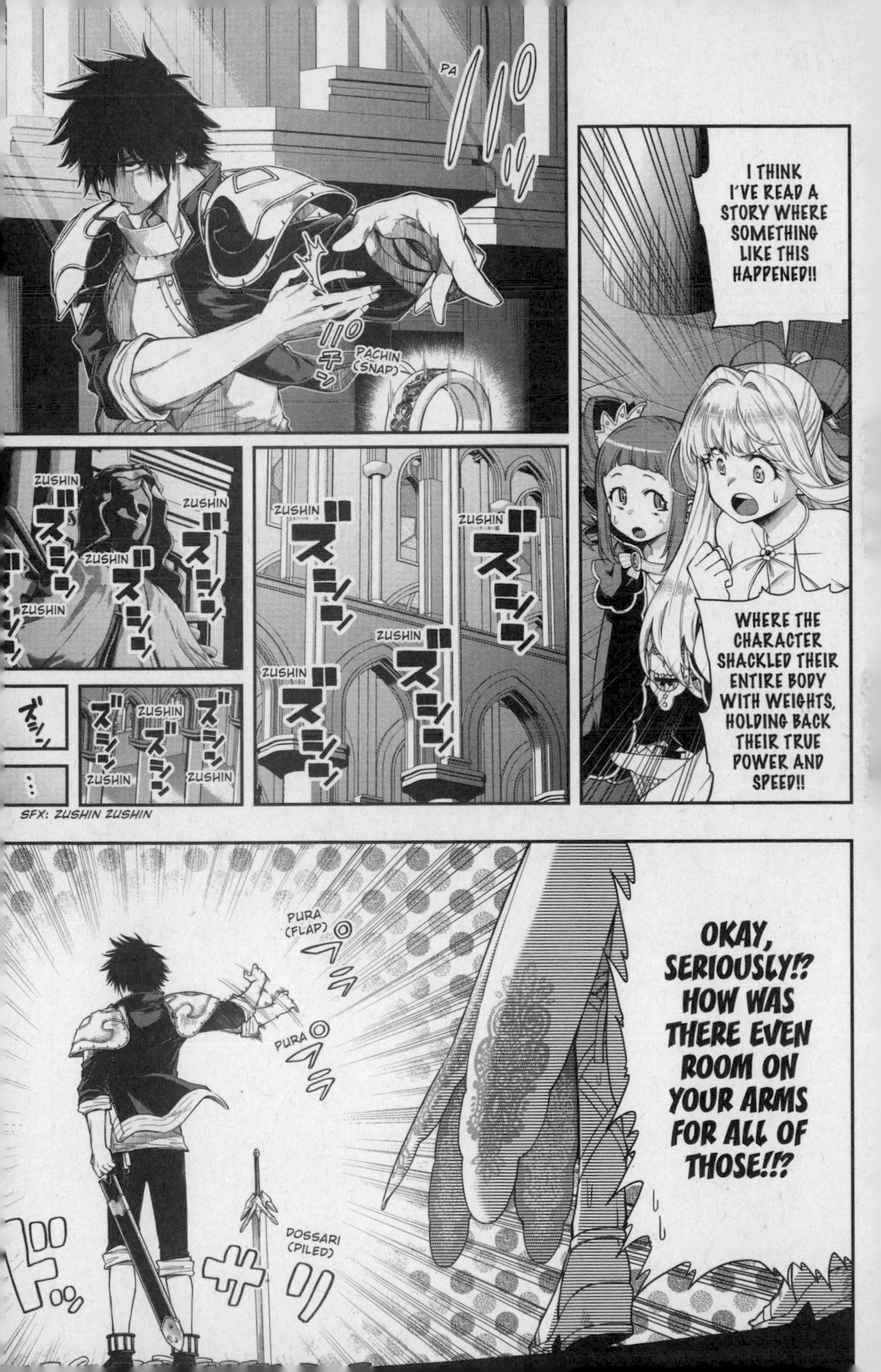

I THINK I'VE READ A STORY WHERE SOMETHING LIKE THIS HAPPENED!!
WHERE THE CHARACTER SHACKLED THEIR ENTIRE BODY WITH WEIGHTS, HOLDING BACK THEIR TRUE POWER AND SPEED!!
PA
PACHIN (SNAP)
ZUSHIN
ZUSHIN
ZUSHIN
ZUSHIN
ZUSHIN
ZUSHIN
ZUSHIN
ZUSHIN
ZUSHIN
ZUSHIN
ZUSHIN
...
SFX: ZUSHIN ZUSHIN
OKAY, SERIOUSLY!? HOW WAS THERE EVEN ROOM ON YOUR ARMS FOR ALL OF THOSE!!?
PURA (FLAP)
PURA
DOSSARI (PILED)

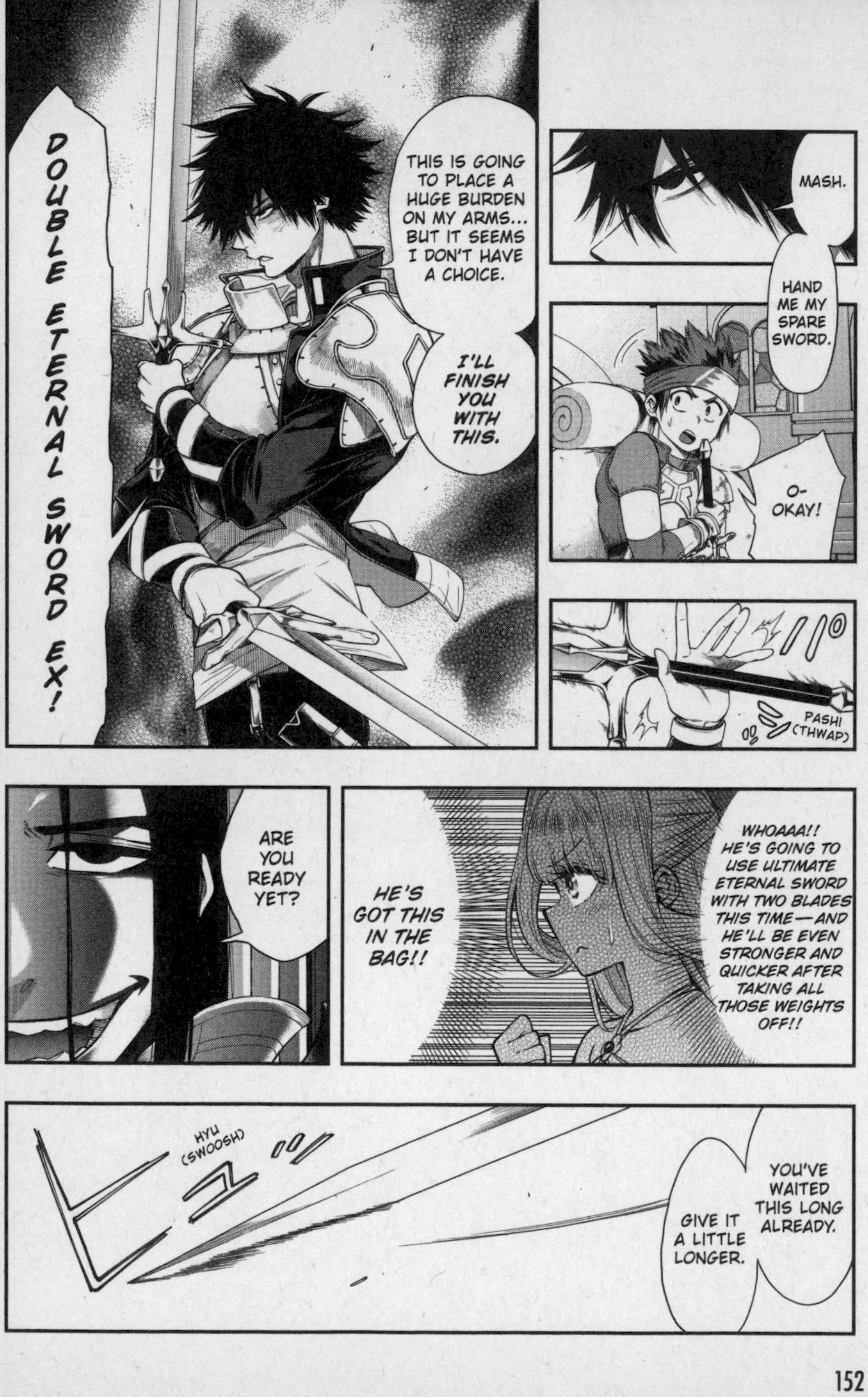
MASH.
HAND ME MY SPARE SWORD.
O-OKAY!
PASHI (THWAP)
THIS IS GOING TO PLACE A HUGE BURDEN ON MY ARMS... BUT IT SEEMS I DON'T HAVE A CHOICE.
I'LL FINISH YOU WITH THIS.
DOUBLE ETERNAL SWORD EX!
WHOAAA!! HE'S GOING TO USE ULTIMATE ETERNAL SWORD WITH TWO BLADES THIS TIME—AND HE'LL BE EVEN STRONGER AND QUICKER AFTER TAKING ALL THOSE WEIGHTS OFF!!
HE'S GOT THIS IN THE BAG!!
ARE YOU READY YET?
YOU'VE WAITED THIS LONG ALREADY.
GIVE IT A LITTLE LONGER.
HYU (SWOOSH)

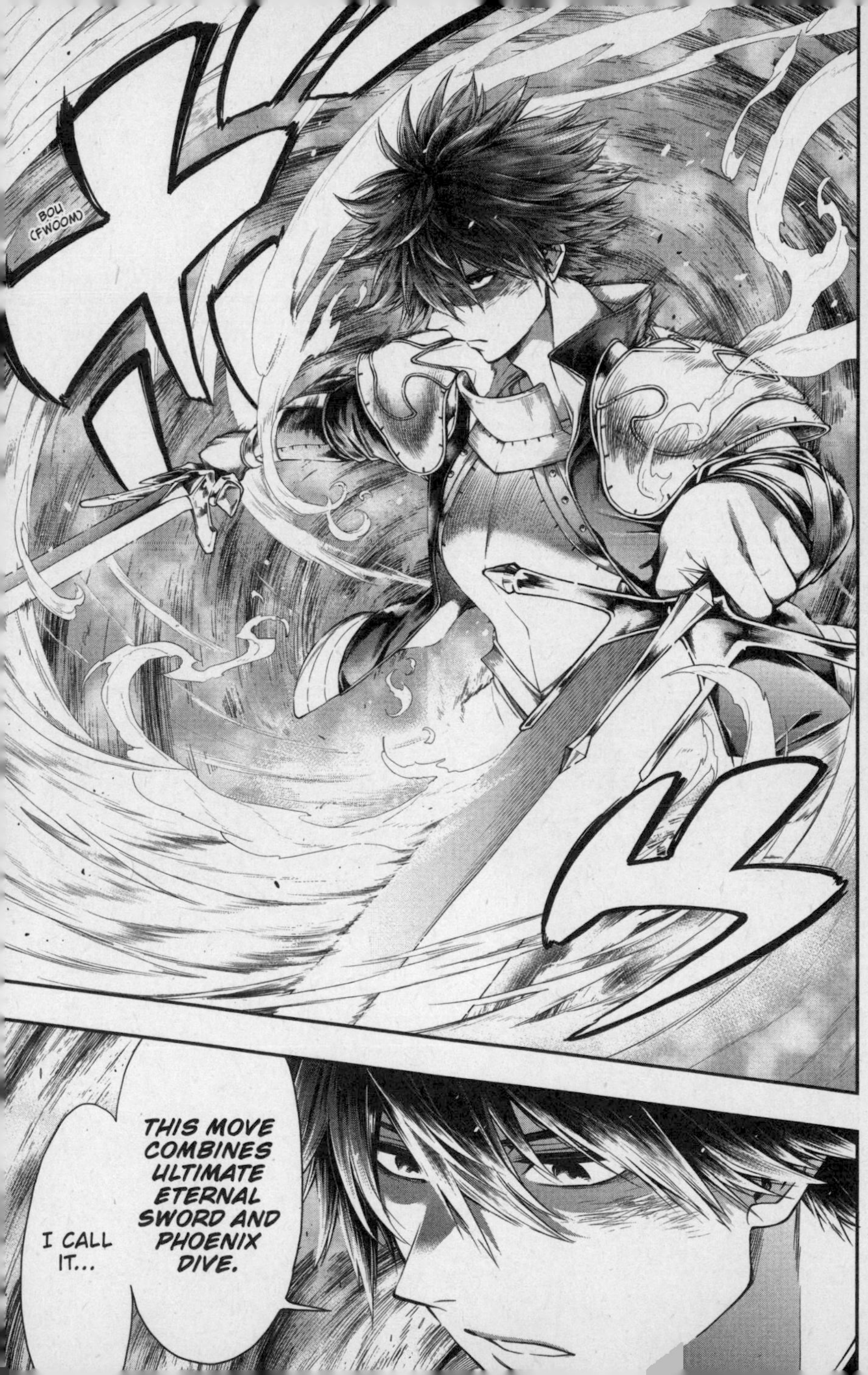
BOU (FWOOM)
THIS MOVE COMBINES ULTIMATE ETERNAL SWORD AND PHOENIX DIVE.
I CALL IT...

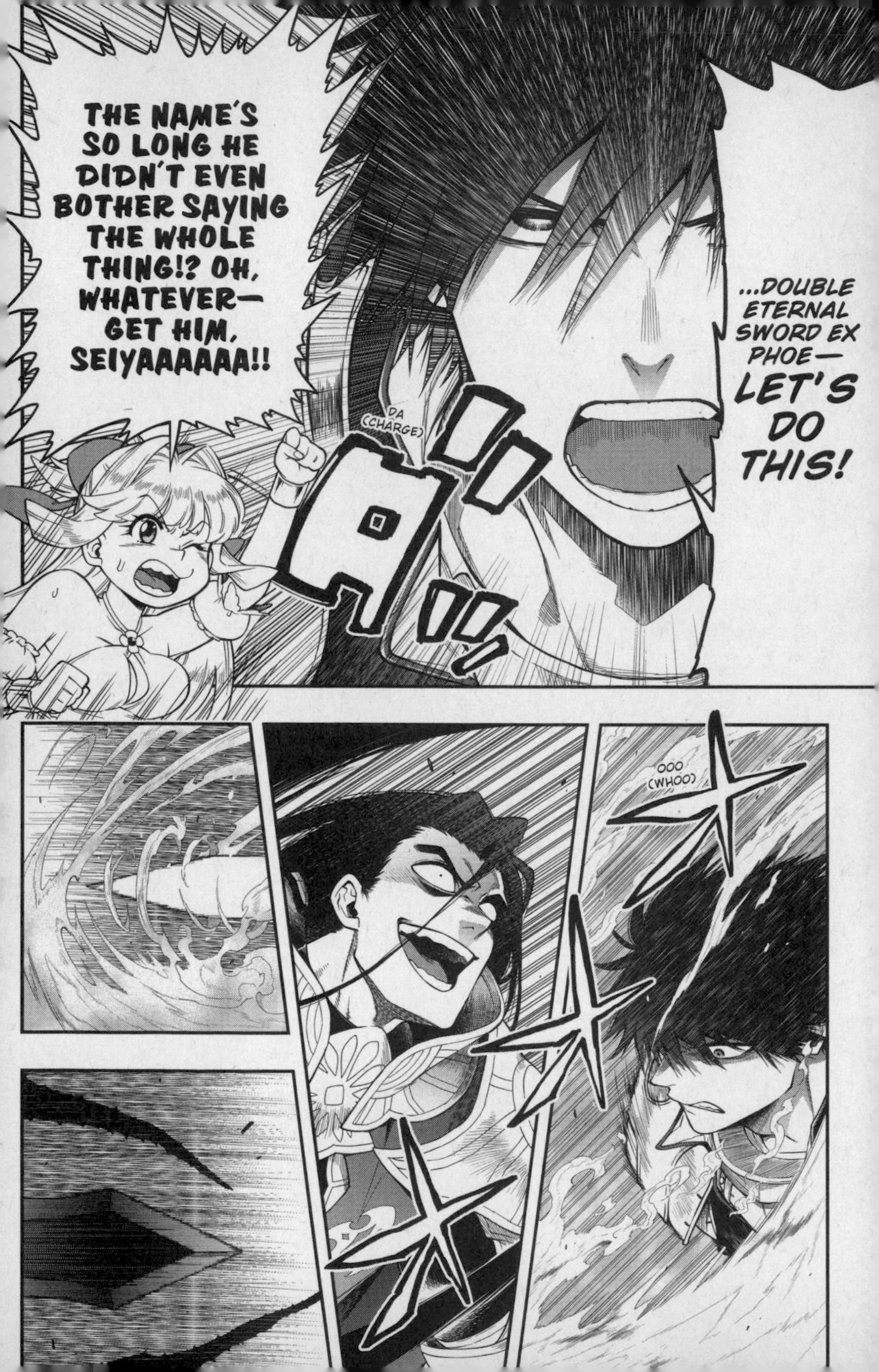
...DOUBLE ETERNAL SWORD EX PHOE— LET'S DO THIS!
DA (CHARGE)
THE NAME'S SO LONG HE DIDN'T EVEN BOTHER SAYING THE WHOLE THING!? OH, WHATEVER— GET HIM, SEIYAAAAAAA!!
OOO (WHOO)

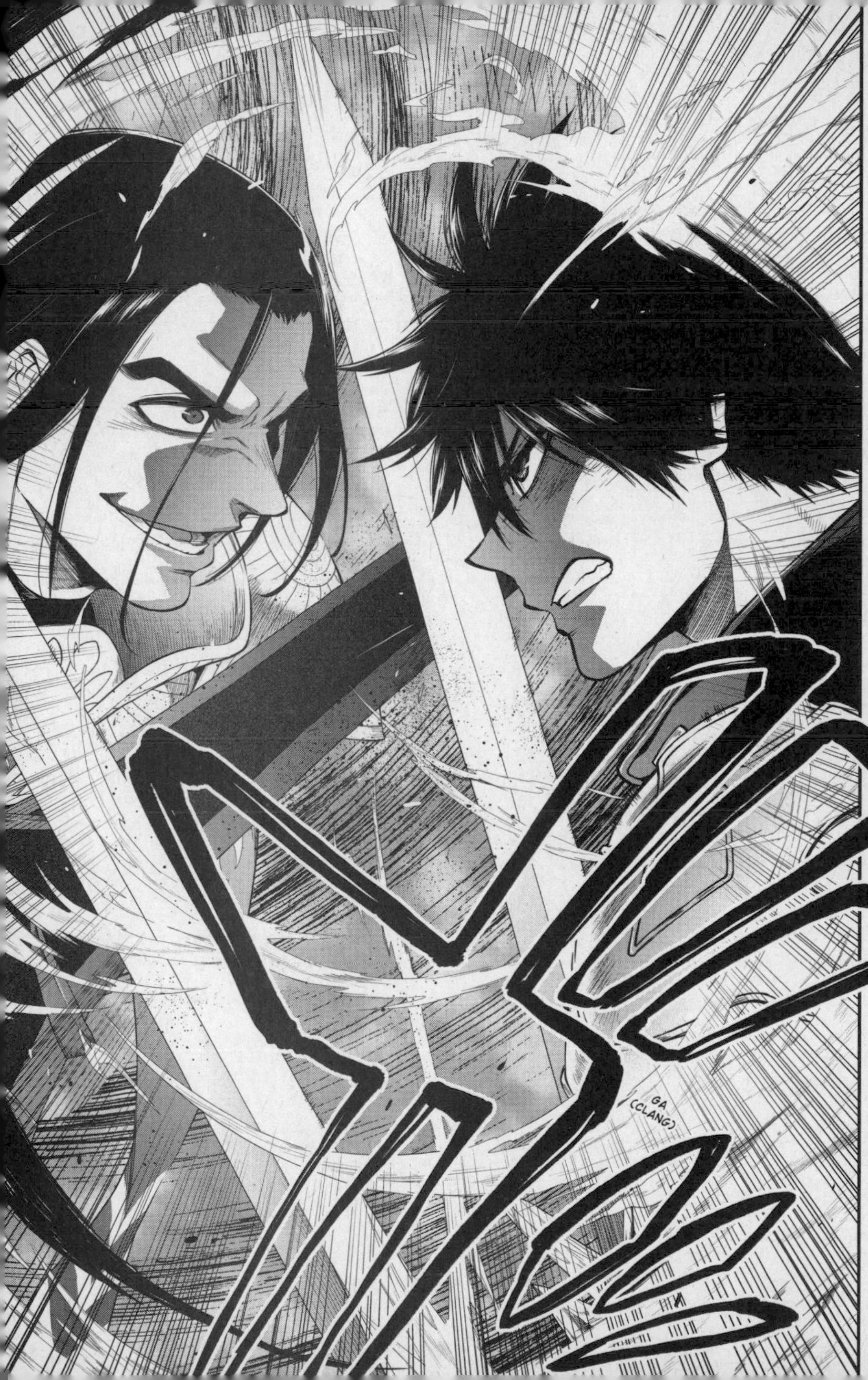
GA
(CLANG)

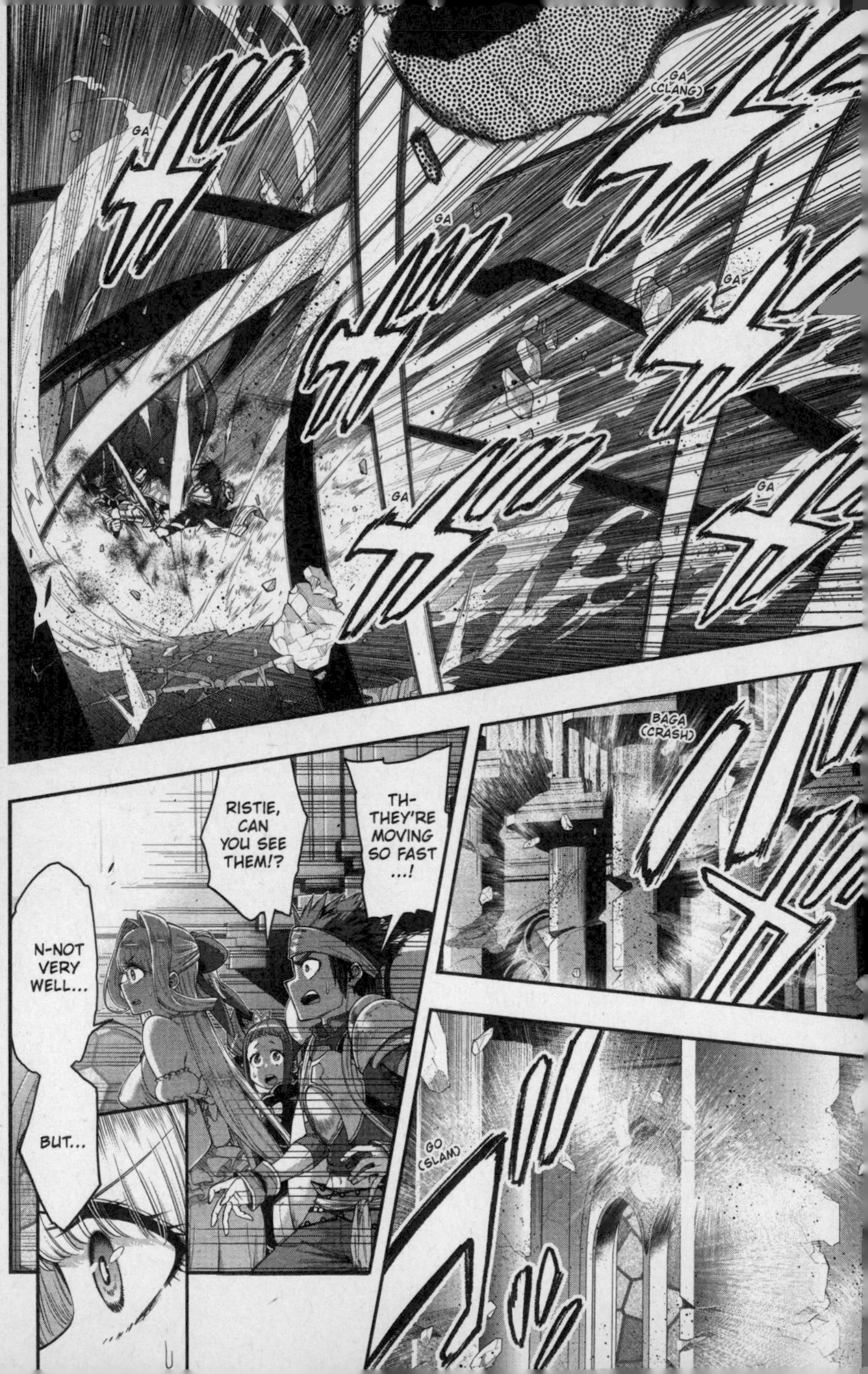
GA
(CLANG)
GA
GA
GA
GA
GA
BAGA
(CRASH)
GO
(SLAM)
TH- THEY'RE MOVING SO FAST ...!
RISTIE, CAN YOU SEE THEM!?
N-NOT VERY WELL...
BUT...

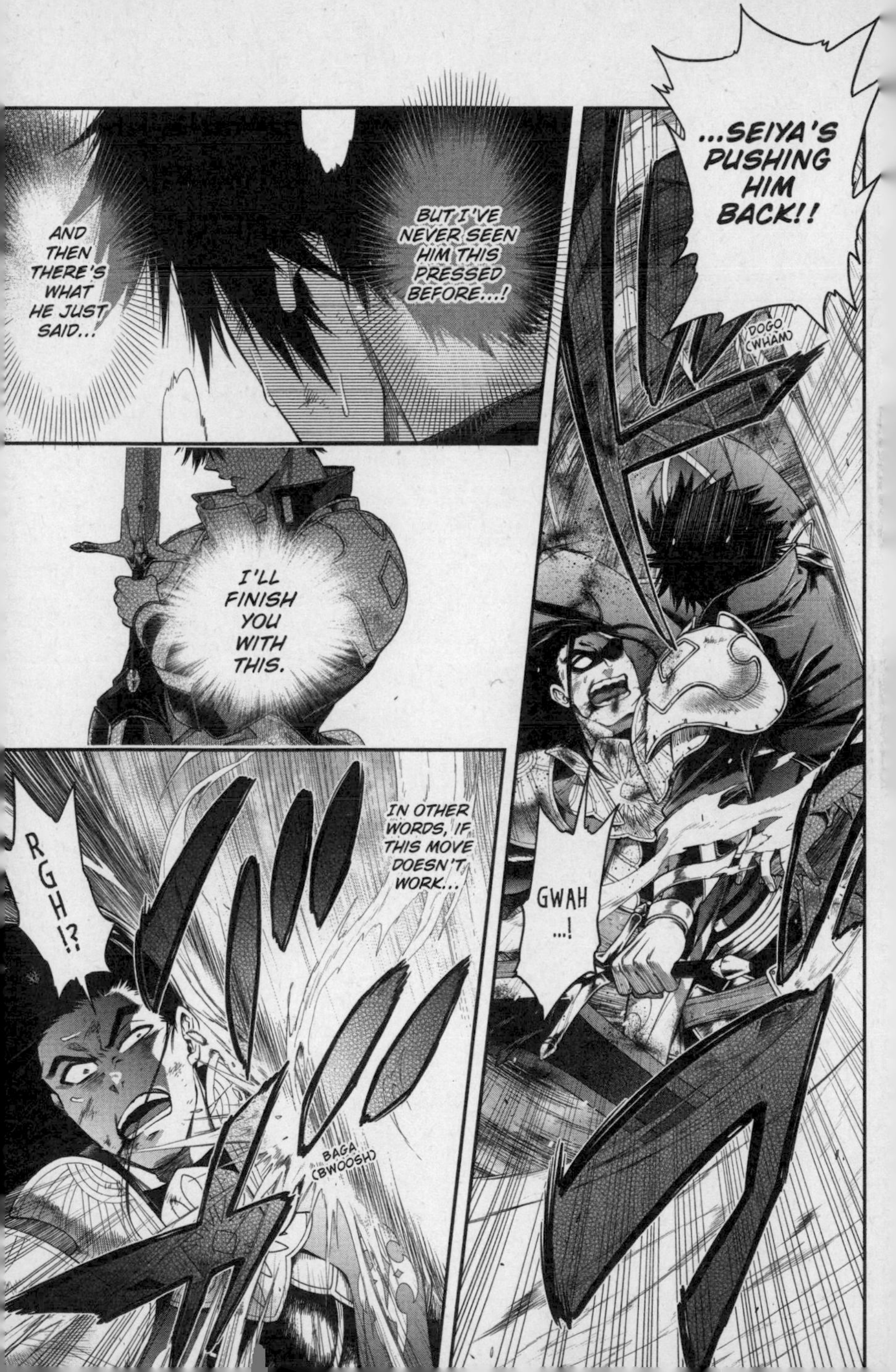
...SEIYA'S PUSHING HIM BACK!!
DOGO (WHAM)
GWAH ...!
AND THEN THERE'S WHAT HE JUST SAID...
BUT I'VE NEVER SEEN HIM THIS PRESSED BEFORE...!
I'LL FINISH YOU WITH THIS.
IN OTHER WORDS, IF THIS MOVE DOESN'T WORK...
RGH!?
BAGA (BWOOSH)

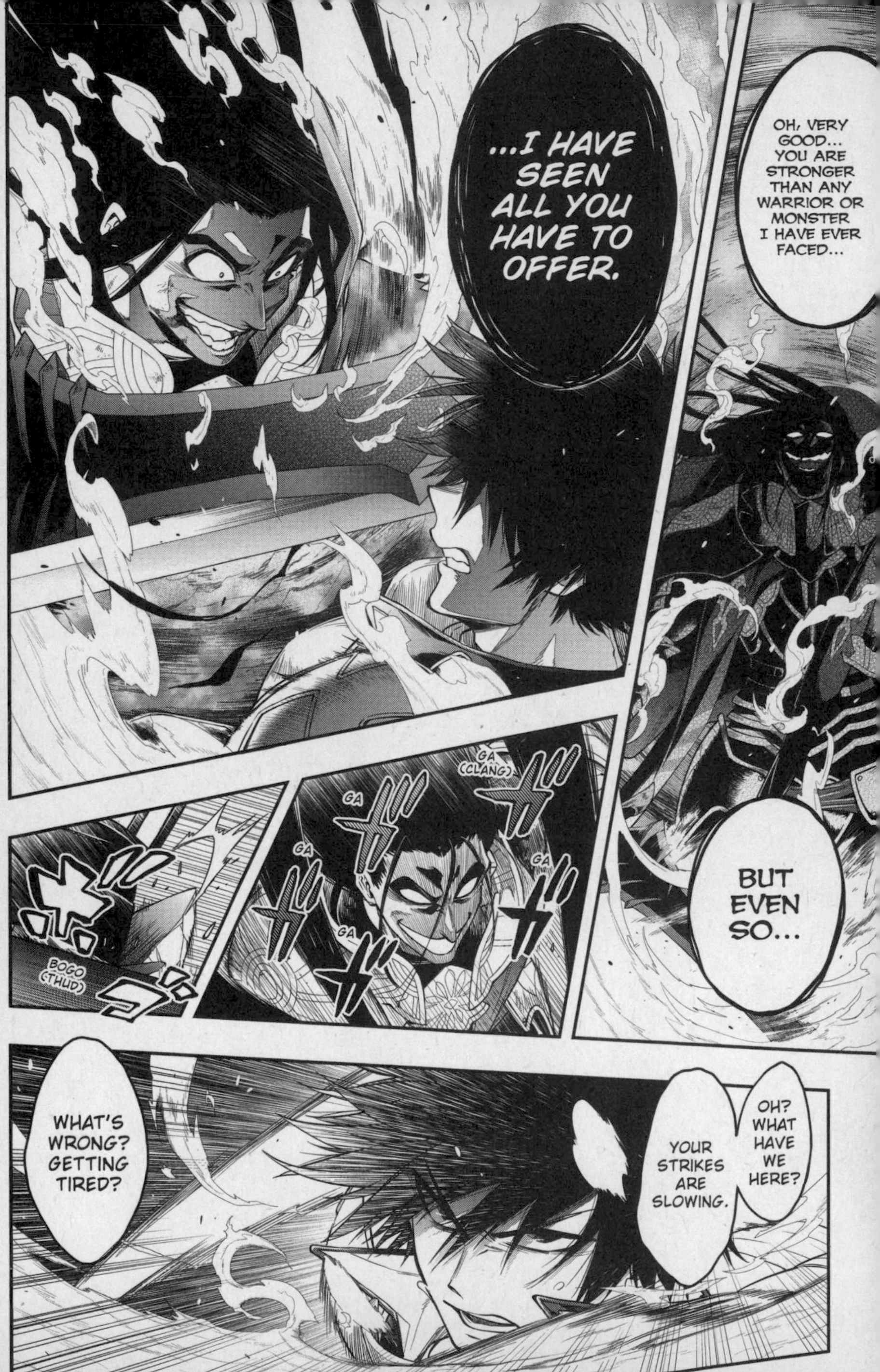
OH, VERY GOOD... YOU ARE STRONGER THAN ANY WARRIOR OR MONSTER I HAVE EVER FACED...
BUT EVEN SO...
...I HAVE SEEN ALL YOU HAVE TO OFFER.
GA (CLANG)
GA
GA
GA
GA
BOGO (THUD)
OH? WHAT HAVE WE HERE?
YOUR STRIKES ARE SLOWING.
WHAT'S WRONG? GETTING TIRED?

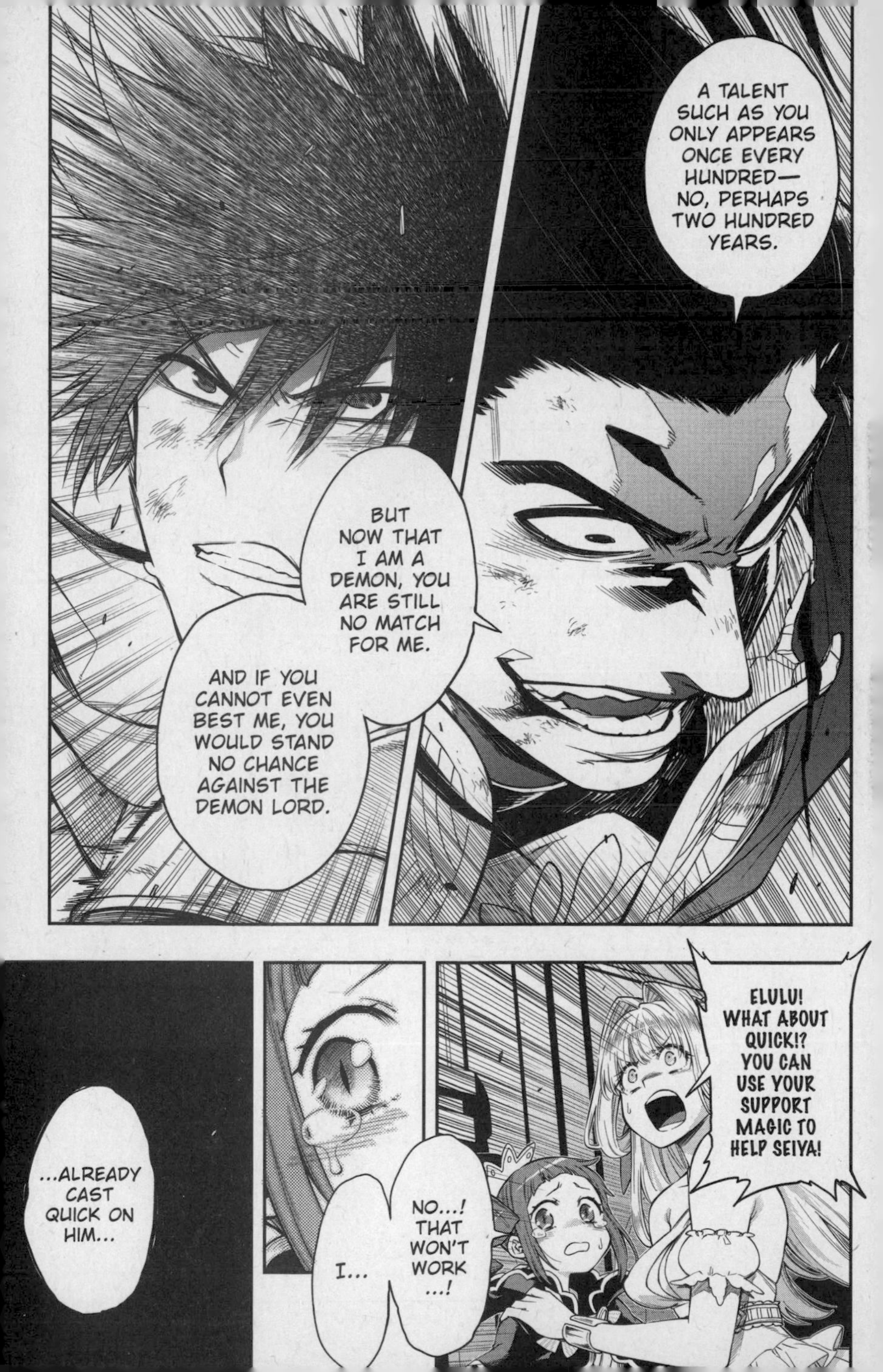
A TALENT SUCH AS YOU ONLY APPEARS ONCE EVERY HUNDRED— NO, PERHAPS TWO HUNDRED YEARS.
BUT NOW THAT I AM A DEMON, YOU ARE STILL NO MATCH FOR ME.
AND IF YOU CANNOT EVEN BEST ME, YOU WOULD STAND NO CHANCE AGAINST THE DEMON LORD.
ELULU! WHAT ABOUT QUICK!? YOU CAN USE YOUR SUPPORT MAGIC TO HELP SEIYA!
NO...! THAT WON'T WORK ...!
I...
...ALREADY CAST QUICK ON HIM...

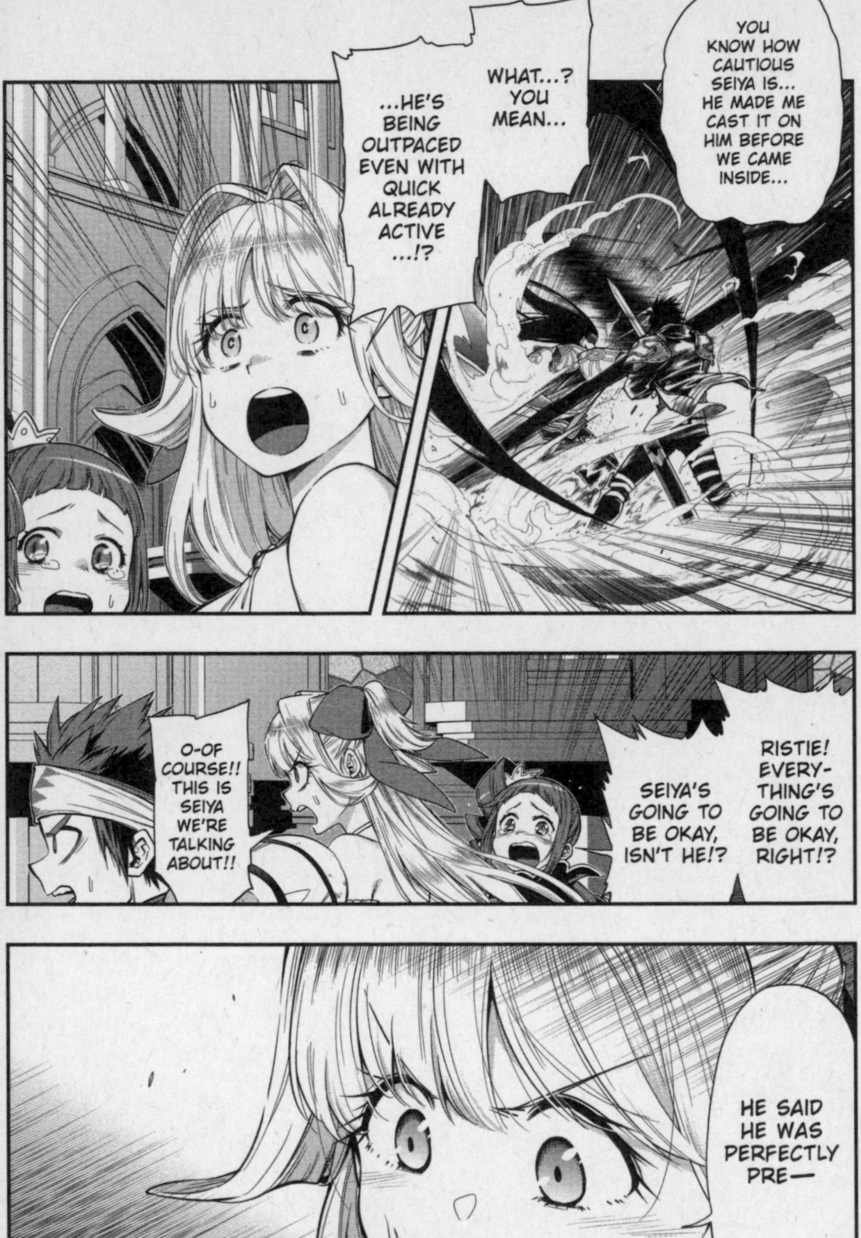
YOU KNOW HOW CAUTIOUS SEIYA IS... HE MADE ME CAST IT ON HIM BEFORE WE CAME INSIDE...
WHAT...? YOU MEAN...
...HE'S BEING OUTPACED EVEN WITH QUICK ALREADY ACTIVE ...!?
RISTIE! EVERY-THING'S GOING TO BE OKAY, RIGHT!?
SEIYA'S GOING TO BE OKAY, ISN'T HE!?
O-OF COURSE!! THIS IS SEIYA WE'RE TALKING ABOUT!!
HE SAID HE WAS PERFECTLY PRE—

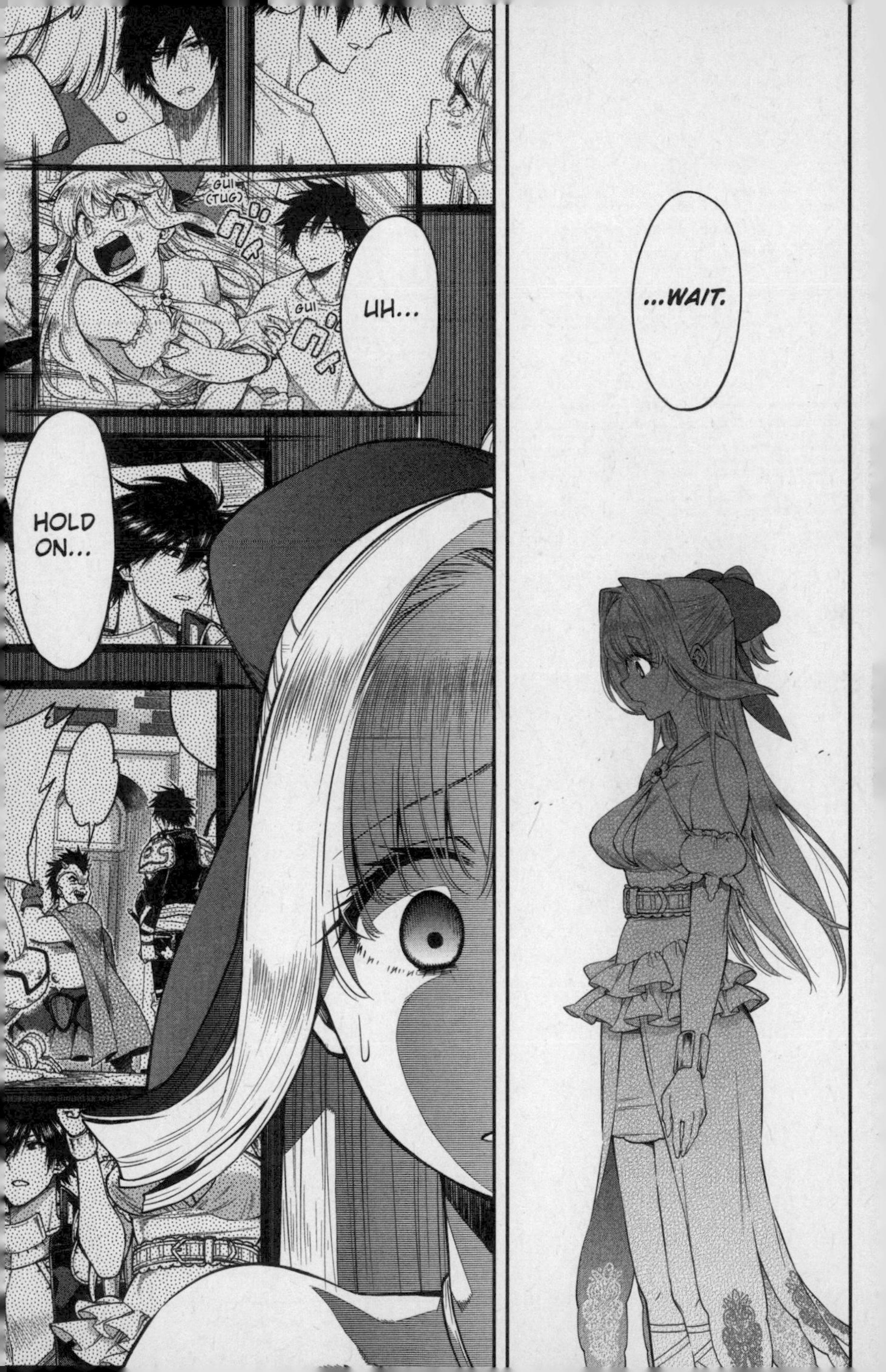
...WAIT.
UH...
GUI
(TUG)
GUI
HOLD ON...

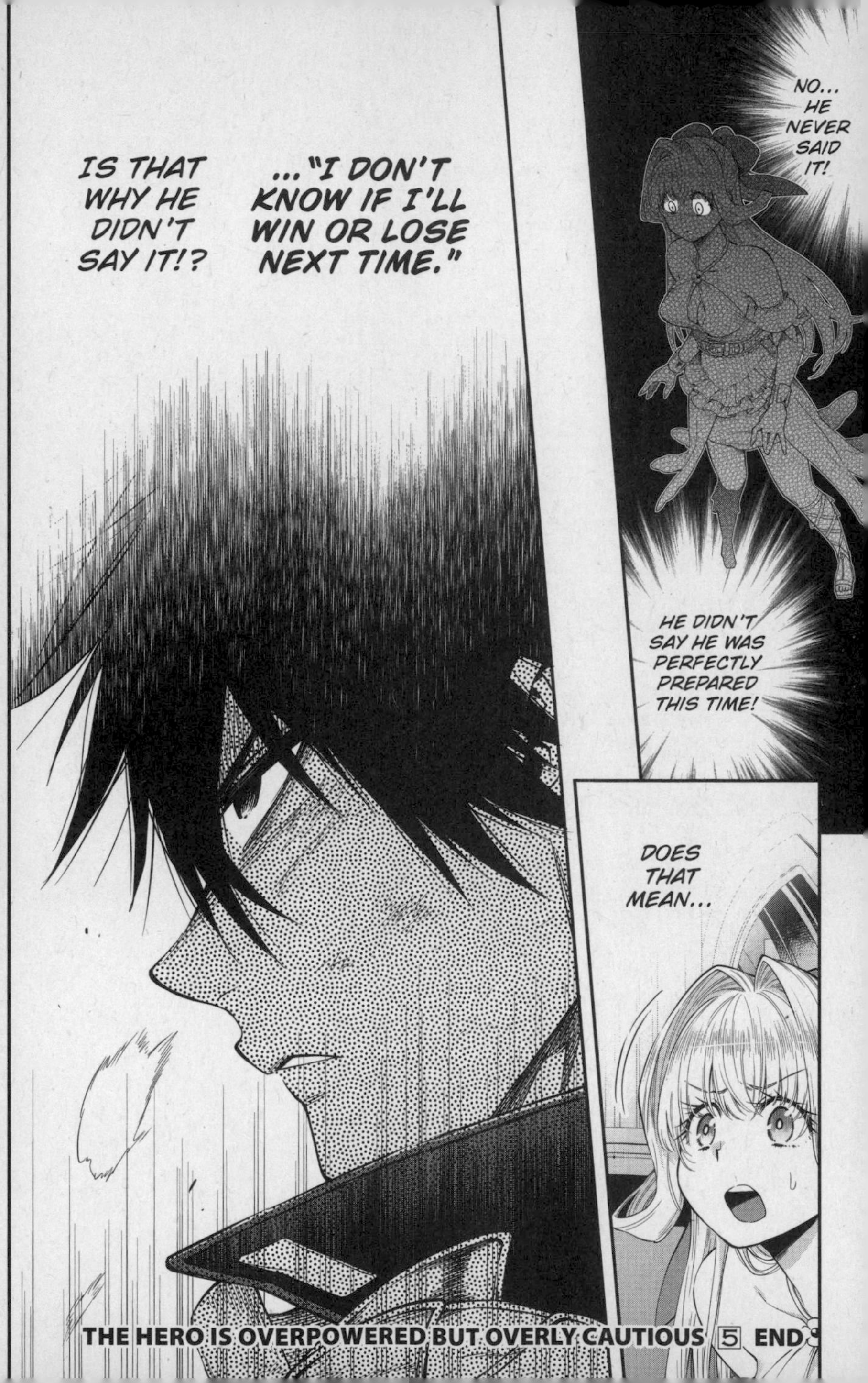
NO... HE NEVER SAID IT!
HE DIDN'T SAY HE WAS PERFECTLY PREPARED THIS TIME!
DOES THAT MEAN...
..."I DON'T KNOW IF I'LL WIN OR LOSE NEXT TIME."
IS THAT WHY HE DIDN'T SAY IT!?
THE HERO IS OVERPOWERED BUT OVERLY CAUTIOUS 5 END

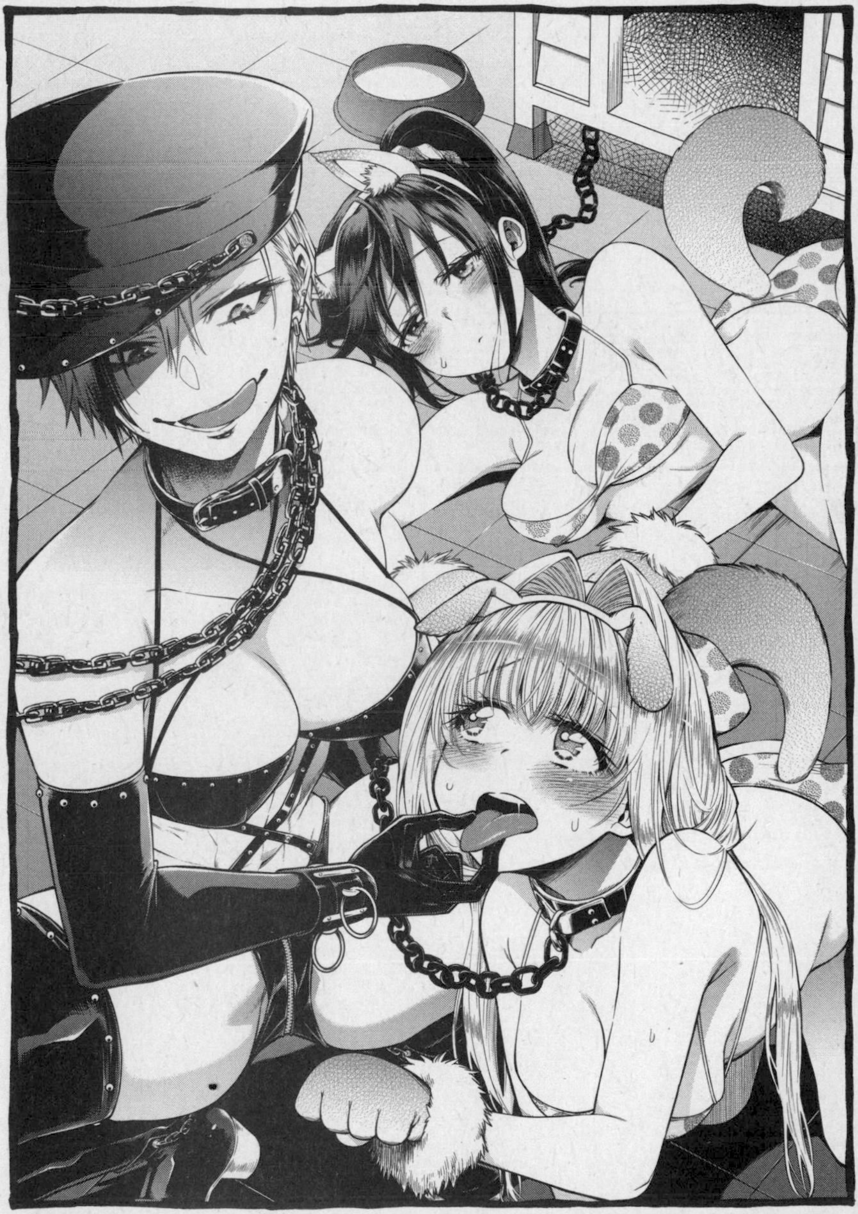

The Hero Is Overpowered but Overly Cautious 5

THE HERO IS OVERPOWERED BUT OVERLY CAUTIOUS 5

ORIGINAL STORY: **LIGHT TUCHIHI**
CHARACTER DESIGN: **SAORI TOYOTA**
ART: **KOYUKI**

Translation: **MATT RUTSOHN** ✳ Lettering: **CHIHO CHRISTIE**

KONO YUSHA GA ORE TUEEE KUSENI SHINCHO SUGIRU Volume 5
© Koyuki 2022
© Light Tuchihi, Saori Toyota 2022
First published in Japan in 2022 by KADOKAWA CORPORATION, Tokyo.
English translation rights arranged with KADOKAWA CORPORATION, Tokyo.
Tokyo through TUTTLE-MORI AGENCY, INC., Tokyo.

English translation © 2023 by Yen Press, LLC

Yen Press
150 West 30th Street, 19th Floor
New York, NY 10001

Visit us at yenpress.com
facebook.com/yenpress
twitter.com/yenpress
yenpress.tumblr.com
instagram.com/yenpress

First Yen Press Edition: February 2023
Edited by Yen Press Editorial: Riley Pearsall
Designed by Yen Press Design: Eddy Mingki, Wendy Chan

Yen Press is an imprint of Yen Press, LLC.
The Yen Press name and logo are trademarks of Yen Press, LLC.

The publisher is not responsible for websites (or their content)
that are not owned by the publisher.

Library of Congress Control Number: 2019953328

ISBNs: 978-1-9753-6285-0 (paperback)
978-1-9753-6286-7 (ebook)

10 9 8 7 6 5 4 3 2 1

WOR

Printed in the United States of America

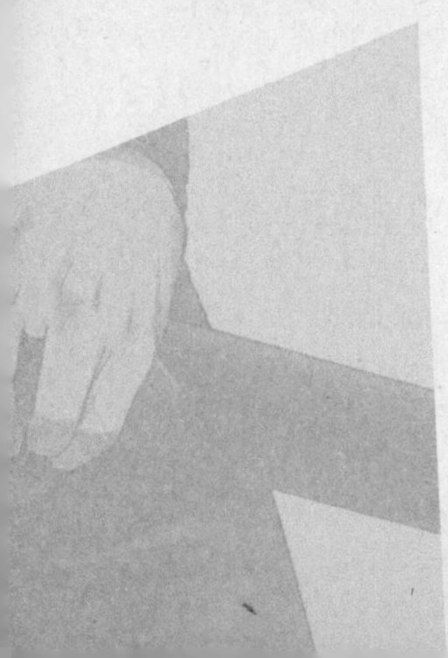